IRISH PARLIAMENTARY POLITICS IN THE EIGHTEENTH CENTURY

VOLUME II: 1730-1760

ROBERT E. BURNS

IRISH PARLIAMENTARY POLITICS IN THE EIGHTEENTH CENTURY

VOLUME II: 1730-1760

THE CATHOLIC UNIVERSITY
OF AMERICA PRESS
WASHINGTON, D.C.

Publication of this book has been funded in part by a gift from the
Associates of the Catholic University of America Press.

Copyright © 1990
The Catholic University of America Press
All rights reserved
Printed in the United States of America

LIBRARY OF CONGRESS
CATALOGING-IN-PUBLICATION DATA
(Revised for vol. 2)

Burns, Robert E., 1927–
Irish parliamentary politics in the eighteenth
century.

Includes bibliographies and indexes.
Contents: v. 1. 1714–1730 — v. 2. 1730–1760.
1. Ireland. Parliament—History–18th century.
2. Ireland—Politics and government—18th century.
I. Title.
JN1467.B87   1989   328.415'09   88-20941
ISBN 0-8132-0673-1 (v. 1)
ISBN 0-8132-0710-X (v. 2)

CONTENTS

ILLUSTRATIONS

PREFACE

This volume continues my previous work on the history of eighteenth century Irish parliamentary politics. The years between Carteret's dismissal in 1730 and Bedford's resignation in early 1761 had their share of political crises and charismatic men. Eighteenth century Irish Protestant politicians of this second generation often uncertain about their national identities, were important because they ran the country for thirty years, bewildered and challenged the great men of English politics, and charted the direction of future state- and nation-making in Ireland.

Mid-eighteenth century Irish Protestant politicians developed political techniques and created a political style which succeeded grandly in their own time. The techniques and style developed for success in mid-eighteenth century Irish parliamentary politics by Henry Boyle, Thomas Carter, Anthony Malone, Sir Richard Cox, Edmund Sexton Pery, John Hely Hutchinson, expanded and extended by Archbishop George Stone, and abetted by those two extremely talented chief secretaries, Lord George Sackville and Richard Rigby, turned out to be marvelously adaptable for later democratic ages. Taken over and refined by Irish Catholic politicians in the next century, this political style, so aristocratic and Irish Protestant in origin, was spread throughout the English-speaking world by the largely Irish Catholic diaspora and absorbed by local political cultures. This period of Irish political history, which some scholars have described as the age of the undertakers or perhaps as politics without a serious purpose, was, in my judgment, at once more complicated and creative than those pejorative appellations would suggest.

No one working in this field does so alone. I have profited greatly from the books and articles of J. C. Beckett, J. L. McCracken, Edith Mary Johnston, F. G. James, David Hayton, Declan O'Donovan, J. C. D. Clark, and Anthony Malcomson. As was the case with my first volume on this subject, I owe a special debt of gratitude to Anthony Malcomson for direction and guidance through eighteenth-century manuscript collections. It must be said that none of the persons mentioned above share any responsibility for errors of fact, substance, or style. They are mine.

For permission to draw on the Macartney Papers and the Wilmot Correspondence and other manuscript materials on deposit in the Public Records Office of Northern Ireland, I should like to thank the Deputy Keeper of Public Records of Northern Ireland and also the following owners and depositors of family collections in that records center and elsewhere: the Derbyshire County Council and the Derbyshire Records Office, the Trustees of the Chatsworth Settlement, the Trustees of the Bedford Estates, the Earl of Shannon, the House of Lords Records Office, and the late General Sir Eustace Tickell.

Also, special thanks must be given to the staffs of the Manuscript Division of the British Library, Public Records Office, London; Public Records Office, Belfast; The National Library, Dublin; Trinity College Library, Dublin; and the Faculty Steno Pool at the University of Notre Dame.

University of Notre Dame   ROBERT E. BURNS
Notre Dame, Indiana
February 1989

CHAPTER I

Irish Parliamentary Politics, 1730-1736

The Duke of Dorset's Political Style

When John, Lord Carteret took leave of his friends and servants and departed from Dublin Castle for England in mid-April 1730, few of those gentlemen and ladies wishing his excellency *bon voyage* expected him to return to Ireland as their chief governor. Carteret had held the office of Lord Lieutenant of Ireland longer than any other nobleman since the accession of George I. He had come to Ireland at a moment of acute crisis in Anglo-Irish political and constitutional relations. Carteret managed to resolve the crisis over Wood's Halfpence in ways that satisfied most of the political influentials in Dublin. Moreover he had been chief governor when three of the most important political leaders in Ireland died within fifteen months of one another. Archbishop William King, Lord Midleton, and William Conolly had dominated Irish politics for the last thirty-five years and their disappearance from public life signaled major changes in how the Irish parliament had been managed and how the country would be governed.

Conolly's death was particularly heart-felt by all of the chief governors of Ireland who had known and trusted him. He had been the mainstay of every Irish administration since 1715. Because of his position as speaker of the Irish house of commons, his great wealth and mind for business, his knowledge of parliamentary procedures and personnel, and his extensive network of political friends, Conolly had been an extraordinarily successful parliamentary manager that no lord lieutenant had been able to do without. It was Conolly who, on most occasions, had delivered the votes required to enact the money bills and complete the king's business.

He was irreplaceable, and his advice and service would be sorely missed. When Carteret boarded the viceregal yacht for Parkgate on April 21, 1730, one generation of Irish Protestant political leadership had passed and another had not yet taken its place.

Carteret's political successes and failures in Ireland had virtually no effect on his relationship with the king's first minister. Walpole despised Carteret and had sent him off to Ireland in 1724 to get him out of London and away from the court. Sir Robert had every intention of turning Carteret out of office whenever circumstances permitted it to be done. Walpole used the opportunity of disputes over foreign policy within his ministry to reshuffle his cabinet. In the course of this reshuffling, Carteret's Irish post was promised to a friend of Walpole's new political ally, Lord Wilmington. Carteret was dismissed in mid-June 1730, two months after he had left Ireland.

A new lord lieutenant for Ireland was not formally appointed until June 23, 1730. Lionel Cranfield Sackville, first Duke of Dorset, was in a very real sense a child of the glorious revolution. As Lord Shelburne observed, being born in 1688 the duke came into the world with the whigs and shared their fortunes ever since. As the young Earl of Dorset during the last years of Queen Anne's reign, he identified closely with whig politicians and was an outspoken champion of the Hanoverian succession. He served the new dynasty in a variety of household and state offices until 1717, was created Duke of Dorset in 1720, and five years later was appointed Lord Steward of the Household. After the coronation of George II in October 1727, the duke appears to have wanted to go to Ireland as chief governor as soon as an opportunity to do so arose.

Lord Percival reported rumors about an intended change in the government of Ireland as early as April,[1] but formal appointment of Dorset as lord lieutenant was delayed until June 23, 1730. In personality, Dorset was very different from Carteret. The duke drank much less and was more formal in personal relations than had been the earl. Contemporaries agreed that the duke was well informed about public affairs but had little aptitude for administra-

1. *Manuscripts of the Earl of Egmont, Diary of Viscount Percival, Afterwards First Earl of Egmont*, Vol. 1, 1730–1733, Historical Manuscripts Commission, published by His Majesty's Stationery Office, London, 1920, 93. Hereafter cited as HMC Egmont.

tion. However, Dorset fancied himself as an excellent judge of men and as being politically astute. In practice, he turned out to be neither.

For chief secretary and leader of government business in the house of commons, Dorset chose a longtime friend of Lord Wilmington, Walter Cary. He was a man of high intelligence but of limited industry. Cary always preferred play to work, and the kind of work required of chief secretaries in Ireland was particularly distasteful to him. He was by nature more disposed to receive favors than to do them for others. Also in the duke's entourage was a bright young clergyman with excellent English political connections. George Stone, brother of Newcastle's private secretary, Andrew Stone, chose to come to Ireland as Dorset's chaplain. George Stone was able, ambitious, a man of great personal charm, and possessed of extraordinary industry. Once in Ireland, he decided to stay and build a career in church and state, which he did with remarkable rapidity.

Among those in Ireland most interested and concerned over the appointment of Dorset was Hugh Boulter, Archbishop of Armagh and lord justice. Since arriving in Ireland in 1724, Boulter had enjoyed a special relationship with Sir Robert Walpole and the Duke of Newcastle. Neither the first minister nor the secretary of state had trusted Carteret, and Boulter's advice had enabled them to endure a political opponent in a sensitive, high-level position during a very difficult period. Boulter was anxious to know whether that special relationship would continue now that Carteret had been replaced.

Boulter had supported Carteret's recommendations on most matters and had been generous in praising the lord lieutenant's tireless ability in dealing with obstreperous influentials and party leaders in the Irish house of commons. However, Boulter had objected to Carteret's willingness to obtain short-term objectives by responding to patronage demands of influential Irish politicians. In Boulter's judgment, Carteret had been inclined to purchase cooperation by recommending jobs and honors for faction leaders or their friends. Boulter saw no virtue in trying to convert troublemakers into supporters with favors. He believed only demonstrated good behavior should be rewarded.

Newcastle wrote to Boulter and also to Thomas Wyndham, Lord Chancellor of Ireland, and Sir Ralph Gore, Speaker of the House of Commons, both serving with Boulter as lords justices on June 20, 1730. The duke apprised them of Dorset's appointment and indicated that henceforth all appropriate correspondence should be directed to him.[2] On the same day, Newcastle wrote a separate and private letter to Boulter explaining that the Duke of Dorset and Lord Wilmington were in perfect concert and union with the present ministers and that the change in chief governors had been made with "the approbation of all your friends here."[3] Newcastle urged the primate to write to Dorset in the same open manner as he would to any other of the king's servants in England without any reservations whatsoever. Thus assured that his present role in Irish affairs would continue, Boulter began corresponding regularly with the new lord lieutenant about the state of the country.

According to Boulter, new Protestant schools were needed in the country because the popery laws had failed to achieve their purpose. Catholicism in Ireland in 1730 was as strong and threatening as ever. The primate believed that the condition of most of the adult Catholics in Ireland was simply beyond the power of well-intentioned men to repair. The future of the country, he continued, depended on doing "much good among the generation that is growing up." He sought Newcastle's support to obtain charters of incorporation for both day and boarding schools which would teach Catholic children "in the English tongue and in the principles of Christianity,"[4] The primate was absolutely committed to this project and successfully communicated his enthusiasm to others. Large subscriptions were collected from the public. Dorset supported Boulter's project because he believed in the value of it and because it was a very popular thing to do.

When talking with friends and advisors in England about the problems awaiting any lord lieutenant in Ireland, Dorset hoped to profit from Carteret's experience. Dorset wanted to believe that the Irish parliament could be managed. With that objective in mind the duke tried to cultivate some of the disorganized remnants of the

2. Newcastle to Lords Justices, June 20, 1730. SP63/392/140.
3. Newcastle to Boulter, June 20, 1730. SP63/392/142.
4. Boulter to Newcastle, May 7, 1730. SP63/392/120.

old Conolly party. The occasion for this effort was the death of Thomas Dalton, Lord Chief Baron of the Irish Court of the Exchequer in June 1730. The three lords justices met to recommend a successor. First, they discussed the matter of a successor with Henry Singleton, prime serjeant, and with Robert Jocelyn, solicitor general. Both declined in favor of the senior law officer, the attorney general, Thomas Marlay. The lords justices then recommended Marlay. The lords justices urged that if Marlay, a man of Irish birth, was approved for the post of chief baron, an Englishman, Robert Jocelyn, should be advanced from solicitor general to attorney general and another Englishman, John Bowes, presently third serjeant-at-law, should be appointed solicitor general.[5]

In a separate letter to Newcastle sent off in the same posting as the letter from the lords justices, Boulter implied that Marlay was Sir Ralph Gore's choice. The primate and lord chancellor had supported Marlay only as "the best person on this side of the water."[6] They saw great advantage to the king's service in Ireland if someone were sent from England for Dalton's post. Newcastle quietly and adroitly passed the making of this decision to the new lord lieutenant.

Dorset decided at once that Marlay was the proper person for the post. Though Marlay had no distinguished reputation as a lawyer, he had rendered good parliamentary service as attorney general. Most important, Marlay had been an admired protégé of the late speaker and had been brought into the house of commons by him. If the individuals and factions formerly united under Conolly were to be regrouped under Gore, then any appointment likely to facilitate that process was worth making. Promoting a prominent member of the old Conolly party was one way of reaching that objective, and establishing a clear line of ascent from law officer to the bench was another.[7]

Dorset was aware that he needed good speakers and men with influence committed to support his administration before parliament opened, and in order to obtain that sort of strength an ap-

5. Lords Justices to Newcastle, June 24, 1730. SP63/392/144.
6. Boulter to Newcastle, June 24, 1730. SP63/392/146.
7. F. Elrington Ball, *The Judges in Ireland, 1225–1921* (Dutton, New York, 1927), II, 119.

proach was made to Thomas Carter. Dorset was willing to overlook
the past for the sake of the present and had no reservations about
seeking support from members who had harassed his predecessor.
The discussions between Dorset and Carter were complicated. Carter presently held the honorific post of deputy master of the rolls.
He wanted to succeed to the well-paid sinecure of master of the rolls
presently held by Lord Berkeley for life. However, the succession of
anyone was blocked by the reversion of that office held by Lord
Barrington. Carter was prepared to purchase the surrender of the
office and of the reversion and then agree to hold the office itself
during the king's pleasure.

To be sure, Carter expected some further advantage from the
king in the future for the very heavy expense of recovering for his
majesty's disposal an office that had been encumbered for two lives.[8]
Dorset not only facilitated Carter's purchase of a sinecure worth
£800 a year and then added him to the privy council in 1732, but
he entrusted the social and political education of his teenage son,
Lord George Sackville, to Carter as well. Opening viceregal confidence to Thomas Carter was indeed a new beginning for any Irish
government. Boulter and other more experienced Castle hands
must have doubted whether Carter was capable of serving anyone
except himself. In any case, the king approved Carter's purchase
of the office in late October.[9]

Dorset was determined to succeed in Ireland. The duke believed
that with proper preparations the Irish house of commons could
be managed. Dorset and Cary arrived in Dublin on September 11,
1731, and descended on social Dublin like the proverbial whirlwind.
A popularity campaign began as soon as the viceregal party disembarked. The duke's progress from the waterside to Dublin Castle
on September 11 was a carefully orchestrated display of splendor
and pomp. What was begun at the Dublin landing was continued
in other ways during the next two weeks. The duke reported many
discussions and much socializing with members and being very busy
"making the best disposition I can for meeting of Parliament."[10]
Cary was also heavily involved in meetings and visitations. He com-

8. Dorset to Newcastle, September 29, 1731. SP63/394/75.
9. Harrington to Dorset, October 30, 1731. SP63/394/103.
10. Dorset to Newcastle, September 15, 1731. SP63/394/69.

plained to friends in England that his back was almost broken from bowing, his belly was stuffed from eating. What was to become of his head from drinking, he could not tell. Though the chief secretary enjoyed the festivities, he doubted whether they would have any significant affect on the progress of the session. Only a few members had actually arrived in Dublin, so "in our cups" not much real business had been done.[11]

Most of the Irish lords and gentlemen were favorably impressed by Dorset's style. All agreed that Dorset lived in a splendid and elegant manner. Three mornings a week he saw company at levees. These gatherings were usually disappointing because the duke spoke only to a very few and did not stay very long. Observers reported that "entertaining of a mixt company is not his talent."[12] Yet, when his grace entertained at dinner or supper he did so magnificently. However, when all was said and done, the true test of how well Dorset's popularity campaign had succeeded would come on October 5, 1731, when the duke opened the first session of the Irish parliament to meet in the country's stunning new parliament house.

Dorset's objectives for this session were very limited ones. The duke believed that among most members there was "a disposition to make the session tolerably easy," and he intended nothing that might change that mood.[13] The only request for additional funds would be a provision for paying the interest on the debt. When the duke outlined his scheme to Newcastle, he admitted that it was fraught with difficulties. "I dare not promise success," he wrote, "nor will I despair of it."[14]

Dorset opened the session on October 5, 1731. In the speech from the throne, the duke expressed concern about the great deficiencies in the public revenues, asked for supplies for the usual period, and sought some provision for interest payments and debt retirement. In the addresses following the lord lieutenant's speech, the commons promised to do what the resources of the nation

11. Cary to Delafaye, September 26, 1731. SP63/394/73.
12. Robert Clayton to Lady Sundon, November 9, 1731. Add. Mss. 20102, 152–154.
13. Dorset to Newcastle, October 8, 1731. SP63/394/93.
14. *Idem.*

would allow but took notice of the distressed state of the country and the decay of trade.[15] The duke's parliamentary managers seized upon the cooperation evidenced by the addresses and brought in the money bills very early. By November 13, the committee on ways and means had completed its work and was ready to report the bills to the entire house. When the voting was over on November 14, the duke had obtained almost everything he requested and came very close to getting a permanent provision for a sinking fund to discharge the debt.

When Carteret had tried to obtain long-term funding of the debt in 1729, he had been defeated by five votes. Dorset failed in this session by only one vote. His grace hoped that all of his friends in England would be pleased by how well the Irish parliament had been managed.[16] Others in Ireland, however, were much less sanguine about what Dorset's government had done and what it could do. For example, the loss of long-term debt funding in 1731 was proclaimed in a pamphlet published during a major Anglo-Irish political crisis two decades later as a great victory for patriotism and the popular party. According to the anonymous author of *The Ministerial Conduct of the Chief Governors of Ireland*, this victory had been won by the late arrival of Colonel Charles Tottenham, member for New Ross, who dashed into the house in boots and riding clothes splashed with mud to cast his tie-breaking vote against the government and against long-term debt funding. Thereafter, according to this pamphlet, "to Tottenham in his boots" became one of the more popular patriotic toasts drunk in drawing rooms and public houses throughout the city.[17] Scarcely any contemporary viewed the loss of long-term debt funding in 1731 as any sort of major political victory or defeat. It was a disappointment but nothing more. However, in the opinion of Robert Clayton, Bishop of Killala, it was a disappointment that could have been avoided.

Bishop Clayton admitted that Dorset's entertainments had been grand affairs. Nonetheless, he believed they had been ineffective. According to Clayton, the chief secretary was far too busy in public

15. Address from the House of Commons, October 5, 1731. SP63/394/86.
16. Newcastle to Dorset, November 29, 1731. SP63/394/129.
17. *The Ministerial Conduct of the Chief Governors of Ireland* (Dublin, 1751).

and less so in private for the bishop's liking. In the house of commons, where in Clayton's judgment he should have sat still, Cary was "perpetually running about speaking to members even in the midst of a debate, whereas people don't love to have all the world know how they are directed."[18] If the truth were known of the division on long-term debt funding, wrote the bishop, with proper precautions what had been lost by one vote should have been carried by twenty.[19]

Toasts to Tottenham and misgivings about Cary notwithstanding, Dorset never let affairs in the house of commons get out of control. When a crisis arose, the chief governor acted with dispatch. For example, some gentlemen from Cork banded together in an effort to make a representation to the king on the state of the nation. According to Thomas Tickell, secretary to the lords justices, Dorset received "early intelligence of such a design and found means to defeat it."[20] He prevailed upon Sir Ralph Gore to meet with them and explain the virtues of good behavior.[21] The gentlemen dropped their scheme when they calculated probable defeat by a margin of six to one.[22] Bishop Clayton had a much different explanation for why and how the intended representation was abandoned. He described the proposed resolutions as "in reality a complaint against the administration" and blamed their rise on Cary's mismanagement.[23]

The return of the money bills from England was delayed by weather. The packets had been held up at Holyhead for several days by contrary winds. In Dublin Castle this delay was a source of anxiety. One untoward parliamentary representation had been stopped, but until the money bills were returned and approved there was always the possibility of another. Cary described what the delays at Holyhead had done to the mood of the Irish government. "I never thought I should desire or have been fond of an Easterly wind," he wrote. "But any wind is better than being kept in continued alarm with daly [sic] motions of Patriots."[24] The chief secretary

18. Robert Clayton to Lady Sundon, November 9, 1731. Add. Mss. 20,102, 152–154.

19. Idem.

20. Tickell to Delafaye, December 8, 1731. SP63/394/136.

21. Robert Clayton to Lady Sundon, December 1, 1731. Add. Mss. 20,102, 154.

22. Tickell to Delafaye, December 5, 1731. SP63/394/136.

23. Robert Clayton to Lady Sundon, December 1, 1731. Add. Mss. 20,102, 154.

24. Cary to Delafaye, December 8, 1731. SP63/394/136.

got an easterly wind. The money bills arrived on December 10 and were quickly approved. They received royal assent on the day before Christmas, and the lord lieutenant immediately adjourned parliament until February 3, 1732.[25]

The December packets also brought reports of another development which promised great difficulties when the Irish parliament reassembled. Approval of a bill for disarming papists sent to England in early December had been delayed in the English privy council. This bill was a matter of serious concern to Irish Protestants. An extensive examination of the present state of popery in Ireland was underway in the Irish house of lords and the primate and other bishops were distressed by the information collected. One of the first reports of the returns published in November indicated that popery was flourishing. Boulter had written a long letter to Newcastle in early December about the present disarming bill explaining how Catholics had succeeded in finding loopholes in that obsolete measure enacted in King William's time. Because Protestants were so outnumbered by Catholics in Ireland, the security of Irish Protestants depended on keeping Catholics disarmed. The archbishop had urged Newcastle to use all of his influence to get this new disarming bill quickly approved in the English privy council and promptly returned. Before the end of the year, the Irish ministers learned that the delay of the bill in the English privy council was not accidental. Walpole and his cabinet colleagues had been so impressed by the lord lieutenant's success getting the money bills through the Irish parliament that they sought his opinion about pressing for repeal of the test clause that discriminated against Protestant dissenters.

Walpole himself wrote to Dorset explaining that action on the disarming bill had been delayed until his grace's sentiments on repealing the test could be known. Sir Robert believed that "the time seems not only favourable, but the present occasion seems to call for all possible means of strengthening the hands of the Protestants in Ireland."[26] He proposed to carry repeal by adding such a clause into the disarming bill pending before the English

25. Dorset to Newcastle, December 10, 1731. SP63/394/139.
26. *Historical Manuscripts Commission Report on the Manuscripts of Mrs. Stopford-Sackville*, HMSO, London, 1904. Vol. 1, 147, Hereafter cited as HMC Stopford-Sackville.

privy council. Walpole concluded his message to Dorset with some optimistic intelligence and a compliment. He had been advised that the Irish house of lords was strongly in favor of taking off the test now and that opposition in the commons would be much less than ever before. He was especially pleased that "the honour of passing a Bill to relieve the Protestant Dissenters from a burthen . . . which they have a long time unjustly and unreasonably groaned under"[27] would go to Dorset.

Walpole's intelligence about the disposition of the Irish parliament to repeal the test was absolutely wrong. Newcastle suggested what might have been its source. A delegation of Presbyterians had gone to London,[28] appealed to the government for relief, and suggested the strategy of adding a repeal clause to the disarming bill. When Boulter learned of Walpole's intentions, he was shocked by the minister's misinformation. The primate had heard about an intended application of the Presbyterians for repeal of the test but expected that such an application would have been begun in Dublin. No one, Boulter insisted, had any "suspicion of the thing being done by inserting an additional clause in a bill sent from here of quite another nature."[29] About the prospects of a repeal measure in the Irish parliament the primate had no doubt. He informed Newcastle that if repeal were attempted in either house of parliament, it would probably fail. If repeal came over from England as a clause added to some Irish bill, failure would be absolutely certain. There were too many young giddy members in the house under no direction, Boulter complained, who were so full of false patriotism that they would "throw out a thing they liked merely for its coming from England."[30]

The primate made a number of discreet inquiries and held several conversations with members in town in order to get a more precise estimate of repeal strength in the house of commons. The dissenters themselves reckoned they had about fifty votes or one third of the sitting house; and, like the Duke of Newcastle, they hoped the

27. *Idem.*
28. J. C. Beckett, *Protestant Dissent in Ireland, 1687–1780*, Faber and Faber, Ltd., London, 1946, 91.
29. Boulter to Newcastle, January 15, 1731/32. SP63/395/3.
30. Boulter to Delafaye, January 4, 1731/32. SP63/395/17.

weight of the government would give them a majority. Boulter doubted whether government whipping could make that much difference. Since not more than twenty dissenting gentlemen would benefit from repeal, Boulter saw no point in pressing for it in this fashion at this time. He strongly urged Newcastle to return the disarming bill without the addition of a repeal clause.[31] In separate letters sent to London, the other leaders of the Irish government— lord lieutenant, lord chancellor, and speaker of the house—agreed with the primate. Repeal of the test had no chance of getting through the Irish parliament.

Next, Boulter met with some of the leading dissenters in Dublin and encouraged them to write to their friends in England about the impossibility of carrying repeal at the present time. According to the primate, they accepted his analysis of the situation and promised to write to London forthwith.[32] Some of these dissenters must have written such letters, because in early February, Newcastle advised Boulter that the crisis was over. The English ministry had decided to "lay aside thoughts of repealing the Test for the present."[33]

Although the crisis was over, the fact that it had occurred made ending the session more difficult. Apprehensions about the test had drawn more members to Dublin after the Christmas recess than had been expected. Cary observed that when members were together, they were "apt to give themselves and the Government more trouble than could be wished."[34] That circumstance, he added, put the king's servants to the necessity of strict attendance and careful attention to detail. Finally, when the last of the bills—including the disarming bill without a clause repealing the test—had been returned, Dorset closed the session on March 10.

With the session over and while preparations for the viceregal departure were being made, Cary reflected on what had been accomplished and concluded that the session had been a successful one. "I flatter myself," Cary wrote, "that his Grace has made a glorious campaign especially if his troops be considered, as they really are, a divided, undisciplined militia, without leaders and

31. Boulter to Newcastle, January 15, 1731/32. SP63/395/3.
32. Boulter to Newcastle, January 18, 1731/32. SP63/395/5–6.
33. Newcastle to Boulter, February 5, 1731/32. SP63/395/7.
34. Cary to Delafaye, February 22, 1731/32. SP63/395/64.

without pay."[35] The chief secretary was perhaps too theatrical in his description, but he was correct. No settled system for managing the Irish house of commons had been devised. Though no system operated in the house, the king's business had been completed. However, as March turned into April, neither Dorset nor Cary had many thoughts about system building or party organizing. They had completed their work and both were very anxious to leave. The viceregal party boarded the yacht on April 22, and despite heavy weather they departed immediately for Parkgate.[36]

Dorset's First Encounter with Henry Boyle

Impressions of Dorset's performance in Ireland reached London before he did, and they were not all favorable. Lord Wilmington inquired of friends with correspondents in Ireland about how Dorset had fared. The responses faulted the duke for acting injudiciously by committing government's authority to matters that were unimportant and then losing the point intended to win. After only one session in Ireland such reports did not enhance the duke's reputation in ministerial circles, but they did no serious damage to it either. There were no doubts in anyone's mind that he would return.

Decisions about appointments and patronage pursued the lord lieutenant wherever he went and some important judicial ones no longer could be avoided. John Pocklington, second Baron of the Irish Court of the Exchequer since 1714 and an Englishman, had died in October; and though both Dorset and Boulter had favored John Wainwright, a scholarly English lawyer and friend of the Duke of Newcastle, they had agreed to keep the post vacant until the late session of the Irish parliament had ended.[37] Dorset recommended Wainwright for the Court of the Exchequer on May 30, 1732, and then offered the names of Thomas Carter, Henry Boyle, and Welbore Ellis, Bishop of Meath, for the Irish privy council.[38]

Throughout the rest of 1732 the lords justices kept the duke

35. Cary to Delafaye, March 11, 1731/32. SP63/395/98.
36. Lords Justices to Newcastle, April 24, 1732. SP63/395/116.
37. Dorset to Newcastle, October 27, 1731. SP63/394/101.
38. Dorset to Newcastle, May 24, 1733. SP63/395/124.

informed about the state of the country. Except for a large and detailed correspondence about the wreck of a Danish East Indian-man, *Golden Lion*, off the Kerry coast and the subsequent theft of a dozen chests of silver bars salvaged from her, Irish affairs did not heavily intrude upon the Duke of Dorset's other activities and diversions until February 1733, when Sir Ralph Gore suddenly became ill and died. As lord justice, speaker of the house of commons, and leader of the old Conolly party, Gore had been an important, if not always effective, member of the government of Ireland. His passing left a leadership vacuum in the Irish house of commons which would not long remain unfilled. Selection of a successor had to be done carefully and quickly.

Speculation about a new speaker began with Gore's illness in January and intensified after his death. On the day after Gore died, Robert Clayton, Bishop of Killala, observed to Lady Sundon that Gore's demise would "occasion a great revolution in the political affairs of this kingdom."[39] What Bishop Clayton had in mind was clear enough to persons whose knowledge of Irish politics went back ten years. Henry Boyle was the first person publicly to declare his intentions to seek the chair, but the names of Coghill, Carter, and Singleton were also frequently mentioned as candidates. Coghill took himself out of consideration even before Sir Ralph succumbed. Carter and Singleton both declared early for Boyle but did not discourage rumors about their own prospects. However, neither Carter nor Singleton possessed fortunes or territorial influence comparable to that of Boyle. At one time Carter's father had been a footman for Lord Percival's uncle. Furthermore, Boulter would have moved heaven and earth to stop Carter, and Dorset was not disposed to make a special effort on behalf of Singleton. In several ways Boyle's accession to the chair would be a new departure in Irish politics, but his pretensions were too strong to be opposed.

In the end, there was not much for the lord lieutenant or the lords justices to discuss or do about selecting the person to succeed Gore. Boyle could not be stopped, and the matter was virtually settled two weeks after Sir Ralph died. The two lords justices—

39. Robert Clayton to Lady Sundon, February 23, 1732/33. Add. Mss. 20, 102, 174.

Boulter and Wyndham—met several times during the last week of February and the first week of March and presented their collective views to Dorset and then to Newcastle. Given the present undirected state of the house of commons, the Irish government simply could not manage the outcome of an election for the speaker's chair. The Irish government had no choice except to recommend Henry Boyle and facilitate an easy access to the chair for him.

Boulter described Boyle as a member of a younger branch of the Burlington family and acknowledged that the lords justices had received a request from Lord Burlington for a positive recommendation from the lord lieutenant. Both the lord chancellor and myself, wrote Boulter, "think in our present circumstances, it will be the most for his Majesty's service, and for the good of the common interest of England and Ireland, that he should be supported by the government in this affair."[40] Having made that point to Newcastle, his grace of Armagh tried to make another. I cannot omit taking this occasion, he observed, to suggest that the present situation provided a "proper occasion of appointing a lord justice who is not speaker of the house of commons." In time, he added, "it may be of ill consequence to the Crown to have it thought here, that a Speaker by virtue of that station is entitled to be one of the Lords Justices."[41]

However, if Boyle could not be kept out of the speaker's chair, there was no basis for supposing that he could be denied appointment as a lord justice. The primate recommended Gore's vacated sinecure of chancellor of the Irish exchequer for Boyle and urged that a public declaration about the succession to the chair be made as soon as possible to forestall future mischief. Apparently no such declaration was issued until Dorset returned to Dublin in September 1733. What Boulter feared would happen did happen. The new speaker believed himself unkindly used and stated that the lord lieutenant's belated declaration for him had been meaningless.[42] Convinced that he owed the lord lieutenant nothing, Boyle proceeded to behave accordingly.

Boyle's assertion of independence came at a most inopportune

40. Boulter to Newcastle, March 6, 1732/33. SP63/396/15.
41. *Idem.*   42. HMC Egmont, I, 463.

Marble bust of Henry Boyle, First Earl of Shannon.
Courtesy of Public Record Office of Northern Ireland

time. Before leaving England for Dublin in September, Dorset received explicit instructions to attempt repeal of the test. While traveling from London to Holyhead, Dorset gave serious thought to ways that support for repeal could be organized. On a matter such as repeal of the test, the duke knew he could not count on the influence of Boulter. Carter might be helpful because in the distant past the Midleton party had been sympathetic to the cause of repeal. Dorset decided to oblige Carter beforehand with a favor worth £500 a year.

The lord lieutenant and his party were windbound at Holyhead for about a week and his grace did not arrive in Dublin until September 17. Once the formalities and pomp of arrival were over, Dorset met with representatives of the dissenters and told them of his intentions about the test.[43] Immediately, Cary began trying to organize parliamentary support, and the duke spoke to "everyone dependent on the government as well as all others he could hope to influence to dispose them to concur in this design."[44] However, the more Dorset talked to gentlemen about the test, the more he became convinced that opposition to repeal had not diminished at all since the last session. Committed to attempt repeal in both his private and public capacities, the lord lieutenant could not retreat without disgrace. Yet without some miraculous revolution in opinion, he could not succeed. Caught between the hammer of ministerial instruction and the anvil of political reality, the lord lieutenant opted for political reality. He decided against raising the issue of repeal in either house of the Irish parliament until after the money bills had been approved.[45]

The session opened on October 4 and began well. Boyle was unanimously elected speaker of the house of commons. In the speech from the throne, the duke asked for nothing from the commons except the usual financial supplies and provisions for the national debt. He made no reference in the speech to repeal of test.[46] The addresses were polite and complimentary. Cary was not deceived by the tranquility of the opening, and he confided to one of his English correspondents that the session was likely to be very

43. Boulter to Newcastle, December 18, 1733. SP63/396/117.
44. *Idem.*
45. Boulter to Newcastle, December 18, 1733. SP63/396/117.
46. Lord Lieutenant's Speech, October 4, 1733. SP63/396/70–75.

troublesome.[47] The main cause of difficulty would be the government's commitment to repeal, but there were others. The most important one was that no progress had been made toward improving the management of the house of commons. The heart of the management problem seemed to be that from either choice or circumstances the government continued to deal with individuals rather than with blocs. Because so many gentlemen had to be solicited, scarcely any had been actually taken into viceregal confidence. In this last particular, the former friends of Lord Carteret were much chagrined. They perceived themselves to be "treated with great coldness and indifference."[48]

Among those former friends of Lord Carteret most sensitive to this perceived viceregal coldness and indifference was Marmaduke Coghill, who communicated those sentiments along with other information to English friends close to Newcastle and Walpole. According to Coghill, Boyle had not brought much strength to the government. Several of the new speaker's friends had announced their intentions to vote against the court if and when the repeal issue came before the house of commons. Even more important than pronouncements by Boyle's friends was the relationship of Boyle himself to the government. Coghill was unable to discover just what the nature of that relationship was. He did not know whether the speaker and the lord lieutenant shared any confidence at all.[49] Thus divided and angry the Irish house of commons turned to the money bills.

When the committee of accounts took up the money bills, the house was unusually full. Rumors about the test had brought in members and other interested persons from far and wide. Agents of the dissenters came down from the north and openly solicited among members for support. Apprehension over the prospect of repeal made the committee of accounts dilatory and uneasy. Members opposed to repeal tried by all means to delay the progress of the money bills, being well assured that nothing would be attempted for the dissenters until those bills had been approved.[50]

47. Cary to Delafaye, October 5, 1733. SP63/396/71.
48. Coghill to Southwell, October 20, 1733. Add. Mss. 21,123.
49. HMC Egmont, I, 463.
50. Cary to Delafaye, November 20, 1733. SP63/396/99.

Even though the Dorset administration had obtained greater savings than any of its predecessors, the accounts were scrutinized in committee with great care. Nothing was allowed to pass without question. No one was in a hurry to report progress or complete committee action. Proceedings in the committee continued to be protracted until mid-November when a new strategy for stopping repeal of the test was devised. Thereupon, the committee of accounts reported to the full house; the money bills were approved and sent off to England on November 20, 1733.[51]

Prevented from trying the strength of repeal in the house by the government's refusal to bring in a bill, opponents of the measure found a way to raise the issue on their own. Sir Richard Meade, member for Kinsale and long time friend of Boyle, moved a resolution fixing a day beyond which the house would not receive a bill to repeal the test. Though some of the lord lieutenant's friends spoke against Meade's motion, as Boulter reported, there was "such warmth against repeal of the Test, it was not thought prudent to divide the House on this resolution."[52] The cause was hopeless and the whole world knew it. When Cary dined with Boyle shortly thereafter and chided him about the behavior of his Cork friends on the repeal issue, the speaker exploded, replying that his friends were all loyal and good subjects. Any man who loved his country, Boyle continued, would be against taking off the test.[53] Clearly, something had to be done. Two meetings with agents of the dissenters present were held at the Castle. A majority of the gentlemen at these meetings urged Dorset to press no further for repeal.

To the politicians at these meetings it appeared that matters relating to the test had already progressed too far. Great heats had been generated in both houses, wrote Boulter, "with more than the usual obstruction of public business."[54] What sense was there in uniting a majority of the house of commons against the intentions of the government by continuing to press for a measure that had absolutely no chance of getting through the Irish house of lords? There was no sense in that course at all. At a meeting held in Dublin

51. Dorset to Newcastle, November 20, 1733. SP63/396/103.
52. Boulter to Newcastle, December 18, 1733. SP63/396/117.
53. HMC Egmont, I, 453.
54. Boulter to Newcastle, December 18, 1733. SP63/396/117.

on December 13, 1733, the agents and friends of the dissenters agreed to drop further proceedings. Dorset assured Newcastle that although he had this affair much at heart and that the government had done its utmost, the votes for repeal were just not there.[55]

Boulter was much relieved by the lord lieutenant's decision to end the push for repeal. He hoped that once this "uneasiness and handle of discontent" was over tempers would cool and things would return to their normal course.[56] However, tempers did not cool and suspicions once aroused were not easily allayed. A party of lay lords during the repeal had mistakenly imagined that the bishops would bow to government pressure and vote for repeal. This party of Irish lay lords found a precedent in their own journals with which they believed they could stop the bishops from forcing repeal through their house. The Irish lords discovered that in 1716 their house had passed a resolution recommending that bills originating in one house should be communicated to the other house before being sent to the Irish privy council. This discovery led to immediate action. According to Wainwright, these lay lords "perceiving it in their power to carry one point against the bishops did it sword in hand without giving the opponents any time to deliberate."[57] On December 5, 1733, the house of lords passed a resolution requiring that all bills be communicated between the two houses before being presented to the lord lieutenant. The commons also "went headlong in the same proposal."[58] Two days later they passed a similar resolution.

News of the communication resolutions raised anxiety levels several degrees in Westminster. Some English ministers urged enactment of legislation prohibiting the Irish parliament from employing this or any other procedure calculated to increase the initiative and powers of that body.[59] In Ireland, both Cary and Wainwright assured the ministry that this procedure was not new, that it meant nothing, changed nothing, and most likely would not last. However,

---

55. Dorset to Newcastle, December 18, 1733. SP63/396/121.
56. *Idem.*
57. Wainwright to Newcastle, January 16, 1733/34. SP63/397/17–20.
58. *Idem.*
59. *Historical Manuscripts Commission. Manuscripts of the Earl of Egmont, Diary of the First Earl of Egmont* (Viscount Percival), Vol. II, 1734–1738, 19. Hereafter cited as HMC Egmont, II.

even if it did survive, Wainwright would not be disappointed. He saw some positive advantages for the Irish government if both houses continued to use it.

In the first place, this procedure was not new; it only had the appearance of innovation. Moreover, every time the procedure had been taken up and tried, it had been found wanting and was quickly abandoned. The procedure only required communication between the two houses. What one house did with a bill received from the other house did not matter. All bills would still have to be presented to the lord lieutenant and Irish privy council by the originating house.[60] Wainwright reported that, in the past, communication of bills had delayed proceedings in parliament, and that he believed that members would quickly tire of it. He suspected that sooner or later the two houses would disagree over a tithe bill and the procedure would be terminated. Disagreement between the houses over a bill before it reached the council would provide the government with a perfect justification for rejecting "popular and improper bills." This new procedure put the onus of rejection one step farther from the throne.[61]

The advice of Cary and Wainwright was received but not believed. The English ministers simply could not be talked out of their anxieties over the new procedure. Dorset decided to put their minds at ease. He gave his friend Carter a chance to demonstrate his political skill. Carter and others contrived to foment a dispute between the two houses.[62] A tithe limitation bill was sent up from the commons to the lords, whereupon their lordships rejected consideration of it forthwith without dividing the house or giving reasons for their rejection.[63] Disenchanted with the procedure and affronted by the lords on an issue that had great support in the commons, on January 9, 1734, members voted 102 to 27 after a heated discussion to end communication of bills.[64] One week later, the lords voted unanimously for the same resolution. The matter was closed and no one in the Irish government had any fears that it would be

60. Cary to Delafaye, January 10, 1733/34. SP63/397/117.
61. Wainwright to Newcastle, January 16, 1733/34. SP63/397/17–20.
62. HMC Stopford-Sackville, I, 149.
63. HMC Egmont, II, 13.
64. HMC Stopford-Sackville, I, 149.

revived. In Ireland, it had been a tempest in a teapot that lasted less than five weeks. Only four bills actually had been communicated. At no time was the communication procedure an assertion of constitutional independence by the Irish parliament against the parliament and government of England.

English ministers were very pleased that both houses of the Irish parliament had decided to reject the communication procedure, but very few of them praised Dorset for his role in ending it. According to Doddington, the king, queen, Walpole, Lord Wilmington, and others were much alarmed over what they perceived as the outrageous pretensions of the Irish parliament. They regarded the resolution establishing the communication procedure "as a subversion of the royal prerogative and (either by mistake or design) the total dissolution of the dependence of Ireland upon England."[65] When news of the final rejection of the communication procedure reached London, official anxieties lessened. The four bills that had been communicated were quietly approved by the English privy council, but Dorset's reputation as an administrator and political manager had been severely damaged.

Though Dorset had done well by transmitting the money bills in mid-November and then getting them quickly approved after their return in early December, the miscarriage of the repeal effort and the communication business were enough to convince Walpole and others that Dorset's usefulness in Ireland was over. To the lords and gentlemen in Westminster it appeared that his grace either could not or would not attend to business and manage the Irish parliament. Boyle had stated publicly that he no longer felt any responsibility to oblige the lord lieutenant.[66] Dorset's friends at court kept him apprised of what people were saying, and some of them urged him to return to England as soon as possible. The duke turned all of his energies toward ending the session and obtaining an early departure.

The only matters remaining unsettled after the Christmas recess were some ecclesiastical appointments, a decision about who should be appointed as the third lord justice when the duke departed, and

65. HMC Stopford-Sackville, I, 152.
66. Coghill to Southwell, December 4, 1733. Add. Mss. 21,123.

an important bill to relieve the creditors of a recently failed Dublin bank. Welbore Ellis, Bishop of Meath, had died on January 1, 1734, and a succession of translations followed. Dorset recommended Arthur Price, Irish-born Bishop of Ferns, for the vacancy at Meath. Another Irishman, Edward Synge, left Cloyne for Ferns, and against the primate's better judgment[67] the eminent philosopher George Berkeley was installed at Cloyne. Boulter could not abide Berkeley and thought him a madman.[68] Because the matter had been settled in England, the primate accepted what he could not prevent. Dorset's chaplain and confidant George Stone was given Berkeley's old post as Dean of Derry.

The question of who should be the third lord justice was a difficult one, but it had to be answered quickly if Dorset was to have any hope of an early departure. The duke was of the same mind as Boulter about the desirability of keeping the offices of speaker and lord justice separated. However, what might be desirable in Irish politics was not always possible. The lord lieutenant confessed that he could find no alternative to Henry Boyle to serve as the third lord justice.[69] With more hope than conviction, Dorset assured Newcastle that "I can therefore no longer doubt but that he will be the most proper person for the third lord justice."[70]

Once the decision about Boyle's appointment as lord justice had been made, the only issue of importance unresolved was whether or not the creditors of Burton's Bank would be paid. This highly respected Dublin bank, which had served the government and financial community since 1700, closed its doors in June 1733. When the bank failed, liabilities exceeded assets by almost £180,000, and nine hundred customers faced the prospect of losing their savings.[71] However, many of those customers were not ordinary people—they included Archbishop Boulter, other members of the government, and many members of parliament. Consequently, several bills were brought into parliament requiring compulsory sales of lands held

67. Boulter to Newcastle, February 25, 1733/34. SP63/397/58.
68. HMC Egmont, I, 224.
69. Dorset to Newcastle, February 22, 1733/34. SP63/397/53.
70. Idem.
71. F. G. Hall, History of the Bank of Ireland, (Hodges, Figgis and Co., Dublin, 1949), 7.

by the heirs of the bank partners and directors in order to compen-
sate the bank's creditors. The heirs and other interested parties
sought unsuccessfully to block approval of these measures in Dublin
and again later in the English privy council.

Cary described the entire business as "like the South Sea Affair
in 1720" and that members were determined that all banks would
be more closely regulated in the future.[72] Debates on this bill continued for eighteen days. At the head of the opposition to the bill
in the Irish parliament was none other than Lord Chief Justice
Rogerson. As Boulter told the story, Rogerson was not an heir of
the bank partners but the motives for his opposition were no less
personal. Rogerson's son-in-law Abraham Creighton was a major
creditor of the bank. If the demands of all nine hundred creditors
were accepted as *bona fide* debts worthy even of partial payment out
of the proceeds of compulsory land sales, Creighton's prospects
for full compensation would be greatly diminished.[73] Rogerson's
opposition notwithstanding, a bill cleared the house of commons at
the end of January 1734. Though the bill was hotly contested in the
Irish privy council for several days, it was approved and sent off to
London in early February.

At the end of March, Cary wrote to friends in England urging
them to use their influence to get the bill approved and returned
as soon as possible. The whole credit of the country, the chief
secretary insisted, "depends on the success of the bill, and if it
should miscarry, there would be a run on all banks in this Kingdom,
and everything would be in confusion."[74] Finally, in mid-April the
English privy council acted and approved the bill. It was dispatched
to Dublin, arriving there on April 23. The bill was quickly approved
by the parliament and given royal assent.

Five days after the bill arrived, Dorset brought this frustrating
session to an end. Concerned about the state of his reputation with
Walpole and the other English ministers, Dorset wrote to Newcastle
on the eve of his departure requesting a meeting in the very near
future.[75] The lord lieutenant and chief secretary boarded the yacht
on May 1 and with fair winds immediately set out for Parkgate.

72. Cary to Delafaye, January 26, 1733/34. SP63/397/34.
73. Boulter to Walpole, March 28, 1734. Boulter's Letters, II, 119.
74. HMC Various Collections, VI, 61.
75. Dorset to Newcastle, April 30, 1734. SP63/397/131.

Patronage, The Tithe of Agistment, and Prudential Politics

Dorset knew that the events and disappointments of the late session had damaged his reputation with the English ministry. He did not know how serious that damage was and he certainly did not imagine that Walpole had begun to think about finding a new lord lieutenant for Ireland. When Dorset reached London and spoke with friends there, he discovered that Sir Robert seemed willing to forgive the failure to carry repeal of the test and had forgotten the business of the communication resolutions but was absolutely incensed over Dorset's efforts to appoint Hugh Dickson, member of parliament for Cork city and close friend of Henry Boyle, to be collector of customs for that city.

The affair of the Cork collectorship began when that post became vacant in March 1734. Boyle had strongly recommended Dickson as the person most worthy and qualified to take over the post at Cork. The lord lieutenant met with the revenue commissioners and prevailed upon them to appoint Dickson even though they informed him that Walpole had recommended John Love, then collector at Mallow, to succeed at Cork.[76] The commissioners agreed to appoint Dickson, which they did on April 8,[77] but only after Dorset personally promised to straighten out the entire matter with Walpole after he arrived in England.[78] Dorset left the country on May 1, whereupon shortly thereafter Love arrived in Dublin with a letter from the English treasury authorizing his appointment to Cork. The commissioners were in a quandary. They had no choice except to obey the treasury order and replace Dickson with Love, which they did on June 6, 1734.[79] However, the process by which that decision was reached was extremely painful.

When the lords justices learned about the English treasury order, they commanded the commissioners to appear before them at Dublin Castle and asked if the commissioners intended to remonstrate

76. *Historical Manuscripts Commission. Manuscripts in Various Collections*, HMSO, Dublin, 1909, Vol. VI, 61. Hereafter cited as HMC Various Collections.
77. *Eighteenth Century Irish Official Papers in Great Britain, Private Collections*, HMSO, Belfast, 1973, I, 97. Hereafter cited as Irish Official Papers, I.
78. HMC Various Collections, VI, 62.
79. Irish Official Papers, I, 97.

against the treasury order.[80] The commissioners responded politely but firmly that they did not believe it was their duty to do so. At that moment, Lord Justice Boyle "fell into a most violent rage, scarce to be imagined, setting forth the disquiet it would give in the country if Mr. Dickson should be superseded."[81] The commissioners responded by lamenting "their unfortunate situation to be between two great powers" and contended that if such a remonstrance was in order, it was more appropriate for the lords justices to do it. According to one of the commissioners, neither Boulter nor Wyndham showed any disposition for that undertaking, "so we left Mr. Boyle full of resentment."[82]

Much of that resentment was poured out by Boyle in a letter to an English correspondent after his meeting with the other lords justices and revenue commissioners. In this letter, Boyle also set out a most explicit statement of his own role in the parliamentary politics and the government of his country. If Dickson was demolished, Boyle wrote, we are all undone unless he is timely and effectually relieved. If everyone here is to understand that Dickson is to be laid aside, he complained, where is my credit, where is my influence, or what business do I have here when I can no longer be of use to his majesty's affairs? Boyle's personal interest would not suffer much because of Dickson's denial, but how his friends would behave in the future, no one could predict. You, sir, Boyle continued, "very well know the difficulties I laboured under at my first setting out, and the pains I was frequently obliged to be at from four in the afternoon to five or six in the morning to persuade my troops to fight in a cause foreign to their own principles or natural inclinations, and, now just as they are brought into a good discipline, I can expect no less than a revolt if they find their endeavours to support me have proved altogether ineffectual."[83] If Boyle could not reward his supporters as promised, "if the foundation I stand on be sapped,"[84] there were others in the house ready to argue that conspicuous opposition would pay more, that is, opposition would win more from the present Irish government than regular support under the speaker's direction.

80. HMC Various Collections, VI, 62.
81. *Idem.*   82. *Idem.*
83. *Ibid.*, 61–62.   84. *Idem.*

While Dorset and Cary would have disagreed with Boyle's estimate of how hard he had worked during the late session to persuade
his friends to take up causes foreign to their own principles or
natural inclinations, the lord lieutenant and chief secretary both
would have admitted that Boyle's friends were the closest thing to
an organized government party in the Irish house of commons. As
lord justice, speaker of the house of commons, and leader of the
government party in that house, Boyle perceived himself as being
the king's first minister in Ireland. Similar to his predecessors Gore
and Conolly, Boyle saw himself as the link between the house of
commons and the crown. All other members of the Irish executive
were appointed. Boyle was the only Irish office holder who was in
any formal sense responsible to the house of commons. Boyle saw
himself cast for the same role in Irish politics that Walpole was
playing in England.

Boyle had no truck whatsoever with patriot notions of independency. He was the chief Irish minister given to the king by the
commons. In that role, his principal tasks were to see that the king's
business in the Irish parliament was done and that the enemies of
the present Irish constitution in church and state, inside and outside
of parliament, were kept powerless. The present undirected state
of Irish parliamentary politics was fraught with all sorts of dangers.
The late session had been proof positive of that condition. The
house of commons was manageable, but management required
resources and of late the meager resources of the present Irish
government had been diverted to other purposes. The English
ministers either had to trust someone like Boyle and his friends
with sufficient patronage to manage the politicians of the country
or resign themselves to the prospect of continuing political difficulties with the Irish parliament. In the summer of 1734, Walpole
decided that for the moment at least Boyle would get his way. The
Irish house of commons was his to manage if he could. Tranquil
parliamentary sessions were worth a few jobs.

This decision was not lightly made or easily obtained. Dorset met
with Walpole in early June and argued that the king's business in
Ireland would suffer if those members of that parliament who had
usefully served the court were not properly rewarded.[85] Walpole

85. HMC Egmont, II, 109.

insisted that all places in the Irish revenue were in the gift of the English treasury. Moreover, Walpole contended that entrusting a collectorship as important as Cork to a man whose financial circumstances were as broken as were those of Dickson was dangerous. Whatever else was said on the matter at the time is unknown. The result was that Dorset and Boyle prevailed over Walpole, but in the long run Walpole's judgment proved to be the correct one. Love agreed to resign the post for a pension of £400,[86] and in November Dickson was formally reinstated.[87] Dickson held the collectorship for seven years, and his performance in office absolutely confirmed Walpole's worst fears. When Dickson died in 1741, he owed just about anyone who had the misfortune to do business with him. But most of all, Dickson owed large sums to his majesty's commissioners of the revenue. Dickson's estate had to be sold to pay his debts and because of encumbrances on it an act of parliament was required to enable the sale to be completed.[88]

Dorset's role in the affair of the Cork collectorship could not be forgotten. When the king was in Hanover during the spring of 1735, Walpole obtained the queen's permission to remove Dorset from the lord lieutenancy. At that time, Walpole secretly offered the post to Lord Scarborough, who shocked the minister by refusing the appointment. If Lord Hervey can be believed, the duke was only partially aware of what had transpired. When he went back to Ireland in September, 1735, he was confident that his own political strength had been too much even for Walpole to overcome.[89] Walpole was content to let Dorset enjoy his fantasy.

Dorset arrived in Dublin from Holyhead on September 25, 1735, and proceeded to the Castle with another of his now-customary displays of pomp and circumstance. The chief secretary expected fair weather but added, "how long it will last, I can't say; for there is a most uncertain climate and storms arise in a minute, some squall we must expect."[90] In his speech from the throne, Dorset asked only for supplies sufficient to maintain the establishments and to service

---

86. Irish Official Papers, I, 72.   87. *Ibid.*, 97.
88. Richard Terry to Boyle, June 6, 1741. Shannon Mss., D.2707/A/1/11, PRONI.
89. Lord John Hervey, *Some Materials Toward Memoirs of the Reign of George II,* ed. Romney Sedgewick (Eyre and Spottiswoode, Ltd., London, 1931), II, 163–164.
90. Cary to Andrew Stone, October 9, 1735. SP63/398/52.

the debt.[91] The addresses were polite and routine. The squall Cary expected never struck. Henry Boyle commanded the parliamentary winds to abate, and abate they did. The issue that Cary had in mind as a source of difficulty and that should have inspired patriots to hitherto unreached heights of denunciation was that of paying a salary from an Irish sinecure to an English politician. As Clerk of the Pells, George Doddington—confidant of the Prince of Wales and opponent of Walpole—had fees worth £3,000 owed to him. What was owed could be paid only if the committee of ways and means of the Irish house of commons approved an authorizing resolution.

In the previous session Carter and others had spoken out sharply against giving Irish money to English politicians, and Doddington's petition for payment had been rejected 93 to 76.[92] In this instance, however, the lord lieutenant supported Doddington's case. So also did Boyle, who described the Clerk of the Pells as a sincere man.[93] Carter had reversed himself from his position of last session and found Doddington worthy and deserving. As a matter of fact, there were only three or four prominent politicians ready to declare open war on the petition,[94] and in the end the question carried without a division.[95]

This remarkable revolution of parliamentary opinion can be attributed to two circumstances. First, most members believed that Doddington had helped Boyle resolve the Dickson matter. Second, Doddington's petition was an opportunity for Boyle to show just how well he could manage the Irish house of commons, and he took it. What could have been an embarrassing and protracted struggle for the Irish government turned out to be an almost routine committee approval. Clearly, Irish parliamentary politics had changed. A new system of managing the Irish parliament was in place. Henceforth, if and when the speaker and his friends and the lord lieutenant were of the same mind, there would be few in the house of commons to oppose them. The new system also worked wonders with the money bills. While the lord lieutenant asked for nothing

91. Dorset's Speech, October 7, 1735. SP63/398/56.
92. HMC Egmont, II, 450.
93. HMC Various Collections, VI, 64.
94. *Idem.*   95. *Ibid.*, 66.

new, he got what he wanted quickly and with minimum difficulty. Dorset reported the money bills in a remarkable state of forwardness on November 6, 1735.[96] Within a week they had cleared the house and were approved by the privy council and sent off to England.[97]

Matters proceeded expeditiously in the Irish parliament until early December. Though the money bills were returned by December 7 and obtained quick approval shortly thereafter,[98] two events occurred—one in England and one in Ireland—which created an uproar in the Irish house of commons. In England, Lord Clancarty succeeded in introducing a bill which would give him leave to sue in court for recovery of Irish estates forfeited by his father during the revolution of 1688. Lord Clancarty contended that his father, being only nineteen years old at the time, could be himself debarred from the property but was too young to forfeit for his unborn offspring, because the estates in question had been entailed.[99] News of the introduction of this bill spread rapidly throughout Dublin. Irish Protestants were enraged by the fact that leave had been given to proceed with such a measure. Dorset reported that an address on this matter would be forthcoming, and on December 19 an address protesting the Clancarty bill was presented to his grace by the speaker, attended by the entire house. The address was sent off immediately and was graciously received and answered by the king. In his answer, the king promised to discourage all future attempts at reversing outlawries imposed after the rebellion of 1641 and the revolution of 1688. Completely satisfied with the royal answer, the house of commons voted an address of thanks to his majesty[100] and then turned their attention to another issue that also touched many of the landlords of the country.

The issue of the tithe of agistment or tithing of pasturage grazed by dry and barren cattle was an old one given new life in December 1735. Moreover, tithe of agistment was an issue that divided Protestant lay lords and commoners from their bishops and clergymen.

96. Dorset to Newcastle, November 6, 1735. SP63/398/74.
97. Dorset to Newcastle, November 15, 1735. SP63/398/82.
98. Dorset to Newcastle, December 7, 1735. SP63/398/92.
99. Southwell to Coghill, April 22, 1735. Mss. 875, NLI.
100. Dorset to Newcastle, February 9, 1735/36. SP63/399/42.

Resistance to paying this tithe went back to the Duke of Ormonde's time and continued sporadically until 1722. In that year, the rights of the clergy to collect it were legally established by a suit brought into the Irish Court of the Exchequer by Archdeacon Neale of Leighlin, whose claims were subsequently upheld by an appeal to the King's Bench in England.[101] Nonetheless, lay resistance continued, and in early December 1735 a petition was introduced into the house of commons by several "Gentlemen, in behalf of themselves and the Rest of the Farmers, Grasiers of Ireland."[102] In this petition the gentlemen prayed for relief against suits demanding the tithe of agistment and argued that according to the best "Information . . . no such Tythes have ever been paid, or even demanded in this kingdom until a few years since."[103] The petition was received but nothing happened. Parliament adjourned for the holidays and did not meet again until mid-February 1736.

Thus matters stood on the issue of the tithe of agistment until mid-March when a second petition protesting against suits demanding payment of that tithe was presented by another group of gentlemen and freeholders. Action came in the form of resolutions alleging that the clergy were amply provided for by glebes, undisputed tithes, and other emoluments; that a demand for the tithe of agistment was new, grievous, and burdensome to landlords and tenants; that this new demand weakened the Protestant interest by encouraging emigration; that pressing for this unlawful tithe had allowed popery and infidelity to gain ground by creating dissensions between clergy and laymen; and that this tithe ought to be resisted by all legal means until a proper remedy could be provided by the legislature.[104] No more than fifty of the sitting members dissented from the resolutions.

Though not having the effect of law, these resolutions effectively deterred tithe owners from trying to collect the tithe of agistment. Irish landlords formed associations to resist this tithe, and funds were collected to support those who might be sued by the clergy.

101. Louis A. Landa, *Swift and the Church of Ireland* (New York: Oxford University Press, 1954), 136.
102. *Idem.*   103. *Idem.*
104. Donald Harman Akenson, *The Church of Ireland: Ecclesiastical Reform and Revolution, 1800–1885* (New Haven, Conn.: Yale University Press, 1971), 96.

Judges who had gone on circuit told the primate that "there was a rage stirred up against the clergy . . . equalling anything they had seen against popish priests in the most dangerous times they remembered."[105] Inside the house, members succeeded in intimidating the clergy. Some gentlemen threatened to move for a committee to inquire into how well bishops and clergymen were performing their pastoral duties. This threat proved to be enough. The tithe of agistment could not be collected and was abandoned. In all of these proceedings, except for Archbishop Boulter the government remained neutral, and by remaining neutral the lord lieutenant was able to close the parliamentary session with dignity and ease. As a matter of fact, if the addresses presented by both houses of the Irish parliament to Dorset are fair indicators of viceregal popularity, the duke was one of the most popular chief governors of the century. No final addresses had been more complimentary; none had been more effusive.

Indeed, the session had been an easy one with the Irish government doing more following than leading. Some members, such as Coghill, thought the session had begun well and ended poorly, and were very glad that it was over. Others, such as Wainwright, sensed that something important had happened in Irish politics and that the immediate future would be much different from the past. "All things go on quietly," he wrote to Doddington, "and respect to the Duke has kept them more so than ever I expect to see them again."[106] All things were out soon, he continued, and tarnish in this Irish air, and nothing tarnishes faster than friendship. As an Englishman in Ireland since 1732, Wainwright had become tired of the country and of its politicians. There was simply no comfort in trying to do one's best. Reputation was much less important in Ireland than in England. Cunning was the science upon which the "masters that mount the stage depend."[107] Cunning was a quality that the new masters of Irish parliamentary politics had in great abundance. According to Wainwright, a majority of the members of the house of commons returned from Munster and Connaught constituencies professed unity under the speaker. Yet, over all cups except Boyle's,

105. Boulter to Angelsey, June 8, 1736/37. Boulter's Letters, Vol. II, 150.
106. HMC Various Collections, VI, 67.
107. Idem.

these same members swore that the speaker did nothing but under the direction and influence of Carter or Bettesworth, or someone else.[108]

A clerical observer, writing to the Archbishop of Canterbury many years after the parliamentary session of 1735–36, considered the failure of the house of lords and the lord lieutenant to prevent spoliation of the clergy over the agistment issue to be a turning point in Irish constitutional and political history. According to Dr. Henry, the house of commons became the paramount force in the Irish constitution, and the power of the house of commons became centered in the speaker. Henry claimed that though Boyle was himself personally sympathetic to the cause of the clergy, in this instance he was obliged to "suffer himself to be borne as the majority pleases or fall to the ground . . . . [P]olitical interests seemed to have prevailed over his virtue."[109] That the Irish house of commons had a leader in the session of 1735–36 was a fact. Conolly had been replaced. That the new leader of the Irish house of commons was disposed to be led by others, there was little doubt. About who was currently helping Boyle to make up his mind, there was much less certainty. Carter and Bettesworth had done so in the past and any number of gentlemen aspired for that role in the future.

Truly, Irish parliamentary politics had changed from its confused and undirected state upon Dorset's arrival. The Irish house of commons had become more manageable and the leadership of that body more managerial. There was a connection in the Irish house of commons under the direction of the speaker that was ready and able to undertake the king's business in that body with fair prospects of carrying it through with success. At the same time, the leadership of this connection was prepared to offer patronage advice and occasionally policy suggestions to the lord lieutenant, which he was disposed to accept and recommend to the English ministry. Dorset would not have admitted or perhaps did not even know that he was also being influenced by the speaker and his friends. What Boulter described as repeated instances of "mild and prudent behavior"[110]

---

108. *Idem.*
109. Dr. Henry to Archbishop of Canterbury, December 21, 1753. Add. Mss., 35,592, 225–232.
110. Boulter to Newcastle, January 8, 1736/37. SP63/400/19.

by the lord lieutenant had been exploited by the Boyle connection for their own advantage. Dorset took advice from influentials in the Irish parliament more often and with better grace than any lord lieutenant since accession of the present royal family. In any case, six weeks after parliament closed on May 17, 1736, the duke boarded the yacht for Parkgate[111] satisfied with himself and wanting to return.

However, Walpole had forgotten nothing and forgiven little. Six years had been long enough for any lord lieutenant and was perhaps too long for this one. As early as February 1737, William, third Duke of Devonshire, was rumored to be Dorset's successor; and Edward Walpole, Sir Robert's second son, was mentioned as the new chief secretary.[112] Walpole had decided to take the government of Ireland out of the hands of a friend of Lord Wilmington and give it to someone closer to himself. The actual appointment of Devonshire as lord lieutenant was delayed until April, and at that time Dorset was reappointed to his old post as Lord Steward of the Household. Though Dorset had been turned out because Walpole lacked confidence in the duke's ability to manage Irish affairs, His Grace of Dorset did not attribute his removal from office to poor performance. He believed that his administration had been a successful one, and he could never rid himself of a desire to return to Ireland once again as chief governor. In time, English politics would present Dorset with another chance to be lord lieutenant of Ireland. At that time, the duke would discover that the passage of sixteen years had not much improved his relationship with the then veteran speaker of the Irish house of commons, Henry Boyle.

111. Lords Justices to Newcastle, May 19, 1736. SP63/399/102.
112. HMC Egmont, II, 342.

CHAPTER II

The Duke of Devonshire and the Rise of the Ponsonby Family, 1737-1744

Devonshire, Boulter, and the English Interest

The Duke of Dorset's successor was the head of one of England's grandest families. William Cavendish, third Duke of Devonshire, was not only the master of the magnificent country estate of Chatsworth and lord of many English and Irish acres, he was also a power in English politics. The duke's close connection with Sir Robert Walpole was evidenced by the fact that the new lord lieutenant chose Edward Walpole, the minister's second son, to be his chief secretary. Devonshire was formally appointed on April 9, 1737, but news of a coming change in the government of Ireland had been widespread as early as February 1737. Wyndham and Boyle both wrote Devonshire congratulatory letters promising assistance and cooperation.[1] Boulter sent off a similar letter,[2] but the primate more than most was anxious to discover what kind of man Devonshire was and where he stood with him.

Boulter's great concern about relating well to the new lord lieutenant derived neither from insecurity nor ambition. The archbishop cared not at all about his own personal political future. He cared very much about the Church of Ireland and about what the recent house of commons' resolution against the tithe of agistment might do to it. The intimidation of the clergy over the tithe of agistment begun by county associations during the last session of

---

1. Wyndham to Devonshire, April 28, 1737. Chatsworth Mss., T.3158/19, PRONI; Boyle to Devonshire April 29, 1737. Chatsworth Mss., T.3158/21, PRONI.
2. Boulter to Devonshire, April 28, 1737. Chatsworth Mss., T.3518/20, PRONI.

parliament had continued during the long recess. Boulter wrote numerous letters to English politicians and churchmen soliciting support for the Irish clergy on the tithe of agistment matter. He warned his friends that these confederacies might well divert their animosities from the Irish clergy to the Irish government and then perhaps to laws enacted for Ireland by the British parliament.[3]

The archbishop had no illusions about where the vast majority of gentlemen in the Irish house of commons stood on the tithe of agistment and had given up all hopes of changing their minds with argument. He now resorted to power. Specifically, Boulter wrote to Walpole and Newcastle urging that these two ministers persuade the king to instruct the new lord lieutenant to protect the rights of the Irish clergy.[4] Boulter's letters had no effect whatsoever. The appeal to power failed. Neither the king nor any of his English or Irish ministers were willing to intervene in any way. Devonshire received no special instructions about the tithe of agistment; and like his predecessor in the last session, the new lord lieutenant left resolution of the issue to the parties involved. The tithe of agistment was dead, though formal abolition did not occur until the end of the century.

Irish lords and gentlemen, bishops and clergy were all favorably impressed by what they heard and saw of his grace of Devonshire. The duke was a sociable man who liked sociable occasions. He was much less formal than his predecessor, and he loved to drink. Devonshire was not as accomplished in that regard as had been Carteret, but few men were. Social Dublin fully expected that Devonshire's levees would be grand affairs and few who attended them ever went away disappointed.

Devonshire arrived in Dublin from Holyhead on September 7, 1737, with his Duchess, seven children, and an entourage of servants. Once installed in accommodations suitable to their rank and numbers, the Cavendishes began to socialize with the Ponsonbies. Brabazon Ponsonby, now Viscount Duncannon, became a confidant of the duke, and his younger sons, William and John, were frequent escorts for the two eldest Cavendish girls, Lady Caroline and Lady

3. Boulter to Walpole, August 9, 1737. Boulter's Letters, Vol. II, 183.
4. Boulter to Newcastle, August 16, 1737. SP63/400/33.

Elizabeth. Thus developed a close social relationship which was to have a profound effect upon Irish politics. Duncannon was one of the last remnants of the old Conolly party who was still active and independent. He had friends and electoral interests in a string of constituencies running from Cork to Down. Duncannon was intensely ambitious for the political advancement of his family and made the most of his friendship with the lord lieutenant.

As parliament's opening approached, an old controversy over the relative value of silver and gold coins threatened to divide existing political connections in the Irish house of commons and complicate the prompt dispatch of the king's business. Because of premiums paid for silver coins by the East India Company and others in England, large quantities had been exported there by Dublin bankers and Cork merchants. Consequently, Ireland suffered from an acute shortage of silver coins. Generally, silver had been replaced in Irish commercial transactions by over-valued large denomination foreign gold coins with the effect of making small cash transactions difficult and complicated. When Boulter managed, after many efforts, to get the Irish privy council to approve a proclamation lowering the value of foreign gold coins in August 1737, Dublin bankers and Cork merchants believed themselves threatened with financial loss and became incensed at the archbishop. For many years, Boulter had argued that lowering the price of gold would have the effect of increasing the supply of silver in the country and thereby would facilitate commerce and trade. In the long run, the August proclamation equalized gold to silver ratios in England and Ireland, but did nothing to alleviate silver shortages, which continued to be severe until the end of the century.

When issued, this proclamation generated great controversy in Dublin and Cork. Right in the center of this controversy was the aging but still vigorous Dean Swift. He denounced the proclamation as soundly as he had ever damned Wood's halfpence. As principal author and promoter of the proclamation, Boulter was singled out for special popular harassment. However, the climax of public uproar over the proclamation did not occur until the lord mayor's banquet in early October, shortly before parliament opened. On that occasion, Swift spoke out bitterly against lowering the value of gold coins. He ended his harangue by telling the primate to his face

that had it not been for himself, the mob would have torn Boulter
to pieces, and that "if he held up his finger he could make them do
it at that instant."[5]

Surely, Swift had exaggerated the depth of popular outrage over
the proclamation and also the extent of his own influence over
the Dublin mob, but not by much. Boulter himself reported that
reducing the gold had "occasioned a great deal of heat."[6] Boulter
believed himself to have been particularly ill-used by persons who
should have known better and complained about the deliberate
circulation of monstrous stories to enrage the people. In Cork the
situation was at once even more outrageous and more organized
than in Dublin. A petition to the house of commons from Cork had
been prepared which urged that house act in this matter and "get
their money put back upon the old footing."[7] When Boulter heard
about the Cork petition he persuaded himself that more than restoring the old value of gold was intended by it.

In part an exculpation of his own role in pressing for the proclamation and in part the result of a dozen years in Irish politics, the
primate saw the Cork petition as the opening cannonade prior to a
full-scale assault on the powers and authority of the Irish privy
council, the body that had issued the proclamation. Boulter urged
Newcastle to advise his majesty to support the present constitutional
position of the Irish privy council at all costs. In this whole business,
he continued, "the aim of several is to depress the English interest
here, which the more some labor to depress, the more necessary
will it be to support by his Majesty's authority."[8]

Boulter's concern for the English interest in the government
of Ireland was genuine and is understandable. For the primate,
preserving the English interest in state and church was a self-evident
principle that only fools with short memories would challenge.
However, there were others in the government of Ireland who
questioned how important and meaningful the primate's distinction
between an English and Irish interest really was. People did not
speak much about whigs and tories anymore and place of nativity

5. HMC Stopford-Sackville, I, 166.
6. Boulter to Newcastle, September 29, 1737. SP63/400/8.
7. HMC Stopford-Sackville, I, 166–167.
8. Boulter to Newcastle, September 29, 1737. SP63/400/8.

was no accurate predictor of anyone's politics. Ten years in Ireland could make an Irishman out of anyone. Boulter was himself proof positive of that fact. He had deep affection for the land and the church in which he had chosen to live and work. Other Englishmen in Ireland, Robert Jocelyn, attorney general, John Bowes, solicitor general, and several on the judicial and episcopal benches had made permanent career choices in Ireland, acquired property in the country, formed strong and lasting social and political connections, and some had even married Irish women and were fathers of Irish children.

Nonetheless, Boulter believed in the existence of an English interest in Irish politics and in the necessity of it. In the present state of unrest over the proclamation, and with so much uncertainty over what its political consequences in parliament might be, Boulter offered to make the ultimate sacrifice and retire.[9] As events were quick to show, no such sacrifice was necessary. Boulter did not retire, but he did withdraw from the forefront of Irish politics. Already past sixty-five, the primate's role in the Devonshire's administration was not to be what it had been under Dorset and Carteret. He devoted most of his attention in the years of life remaining to church matters, expansion of the charter schools, and other charitable and welfare projects.

Despite Boulter's anxieties, the session began well. In the month before parliament opened, Devonshire and Edward Walpole had been busy, drinking, talking, arranging, and promising. The duke opened parliament on October 4, 1737, and continued the policy of his predecessor by asking for nothing more in his speech than "the usual and necessary supplies for the support of the Establishments."[10] Serious business did not begin until the Cork petition was presented on October 18, 1737. On that day the petition was presented and committal was scheduled for October 26. The primate's friends complained bitterly. They had urged immediate rejection, and they believed that they had the votes to obtain rejection. In their opinion, assigning a day for hearings gave the business more honor than it deserved. The speaker found himself in a very

9. *Idem.*
10. Devonshire's Speech, October 14, 1737. SP63/400/96.

ugly situation: he was being forced to choose between his Cork interests and Castle obligations. Boyle convinced Devonshire that, given a little more time, he would be able to bring people to a moderate way of thinking and have the petition dropped.[11] At the same time, Boyle could tell his friends in Cork that if he had not stood between them and the Castle their petition would have been immediately and scornfully rejected. By these means Boyle was able to serve both sides.

How much the speaker truly served himself or anyone else was problematic. He gained no advantage with the lord lieutenant and stirred up political difficulties in Cork that took several months to resolve. In any case, the fate of the Cork petition was settled and further parliamentary debate on lowering the value of gold coins was adjourned indefinitely on October 26. Though the entire matter had been troublesome, the lord lieutenant was satisfied with the outcome and had reason to hope that the progress of the money bills would not be clogged by the dissident friends of Henry Boyle.

The committee of accounts took up the money bills in early November and proceeded through them very slowly. Led by Sir Richard Cox and Eaton Stannard, opposition was very strong. They succeeded in proposing and carrying a resolution that the overruns in several accounts were "a great cause of the debt of the nation and tended to the impoverishment of the kingdom."[12] Lord George Sackville reported to his father that through all of this "The Speaker has behaved with great indifference, and I believe was pleased with what was done."[13] Lord George may have confused surprise with indifference, but in any case the resolution proved to be an embarrassment, nothing more The money bills were passed and dispatched by Devonshire on November 22, 1737, with the usual request that they be given prompt attention by the English privy council and returned to Ireland before Christmas day.[14]

Once again Newcastle obliged the lord lieutenant. He guided the money bills through the English privy council and returned them to Ireland for approval and royal assent by December 11, 1737.

11. HMC Stopford-Sackville, I, 167.
12. HMC Stopford-Sackville, I, 168; Irish Official Papers, I, 34.
13. HMC Stopford-Sackville, I, 168.
14. Devonshire to Newcastle, November 22, 1737. SP63/400/126.

With the business of the session virtually completed, Devonshire dispatched a packet of other bills along with several addresses of condolence upon the death of Queen Caroline and adjourned parliament for the Christmas recess.

With parliamentary business concluded, Devonshire applied for leave to return to England as soon as convenient and to appoint the primate, lord chancellor, and speaker as lords justices. Leave to return was granted. The duke prorogued parliament on March 24, 1738, received flattering addresses for his conduct as chief governor, and embarked with his family for Parkgate on March 26, 1738.[15]

Devonshire, Irish Politicians, and the Catholics

Devonshire had concluded his first session with credit. There had been some difficult moments in the session but Lord George Sackville certainly exaggerated when he described it in November 1737 as by much the most troublesome session he remembered.[16] The troubles which had occurred were not between the duke and any of the political connections in the house of commons. Devonshire was no less popular in March 1738 when he left the country than he had been at the time of his arrival in September 1737. The principal troubles of the last session had been between the speaker and some of his more articulate and ambitious friends. The extent of those troubles was not apparent until after Devonshire had left the country, and Boyle had been once again installed as a lord justice. Boyle had been embarrassed by his Cork friends on the coinage business and had been surprised by their success in carrying a resolution against the over-runs in the accounts. He communicated the extent of his embarrassment and surprise along with some remarks about the behavior of his friends in a confidential conversation to Robert Clayton, Bishop of Cork. The bishop then wrote letters to persons in Cork in which he repeated remarks made by Boyle about Sir Richard Cox, Eaton Stannard, and Anthony Malone. Cox learned about the bishop's letters and thereupon followed a heated correspondence between Cox and Boyle and Cox and the bishop.[17]

15. Lords Justices to Newcastle, March 28, 1738. SP63/401/132.
16. HMC Stopford-Sackville, I, 168.
17. Irish Official Papers, I, 33–34.

According to Cox, the bishop had told friends in Cork that Boyle had said that Cox had promised to get into the counsels of Stannard, Malone, and others and betray them to Boyle. Cox also contended that the bishop had assured several gentlemen in Cork that Boyle had authorized the bishop to repeat this conversation about Cox and that Boyle would avow it to Cox's face.[18] However, Cox categorically denied that he had ever made any promise to get into the counsels of Stannard and Malone or betray anyone.[19] Boyle answered Cox on April 11, 1738, and admitted that he had repeated to the bishop some of the things that Cox had told him. Boyle professed not to understand the reference to Cox's offer to get into the counsels of Stannard and Malone. Apparently Boyle, Cox, and the bishop had been unable to keep their mouths closed. Each one seems to have been telling tales about the other.

If Boyle's reply of April 11, 1738, to Cox was intended to end the matter, it failed. In a long letter to Boyle written on April 20, 1738, Cox tried to guess Boyle's motives for betraying their conversation to Bishop Clayton. He attributed Boyle's hostility to his own refusal to follow the speaker blindly on every question. With regard to Stannard and Malone, Cox insisted, the idea that he would betray his friends was preposterous.

The speaker had read and heard enough. There was no reason to go on with this exchange. In order to end this business in a civil fashion, on May 2, 1738 Boyle proposed a meeting with friends present on both sides where he and Cox could resolve their differences. Cox rejected this proposal out of hand. He saw no useful purpose in such a meeting because Boyle's letters had failed to answer satisfactorily any of the points which he had raised.[20] However, when passions cooled, they would be friends again.

While Cox and Boyle for the moment seemed intent upon losing friends and making enemies, Lord Duncannon was doing exactly the opposite. He had established an extremely close personal and political friendship with the lord lieutenant, and in the summer of 1739 that friendship became a family alliance. William Ponsonby married Lady Caroline Cavendish at Chatsworth on July 5, 1739.

18. *Ibid.*, 33.   19. *Ibid.*, 33–34.
20. *Ibid.*, 34.

This union of a Ponsonby with a Cavendish had immediate social and political consequences. The father of the bridegroom, Brabazon, Viscount Duncannon, became Brabazon, first Earl of Bessborough and obtained appointment as a commissioner on the Irish revenue board. The bridegroom, William Ponsonby, assumed the courtesy title of Lord Duncannon and began functioning as an assistant to the chief secretary.

During the summer of 1739, England drifted into war with Spain which quickly turned into a larger one of nine years' duration with France and Prussia. When Devonshire returned to Ireland in late September 1739, he faced the opening of his second parliamentary session with a new lord chancellor and new law officers. In the summer of 1739 Thomas Wyndham unexpectedly resigned the lord chancellor's seals. Though only in his fifty-eighth year, Wyndham had enough of Ireland. He pleaded fatigue and ill health and departed for England only six weeks after writing his letter of resignation. Boulter discussed the problems of finding a successor with Wyndham and Boyle and then recommended to Devonshire either Chief Justice Reynolds or John Bowes, solicitor general. Boyle made the same recommendation. Reynolds was the first choice and, failing him, Bowes was worthy because of helpful service in the house of commons.[21] However, the great prize went to neither of these men. Somehow Robert Jocelyn, attorney general, learned of Wyndham's intention to resign and applied to Lord Hardwicke, the lord chancellor of England, who was an old and close friend[22] to Jocelyn and the lord lieutenant.[23] Hardwicke met with Walpole and Newcastle;[24] Jocelyn was appointed and became Baron Newport.

Immediately after the English ministers had settled on Jocelyn and had made the appointment, the lord lieutenant wrote to Hardwicke to ask a favor. Devonshire explained that the primate and the speaker in private letters to Newcastle and Walpole had favored Reynolds and Bowes over Jocelyn. The favor which the lord lieutenant solicited was for a few words from Hardwicke to his fortunate

21. Boyle to Devonshire, August 7, 1739. Chatsworth Mss., T.3158/98, PRONI.
22. Jocelyn to Hardwicke, July 31, 1739. Add. Mss. 35,586.
23. Jocelyn to Devonshire, August 1739. Chatsworth Mss., T.3158/93, PRONI.
24. Walpole to Devonshire, August 7, 1739. Chatsworth Mss., T.3158/99, PRONI.

friend recommending that the new lord chancellor make a special effort toward "keeping up that harmony in the government which his majesty's service requires."[25]

The lucky winner of this contest for the highest judicial post in Ireland was English-born but had been in Ireland since 1719. Jocelyn was married to a sister-in-law of Timothy Godwin, late Archbishop of Cashel, and moved very easily in the select company of Irish bishops of English birth. Jocelyn had done well in Ireland partly because of his long association with Lord Hardwicke, who had missed no opportunities for advancing the career of his protégé, and partly because he fully understood the conventions and realities of politics in England and Ireland. As Jocelyn once observed to Hardwicke, when the latter had tried but failed to obtain for him a minor legal appointment at the Irish revenue board, "How beautiful is Interest and power when attended with an inclination to serve ones Friends."[26] Jocelyn was an Englishman who had become a very successful Irish politician.

Jocelyn's post was given to John Bowes, solicitor general since 1730. Like Jocelyn, Bowes was an Englishman who had come to Ireland to build a legal and political career and had fared extremely well. Bowes' successor as solicitor general was St. George Caulfield, an Irishman and son of a former justice of the king's bench. With Jocelyn as speaker of the house of lords and with Bowes and Caulfield in the house of commons, Devonshire had enough experienced men around him to avoid surprises in parliament if he had chosen to listen to them. That he did not, and so was surprised and embarrassed, was because he listened to his new son-in-law first, and because of his preoccupation with war preparations.

Immediately after arriving at Dublin Castle in September, Devonshire received a private communication from Newcastle asking him to inquire into the state of an important and potentially very dangerous situation. Newcastle had received an unusual but unsigned paper purportedly coming from the Roman Catholics of Ireland. It was addressed to his majesty and had been brought directly to Newcastle's office. Though Newcastle was very clear that little

25. Devonshire to Hardwicke, August 28, 1739. Add. Mss. 35,586, 178.
26. Jocelyn to Hardwicke, January 1, 1722/23. Add. Mss. 35,585.

attention should be "given to a Paper sent in this manner, and consequently no orders [were] to be given upon it,"[27] he sent it along to the duke for his information and consideration. Newcastle also suggested that the lord lieutenant might "have a strict Watch upon the Behaviour of the Papists in Ireland at this Conjuncture, whether They may be forming This, or any Cabal, of any other Nature that may affect His Majesty's Service."[28]

For its time, the paper Newcastle had sent to Devonshire was most unusual. It was one of the earliest formal attempts by Irish Catholics to improve their situation. The authors of this paper saw in the outbreak of a war with Catholic Spain an opportunity to profess their unconditioned loyalty to the Protestant succession and to seek relief from some of the more oppressive provisions of the popery laws.

According to this address, the king's faithful Catholic subjects had suffered during the last thirty years under laws which were "the most severe, that could be thought of or invented." They also wanted to acquaint the king that since trade had been the only enterprise open to Catholics during the last thirty years, some of their number had acquired "Fortunes which chiefly consist in ready Money, which . . . lyes dead in the hands of several Thousand [of us]." Since Catholics could not live as did other loyal subjects because of the laws enacted against them, they begged leave from the king to be allowed to withdraw to a foreign country where they might "reap the benefit of our Labour, and leave some Stake in lands to our Posterity, that will secure them to be true and faithful Subjects to that Prince under whom they live."[29]

For all of its novelty, this address had no ameliorative effect upon the Protestant lords and gentlemen in and close to the government of Ireland. The prospect of war with Spain resurrected terrible fears and bitter memories from both the near and the distant past. Ireland's Protestant leaders responded to this new crisis in highly traditional ways. They advised the lord lieutenant to include in his speech from the throne an exhortation

27. Newcastle to Devonshire, October 2, 1739. SP63/402/26.
28. *Idem.*
29. Humble Address of the Roman Catholics of Ireland, October 1739. SP63/402/28–29.

to put into immediate execution all of the laws against popish priests.[30]

Though Devonshire was hesitant about the chief governor taking initiative in such matters, Lord Duncannon and others that he trusted persuaded him that something of that sort was absolutely necessary.[31] Having been advised that his speech opening parliament should make some mention of threats to internal security, Devonshire decided to deal with it in as inoffensive and obtuse a manner as possible. He refused to use the words "Popish Priests" in his speech. After declaring that affairs in Europe had made it necessary for his majesty to exert his power for the protection of overseas trade and commerce, he urged the lords and gentlemen present "to show Utmost zeal at home for the support of His Majesty's government and the Protestant Religion against such as shall dare to disturb the Peace and tranquility we so happily enjoy."[32]

While this language was much more subdued than that employed by some of his predecessors, Devonshire suspected that it might be viewed in England as being too severe. To be sure, the king's English ministers were not pleased by the part of the speech dealing with Catholics, but they thoroughly understood the lord lieutenant's difficult position and did not rebuke him. Instead, Newcastle tried to explain what the position of the English government was on this matter and give Devonshire some guidelines for the future.

Newcastle insisted that the king was always ready to "concur in anything that is for the support of the Protestant religion and for the security of Protestants in Ireland."[33] However, because the parliament of Ireland had "at all times been of themselves very watchful upon that head, His Majesty does not think it necessary for your Grace to promote or encourage anything on that head."[34] However, if any proposal for that purpose should arise from the Irish parliament, he added, "your Grace will then do in it according to the nature of such proposal and as it shall appear to you to be most for H.M. service."[35] Devonshire was much relieved and promised to follow Newcastle's directions as closely as possible.

30. Devonshire to Newcastle, October 12, 1739. SP63/402/50–52.
31. *Idem.*
32. Lord Lieutenant's Speech, October 11, 1739. SP63/402/46.
33. Newcastle to Devonshire, November 8, 1739. SP63/402/89.
34. *Idem.*   35. *Idem.*

With regard to the rest of Devonshire's speech from the throne, it was well received in both Ireland and England. Once again the lord lieutenant asked for nothing except the usual supplies and promised that whatever was given would be frugally managed and applied.[36] The addresses were loyal and patriotic. The house of commons pledged adequate supplies cheerfully granted and zealous support of the king's government and of the Protestant religion against all who would challenge the one or disturb the other. Once the addresses had been transmitted, the commons turned to the accounts and the lords adjourned for want of business. Devonshire advised the English ministers that he saw "no sort of Reason to apprehend any trouble in Parliament here this session and everybody here seems disposed to do what is right."[37]

Parliamentary business proceeded in an orderly fashion. The formal declaration of war on Spain was received by the lord lieutenant on October 29, 1739, and the money bills were ready for the Irish privy council by mid-November. However, anxieties in parliament over the loyalty and possible machinations of Catholics had not diminished one whit. Devonshire reported that bills explaining and amending the act for disarming papists had been brought in and that both houses "were ready to do something in relation to the priests who were extremely numerous."[38]

Within a week Devonshire reported what the gentlemen in the house of commons had in mind. First, he assured Newcastle that he had tried in all respects to conform to the directions lately received about anti-papist measures. However, notwithstanding the confidence which he had given to Lord Duncannon and the diligence of Bowes and Caulfield, bills amending the act for disarming papists had been brought into the house without his knowledge. On this matter the house of commons simply would not and could not be put off. What had happened was that a group of Catholics had presumed to petition the Irish house of commons against tampering with the disarming law. According to the lord lieutenant, this petition "put the House into a great flame."[39] Nonetheless, the

---

36. Lord Lieutenant's Speech, October 11, 1739. SP63/402/46.
37. Devonshire to Newcastle, October 11, 1739. SP63/402/48.
38. Devonshire to Newcastle, November 11, 1739. SP63/402/91.
39. Devonshire to Newcastle, November 21, 1739. SP63/402/127.

house agreed to receive the petition and set a day for it to be heard. However, before that day arrived, the house unanimously passed an address to the lord lieutenant requesting him to take all legal measures "for disarming the Papists of this Kingdom as may preserve the public peace and tranquility."[40] This address was presented to Devonshire as he was proceeding to the privy council to act on the money bills. After approving the money bills, the privy council agreed to meet again that very evening to act upon the address. Meet they did and act they did. The council issued a proclamation requiring Catholics to surrender all unlicensed and illegal arms and appended the address of the house of commons to the lord lieutenant on disarming to it.

Devonshire was deeply concerned that the English ministers understand that he had not departed from their instruction by encouraging either the address or the proclamation.[41] Though embarrassed by what had happened, from Devonshire's point of view this affair ended happily. The Irish house of commons remained remarkably and predictably consistent. They had received and rejected the Catholic petition against the proposed amendments to the disarming act. The amendments themselves were quickly passed by the house of commons and easily approved by the Irish privy council. The English ministers accepted the lord lieutenant's explanation of the origin and progress of the amendments, address, and proclamation and said no more about them or about their instructions on anti-papist measures. Having been embarrassed once, Devonshire gratefully turned to other matters. He dispatched the money bills on November 19, 1739, collected information about wool running, acted on military appointments, attended to troop dispositions, and remained generally occupied with public affairs until the Christmas recess.

The lord lieutenant and the lords and gentlemen in the Irish parliament welcomed the recess, but there was little joy in Dublin during this holiday season. Goods and commodities of all sorts were in short supply and the winter of 1739–40 was appalling. An extraordinary frost descended upon the entire British Isles in October 1739 before the harvests were in and continued without

40. *Idem.*   41. *Idem.*

much relief until May 1740. People of all classes shivered and suffered. Hundreds of farm laborers and workers died from food shortages and exposure. The cold was so severe that wells froze everywhere; hens, ducks, and even sheep and cattle died in the cold, and there were reports of crows and other birds falling to the ground frozen in their flight.[42] While the bitter cold had a profound effect upon personal comforts, trade, employment, and general living standards it had little meaning for Irish politics.

When the session reopened at the end of January, a new customs enforcement bill received quick approval. The particular concern of this bill was wool running to foreign countries. This illegal trade was a matter of great interest and passion in England. Wool running was a well established enterprise in the Cork region and everyone knew that, without close cooperation between the principal land-lords and customs officers in that part of the country, it would continue undiminished no matter what the Irish parliament tried to do about it. Henry Boyle's estate agent in Clonakilty reported that one of the reasons why some of his tenants in that place had pleaded poverty and an inability to pay their rents was because customs officials had lately seized a ship "laden with wool just going off from Clonakilty."[43] Notwithstanding the strong encouragement that Boyle had given them "to turn their industry another way," the agent added, "they will not quit that pernicious trade whilst they have wherewithal to carry it on."[44]

In the end, Boyle and his friends decided against tampering with economic realities. The lord lieutenant got a bill, but the final version contained nothing that was new and wool running was scarcely affected by it. A Dublin Castle official reported that there was a wrong spirit in the house and "the conduct of some who ought to assist, and said they would assist is monstrous."[45] Few of the king's servants in the house of commons would support any sort of strong measures against wool running.

---

42. T. S. Ashton, *Economic Fluctuations in England, 1700–1800,* (Oxford University Press, 1959), 19. New York.
43. William Corner to Henry Boyle, May 5, 1741. Shannon Mss., T.3019/226, PRONI.
44. *Idem.*
45. Potter to Legge, February 12, 1739/40. Wilmot Mss., T.3019/226, PRONI.

On February 16, 1740, Newcastle informed Devonshire that intelligence sources reported the Spanish had established a camp in Galicia where great preparations were underway for a possible descent upon Ireland or England. Newcastle advised the lord lieutenant "to be provided against all Events."[46] Newcastle instructed Devonshire to consult with the king's servants in Ireland about the necessity of enacting a temporary law before the present session of parliament ended authorizing the Irish government to quarter any number of troops for a certain period of time "in such Places, as may be for the Safety and Defence of the Kingdom."[47] After reflecting on the state of the country and after consulting with Lord Duncannon, Devonshire rejected Newcastle's recommendations about a new quartering law and proceeded to implement a militia scheme.[48] Instead, he justified his decision on the need to concentrate the army in strategic locations to meet the threat of an invasion or a descent upon the coasts. Militia would be required to protect and police those areas with large Catholic populations from which army units had been withdrawn for strategic concentration.[49]

Having decided to arm a Protestant militia, Devonshire met with a group of influential members of the house of commons and apprised them of the Galicia force. He sought their support in getting an address authorizing the purchase of twenty thousand militia arms. However, to get such an address the duke had to make an important compromise—five thousand of the arms authorized for purchase had to be manufactured in Ireland. Devonshire was furious over what had happened. He believed himself "used in this as in the wool affair." The duke could understand why some members might try to deceive him on the customs enforcement bill, but on the question of militia arms, deception and delay made no sense. After all, he complained to Newcastle, "their Throats are concerned on it."[50] Devonshire began to suspect that there was more to Irish politics than Lord Duncannon and his friends were telling him.

With this business completed, the duke was extremely anxious to end the session and return to England. He prorogued the parlia-

---

46. Newcastle to Devonshire, February 16, 1739/40. SP63/403/39.
47. Idem.
48. Devonshire to Newcastle, March 11–14, 1739/40. SP63/403/61–62.
49. Idem.   50. Idem.

ment on March 31 and began departure preparations forthwith. He approved a number of military appointments, the elevation of the Duke of Dorset's protégé, George Stone, to be Bishop of Ferns, and the advancement of Henry Singleton to the post of Chief Justice of Common Pleas. With these decisions behind him, Devonshire left Boulter, Boyle, and Newport as lords justices and embarked for Parkgate on April 15, 1740.

Famine, War, and Political Change

Though Devonshire did not understand or realize what had happened to him during the late session, the reality of his situation in Irish politics was clear enough to those knowledgeable about Irish affairs. During this session the chief governor of Ireland was himself frequently being governed by Irish politicians. He had been surprised by the disarming bill and the proclamation, deceived on the customs enforcement bill, and led into a militia arms procurement job. As a matter of fact, no other lord lieutenant since 1715 had been surprised, deceived, or led more easily or more often than his grace of Devonshire. The director had been directed. When such direction came in the form of advice from Lord Duncannon and his friends, the duke accepted it with thanks. When it came as a *fait accompli* in the house of commons or privy council staged by the speaker and his friends or by other influentials, the duke accepted it with regret and embarrassment. It was, however, invariably accepted by Devonshire and was always productive of the same result: the lord lieutenant had to explain to the English ministers why and how special circumstances in Ireland had forced a departure from the instructions they had given to him.

The duke's management failures in Ireland were in part a function of his personality and a consequence of the state of the English ministry. The duke was a good friend who enjoyed convivial company, but he was by no means distinguished for quickness of mind or industry. He was typical of the kind of man that Walpole had come to tolerate in cabinet-level positions. At some other time Devonshire's performance in Ireland would have made him a certain candidate for removal, but within Walpole's narrowing circle of trusted mediocrities, there was no one to replace him.

While in England, Devonshire gave little thought to how political and confidence relationships between himself as lord lieutenant and Irish parliamentary leaders were changing. The duke could not, of course, entirely escape from Irish affairs; he heard regularly from the lords justices and from Lord Duncannon. Both Devonshire and the lords justices were much relieved to learn that the Spanish force gathering in Galicia had embarked and sailed for the West Indies. However, as the summer of 1740 progressed, it became evident that Ireland was threatened by something much more serious than a Spanish raid. The terrible winter had left the ground frost hard for so long that planting had been set back. Crop maturation was slow and crop failures were widespread. Provisions were scarce, prices rose, and the prospect of a major famine became real.

As many feared, the Irish harvest of 1740 was a very bad one. People simply could not lay up a sufficient stock of provisions for themselves or for their animals. Once the meager harvests of grain and potatoes had been consumed, survival would depend on the availability of imports. However, the harvests had been poor in England and scarcities there drove the prices of wheat and bread up to the highest levels since the winter of 1708–09. Imports of English meal, flour, and unground grain into Ireland during the critical winter and spring have been estimated at only twenty-six percent of need. This desperate situation needed only one additional circumstance to become a major social disaster. That circumstance the elements provided. The winter of 1740–41 matched the previous one in both severity and duration. When spring finally came in 1741, hardship and distress were everywhere. The country was in a state of shock. If contemporary estimates can be believed, upwards of 300,000 people may have perished from starvation, exposure, and famine fevers.[51]

The rich and powerful responded to this great national calamity with extraordinary generosity. Subscriptions for famine relief were raised everywhere. Henry Singleton spent over £1400 purchasing oatmeal for the people of Drogheda.[52] True to character, Arch-

51. Michael Drake, "The Irish Demographic Crises of 1740–41," in *Historical Studies*, VI, London, 1968, 101–124; "The Groans of Ireland," in *The Gentleman's Magazine*, Vol. XI, 1741, 638.
52. Ball, *op. cit.*, II, 131.

bishop Boulter spent freely on the indigent and distressed people of Dublin. The provost and fellows of Trinity College did the same. Kildare landlords provided make-work employment for their people building obelisks,[53] and without the continuing contributions of Henry Boyle and other landlords, the people of Clonakilty and Bandon would have become desperate.[54]

The Leinster and Munster jails were full. They were so full—upwards of four hundred criminals in Cork jails alone—that the government was obliged to send special judges to try them. Baron Wainwright, John Bowes, attorney general, and Serjeant Bettesworth went south and two of the three contracted an infectious fever from the prisoners appearing before them.[55] Bettesworth died in Cork and Wainwright expired a few weeks later in Dublin. Another judge and old whig politician from the Duke of Ormonde's time, Sir John Rogerson, contracted a fever while on circuit in the northeast and died shortly after returning to Dublin in August 1741.

People from all classes suffered, people from all classes died, and for a while it seemed as if Ireland was destined to become one vast charnel house. However, by the end of summer of 1741, the worst was over. The harvests of that year in both Ireland and England were much improved and the food shortages ended. With the return of an orderly provisions market the incidence of the famine fever declined, and those people having agricultural or commercial employments were thankful to be able to return to them. Those lords and gentlemen who had been preoccupied with the plight of their people could once again think about the war, politics, and what the next session of parliament would be like.

While preparing for his return to Dublin, the Duke of Devonshire also must have wondered about that subject. His chief secretary had resigned. The duke's search for a successor was brief and limited. He offered the post to his son-in-law. Lord Duncannon accepted at once, and shortly before departing for Ireland the duke recommended him for a place on the Irish privy council.[56] Devonshire

53. Lecky, *op. cit.*, I, 188.
54. William Conner to Henry Boyle, May 5, 1741. Shannon Mss., D.2707/A/1/4.
55. Jocelyn to Hardwicke, March 29, 1741. Add. Mss. 35,586, 335–337.
56. Devonshire to Harrington, August 11, 1741. SP63/404/86.

also had to find replacements for the judicial posts vacated by the deaths of Wainwright and Rogerson. Solicitations were heavy, and after lengthy discussions with Duncannon, the duke made a series of recommendations that he believed would advance worthy men and strengthen his administration. Thomas Marlay, the Irish-born Chief Baron of the Exchequer, was chosen to succeed Rogerson as Chief Justice of the King's Bench. John Bowes, an Englishman of sixteen years' standing at the Irish bar and attorney general since 1739, replaced Marlay as Chief Baron. Richard Mountney, a lawyer and writer, came over from England and assumed Wainwright's place as a Baron of the Court of the Exchequer. St. George Caulfield, an Irishman, was advanced from solicitor general to succeed Bowes as attorney general, and Warden Flood, a well-known Irish lawyer and member of the house of commons for many years, replaced Caulfield as solicitor general. Devonshire submitted these recommendations to the English ministry, bid farewell to Chatsworth house, proceeded to Holyhead, and arrived in Dublin ready for business on September 23, 1741.[57]

On the basis of information collected by Lord Duncannon, Devonshire had strong hopes for an easy session and prepared his speech from the throne accordingly. When parliament opened on October 6, 1741, attendance was thin. The lord lieutenant first spoke about the terrible famine and sickness which ravaged the country and invited members to consider ways that similar future calamities could be prevented. Next, he mentioned the progress of the war; and though the establishments were much in arrears, he asked only for financial supplies sufficient to support the establishments at present levels and to service the national debt.[58] The addresses which followed the speech were agreeable and complimentary. Want of money was evident everywhere; it had certainly ruined the social season. The duke could not remember a time when Dublin had been so empty during a parliamentary winter.[59]

The duke's immediate problems were two-fold. He had to collect ships at Cork and embark reinforcements for Admiral Vernon's forces in Jamaica, and he had to find some way of raising money

57. Duncannon to Newcastle, September 23, 1741. SP63/404/112.
58. Devonshire's Speech, October 6, 1741. SP63/404/154.
59. Devonshire to Newcastle, November 11, 1741. SP63/404/212.

for the establishments without increasing taxes. Within five weeks of parliament's opening, troops and drafts had been marched to Cork, put on board the ships, and sent off to the West Indies. Raising new money for the establishments took about as long to accomplish and turned out to be far more complicated and consequential than the Cork embarkation. To get the money required to make up existing arrears and to carry out the king's business, Devonshire had to put himself into the hands of those who could devise ways and means of procuring it. Those who devised such ways and means were Thomas Carter and Henry Boyle.

Approximately £125,000 of new money was needed to reduce arrears and maintain the establishments for two more years.[60] Carter proposed raising these funds by borrowing on the credit of an existing loan authorization. Implementation of this strategy required nothing more than obtaining from the house of commons a vote instructing its committee on ways and means to consider some accounts and ordering the vice treasurer, Luke Gardiner, to seek additional subscriptions to the old loan from his friends in the financial and banking community.[61] After consideration by the principal crown servants in several meetings, the strategy was approved and then implemented on November 11, 1741. Carter moved that the committee on ways and means be instructed to consider some accounts and, after a debate extended several hours by the zeal and numbers of those speaking for the motion, it carried 93 to 33.[62] Despite the great care and labor devoted to this business in October and early November, it had not been firmly and finally arranged until shortly before Carter rose to make his motion. This apparent paradox of winning big while remaining so long uncertain required explanation; and in doing so for Newcastle, the lord lieutenant also had to explain how Irish politics had changed in the last four years.

The outbreak of war with Catholic Spain had the effect of uniting all Irish Protestants behind the Irish government. As Devonshire explained, "All those who have ever voted with the Government expressed so much zeal that opposition seems to me to be pretty

60. Devonshire to Newcastle, November 17, 1741. SP63/404/224.
61. Devonshire to Newcastle, November 11, 1741. SP63/404/212.
62. Devonshire to Newcastle, November 17, 1741. SP63/404/224.

much shocked."[63] However, while the government interest was large, it was not disciplined. There were factions and jealousies among the lord lieutenant's supporters that caused him great anxiety and no end of difficulty. The duke had to be constantly aware of and very sensitive to the delicate state of personal relationships that existed among his parliamentary friends. He described himself as being "obliged to be very attentive lest private picque might prevail on some of our friends and vary [them] from the method agreed on."[64] Devonshire had been given information that a scheme to defeat Carter's motion was being concerted between some friends of the government and political enemies of Carter and Boyle. The duke intervened personally and the scheme collapsed.[65]

Though persons unacquainted with Ireland might think otherwise, Devonshire assured Newcastle that the government of Ireland was firmly in control of Irish affairs. There was a system operating here. The size of the government interest in the Irish house of commons had never been larger, public business had rarely ever been dispatched more expeditiously, and the present parliamentary session promised to be the shortest since 1713. "The way I keep matters on this way," he concluded, "is to show proper regard without partiality to all that do service to the government."[66]

Just what the duke meant by proper regard was very soon apparent. Because the speaker and his friends had supported the government with such ingenuity and zeal during the present session, they deserved whatever proper regard the duke could give—"They have done all I could wish." Fortuitously, the death of a colonel in an Irish regiment provided an opportunity for Devonshire to oblige the speaker. The duke recommended Boyle's brother-in-law, Major Michael O'Brien Dilkes, to succeed to the vacancy. Moreover, the recommendation for Dilkes was in the post within twenty-four hours of the late colonel's demise. It was done so quickly, Devonshire added, "to cut sollicitations short."[67]

The lord lieutenant's system was at once both old and new. Paying

63. Devonshire to Newcastle, November 24, 1741. SP63/405/239.
64. Devonshire to Newcastle, November 17, 1741. SP63/404/224.
65. *Idem.*
66. Devonshire to Newcastle, November 24, 1741. SP63/404/239.
67. *Idem.*

for support with patronage indeed was old. Rewarding crown officers with additional patronage for what crown officers were supposed to do for being crown officers was new. The problem inherent in the duke's system was that once such rewards were given, they would be thereafter always expected. However, Devonshire had little to go to market with. As the duke's system became an accepted convention of Irish parliamentary politics, the chief governors found themselves obliged to make more promises and reach more understandings with crown officers and parliamentary influentials about the disposition of patronage. Boyle, Carter, and the new Bessborough faction sought patronage and were ready to provide parliamentary service for it. These men and their friends not only asked for favors; they also gave advice and sometimes proposed policy initiatives. Boyle and Bessborough exercised more influence over the affairs of their country than any other Irishmen since Lord Midleton, Archbishop King, and William Conolly. The functioning of this new political system was perhaps most succinctly described by one of Boyle's kinsman, who wrote to the speaker in June 1741. "Since you have been in the chair, you have not been foiled in anything you made a point of, nor has there been a division about the public accounts."[68] The lord lieutenant honored the speaker's recommendations and the speaker expedited parliamentary approval of the money bills.

It is doubtful whether Devonshire understood how much Irish politics had changed since Lord Carteret's time. At the moment, the duke probably did not care. He was preoccupied with completing action on all pending bills and ending the session as soon as possible. Great events were occurring in England. Sir Robert Walpole's long ministry was on the verge of collapse and Devonshire believed that his presence in England was desperately needed. The money bills were dispatched to England in mid-November and received prompt attention and approval by the English privy council. They were received in Ireland before the Christmas recess, whereupon Devonshire asked for the usual permission to return to England and appoint Boulter, Boyle, and Jocelyn as lords justices.

---

68. Bellingham Boyle to Henry Boyle, June 16, 1741. Shannon Mss., D.2707/A/1/4/16, PRONI.

All that delayed prorogation and the duke's departure was imposition of a ban on trade in beef with France and French possessions[69] and resolution of a breach of privilege complaint in the Irish house of lords.

The affair in the Irish house of lords followed from a complaint brought by Robert Clayton, Bishop of Cork. It related to a personal dispute between Cork gentlemen and the bishop in that county. After the controversy between Boyle and Sir Richard Cox and the bishop in 1738, few Cork politicians trusted the Bishop of Cork. Devonshire was certain that the bishop meant no trouble but, fearing that continuation of such a dispute might occasion some difficulties about quartering troops there, he decided to intervene and put an end to it. His agent for so doing was George Stone, Bishop of Ferns, who persuaded Clayton to drop the matter. The duke was much pleased by the skills and tact Stone displayed in this affair and commended him accordingly to Newcastle.[70]

With all parliamentary business concluded, Devonshire prorogued his third session on February 15, 1742, and boarded the yacht for Parkgate on the following day. While crossing the Irish Sea, Devonshire must have wondered whether he would return to Ireland. Walpole's long tenure as the king's first minister had come to an end. Suffering several defeats in January, Walpole gave up after losing a division on the Chippenham election petition on February 2, 1742. On that same day, Walpole wrote to Devonshire in Dublin informing his friend that he had resigned.[71] The king adjourned the English parliament for a fortnight while he constructed a new ministry. On the day that Devonshire arrived at Parkgate, February 16, his majesty announced a new ministry with Lord Wilmington at its head and with Lord Carteret as its principal member.

The Progress of the Parties

Walpole's resignation was the fall of a minister, not the end of a ministry. No one expected the king to dismiss all of his servants and

---

69. Devonshire to Newcastle, December 29, 1741. SP63/404/270.
70. Devonshire to Newcastle, January 10, 1741/42. SP63/405/13.
71. Walpole to Devonshire, February 2, 1741/42. Chatsworth Mss., T.3518/206. PRONI.

take in new ones just because his first minister had been forced to resign. Lord Wilmington became first lord of the treasury and Lord Carteret came in as a secretary of state. Newcastle, Henry Pelham, Lord Hardwicke, and the Duke of Devonshire all retained their current posts. Changes would come in time, and ultimately, the effects of them would be felt in Ireland.

However, even though the uncertain state of English politics in 1742 promised no immediate changes of men or measures for Ireland, the country lost one of its most important public men in that year. Archbishop Boulter sought permission in mid-May to go to England for his health. Permission was granted. Boulter went to Bath and then to London where, after two days of illness, he died on September 27, 1742. History has been unkind to the reputation of this very decent man. Indeed, the goodness of his life was interred with his bones. He is best remembered as an enemy of Archbishop William King and Jonathan Swift and as a strong proponent of appointing Englishmen to important Irish ecclesiastical and civil offices. While Boulter distrusted King and advocated such a policy, he was also a dedicated churchman and one of the most active and generous philanthropists of his time in Ireland.

Coming to Ireland at the height of the halfpence crisis, Boulter became quickly convinced that Anglo-Irish relations would never be congenial and that orderly government in Ireland would be impossible so long as the highest offices in the state and church were held by persons connected with any of the principal Irish political factions. In his view, the most effective way of assuring the appointment of independent men to public offices in Ireland was to appoint only men born in England. While this strategy was not original with Boulter, he became its most public advocate—especially during his early years in Ireland. However, Boulter was never absolutely single-minded on this subject. He recognized that the claims of many Irishmen for office were too strong to be denied, and he accepted and recommended such persons for advancement. At no time did he ever argue for anything close to total exclusion of Irishmen from public offices. His purpose was to introduce greater stability into the public affairs of Ireland by increasing the presence of what he called the English interest in the government and in the Church of Ireland. Boulter also thought that some offices were more important than others and that the office of lord justice was the most important of all. Boulter believed strongly that all present and future lords justices should be men of English birth. Since two of the persons sworn as lords justices were by precedents running back to the beginning of the century the lord chancellor and the primate, those places should be reserved for Englishmen. The third lord justice had been the speaker of the house of commons only since 1717. Because the speaker invariably would be one of the principal party leaders in the house, Boulter strove mightily but unsuccessfully to invest someone other than the speaker with the authority of lord justice.

Except for the primacy, which Boulter himself held, and the office of lord chancellor and the Archbishopric of Dublin, which were reserved for Englishmen, the exclusion of Irish-born candidates from Irish ecclesiastical and judicial offices was no more systematically applied during all of Boulter's years than was the case earlier or later. Statistics reveal how far the policy of appointing Englishmen to important Irish offices went. Of the twenty-three bishops appointed or translated during Boulter's incumbency, thirteen were English-born. While a majority of those new appointments and translations were Englishmen, a majority of the bishops in the Church of Ireland before Boulter came to Ireland had been English and a majority continued to be so after him. Of the 310 appointments made to Irish sees between 1690 and 1840, 157 were men born in England.[72] During Boulter's time, at the four courts the policy of excluding Irishmen from judicial posts was even much less systematically applied. Of the fourteen men filling the eleven major judicial appointments plus the posts of attorney general, solicitor general, and prime serjeant in Ireland at the accession of George II in 1727—three years after Boulter's arrival—seven had been born in England. When Boulter died in 1742, only three of those fourteen posts were occupied by men of English birth, and two of them—Jocelyn and Bowes—had been members of the Irish bar for twenty-three and seventeen years, respectively. As a matter of fact, between 1728 and 1742, only three men of English birth came directly from England to be appointed to one of these four-

72. "The Church of Ireland," *Church Quarterly Review*, 29, January, 1885, 454.

teen judicial or law officer posts without first being a member of the Irish bar and having lived and worked in Ireland for a number of years.

There is no doubt that Boulter strongly supported the policy of excluding Irishmen from the highest places in the established church and in the Irish government in his early years. This policy seemed to be an appropriate response to the halfpence crisis. However, as the memory of that crisis receded in time, the necessity for continuing such a policy diminished. Boulter wrote less about preserving and expanding what he called the English interest in 1730 than he had in 1725, and after 1735 he hardly wrote about it at all. The immunity from Irish political factionalism which English birth was assumed to provide turned out to be of short duration. Living and working in Ireland could make an Irishman out of anyone. In any case, by the time of Boulter's death, except for the office of lord chancellor, being properly connected in Irish politics had become a much more valued qualification for public office than place of birth.

As a successful projector and philanthropist, Boulter was unsurpassed by any of his contemporaries. He had married a lady of great fortune and since they had no children the archbishop and his wife used the bulk of their fortune for public and charitable purposes. He played a leading role in the design and provided some of the money for the construction of a canal from Newry to the river Bann, thus opening an inland water route between Newry and Lough Neagh. While serving on the Linen Board, Boulter helped raise a voluntary subscription of £30,000 in 1737, whereby a thriving cambric manufacture was established at Dundalk. He built and endowed with his own money four houses for clergymen's widows and constructed a new market house in Armagh town. He did the same in Drogheda. Boulter also provided scholarships for the needy sons of his diocesan clergy to attend Trinity College. He contributed £1,000 toward rebuilding the Blue Coat Hospital in Dublin. Similarly, Steeven's hospital and other Dublin charitable institutions received frequent and substantial gifts from this most generous man.

During the food scarcities of 1727 and 1728, Boulter launched a subscription to purchase corn for the poor with a substantial personal contribution. Large quantities of corn were purchased and distributed throughout Ireland, and by his order all houseless wanderers were to be received into the Dublin poorhouses and fed at his expense. The house of commons responded to this extraordinary display of disinterested charity by a public vote of thanks. Again, during the terrible winter of 1739–40, Boulter's bounty was unlimited. From his own funds, Boulter supported the poor from all parts of Ireland without distinction of religion in the Dublin poorhouses. Moreover, as a memorial to his many charities during the famine of 1741, a full length portrait of him by Francis Bindon was placed in the hall of the principal Dublin poorhouse. True to character, Boulter had no intention of allowing his good works to end with his death. After providing for his wife during her life, he bequeathed the remainder of his property, valued at more than £30,000, to charitable purposes, and appointed the Archbishop of Dublin, Bishop of Kildare, and Thomas Morgan as executors.[73] Dying in London, he was buried in the north transept of Westminster Abbey, where a marble monument and bust were placed over his remains. Appropriately, one of the lines from the inscription on that monument best summarizes the man and his life—"His virtues he manifested in his good works."

Boulter's demise left a void in the hearts of those who knew him well that could not be filled. His passing left a void in the government and Church of Ireland that had to be filled, and Devonshire made up his mind quickly. All solicitations were wasted effort. Devonshire wanted John Hoadley, present Archbishop of Dublin, to be translated to Armagh and he was. The nomination was announced on October 6, 1742, and Hoadley was sworn as a lord justice on December 3, 1742. Though quickly and decisively determined, Hoadley's appointment was popular with most of the people who mattered in the Irish parliament. He was English-born but had been in Ireland since 1727 and had become Irish in many ways. Hoadley was a good example of what frequently happened to Englishmen who spent fifteen years as bishops or archbishops in the Church of Ireland. They socialized completely. Accepting the customs and conventions of their adopted country many of them be-

73. *The Gentleman's Magazine*, XII, October 1741, S47.

came as Irish in outlook as any of their native-born colleagues on the episcopal bench. This is what appears to have happened to Hoadley. His only daughter, Sarah, had married Bellingham Boyle, a nephew of the speaker and member of parliament for Bandonbridge. The new primate loved his daughter dearly, and he spared no effort to see that the public career of his son-in-law was quickly and profitably advanced.

Hoadley's translation to Armagh left Dublin vacant and the lord lieutenant received solicitations and recommendations from several quarters. Ultimately, Devonshire settled on Charles Cobbe, Bishop of Kildare, a man with twenty-two years of service on the Irish episcopal bench. For the see of Kildare, the lord lieutenant nominated the brilliant and useful George Stone, only lately installed at Ferns. By early 1743, all decisions about vacant Irish episcopal appointments had been made and implemented. The duke next turned his attention to a vacancy on the court of the king's bench. Henry Rose, a judge of almost ten years' standing and well-connected in Limerick and Kerry, died suddenly. Devonshire chose Arthur Blennerhassett, prime serjeant since 1741 and an Irish lawyer of many years experience, for the appointment. The post of prime serjeant was considered first for Phillip Tisdale, who was later put aside in favor of Anthony Malone. The speaker supported Tisdale strongly,[74] but he accepted the choice of Malone. The Earl of Bessborough pressed very hard for Malone and succeeded. Bessborough believed that a man of Malone's ability in the king's service would be a great asset. Malone was a gifted speaker and a man of integrity and honor as well. The earl believed so strongly in Malone that he offered to be "bound body for body for him." Furthermore, Archbishop Hoadley and the lord chancellor were very much for him.[75] Devonshire was persuaded about Malone. With speakers and parliamentary managers such as Carter and Malone firmly attached to the government, Devonshire had every reason to hope that his next session would be easy and brief.

Thus prepared for the future, the duke could now turn his

74. Boyle to Devonshire, October 7, 1742. Chatsworth Mss., T.3158/232, PRONI.
75. Bessborough to Duncannon, February 2, 1742/43. Chatsworth Mss., T3158/235; Jocelyn to Devonshire February 12, 1742/43. Chatsworth Mss., T.3158/237, PRONI.

attention to more personal matters. His grace was about to gain another Irish son-in-law. On September 23, 1743, the Earl of Bessborough's second son, John Ponsonby, married Lady Elizabeth Cavendish at Chatsworth. At age thirty, John Ponsonby was a pleasant, attractive young man. Unlike his father and brother, John was not especially noted for ambition or industry. He had been a member of parliament for the borough of Newtown in county Down since 1739, where the Earl of Bessborough exercised a powerful interest through property held by his wild and distraught stepson, Robert Colvill. Moreover, Bessborough, a member of the Irish revenue board since 1739, obtained the place of secretary of the revenue board for his son John in 1742. The earl also provided for his son and daughter-in-law in other ways. Shortly before the marriage of John to Lady Betty, the earl purchased an estate worth £2,300 a year and settled it on him.[76] Bessborough had great plans for his much loved son, and in the course of the next fifteen years he managed to realize most of them. No matter how fast or how far John Ponsonby rose in the rugged and sometime bruising world of Irish politics, he was always his father's son. Until the old earl died in 1758, John Ponsonby lived very much in his shadow and seemed very content doing so. One week after the wedding, Devonshire, Bessborough, and Duncannon all made their way from Derbyshire to Holyhead and embarked for Ireland.

After arriving in Dublin, Devonshire conferred with the lords justices and learned that in most things all was well in the country. Except for the eruption of a noisy dispute the previous spring between several members of the Dublin common council—led by a well known apothecary, Charles Lucas—and the board of aldermen over the rights of freeman to elect the mayor and sheriffs, choose guild representatives to the common council, and fill aldermanic vacancies, Irish politics and politicians were as he had left them. Henry Boyle and his many friends had parliamentary politics well under control. Devonshire paid no heed to the Lucas matter and after several discussions with the lords justices and others the duke reported to Newcastle that "[e]verything here is quiet and every-

76. Irish Official Papers, I, 35.

body in good behavior." He promised the secretary of state that he would try to obtain another short session.[77]

True to his word, Devonshire's speech from the throne was non-controversial. He commented on the progress of the war, and asked only for the usual supplies. The addresses were complimentary and patriotic. All in all, the opening of parliament went very well, but everyone there knew that elsewhere things were not going well at all. The war and its management were matters of grave concern. The prospect of a self-contained war between England and Spain had vanished in 1740 with the outbreak of the War for the Austrian Succession. Soon all of Europe was involved. Though France and England were not officially at war with one another until the spring of 1744, Englishmen and Frenchmen shot at one another throughout 1742.

Attacks on British policy and its principal author, Lord Carteret, by Pitt in the English house of commons and by Chesterfield in the English house of lords became frequent and ferocious. Lords and gentlemen in both houses were being told daily that English blood and treasure was being wasted and that English interests were being sacrificed to protect and preserve his majesty's beloved Electorate of Hanover. Carteret denied that Hanoverian interests had ever been paramount and insisted that all of his policies since coming into office in 1742 had been based on the two assumptions: that France was the enemy and that France had to be contained. On France being the real enemy there was no dispute. Controversy raged around how best to deal with the real enemy. Intelligence reports in the fall of 1743 disclosed that major military and naval preparations were underway at Dunkirk and Brest and that the pretender's son was on his way to northern France.

Before the prospects of a Jacobite descent upon some part of the British Isles and open war with France, the concerns and the conflicts of Irish politicians at the College Green seemed insignificant. Irish parliamentary politics were suddenly and thoroughly tranquilized. Though most of the parties and connections retained their separate identities, organized opposition in the Irish parliament virtually disappeared for the duration of the war. Devonshire got

77. Devonshire to Newcastle, October 7, 1743. SP63/405/155.

the short and easy session he had predicted. Boyle, Carter, Malone, and their friends did all that was asked of them. Despite the fact that parliament did not open until early October, the money bills were approved by November 9 and all other bills were ready for dispatch the day after Christmas. Members could not remember a quieter session. Devonshire's moderation and the general satisfaction of buying arms of Irish manufacture cut off all occasions for opposition.[78] In fact, all parliamentary business was completed by December 29, 1743, and the duke asked for the usual permission to leave and to appoint the speaker, primate, and lord chancellor as lords justices.[79]

Devonshire intended to leave Ireland on February 7, 1744, as his presence was much needed in the English house of lords, but receipt of a private letter from Newcastle at the end of January altered his plans and extended his stay. Newcastle informed the lord lieutenant that intelligence sources reported a squadron of ships under the command of the Count de Roquefeuil was outfitting in Brest. These ships had large quantities of small arms on board and might be headed for Scotland. The secretary of state instructed Devonshire quietly to concentrate troops in those parts of Ireland closest to the northern regions of Scotland and to prepare them for immediate transport. Furthermore, the lord lieutenant was to tell no one that he had been ordered to make such preparations.[80] After reading Newcastle's letter, Devonshire immediately discussed the situation with the lords justices and with Luke Gardiner, deputy vice treasurer and a man of great experience and knowledge in embarking and quartering troops.

Devonshire agreed that the current emergency required that troops be concentrated at some convenient place for possible transport to Scotland, but cautioned about withdrawing troops from the west and southwestern parts of Ireland. If troops had to be sent to Scotland, he suggested sending them from the Dublin garrisons and from the northern and midland counties. In those parts of the country there were sufficient numbers of Protestants to arm and enroll in a militia, "who if no regular troops invade us will be able

78. Congreve to Wilmot, February 8, 1743/44. Wilmot Mss., T.3019/504, PRONI.
79. Devonshire to Newcastle, December 29, 1743. SP63/405/155.
80. Newcastle to Devonshire, January 26, 1743/44. SP63/406/24.

to keep the Papists quiet."[81] Devonshire's understatement of the anxieties felt by Irish Protestants whenever regular troops were sent out of Ireland for any purpose obscured the fact that, even before the need for an embarkation to Scotland arose, the country was dangerously short of regular troops. On February 1, 1744, Newcastle dispatched a warning to Devonshire that de Roquefeuil's squadron of twenty-one ships had left Brest on January 26, 1744, and appeared to be heading for Ireland. Since the passage north to Scotland was so dangerous in February, the secretary of state suspected that the apparent Irish heading was a feint and that they might be really going to the Mediterranean.[82]

The lord lieutenant's advisers were gravely concerned over de Roquefeuil's departure, but most of them believed that the French were bound for some place other than Ireland. They based this opinion on analyses of all available intelligence about the Brest squadron and from informants among Irish Catholics. Careful examination of the private correspondence of leading Catholics and reports from informants indicated that nothing appeared to be stirring among them.[83] Speculation about the whereabouts of de Roquefeuil ended on January 29 when his ships were sighted in the English Channel on an easterly course passing the Scilly Islands. De Roquefeuil's squadron was bound for Dunkirk in order to cover a possible invasion of England. Once the danger was known, things began to happen.

In England, Admiral Sir John Norris, the eighty-four-year-old commander-in-chief of the channel fleet, put to sea with orders to seek out and destroy all French troop transports. However, a sudden and vicious channel storm did the job for him. Easterly gales scattered de Roquefeuil's ships and damaged or wrecked most of the Dunkirk invasion flotilla. In Ireland, Devonshire prorogued the Irish parliament on February 9, 1744, and sent over to London a list of completed bills and a packet of loyal addresses. Next, the lord lieutenant met with the Irish privy council and issued a series of proclamations and orders. Rewards for the capture of officers enlisting for foreign service without licenses were posted. Orders were

81. Devonshire to Newcastle, January 31, 1743/44. SP63/406/32.
82. Newcastle to Devonshire, February 1, 1743/44. SP63/406/34.
83. Devonshire to Newcastle, February 7, 1743/44. SP63/406/50.

issued for the arrest of popish bishops and regulars and for the suppression of all monasteries and nunneries. This last order troubled Devonshire. It was absurd, he wrote to Newcastle, to alarm the papists before we are in the best state of defense. But, he continued, "[t]hey were so set on it I would not stop it."[84]

However, before bishops and regulars could be taken up they had to be identified and located. Instructions were sent to sheriffs, mayors, magistrates, and high constables throughout the country, requiring them to inquire and report back to the privy council the names and residences of all persons being or suspected of being popish bishops, regulars, or papists exercising ecclesiastical jurisdiction, as well as the names and residences of all persons with whom they resided. During March and April, these instructions were carried out and a large amount of information was collected and returned to the privy council.[85] Despite the tensions and anxieties raised by the prospect of an invasion, once this information about bishops and regulars was collected, very little action was taken upon it. Few bishops or regulars were actually arrested. Warned by the proclamation, most of those threatened by arrest either went into hiding or simply remained where they were, trusting that the decency and common sense of local Protestant landlords and magistrates would spare them from harassment.

During this crisis, the behavior of all classes of Catholics was remarkably prudent. Devonshire reported that everything was quiet in Ireland; "the Papists are quite dispirited and the Protestants extremely zealous."[86] Few arms had been discovered in Catholic hands. Moreover, after seizing and examining many private papers belonging to Catholics and finding nothing of consequence in them, the lord lieutenant concluded that nothing had been concerted between the French and Irish Papists.[87] By early April there was no longer any reason for Devonshire to remain in Ireland. With defense preparations well underway, the duke put the government of

---

84. Devonshire to Newcastle, February 20, 1743/44. SP63/406/89.
85. Some of the information in these returns has been edited and presented in Rev. William Burke, *The Irish Priests in the Penal Times (1660–1760)*, printed by N. Harvey for the author (Waterford, 1914), *passim*.
86. Devonshire to Newcastle, March 22, 1743/44. SP63/406/143.
87. *Idem.*

Ireland into the now-trusted hands of Boyle, Jocelyn, and Hoadley as lords justices and boarded the yacht for Parkgate on April 9, 1744.

For Devonshire this departure from Ireland was to be his final one. Important changes in English politics occurring in the next seven months would take him out of the office he had held longer than any other man since the first Duke of Ormonde in the seventeenth century. The combination of Devonshire's long tenure and the outbreak of England's first war in twenty-six years had a profound effect on the evolution of Irish politics. Devonshire had not been a strong lord lieutenant. He began his first parliamentary session with a strong dependence on Lord Bessborough and ended his last one much beholden to Boyle and his friends. From the beginning of the duke's third session in October 1741 and continuing thereafter for the rest of his time in Ireland, Devonshire appears to have become increasingly more willing to accept advice from Boyle's party and act upon it. To do so was the best assurance for a short and easy session; and during those uncertain and unsettled times, short and easy sessions of the Irish parliament were precisely what the lord lieutenant and the English ministry had to have.

Divided among themselves since Walpole's fall about who should lead the English government, and where and how foreign policy ought to be made, as well as being preoccupied with a major war, the English ministers had little time for Irish politics. They were willing to pay what appeared to be reasonable prices for quick enactment of the money bills and tranquil parliamentary sessions. If there were persons in the Irish parliament who could undertake and complete the king's business expeditiously, let them do it. However, it would be mistaken to attribute entirely the gift of leadership and initiative in Irish affairs to the Boyle and Bessborough parties in the Irish parliament to the weakness and other preoccupations of the English ministry. In a very important sense, Devonshire himself significantly contributed to the new direction given to Irish politics during his long service as chief governor.

Indeed, without the favor and close identification with the duke as lord lieutenant, Bessborough and Duncannon would not have been able to transform their connection of friends and relatives into a major parliamentary party. Also, it was Devonshire who decided that Boyle ought to be rewarded with more patronage for doing what his status as speaker and patronage already held should have guaranteed. Moreover, it was Devonshire on Bessborough's recommendation who agreed to bring Anthony Malone, a brilliant orator with a disposition for independent action, into the government as prime serjeant. At the time, there were alternatives. Devonshire did not have to recommend Malone, but he did. More than any other action, the appointment of Malone symbolized the transfer of leadership and initiative back to the great men in the Irish parliament. Successors to Midleton and Conolly were now in place.

Both of these developments—raising up the Bessboroughians as they were called and accepting Boyle's advice and Boyle's people in exchange for Boyle's votes—would be sources of serious future difficulties. Certainly, the ambitions of the Bessborough faction would not cease growing with the departure of their viceregal benefactor. How Boyle and Carter and Malone would use the influence which Devonshire had allowed them to assume was problematic, and what would happen to those numerous small parliamentary connections and individual members who would not or could not associate with Boyle or Bessborough remained to be seen. Yet, for the moment such concerns troubled no one in the governments of Ireland or England. In the spring and summer of 1744, uppermost in every mind was the progress of the war, and it was going badly. When Devonshire went up to London in the fall for the opening of the English parliament, he found confirmed what he already should have suspected. Carteret, now Earl of Granville, would not long survive the opening of the session. His colleagues in the cabinet— Pelham and Newcastle—would not go on with him or his policies. Changes were coming, room would have to be made for new men. Most certainly Ireland would receive a new lord lieutenant.

After much consultation with opposition groups in the British house of commons, Newcastle delivered to the king on November 1, 1744, a memorandum demanding Granville's dismissal. Virtually all of the lesser members of the cabinet had become so resentful of Granville's lordly dictation of foreign policy that he found himself completely isolated. For three weeks, the king tried desperately to save his favorite minister, but Newcastle and Henry Pelham had prepared their ground very well. His majesty could find no one in the cabinet or out of it with a sufficient following in the British house of commons willing to serve with Granville if Newcastle and Pelham left the ministry. Finally, on November 23, 1744, three days before the session opened, Granville resigned. Lord Harrington gave up the lord presidency of the council and replaced Granville as secretary of state for the northern department. The Duke of Dorset went in as lord president of the council, and some friends of Pitt but not Pitt himself were admitted into lesser offices. Most important, the king was persuaded to replace the Duke of Devonshire as chief governor of Ireland with the Earl of Chesterfield.

A perfervid war hawk in 1739, and scarcely less obnoxious than Pitt when in opposition, Chesterfield had also the additional liability of being married to the king's half sister—the illegitimate daughter of George I and the Duchess of Kendal. George II disliked his half sister and he positively despised her husband. Yet under the circumstances, if he had to take in at least one prominent opposition man, better it should be Chesterfield, who could be sent off to Ireland, than that madman Pitt, who would have to be endured in person in cabinet meetings. The choice was difficult, and it took his majesty six weeks to make it. Lord Chesterfield was formally appointed Lord Lieutenant of Ireland on January 8, 1745.

CHAPTER III

The Chesterfield and Harrington Years,

1745-1750

A Man for One Season

Ireland's new chief governor, Philip Dormer Stanhope, fourth Earl of Chesterfield, was by all accounts a remarkable man. A facile and prolific writer, a brilliant speaker and conversationalist, a supremely ambitious politician of long experience, the earl's appointment was enthusiastically received by social Dublin. However, like many of his class and generation, Chesterfield did not suffer disagreement easily or fools at all. More than that, he had a positive genius for irritating people who might be useful to him. It may be that the earl did not care whom he offended so long as he preserved his own independence.[1] However, by preserving that independence at whatever cost, Chesterfield failed as a political leader. He was in most things his own worst enemy.

While loyal and open to personal friends, associates in politics and in government found Chesterfield difficult and unreliable. Superiors could never be certain that he would carry out orders. Lesser ministers and officials never knew where they stood with him and could never be sure that he would defend their actions or protect their interests. Most men who had to deal with him in official ways knew from bitter experience that beneath his elegant and polished exterior, there was a will of iron, a carelessness about procedures and about means for achieving ends, and a disposition for taking hard lines in most controversies.

1. Bonamy Dobree, *The Letters of Philip Dormer Stanhope, 4th Earl of Chesterfield,* King's Printer's edition (Viking Press, New York, 1932), Vol. I, 81.

The liabilities that Chesterfield's personality and public style brought to the government of Ireland could have been mitigated somewhat by selecting a chief secretary with whom officials and politicians could more easily interact. However, the earl deliberately chose a nonentity that few would even consider worth cultivating. The earl chose Richard Liddell, a member of parliament for Bossiney in Cornwall, whose sole claim to distinction was having been caught *in flagrante delicto* with Lady Abergavenney. Liddell was meant to be ornamental and nothing more. Like it or not, and those who eventually had the experience did not like it, Irish politicians and Irish officials had to deal with the lord lieutenant directly. For many Irish politicians, the greatest mitigating circumstance of Chesterfield's time in Ireland was its brevity.

After his appointment, the new lord lieutenant's first assignment had nothing to do with Ireland. He was dispatched immediately to The Hague on the diplomatic mission to persuade the Dutch government to enter the war. Though Chesterfield did not get exceptionally good terms from the Dutch, they agreed to come into the war but steadfastly refused to declare it.

While at the Hague, Chesterfield's Irish correspondence was substantial. On January 1, 1745, Carew Reynell, Bishop of Derry, died; and, war or no war, decisions had to be made about a successor and about the chain of translations that would inevitably follow the appointment of one. Derry was a great prize. After Armagh it was the most lucrative see in the country, and its disposition prompted a solicitation from even the secretary of state himself. Newcastle wrote to Chesterfield in late January pressing for the translation of his own private secretary's brother, George Stone, from Kildare to Derry. If that were done, the earl would have an opportunity to satisfy the Duke of Devonshire by translating the duke's former chaplain, Thomas Fletcher, from Dromore to Kildare. Chesterfield would then have Dromore to dispose as he pleased. About George Stone, Newcastle was very clear, "My friend, the Bishop of Kildare . . . will not discredit any station you may do the honor to place him in."[2] Similar letters in support of Stone arrived from Dorset,

2. Sir Richard Lodge, *Private Correspondence of Chesterfield and Newcastle, 1744–46* (Royal Historical Society, London, 1930), 4.

Devonshire, and from the candidate himself. Chesterfield readily agreed, and Stone went to Derry. For those who could read the signs a star was rising.

Chesterfield obliged Devonshire by recommending Fletcher to leave Dromore for Kildare and proposed to move John Witcombe from remote Clonfert to Dromore. For Clonfert, he intended his own chaplain of sixteen years standing, Dr. Richard Chevenix. When Newcastle presented Chesterfield's recommendations to the king, all were approved except the latter. His majesty believed wrongly that Chevenix had written political pamphlets against him and would not approve the appointment. When Chesterfield learned of the problem, he exploded and simply would not accept that sort of mistreatment of Chevenix or of himself. "If Dr. Chevenix is not Bishop at Clonfert," he wrote, "I will not be Lord Lieutenant of Ireland."[3]

It is not known for certain whether Chesterfield's threat of resignation was ever communicated to the king. The earl first made his threat in a letter written from The Hague on March 30, and then repeated it in another letter sent from the same place on April 13. Newcastle and Harrington continued to press the king to change his mind, and by April 26, 1745, they had succeeded in getting a warrant for the appointment signed. However, Chevenix did not go to Clonfert. Bishop Whitcome absolutely refused to leave Clonfert for Dromore.[4] Instead, Jemmett Brown agreed to vacate distant Killaloe for Dromore, and Chevenix was nominated for Killaloe.

Upon returning to London, the earl quickly stepped into the role of lord lieutenant and turned his attention to a mountain of packets and papers from his lords justices. In those packets were dozens of requests and recommendations for military appointments. Chesterfield sorted through the papers and once he had convinced himself that a promotion recommendation from the lords justice was regular, he approved it. There was, however, one recommendation in the group that was irregular and yet Chesterfield endorsed it as his "most earnest request." It was to promote Thomas Carter's son from cornet to captain and give him a company in General Irwin's regiment. Chesterfield explained to Harrington why his lords jus-

3. *Ibid.*, 43.   4. *Ibid.*, 53.

tices had pressed for this promotion. The whole truth was that the young cornet was a son to "Mr. Carter, Master of the Rolls in Ireland, who is the leading person in the Parliament there, has great influence over the Speaker, whose party constitutes the great majority in that house."[5] Chesterfield believed that the request was reasonable and that it would be beneficial to his majesty's service in Ireland.[6]

As departure time approached. Chesterfield's spirits lightened and he looked forward to what he described to a friend as a scene which would be "much better suited to my temper and inclinations" and where he could expect to have "business enough to hinder him from falling asleep and not enough to hinder him from sleeping."[7] The earl departed for Holyhead on August 19, 1745, and by the time his party arrived there on August 30, he had heard news which would prevent him from getting much sleep at all during the next few months. The young pretender, Charles Edward Stuart, had landed in the northwest Scottish highlands and three thousand people had rallied to his cause.

Chesterfield arrived in Ireland at noon on August 31, 1745. Once the customary progress to Dublin Castle had been completed and the noise of the drums, trumpets, and cannon had subsided, the lord lieutenant turned immediately to his correspondence to find out what was happening in Scotland and what demands were to be made on Ireland. News about Scotland was late and unreliable. One of Chesterfield's first acts was to send a "trusty smuggler to the north of Scotland for more authenick information."[8]

After dispatching a spy north, Chesterfield requested a warrant for the postmaster to open letters when necessary and began collecting information about the state of military preparedness. He discovered of course what his predecessors had known. The country appeared to be in a most defenseless condition. Nevertheless, the lord lieutenant was ordered to get two of the six regiments in the country—Battereau's and St. Clair's—in readiness for embarkation to Chester if the Scottish rebels marched toward Lancastershire.[9] The earl believed that two additional companies for each of the six

5. Dobree, *op. cit.*, III, 638.   6. *Ibid.*, III, 639.
7. *Ibid.*, 655.   8. Lodge, *op. cit.*, 62.
9. Newcastle to Chesterfield, September 6, 1745. SP63/408/72.

regiments presently in Ireland could be raised in the north at once; and if Battereau's and St. Clair's regiments went off to Chester as anticipated, three new companies for each of the four remaining regiments—an additional 3000 men—could be raised up there without difficulty.[10]

While waiting for permission to go ahead with recruitment plans in the north, the lord lieutenant acted on his own authority to see that all regiments in the country were recruited up to their full strength with undoubted Protestants. Next, the lord lieutenant ordered out the militia everywhere and entrusted the defense of Dublin to the city militia of 5,000 men, a regiment of dragoons, a regiment of horses, three companies of foot, and 300 invalids.

Getting these plans implemented had been hectic and time-consuming. However, Battereau's and St. Clair's regiments went off on October 1. By the end of September, Chesterfield was able to assure Newcastle that, should an invasion or insurrection occur in Ireland, "it shall have no time given it to gather strength; and whatever the numbers may be of either side, the rebels or the invaders shall be instantly attacked . . . I will go myself."[11] He praised the zeal and enthusiasm of the Protestants and admitted that he had found nothing stirring among the Papists. The earl's dispatches from Ireland contained just about the only good news that the English ministers read during August and September. Newcastle told Chesterfield that the "spirit, the solidity, and bravery" of his letters had a wonderful effect, and that he had never seen "so masterly an instruction for our interior situation" as had been presented in Chesterfield's Irish dispatches.[12]

Meanwhile, Chesterfield had to prepare for the opening of the Irish parliament. He did not expect a difficult session but there were problems. Although there was not even a formed opposition in the house of commons, he complained that every connection, almost every family, expected to govern the lord lieutenant. He reported to Newcastle that "Anything propos'd by one is for that very reason oppos'd by twenty."[13] In Chesterfield's judgment, the chancellor—Robert Jocelyn, now Lord Newport—was the most sen-

10. Dobree, *op. cit.*, III, 667–668.   11. *Ibid.*, 673.

12. Lodge, *op. cit.*, 73–74.   13. Dobree, *op. cit.*, III, 73–74.

sible, able, and honest man around in the government. However, if he were to show the kind of preference which the chancellor's advice and support so rightfully deserved, it would be the worse for both of them. When Chesterfield recommended the chancellor's nephew, Cornet Jocelyn, for a new company, he had to couple it with a recommendation that one of Boyle's sons be made a cornet.[14] Such were the necessities and realities of Irish politics. If Chesterfield wanted a successful session, he would have to accept them. All the lord lieutenant really wanted was to conclude his business in Ireland without disgrace and get back to London a soon as possible.[15]

When Parliament rose on October 10, 1745, Chesterfield spoke of the high indignation which all the king's subjects must feel over the attempt by the pretender in Scotland to disturb his majesty's government and whose success would destroy their liberty, property, and religion. He did not break with the immediate past on money matters. Despite the present emergency, like Dorset and Devonshire before him, the earl asked only for the usual and necessary supplies.

The addresses were complimentary, patriotic, and quickly voted. The appropriate committees began examining the accounts and estimates, and by mid-November the money bills had been approved and sent off to England. Loyal addresses poured in from every part of the country in October and November to such an extent that much of parliament's time was taken up receiving them. In late October, Chesterfield reported to Newcastle that business in parliament proceeded with the greatest zeal and unanimity, the only contention being who should be foremost in duty and loyalty to his majesty. Trouble of some sort in parliament was always possible, but in the present session none was likely. Nonetheless, despite the friendliness of all of the principal connections to Chesterfield's government, the strong rivalries that existed between the groups caused some concern. The main problem was that connections and groups in the Irish parliament rose or fell in public esteem in direct proportion to the number of viceregal favors bestowed or withheld from them.

14. *Ibid.*, 690.   15. *Ibid.*, 665.

During the session, Chesterfield had his way with the house of commons in every instance but one. Even though Thomas Carter's son had been promoted from cornet to captain before the session began and a seat in the house of commons had been procured for young Carter by the direct recommendation of Chesterfield, the lord lieutenant had trouble with his master of the rolls.[16] According to Thomas Fletcher, Bishop of Kildare, the master of the rolls had asked for some other "place or commission which could not be granted on account of an engagement to serve a friend of the Chancellor of England." For Thomas Carter that excuse simply would not do. He was heard saying that "if the Chancellor of England was to be served before him, let the Chancellor of England do his business for him here."[17]

The first opportunity for Carter to show his resentment was on some bills that had originated in the Irish privy council. He made a "flaming speech" against a navigation bill on that account and was primarily responsible for the bill being rejected. Chesterfield was outraged at Carter. The earl not only absented himself from a dinner party to which Carter had been invited[18] but, true to his style and reputation, the lord lieutenant summoned the master of the rolls to a private meeting and did what no other chief governor had dared to do. Chesterfield told Carter to his face, "you must do the king's business or be turned out of your employment; and if you are, I shall not do with you as they do in England, for you shall never come in again while I shall have any power."[19]

Though Carter's response to the earl is unrecorded, it is doubtful whether he said or did anything unusual at that moment. Carter was too wise and too experienced to risk ego-saving repartee with a man as powerfully circumstanced as was Chesterfield at that time. Instead, Carter directed his animosity at George Stone, Bishop of Derry, the person who had first introduced him to the lord lieutenant. Carter proclaimed at all social gatherings that he had been severely used by the Bishop of Derry.[20] However, vengeance could

16. Bishop of Kildare to Wilmot, April 23, 1746. Wilmot Mss., C.1827/42/80/67/64.
17. *Idem.*   18. *Idem.*
19. Dobree, *op. cit.*, I, 129; Irish Official Papers, I, 49.
20. Bishop Kildare to Wilmot, April 23, 1746. Wilmot Mss., C.1827/42/80/67/64.

wait. If the earl remained in Ireland for more than the current session, he would have need of Carter's services. When that moment came, compensation for previous indignities could be exacted. However, for the present, in parliament neither Carter nor anyone else attempted to complicate or delay any of the lord lieutenant's measures.

Outside of parliament most matters were well in hand. The Catholics were profuse in public displays of loyalty. Chesterfield had intelligence that even their priests were preaching quiet to them. It was wise and prudent that such was the case because the lord lieutenant had told prominent Catholic leaders what would happen if any disturbances occurred. By comparison, the retribution of Cromwell would appear lenient.[21] Chesterfield's threats were not empty rhetoric. His hatred of the Scottish rebels was intense. He received information that Scots were buying up large quantities of corn and meal in Belfast and elsewhere in the north of Ireland. This matter was brought into the privy council and a proclamation was issued prohibiting the export of all corn, meal, flour, and other foodstuffs until further notice. "This may, I hope," Chesterfield wrote to Newcastle, "contribute to starve the beasts when they return to their dens, as I suppose they will, at the approach of his Majesty's troops."[22]

Before the rebellion was over in Scotland, an almost comic palace revolution occurred in London. When the English parliament opened in October, Scotland was in Stuart hands. William Pitt erupted into opposition. He lashed out at the king and excoriated the ministers. Pitt's message was simple. Recall all British troops from the continent to meet the emergency in Scotland and employ no German mercenaries in England. Deciding that Pitt was needed in the government as secretary at war, Pelham, Newcastle, and Harrington asked the king to bring him in. His majesty could not bear the thought of daily meetings with Pitt and refused to consider him for any ministerial post. The king next turned to Lord Bath and his old friend Lord Granville for advice and support. Thinking them capable of forming a ministry, the king displayed more ill humor and discourtesy toward Pelham and Newcastle than was

21. Dobree, *op. cit.*, 686.   22. *Ibid.*, 691.

usual. Thereupon, all of the ministers, headed by Harrington, with a hitherto unprecedented unanimity marched off to St. James' palace and resigned *en bloc* on February 10, 1746.

For two days the king struggled to form a new ministry around Bath and Granville but could not. His majesty had to take Pelham, Newcastle, and Harrington back on their own terms, which were a monopoly of royal confidence for themselves, exclusion of Bath and Granville and their friends from the king's inner circle, and office for Pitt. Taking back Harrington proved to be more painful for the king than taking in Pitt. Harrington had been unforgivably rude when the ministry resigned and his majesty was never comfortable in his presence again. For a reputed madman, Pitt appeared to the king as remarkably reasonable. He did not insist on coming in as secretary at war; he was content to be a vice-treasurer of Ireland for a month or two before accepting the post of paymaster of the forces.

In Ireland, Chesterfield watched the progress of events in Scotland and at St. James palace with great interest and no small envy. By comparison his concerns in Dublin were uninteresting and unimportant. How he longed to be where the great decisions of his time were being made! During the months of December, January, and February, Chesterfield wrote constantly about what ought to be done in Scotland and what could be done at Westminster. In his view, no provisions of any kind should be allowed into Scotland unless sent directly to the Duke of Cumberland's army. "I would starve the loyal with the disloyal," he wrote, "if the former thought to remain with the latter," and bragged that even the loyalest Highlander" would receive not so much as a single oat cake from Ireland.[23]

Chesterfield took a similar hard line toward Bath and Granville for their roles in the late ministerial revolution at St. James. He urged that these two earls and all of their friends in lesser places be turned out at once. "Good policy still more than resentment," the lord lieutenant wrote, "requires that Granville and Bath should be mark'd out, and all their people cut off, to the dog that pisseth against the wall."[24] Everyone should see and know that the ministry

23. Lodge, *op. cit.*, 123.   24. *Ibid.*, 107.

has power and that they were ready to use it. What troubled Chesterfield most about this entire affair was that time and distance had prevented him from participating in it.

Newcastle promised to facilitate Chesterfield's return by expediting action on the Irish bills and urged Chesterfield not to dally in Ireland once his business had been completed. At a time when nothing seemed to be going right anywhere Chesterfield had kept Ireland under control and quiet. Though Newcastle did not say so directly, he seemed to be suggesting that when Chesterfield returned he had an excellent chance of moving into a higher office.[25]

Anxious to depart, Chesterfield became increasingly impatient in March and April with the demands and maneuvering of Irish politicians. For example, Archbishop Hoadley approached Chesterfield and asked him to facilitate the succession of his son-in-law, Bellingham Boyle, to a place on the Irish revenue commission. Chesterfield forwarded the request stating to Newcastle that he was not pressing for it at all. The earl explained that his letter was no solicitation. He could not refuse to present the primate's request to the secretary of state, but beyond that he promised nothing and cared less. According to Chesterfield, the primate, "a dirty troublesome parson, has married his only daughter to Mr. Boyle of this country, and has set his heart upon enriching him."[26] Newcastle should do whatever he thought proper in this bit of jobbery. Only please, Chesterfield requested, "write me such a letter as I may show the parson."[27]

While Chesterfield was of no mind to please the primate, he decided to look into the matter further. What he discovered was how utterly meaningless Boulter's old distinction between an English and Irish interest had become. In Hoadley's case, he was an English-born primate of the Church of Ireland who had become thoroughly Irish in interest.

Hoadley's request prompted Chesterfield to undertake a general examination of the performance of the revenue commission. In the lord lieutenant's judgment the performance of the three English and two Irish commissioners presently serving on it had been very

25. *Ibid.*, 117. 26. Irish Official Papers, I, 66–67.
27. *Idem.*

poor. According to Chesterfield, two of the English commissioners never bothered to attend the meetings of the board or perform any services at all. Ponsonby, one of the Irish commissioners, attended the meetings, but did not "pretend to do anything but to dispose of such inferior employments as fall to his share."[28] Only Grey, the most senior English commissioner, and Lord Boyne, the senior Irish commissioner, seriously attended to business. Since the presence of at least three commissioners was required for any transaction and since poor Lord Boyne was near death, the business of the commission had come to a standstill. Chesterfield urged that Boyne's successor should be an Englishman and also a man of business. The lord lieutenant informed Pelham that if and when Boyne died, he would have to send over recommendations, but "look on all such letters as letters of form only . . . a man of business is absolutely necessary."[29] This entire affair—Hoadley's behavior and the absenteeism of the two English revenue commissioners—showed that English nativity guaranteed neither independence from Irish political factionalism nor competent performance in office. Pelham acted on Chesterfield's advice. Lord Boyne's successor was Thomas Brian, an Englishman and an accomplished man of business.

By mid-March most of the bills had been returned from England and authorization to appoint lords justices had arrived. Closing addresses were presented and parliament was prorogued on April 12, 1746. Chesterfield completed all of his personal business and left for Parkgate on April 23, 1746. The lord lieutenant's passage from the Castle gate to the harborside proceeded in the manner of a Roman triumph. The earl and his countess made their way on foot through large, friendly crowds, who wished them well and urged a speedy return. Lord Chief Baron Bowes observed that Chesterfield's passion for sobriety would be sorely missed. By example, he had shown that one could be both cheerful and sober, but now that he was gone people were returning to their old habits.[30] What Boyle, Carter, and Archbishop Hoadley thought about their departing lord lieutenant is not recorded, but it is doubtful whether they were as anxious to see him return as were the crowds at the

28. *Ibid.*, 67.   29. *Idem.*
30. HMC Various Collections, VI, 68.

Castle gate, or that they valued his sobriety as highly as did Lord Chief Baron Bowes.

One of Chesterfield's biographers described his subject as the most popular viceroy Ireland ever had and possibly the most successful.[31] That he was popular with the people of Dublin is certain and should not be surprising because he deliberately cultivated it. His celebration of the king's birthday was a grand affair complete with fountains of wine in the lower Castle yard where the populace had an "opportunity to drink his Majesty's health, which they heartily did."[32] That Chesterfield was as popular with the rank and file in the Irish parliament as he was with Dubliners is also probably true. The earl had come to Ireland at a critical time in the midst of a war that was going badly. He took charge and made decisions quickly, and the country experienced neither invasion nor internal disorders. That Chesterfield's viceroyalty, despite its brevity, has been highly regarded by historians and biographers is easily explained. The earl's Irish dispatches were superbly written. For clarity, wit, and humor, they are unsurpassed. Attracted by an extraordinary candor and a magnificent style, historians and biographers have been inclined to see Chesterfield as a man for all seasons. They have assumed that any man who could write so much so well, any lord lieutenant possessed with such intelligence and intellectual power, had to be popular and successful. In this instance, as in others, articulation and style in an historical personality has had the effect of enhancing an historical reputation.

In fact, however, Chesterfield was a man of a single season. He did not serve long enough in Ireland to establish any sort of historical reputation. His ability to manage the Irish parliament was never really tested in normal political circumstances. He had done well in a time of urgent crisis, but what would happen once the dangers from abroad had passed and the intensity of crisis patriotism had diminished? Given the contempt which the earl exhibited towards Irish politicians and their concerns in his correspondence, it is unlikely that he could have avoided a confrontation with one or more of the leading men in the Irish parliament. Devonshire's near

31. Dobree, *op. cit.*, 1, 135.
32. *Dublin Journal* October 29–November 2, 1745.

abdication of leadership and the war had made Boyle, Carter, and their friends so necessary that no lord lieutenant could manage the Irish parliament without them. In future parliamentary sessions, Chesterfield would have been obliged to accommodate or turn them out. He was by nature incapable of doing the former and too outnumbered to attempt the latter. By not returning to Ireland, Chesterfield left those difficult choices to others. In effect, the earl passed on the poison cup which Devonshire had brewed to his successors.

Harrington's Special Problem

When Chesterfield left the Castle gate in April 1746, he fully expected to return to Ireland. Newcastle had implied that there might be possibilities for him at Whitehall, but Chesterfield simply did not want to believe in what might be. There were just too many personality and policy differences between himself and Newcastle for anyone to think that they could work together in the cabinet for very long. One such difference was whether to make peace or continue the war. While in Ireland, Chesterfield, the fierce war hawk of 1739, had become an unashamed dove. In his mind, the war had become hopeless, and England had absolutely nothing to gain by continuing it. With an issue as basic as peace or war dividing them, Chesterfield was genuinely surprised when, shortly after arriving in London, Newcastle asked the earl if he would consider accepting the office of secretary of state for the northern department if Lord Harrington resigned or was turned out.[33] Given the fact that Harrington was his cousin and a friend, Chesterfield refused the proposition by saying that he was content with Ireland.

Newcastle had approached Chesterfield because Harrington had become an extreme liability. The king despised him for his role in the mass resignations of February 1746. At that time, Harrington had flung his purse and seals down on to a table in front of the king and left his majesty almost speechless with anger. Thereafter, Harrington was never again welcome in the royal presence.

Newcastle did not despair of getting Chesterfield. He kept after

33. Dobree, *op. cit.*, I, 136.

the earl, perhaps sensing a willingness in him to accept if only a proper rationalization could be found. On October 28, 1746, such a rationalization was found. Chesterfield still insisted that peace was the best policy for the country. However, since that policy was impossible and the die of war had been cast, far better to pursue the war as vigorously as possible. Since the ministry had agreed to pay the Tsarina £900,000 for 30,000 Russian soldiers to march across Europe and fight in Flanders, Chesterfield agreed to accept the office that Newcastle had been thrusting upon him, provided that his cousin would resign. Newcastle dashed off to court with the news and discovered that Harrington had already quit. A difficult scene with his majesty had been too much. Harrington threatened resignation and the king took him at his word. When Newcastle proposed Chesterfield, the king agreed only on the condition that if he did not like Chesterfield, the duke would help his majesty get rid of him.[34]

Newcastle accepted the king's condition with enthusiasm and then founded another request upon it. After consulting with Pelham, the duke asked the king to send Harrington off to Ireland. Newcastle wanted to be rid of Harrington but was fearful of weakening the government if it were not properly done. To be properly done, it should appear to the political world that what had happened was only an exchange of offices between the two Stanhope cousins.[35] Though initially appalled at the idea of giving Harrington anything, in two weeks time Newcastle persuaded the king of the wisdom of doing so. Harrington would be distant from the court and his friends in parliament would be quiet.

Chesterfield lasted about eighteen months as secretary of state. His initial estimate that further prosecution of the war was hopeless turned out to be accurate. Truly, nothing had been gained by continuing the war. However, toward the end of 1747, the earl had begun to realize that official business was tedious, that conforming to majority opinion was ego-bruising, and that his presence in office had not made much of a difference about anything. Newcastle had

34. *Ibid.*, 139.
35. Lord John Russell, *Correspondence of John, Fourth Duke of Bedford*, Longman, Brown, Green, and Longmans, London, 1842, I, 178. Hereafter cited as Bedford Correspondence.

the king's confidence, and Newcastle determined policy. Chesterfield decided that his own time could be wasted more enjoyably
elsewhere. He resigned his office on February 26, 1748.

The Earl of Harrington's tour as lord lieutenant of Ireland turned
out to be both longer and more critical than his cousin's tenure as
secretary of state. Harrington held the office for forty-four months,
and during that time he enjoyed scarcely a contented moment.
His problem in Ireland was the same that destroyed his career in
England. The king despised him and all the world knew it. Aware
that any mistake or misadventure would mean dismissal and total
disgrace, Harrington strove mightily to avoid them. Given the realities of his situation, Harrington's strategy for political survival was
uncomplicated: simply accommodate those in Ireland who could
embarrass or damage him. Some contend that Harrington actually
made a treaty with Boyle, Carter, Malone, and their friends a week
after he arrived in Dublin.[36] Though evidence of such a treaty is
wanting, the earl clearly seems to have put himself in their hands.
Harrington appears to have decided that if he was to get along in
Ireland he would have to go along with the Boyle connection. In
Dublin during Harrington's time, going along came to mean doing
what the speaker wanted.

William Stanhope, Earl of Harrington was fifty-six years old when
appointed lord lieutenant of Ireland. Born into a prominent whig
political family, he served for many years as a soldier, a diplomat,
and a cabinet level officer. Between 1742 and 1747, Harrington was
deeply involved in virtually every ministerial change that Pelham
and Newcastle maneuvered the king into accepting. However, the
full force of royal frustration and pique was rarely ever directed
against the authors of these sometimes subtle but always unpleasant
political scenarios. Instead, it descended upon the head of Lord
Harrington, who was unlucky enough to be frequently cast as the
leading player.

Harrington was appointed lord lieutenant on November 15,
1746. He chose Edward Weston, a middle-aged under-secretary of
state of long acquaintance, to be his chief secretary and began
receiving correspondence from the lords justices about military

36. Irish Official Papers, I, 50.

appointments forthwith. The first major decision faced by the new lord lieutenant was selection of a new primate for the church of Ireland. John Hoadley had died in July 1746 and remarkably few solicitations had been received for the appointment since that time. The reason for this lack of interest was the general expectation by all parties that Armagh would go to George Stone, Bishop of Derry. George Stone was a brilliant and handsome young man with excellent political connections in England. Known personally to Pelham, Newcastle, and the new chief secretary, Stone had come to Ireland as one of the Duke of Dorset's chaplains in 1731. Since that time he rose steadily and rapidly to a position of recognized leadership in the Church of Ireland. Though only thirty-eight years old when the vacancy at Armagh occurred, Stone was the only serious candidate for it. During the previous fifteen years, Stone had demonstrated political and administrative talents for three successive chief governors that were unmatched by any other clergyman and few laymen of his time. Stone's political knowledge was so great and his many connections with unattached members of the Irish parliament were so promising that no Irish government could afford to do without him. Since Lord Harrington needed all the help he could get, the nomination was approved on February 28, 1747.

Stone began to prove his worth at once. He promised the lord lieutenant that he would make himself as useful to his excellency's service as possible and would keep him informed of all occurrences and developments.[37] According to Stone, Boyle had the largest but not the sole influence in the house of commons and was on occasions driven to make requests for favors. The speaker was "an honest, good natured, and, in his natural temper, not untractable man" and would do his best to make Lord Harrington's administration easy.[38] The lord chancellor through his influence with barristers and solicitors was the other great prince of parliament in Ireland and he "will be found always ready to bring his Assistance without difficulty upon Terms and Conditions." There was a jealousy between the speaker and lord chancellor that some of their respective friends constantly endeavored to cure and others strove regularly to in-

---

37. Stone to Harrington, March 5, 1746/47. Wilmot Mss., T.3019/828.
38. *Idem.*

George Stone, Archbishop of Armagh.
Courtesy of The Governing Body, Christ Church College, Oxford

flame. Stone advised the chief secretary not to worry about this jealousy because he might be able to find advantage, perhaps amusement, but not trouble in it.[39]

Stone described Malone as "by his Abilities the most considerable Man here, and the most usefull to the Government; at the same time, He is of all those in the Service of the Government, the most independent and the least importunate for Favours."[40] The primate recommended that some small mark of the lord lieutenant's attention to Malone would be of great service to the government and suggested a provision in the church worth £200 a year for one of Malone's kinsmen. Small favors of this sort, he concluded, should be used to good advantage, instead of being lost or thrown away, as had been often the case in the past.[41]

With Stone installed as primate and lord justice, Harrington and Weston had access to political information of the most intimate sort. Stone collected gossip. Much of the primate's information was insightful, but some of it was misleading. Because of Stone, the new chief governors were in a position to know more about what was in the minds and hearts of the country's political leaders, but that sort of knowledge did not make decisions easier or wiser.

Harrington arrived in Dublin on September 13 and his progress from the harbor side to the Castle was as splendid as any other in recent memory. If Stone's memory can be trusted, the lord lieutenant met first with himself and then with the lord chancellor, Boyle, Malone, Carter, Bessborough, and others. Though written seven years after the event, Stone asserted that during these meetings in late September and early October 1747, Lord Harrington made a treaty with the Boyle group.[42] In exchange for the promise of a tranquil session and a swift and easy passage of the money bills, Harrington agreed to take the speaker's advice on most things and reward those gentlemen whom the speaker believed should be rewarded. In Stone's view, the lord lieutenant simply did what he had to do. In happier periods of his life, Stone insisted, most assuredly the earl would have done otherwise. But given his relations with the king, the earl decided to accept an arrangement early in

39. Stone to Weston March 19, 1746/47. Wilmot, T.3019/829.
40. *Idem.*   41. *Idem.*
42. Irish Official Papers, I, 50.

his administration by choice and with good grace rather than be driven into it later by necessity.[43] For his part, Stone undertook to make the lord lieutenant's situation as easy as possible by cultivating and cooperating with the speaker.

Harrington's account of these September and October meetings written immediately after they occurred has not the benefit of hindsight. It is different but not contrary to Stone's recollections.[44] According to Harrington, what was learned from these meetings was the deplorable state of the country's defenses. He informed Newcastle that his first priority must be to improve them. To that end, one of his first official acts was to order all governors of counties and mayors to report on the state of the militia and on the condition of all fortresses in their jurisdictions. With regard to politics and to his present and future relations with the Boyle group, all he said was that the "principal people here" were full of zeal and that "from the dispositions so far displayed, I have all possible reason to hope that the affairs of the ensuing session of parliament will be transacted and settled in such a way as may be agreeable to his Majesty."[45] That may have been Harrington's way of saying that a treaty was made and that no trouble was expected from the people who could cause it. Then again it may be evidence of nothing of that sort. Nonetheless, subsequent events suggest that indeed Harrington had done what Stone later attributed to him.

Thus prepared, Harrington opened his first parliament on October 6, 1747. The speech from the throne touched upon the good work of the Protestant Charter Schools and the difficulties encountered installing batteries and new fortifications at Cork Harbor. Once again this lord lieutenant did not break with the financial policy of his predecessors: he asked only for the usual supplies.[46] The addresses were complimentary and noncontroversial. Next, the appropriate committees began reviewing the accounts and business proceeded expeditiously. By early November, the money bills had been reported and approved by the full house of commons. The privy council acted upon them immediately and the lord lieutenant

43. *Idem.*
44. Harrington to Newcastle, October 5, 1747. SP63/410/67.
45. *Idem.*
46. Harrington to Newcastle, October 8, 1747. SP63/410/77.

was able to dispatch the money bills to England on November 17, 1747.[47] With the routine business completed in near-record time, the lord lieutenant turned to the problem of improving Ireland's defenses.

Early in the present session, a committee had been appointed to consider the state of the barracks and to make recommendations about reconstruction and new building. The committee reported its findings to the house on December 9, 1747, in the form of resolutions requiring that an address be presented to the lord lieutenant requesting him to give directions for repairing or building such barracks as he should judge necessary for the security of the kingdom and for the more convenient reception of the king's forces.[48] This resolution precipitated a lengthy and acrimonious debate. Opponents protested that it gave unlimited power to the lord lieutenant. He could select barracks sites and determine the amount of money to be spent on repairs or new construction. If an address founded on this resolution passed, opponents argued, the house would be engaged to provide whatever sums the lord lieutenant chose to spend. It was an unlimited absolute vote of credit.[49]

The opponents of the address were correct in their estimate of what it authorized the lord lieutenant to do. Harrington admitted as much to Newcastle later and described the address as evidence of the great confidence the gentlemen in the house had come to have in his judgment.[50] In any case, when the tellers reported their counts, the address had carried by more than four to one. Elated by his success, Harrington immediately ordered the collection of information about the condition of barracks throughout the country, promised to present Newcastle with a general plan for repair or new building, and then adjourned parliament for the Christmas recess.[51]

When parliament reassembled in mid-January, all pending bills received final action and were passed on to the privy council for approval. In that body, all of the bills presented to it except one

47. Harrington to Newcastle, November 17, 1747. SP63/410/103.
48. Resolutions of the House of Commons, December 9, 1747. SP63/410/145.
49. Harrington to Newcastle, December 12, 1747. SP63/410/142.
50. Harrington to Newcastle, January 18, 1747/48. SP63/410/157.
51. Harrington to Newcastle, December 12, 1747. SP63/410/142.

obtained approval. The exception was a bill for the regulation of corporations, better known as the Newtown bill. The thrust of this measure was to permit Irish corporations to elect nonresidents as burgesses and other officers. Any legislation touching upon who could or could not be a burgess struck at the heart of the Irish electoral system. More than a third of the entire membership of the Irish house of commons were returned from corporation boroughs that would be regulated by provisions of the Newtown bill.

Underlying this bill was a dispute between Lord Bessborough and Alexander Stewart over the disposition of the parliamentary interest of Newtown borough. Bessborough had controlled the parliamentary representation of Newtown, county Down, for many years. He had done so through the interest of his stepson, Robert Colvill, who owned the manors of Newtown and Mount Alexander. However, Colvill broke with his stepfather in 1744 and sold both of those manors to a prominent Presbyterian landlord, Alexander Stewart. After purchasing the property from Colvill, Stewart refused to pay Bessborough for his lordship's interest over the burgesses on the assumption that he could get it for nothing. He began action in the Court of King's Bench to have Bessborough's burgesses disqualified and expelled from office on the grounds of nonresidence. Because the language of the Newtown bill was not retrospective and because Stewart had begun his legal action in 1747, the Newtown bill could have no effect on Stewart's litigation with the burgesses.[52] However, other gentlemen with borough interests to protect became greatly alarmed over what Stewart's case might do to them. According to Primate Stone, there was a general apprehension among the lords and gentlemen in the Irish parliament that some enterprising person might try to bring all corporation boroughs into question, "as they are all open to it," and they have brought in a quieting clause.[53]

The unanimous support which the Newtown bill received in the house of commons was not found in the privy council. The lord chancellor and the two chief justices—Newport, Marlay, and Single-

---

52. A. P. W. Malcomson, "The Newtown Act of 1748: Revision and Reconstruction," *Irish Historical Studies,* XVIII, no. 71. (March 1973), 313. Hereafter cited as Malcomson Newtown Act.

53. Irish Official Papers, I, 36.

ton—strongly opposed the measure in the council, but the arguments of Chief Baron Bowes and Primate Stone were sufficient to carry it through. Because this bill was the first major point of business undertaken by Stone, he suspected that opposition to it in the council proceeded from pique and resentment. Matters had been going so well for the government that a few councillors simply could not resist raising a stumbling block about something. In a long letter to Lord George Sackville, the primate expressed concern that misrepresentations about the bill would be made in London, but insisted that, in his judgment, the measure was both useful and necessary. Even more important, the lord lieutenant strongly recommended it.[54]

Except for revealing something about the primate's perceptions of how his colleagues on the council were reacting to his presence in the government, Stone's concern over the bill turned out to be unwarranted. The bill was returned from England as it had been sent over, and Stewart's litigation with Bessborough's burgesses wound its way through several levels of the Irish and English courts. Ultimately, the case was finally determined by the English courts, and any hopes Stewart ever had for the parliamentary representation of Newtown disappeared. Lord Bessborough's family continued to control the interest of Newtown until 1788, when they exchanged it with James Alexander for a similar interest in the borough of Banagher, Kings county.[55]

The unanimity of parties that had made Harrington's session so easy proved to be shortlived. It began breaking down almost as soon as the money bills were approved. The cause of this breakdown was the fine balance of Irish parties on the revenue board. With one Boyle commissioner, Bourke, and one Bessborough commissioner, Ponsonby, sitting on the board, decisions about the disposition of collectorships and other revenue employments became highly politicized. There were just not enough vacancies available to satisfy both groups.

Harrington reported in early 1748 that a serious dispute had arisen over the disposition of the collectorship of Waterford. Apparently the Boyle group expected that it would go to them when in fact

---

54. *Idem.*   55. Malcomson Newtown Act, 339.

it was already promised to the Bessborough interest. Differences between the two groups became so great, wrote Harrington, that it threatened to throw parliamentary affairs into great confusion. By their behavior during the present session, both parties deserved whatever the lord lieutenant could give. Harrington had no alternative but to find something comparable for the Boyle group elsewhere. The fortuitous demise of an elderly office holder named Copplestone provided such an alternative; but before the matter could be discussed with the speaker, Harrington received a solicitation for the place from none other than Henry Pelham. Actually, the situation was even more complicated than it appeared. Copplestone's death had opened up two places, and Harrington had already given one of the two to a member of his own family. As matters stood, Harrington had three options: he could turn out a near relative, offend the speaker and his party, or disappoint the king's first minister. He chose to disappoint Pelham. Hoping that the minister would understand, Harrington wrote a lengthy account of the entire matter, explaining that "it is not in my power to go back entirely from any engagement to the Speaker and his friends."[56] In the end, the job went to the Boyle group and, for the present, peace between the speaker and Bessborough was preserved.

With faction politics under control, Harrington prepared to end the session. However, before proceeding very far he learned that Newcastle had moved into Chesterfield's post as secretary of state for the southern department and that the Duke of Bedford had succeeded Newcastle as secretary of state for the northern department. Harrington immediately wrote to the new secretary congratulating him on his accession. With all parliamentary business completed in early March, Harrington requested the usual permission to return to England and to appoint the primate, speaker, and lord chancellor as lords justices. Within a month all bills were approved. Harrington prorogued parliament on April 9 and immediately sent off the closing addresses and answers to London. The lord lieutenant met with the primate and several members of parliament about patronage and pension matters during the course of the next week and then embarked for Parkgate on April 18, 1748.[57]

56. Irish Official Papers, I, 71.
57. Lords Justices to Bedford, April 20, 1748. SP63/411/17.

The Politicians Prevail

From Harrington's perspective, the session had been successful. The money bills had been easily and quickly passed, peace had prevailed among the principal parliamentary groups, and nothing untoward or embarrassing had occurred. Truly, everything had been under control. However, ministers in England and gentlemen in Ireland might well ask, under whose control? Harrington had gotten along because he had gone along. The situation was as Stone described it a few years later—a time when "the law was given to and not from the castle."[58] Nevertheless, Harrington had gotten through a session of the Irish parliament without disgrace, and for that he was certainly thankful. Also, the lord lieutenant had reason to be proud of the striking new efficiency exhibited by the Dublin Castle bureaucracy. The elevation of Stone to the primacy and his appointment as lord justice meant that correspondence was more detailed, politically incisive, and quickly dispatched. Moreover, the appointment of Thomas Waite, an industrious young Yorkshireman, strongly recommended by the chief secretary, to succeed William Potter as secretary to the lords justices improved the quality of information flowing out of Dublin.

At the other end of the communication link in Westminster, the employment since 1740 of Sir Robert Wilmot as a private secretary resident in London for the lord lieutenant provided English ministers with information and explanations of Irish affairs that properly could not be included in the official correspondence directed to the secretary of state. In the past, such matters had been sent to the secretary of state in private letters, but after 1748 information of this nature increasingly found its way to English ministers through letters sent to Sir Robert Wilmot. The combination of Stone and Waite in office since 1747 and Wilmot since 1740 had the effect of communicating much more detailed information about the causes and nature of Irish political problems to English ministers than had been received by them hitherto. Though much more was known in English ministerial circles about Irish politics in the years after 1748, one cannot say that greater knowledge of alignments and personalities made the tasks of governing Ireland any easier.

58. HMC Stopford-Sackville, I, 183.

While it is impossible to know what ran through the minds of Harrington and Weston as the yacht made for the Chester shore, they both must have thought about the future. Weston had several conversations with Stone, Boyle, and Newport before leaving Dublin about several pensions for persons in Ireland which the lord lieutenant hoped to obtain before returning. These pensions would gratify the lords and gentlemen receiving them but they might make the house of commons grumble if they came in as new charges and not as replacements for existing ones. However, more important for the next session than possible grumbling over new additions to the pension list were two very difficult problems relating to Thomas Carter and to Charles Lucas, a very popular and assertive pamphleteer and Dublin city politician. After arriving in England and further discussions with Weston, the lord lieutenant decided to try to do something for Carter and for the moment to ignore Lucas.

Carter was fifty-eight years old when serious illness brought him near death in the winter of 1748. For a man of his age and habits recuperation must have been slow. In any case, removed from the house of commons for a month or more, Carter had time enough to think about the future and the past. He thought about the prospects for his family in the years ahead and also about the reversions of offices and sinecures promised to him for his sons as long ago as 1731 but never delivered. Sometime before Harrington left Ireland, Carter made known his concerns to the lord lieutenant, who promised to do what he could on Carter's behalf. On May 11, 1748, Harrington wrote to Bedford urging that the reversions of Carter's offices be given to his two sons, Thomas Carter, younger, and Henry Boyle Carter.[59] The letter was received, and shortly thereafter Henry Boyle Carter was appointed clerk of the crown and prothonotary of the king's bench.[60] No action was taken on behalf of Thomas Carter, younger, and the reversion of the master of the rolls.

The reasons why nothing happened can be guessed. His majesty was reluctant to give reversions to anyone, and any recommendation from Harrington carried little weight with the king. Further-

---

59. Harrington to Bedford, May 11, 1748. SP63/411/27.
60. Carter to Wilmot, May 19, 1748. Wilmot Mss., T. 3019/1017.

more, Carter's reputation in English ministerial circles was not such that any of them would press his case on the king. After waiting a reasonable length of time, Carter accepted the fact that Harrington could not help him. He turned next to the primate in the hope that George Stone's special relationship with Pelham and Newcastle through his brother Andrew Stone might be sufficient to persuade either or both of the ministers to take up Carter's cause. He fancied that he had an influence over the primate because of previous cooperation in common enterprises and because of past services. Carter approached the primate in October 1748 with what he believed was a modified and very modest proposal. He asked only that Stone use his good offices to obtain the appointment of his son to succeed him as master of the rolls.

Affecting surprise at what he described as "a very unexpected and abrupt proposal," Stone refused to do anything.[61] He told Carter to his face that it was an improper request and would never be granted. Carter's son was very young and little known. Moreover, the nature and dignity of the office in question was such that it could not be transferred or handed about without serious regard to the qualifications and experience of the persons seeking it. In this instance, Stone had acted with more honesty and clarity than was usual among Irish politicians; and the experience must have been most instructive because no one ever accused him of acting thus again. He had made a strong point for virtue which affected Carter not one whit. Carter could hardly believe what was happening and exploded. How was it possible that one of the most influential men in the Irish parliament should be denied a favor that two lords lieutenants had approved by a young, smooth-talking over-ambitious cleric? According to Stone, Carter broke out into "the bitterest resentments" and from that moment set himself "to contrive and execute mischief."[62] Stone either clearly had underestimated his man or thought him much closer to eternity than he actually was. Whatever the reason for Stone's affront of Carter, the result was disastrous. The archbishop had created an inveterate enemy out of one of the most gifted, untiring, and unscrupulous Irish politicians of the eighteenth century. Carter's unforgiving animus for Stone and his genius

61. Irish Official Papers, I, 50.   62. *Idem.*

for invective would do much to alter the style and shape the course of Irish politics for the next decade.

Whatever the long-range consequences of Stone's impolitic treatment of Carter, at the time of Stone's scene with him no one in the government of Ireland was pleased with what had happened. Lord Newport was gravely concerned over the misunderstanding between the primate and the master of the rolls.[63] Waite reported that Carter had spread the word all over the city that the primate had refused his request for no other reason "than that of having resolved to keep Irish Men out of Places of Power as much as he could cum multis aliis which are better told than trusted to paper."[64] Stone met with the speaker and tried to explain what had happened and why. Boyle responded by saying that he was not blind to Carter's faults and assured the primate that their relationship would not be damaged by what had occurred between himself and Carter. From that meeting Stone went away entirely satisfied and secure in his own mind that he had nothing to be sorry for and that right had been done. For the present, that assessment was probably correct. However, neither Stone, Boyle, nor anyone else was able to appreciate how determined or how patient Thomas Carter could be.

Throughout the fall the lords justices and other members of the Irish government had been discussing schemes for improving the country's defense posture. Along with other office holders Carter had been apprised of these discussions and had probably participated in them. Waite made some inquiries in late December to try to find out what gentlemen in and out of the government thought about the prospect of increased military spending and got frightening reports about what Carter was saying on this issue. Carter was assuring his friends that the office of master of the rolls would be settled on his son with or without the support of the primate, and to encourage that result he began "ringing the Alarm Bell against the new Establishment."[65]

At the same time that Carter spoke his mind about Stone and

63. Newport to Weston, January 6, 1747/48. Wilmot Mss., T.3019/1219.
64. Waite to Weston, January 18, 1747/48. Wilmot Mss., T. 3019/1224. 96 Irish Official Papers, I, 51.
65. Stone to Weston, January 7, 1748/49. Wilmot Mss., T.3019/1220.

raised questions about the costs of proposed military spending, he communicated directly with the lord lieutenant about the new military establishments and his hope that Thomas Carter, younger, could succeed him as master of the rolls. Carter met several times with several gentlemen in Dublin about military expenses and implied in his correspondence with Harrington that one of those present was Henry Boyle.[66] At these meetings, Carter supported and probably advanced the argument that no funds would be available for increased military spending without introducing a land tax. According to Carter, all of the gentlemen present at these meetings were persuaded that their concern about a land tax and the difficulties that such a measure might cause in the next session of parliament ought to be presented to the lord lieutenant. Apparently, Carter wrote a letter to his son Thomas Carter, younger, who was in England about the concerns of the Irish gentlemen over a land tax and the political consequences of pressing for such a measure. Then young Carter sought out Lord Harrington and showed him the letter.[67]

While the lord lieutenant had the pleasure of meeting young Thomas Carter in London, and learning how concerned the master of the rolls and his Irish friends were that his excellency should be forewarned of serious trouble in the next session, old Thomas Carter prepared another letter for Harrington. On January 19, 1749, Carter advised the lord lieutenant that receipt of additional information from London about the new establishments disclosed that earlier apprehensions about the cost of the new establishments were unfounded. The estimates were about one-half of what had been first supposed.[68] Carter assured the lord lieutenant that insofar as his knowledge of gentlemen's minds extended, most of them wanted "to go as far as they can into Measures that maybe agreeable to H.M." Carter had communicated this information to Harrington not with a view toward any expected favors but so the lord lieutenant could know the real Thomas Carter. He wanted the lord lieutenant to know him through his own work and not through what others might say or write about him.

Stone did not know in February about Carter's correspondence

66. Carter to Harrington, January 19, 1748/49. Wilmot Mss., T.3019/1226.
67. *Idem.*   68. *Idem.*

with Harrington but suspected that there would be one and urged the chief secretary to make no decisions about Carter's requests until he had an opportunity to explain the entire situation to the lord lieutenant.[69] The primate believed his problems with Carter were over. The old man was crippled by an attack of gout; and according to Waite, many of his friends faulted him for unnecessary rudeness toward the primate. Stone made very clear that he would have nothing further to say about or to do with the master of the rolls.[70]

Harrington responded to Carter on February 16, 1749, thanking him for the welcomed assurances of personal regard and friendship and expressing relief that the alarm in Ireland over the proposed new establishments had subsided. The lord lieutenant affected no understanding of the reasons why there was so much concern in Ireland over the possibility of a land tax. He saw no possibility of such an expedient being considered and could not imagine where such an idea that it would be considered had come from. In Harrington's mind, the need for improving the military establishment had been demonstrated and he had no doubt that all members who were attached to the true interests of their country would support the king in this matter. Insofar as Carter himself was concerned, the lord lieutenant assured the master of the rolls that he was not by nature a person influenced by insinuations without proof. Carter should put to rest all fears that unsubstantiated assertions would prejudice him in any way with the lord lieutenant.[71]

Harrington made no promises to Carter but had managed to keep normal channels of communication open with him, and he appears to have requested and very soon received a full statement of the Carter family's pretensions to the office of master of the rolls. Carter explained that he had purchased the interests of Lords Berkeley and Barrington in the office in order that a grant of it might be made to himself during his majesty's pleasure. He paid out more than £11,000 that "I might have the Honr. of being imploy'd in such a Station in H.M.s Affairs—a thing which has not been done by many But where my heart was, there I was resolved

69. Stone to Weston, January 7, 1748/49. Wilmot Mss., T.3019/1220.
70. Waite to Weston January 26, 1748/49. Wilmot Mss., T.3019/1230.
71. Harrington to Carter, February 16, 1748/49. Wilmot Mss., T.3019/1249.

to entrust my fortune."[72] Carter had spent a great deal of money for this office and in his mind he believed that he had a moral if not a legal right to pass it on to his son. For Carter this office had been bought and paid for and should be his to give or bestow provided there was no prejudice to the king's service.

Carter got nowhere with Harrington on the transfer of the office to his son and by late April realized that further efforts at that time would be futile. He decided that enough was enough and begged Harrington's pardon for pressing this matter on him. Because of the opposition "some Ennemy of mine may give to it, and may become troublesome or disagreeable to your Lordp," Carter wrote, "I think it my Duty to tell your Lordp that I had rather the affair were dropd than that your Lordp should have any trouble on my acct, who am Conscious I have already recd. greater favours from you than what I had any the least pretensions to."[73] For the moment the Carter affair was over. However, it was not ended. From Carter's point of view the conflict between himself and Stone was irresolvable. He had suffered heavy financial damage that only ministerial intervention in England could repair. A chain of events had begun that would lead to major crisis between the Irish government and Irish parliament and a temporary exclusion of the primate from public life.

While corresponding with and failing to accommodate Carter, the lord lieutenant elected to ignore the public demands for reform of the Dublin city government being pressed by Charles Lucas. By choosing to do nothing about the Lucas agitation, Harrington began another chain of events that led to the very misadventures and disgrace he had worked so hard to avoid ever since coming to Ireland. Harrington certainly should have taken the time to find out more about this man, because by any standards Lucas was an exceptional person. He was of obscure origins and a partial cripple. Yet almost from the moment Lucas entered Dublin city politics in the 1730s and continuing until his death in 1771, this sometime apothecary and physician was without doubt the country's most irrepressible demagogue and most assertive Protestant patriot.

72. Carter to Harrington, February 16, 1748/49. Wilmot Mss., T.3019/1250.
73. Carter to Harrington, April 25, 1749. Wilmot Mss., T.3019/1311.

Growing up in Dublin in modest circumstances, Lucas served several apprenticeships and was admitted to the Guild of St. Mary Magdalene as an apothecary. Lucas married young, had a large family, and kept a shop in Charles street. Later, political opponents represented him as having been a poor businessman who affected notoriety by advertising his drugs in Latin. On one point about Lucas' early life all accounts agree. He loved controversy and had few scruples about the means of engaging in it.

In public life Lucas was a poor but indefatigable speaker, remembered by one lord lieutenant as a noisy declaimer who usually began a speech by remarking "Of all the days of my life this is the proudest" and invariably concluded it with an exhortation to return him to some public office.[74] As a writer Lucas was prolific and prolix. If not always clearly, he wrote easily and quickly on a variety of political and constitutional subjects. Though his numerous pamphlets and articles were done in a deadly style characterized by crude antiquarian arguments occasionally relieved by passages of spectacular vituperation, Lucas played a major role in the development of Irish political journalism. He also played another more traditional role. Lucas was a determined anti-papist and an outspoken anti-cleric. He was an enemy of priest craft and priestly influences whenever and wherever he found them at work. At various times in his public life he found them at work in the Church of Ireland, in Dublin Castle, and in county and borough elections.

Lucas began his public career in 1735, when, as a keeper of an apothecary shop in Dublin, he published a scheme for preventing frauds and abuses in the pharmacy trade. In 1741, he obtained a place in the common council for the city of Dublin as a representative of his corporation. During the next seven years, Lucas became one of the most hated and best loved men in Dublin politics. The experience of public office convinced him that the Dublin aldermen were corrupt and that he ought to do something about restoring integrity to his city's government.

As presently constituted, the board of aldermen elected its own membership; after inspecting the city's ancient charters and other civic records, Lucas concluded that the board of aldermen had

74. Bedford Correspondence, II, 427.

usurped the right of electing their membership from the entire corporation. With great force and acerbity, Lucas put that conclusion in his pamphlet *Remonstrance against certain infringements on the Rights and Liberties of the commons and citizens of Dublin,* which he published in 1743. He raised a fund by voluntary subscription, and on November 7, 1744, he initiated an action in the court of the king's bench against the alleged aldermanic usurpation of electoral rights. However, Lucas' case against the aldermen did not progress very far; after a hearing of two days the court refused Lucas permission to lodge an information against the aldermen, thereby quashing any further legal proceedings in the matter. Encouraged by the count's action, the victorious aldermen struck the names of Lucas and his supporters from the triennial return of the common council. Thus matters stood until Lord Harrington came to Ireland in September 1747. Lucas prepared a printed statement of the corporation's case against the aldermen—*The Complaints of Dublin*—and presented it to the lord lieutenant on Christmas Day, 1747. Lord Harrington refused to interfere at that time and continued to ignore Lucas during the rest of his time in Ireland in 1748.

Harrington left the country in April, and nothing further happened in the Lucas matter until August 1748, when Sir James Somerville died. One of Dublin's parliamentary seats was now vacant. Although the election was fourteen months away, Lucas immediately offered himself as a candidate. All of the bitterness lately exhibited by the alderman toward Lucas intensified. However, Lucas was not the only announced candidate. James Digges Latouche, wealthy son of a Dublin banker and a cooperator with Lucas in the late proceedings against the aldermen, and Sir Samuel Cooke, an alderman, both declared themselves as candidates. Though Lucas and Latouche professed substantially the same principles, they were both equally ambitious; and neither one would withdraw in favor of the other. Unless something unusual happened, the presence of two popular men in a three-man contest would virtually assure the return of Cooke.

Beginning on August 18, 1748, and continuing until September 1749, Lucas published a series of twenty *Addresses to the Free Citizens and Free-Holders of the City of Dublin,* wherein he alleged and then attacked corruption in the Irish house of commons, insulted Latouche and his friends, and proclaimed himself an advocate of Molyneux's concept of Anglo-Irish constitutional relations. Next, in May 1749, the other incumbent parliamentary representative for Dublin city, Nathaniel Pearson, died, creating another vacancy. Lucas and Latouche became partly reconciled and agreed to cooperate in opposing Cooke and the second aldermanic candidate, Charles Burton. Lucas celebrated this truce with Latouche and the new opportunity for the return of two popular men by publishing a remonstrance, setting forth a long list of grievances, entitled *The Great Charter of the Liberties of the City of Dublin*, on May 15, 1749. The lords justices thought the dedication paragraphs of the pamphlet libelous because of observations made about the lord lieutenant, court of king's bench, and lord mayor and aldermen. On June 16, Chief Justice Marlay bound over the printer for publishing a libel and considered action against Lucas.[75] Stopped by the lords justices and anxious to reach a wider audience, Lucas launched the famous *Censor or the Citizen's Journal,* a weekly newspaper devoted to exposure of scandals and to political reform, on June 3, 1749.

The appearance of the *Censor* was a major event in the history of Irish political journalism. In a verbose and wearying style, Lucas spared nothing and no one. He excoriated the conventions and everyday realities of Irish political life. Patronage was wrong. Sinecures, placemen, and pensioners were evils that honest Protestant freemen need tolerate no longer. Purity was possible, and the Dublin electors could take a greater step toward achieving it by voting for Charles Lucas.

Attacking the world as it was made Lucas a celebrity and increased his chances of getting into parliament, but it also made enemies— determined, unforgiving, and relentless enemies. For example, when the Dublin common council passed a resolution in June 1749 authorizing one of the aldermen to farm the city's revenues, Lucas denounced the proceedings as a colossal job charging that the council meeting in which the resolution had been carried was packed. The council responded on July 21, 1749, by voting Lucas' charges false, malicious, and scandalous and refused to hear anything in his defense. This censure of Lucas was confirmed at a later council

75. Waite to Wilmot, June 17, 1749. Wilmot Mss., T.3013/1329.

meeting in August and again by a vote of thanks to an author of a pamphlet who had attacked Lucas.[76] More important for the immediate future was Lucas' alienation of Sir Richard Cox. Lucas had played havoc with history in an article published in the *Censor* on June 24, 1749, by indicting Cox's distinguished grandfather— Sir Richard Coxe, Lord Chancellor 1703–1707 and Chief Justice of the King's Bench 1711–1714—as an enemy of the people. According to Lucas, old Judge Coxe had been one of those "knighted Ermined villains of the perfidious Ministry of the late abused Queen Anne" who had tried to usurp the authority of the Dublin city government and almost succeeded in ruining the country.[77]

Lucas' published observations on Judge Coxe were not only untrue and unhistorical, they were politically pointless and accomplished nothing except to infuriate Sir Richard Cox. By temperament and personality Cox was a perfect enemy. Though capable of displaying great charm, he had an explosive temper. Cox was easily offended and was intimidated by no one. Most important, Sir Richard Cox had not one particle of democratic sentiment anywhere in his being. Cox hated Lucas as much for who he was as for what he had written about the old judge. With a man as important as Cox leagued with the aldermen against Lucas, the probability that the power of the entire Boyle party would be arrayed against him in some fashion once parliament opened began rising.

While Harrington was in England, it is not certain how much he knew about the way the Lucas situation had developed in Dublin. In what little Harrington wrote to friends during his stay in England, Irish affairs did not loom large. Shortly before leaving London in August, Harrington met with the king and the English ministers and discussed the poor state of Ireland's defenses. The lord lieutenant agreed with the other ministers that the time had come to seek additional funds from the Irish parliament for the repair and improvement of the country's military preparedness.[78] Previous discussions about the condition of the barracks, the state of fortifications, and the number of troops needed in Ireland were formalized into a policy. Harrington left the meeting charged to

76. Munter, *op. cit.*, 176.
77. *Censor*, June 24, 1749.
78. Harrington to Bedford, October 12, 1749. SP63/411/49–54.

obtain from the Irish parliament additional funds sufficient to meet the costs of a new and expanded military establishment.

Burdened with this difficult task, Harrington arrived in Dublin on September 19, 1749. He had less than three weeks to get agreement from his parliamentary managers about the propriety of a tax increase, deal with the Lucas matter, and prepare his speech from the throne. The lord lieutenant met with Stone, Newport, Boyle, the law officers, and others and put directly to them the question "how far it might be expedient to demand new supplies for defraying the increased charge of the military establishment."[79] All of Harrington's advisors responded with the same voice. The present moment was no occasion for making such a demand. Harrington listened to their arguments, personally inspected the accounts of the revenue commission, and agreed that no increase should be requested. He struck all references to a tax increase from his speech and inserted language which asked only for the usual supplies. Next, the lord lieutenant proceeded to explain to the English ministers in detail how and why "persons of Chief weight and figure" in Ireland had managed to persuade him to depart from the specific instruction which had been given to him on this matter.

According to what Harrington had been told by his advisors, the principal impediment to seeking new funds at this time was the presence of a large unspent balance in the exchequer. This surplus derived in part from savings incurred because of the sparse number of troops in the country and from an extraordinary importation of dutiable goods after the peace.[80] To a man, everyone familiar with Irish fiscal affairs insisted that what was on hand plus the growing produce of the revenues ought to be sufficient to support the civil and military establishments for the next two years and also to provide sufficient funds to begin repair and construction of fortifications and barracks. Harrington accepted the arguments of his advisors and prayed that the king and his English ministers would do the same.

Harrington also hoped that his conduct on another matter would be approved in London. After arriving in Dublin, Harrington quickly discovered how divided the city had become over Lucas.

79. *Idem.*   80. *Idem.*

The king's Irish ministers were unanimous in their detestation of Lucas and urged the lord lieutenant to take notice of him in the speech from the throne. If Harrington had any doubts about the propriety of such extraordinary action, they were quickly banished after experiencing two unpleasant personal encounters with Lucas in early October. On October 3, Lucas attended the lord lieutenant at the Castle and presented him with *The Great Charter of the City of Dublin* as well as copies of his other political writings. Though Harrington simply accepted the writings without comment, Lucas interpreted anything less than outright rejection as approval and expected that *The Great Charter of the City of Dublin* would be transmitted to the king. In order to be certain that it had been sent off, Lucas returned to the Castle two days later to attend a public levee. Harrington was told that Lucas had come to the levee for the specific purpose of asking the lord lieutenant in the presence of all those attending whether or not he had transmitted *The Great Charter of the City of Dublin* to his majesty.[81] After a hasty meeting with his advisors, Harrington decided to avoid one embarrassing situation by creating another. An officer was sent to where Lucas was standing in the room and publicly commanded him to leave, which he did at once without further comment or disturbance. However, Lucas must have retired immediately to his workroom because on the next day, October 6, he published an account of the incident in the *Censor* "with thanks to his excellency for the honour he did him."[82] He followed up that piece on October 7 with *An Address to His Excellency William, Earl of Harrington, Lord Lieutenant . . . of Ireland . . . with a preface to the free and loyal subjects of Ireland in general,* which was described by Harrington as being more insolent and dangerous than anything previously written. Clearly, matters had gone too far. Lucas had to be stopped.

Harrington collected copies of several numbers of the *Censor* and sent them off to London with a detailed explanation of who Lucas was and what he had done. Lucas had "aspersed people of all ranks in the kingdom and even the government itself." He had gone so far as "to represent the Irish nation as under a state of oppression

81. *Idem.*
82. *Censor,* September 30 to October 7, 1749.

and to inveigh most indecently against the power assum'd by the British Parliament of making laws to bind Ireland."[83]

Lucas had made so many converts, Harrington continued, that it had become absolutely necessary to put an immediate stop to his proceedings and to do it "in a parliamentary way, by declaring the sense of the nation thereupon, and their abhorrence of his rebellious doctrines."[84] The lord lieutenant decided to initiate parliamentary action against Lucas, because it was the unanimous desire of the king's principal servants in Ireland that he should do so. In the Lucas case as in virtually every other policy or patronage decision which Harrington had to make, it appears that he did exactly what the speaker and his friends wanted.

Ever hopeful that his majesty would approve of his conduct, Harrington opened the Irish parliament and delivered his speech from the throne on October 10, 1749. True to the scenario that had been worked out beforehand, the lord lieutenant commented on the great blessings of peace the king had obtained for his subjects, asked for nothing except the usual supplies, and observed that progress had been made on the installation of gun batteries at Cork Harbor and on the new disposition and repair of army barracks throughout the country. Next, the lord lieutenant turned to Lucas. Though not mentioning Lucas by name, he denounced all audacious attempts to create jealousies between the kingdoms of England and Ireland. The addresses from both houses following the speech were appropriate to the charge given them. What was well begun on October 10 continued for the next three weeks.

First, the house of commons formed itself into a committee of the whole to consider the alleged seditious, libelous, and scandalous nature of Lucas' writings. Next, after finding those writings to be as alleged, the house agreed to a motion, introduced by Sir Richard Cox ordering Lucas and his printers, to appear at the bar of the house to answer for what they had written and published. The printer, Edsall, absconded immediately, but Lucas considered staying and defending his own case in the house. However, after the house passed a series of resolutions also introduced by Cox with

83. Harrington to Bedford, October 12, 1749. SP63/411/49–54.
84. *Idem.*

only one negative vote,[85] declaring Lucas to be an enemy of his country, directing the attorney general to prosecute him for publishing seditious and scandalous papers, and ordering his confinement in Newgate Jail for infringement and violation of the privileges of the house of commons,[86] he thought otherwise and fled first to the Isle of Man and then to London. Gentlemen connected with the government were well pleased by this result. The chief secretary described the great mischief nearly done to this kingdom by one poor apothecary as hardly credible; but, Weston concluded, "you will see in our Votes how we have handled him; and indeed it was high time."[87]

Lucas' departure did not end the matter. The lord mayor, sheriff, and common council attended the lord lieutenant in a body on October 21, 1749, and presented a loyal address denouncing Lucas' writings as seditious and expressing satisfaction with the censure passed on him by the house of commons.[88] In early November, Lucas was indicted by the grand juries of the city and county of Dublin as a common libeler; and at the direction of the house of commons, the lord lieutenant issued a warrant for his apprehension. Undaunted by what had happened, Lucas continued to send materials from England for publication in the *Censor;* and in December his printer's wife, Mrs. Edsall, was summoned before the bar of the house of commons for printing an offensive article. When the speaker learned that the manuscript Mrs. Edsall had printed had been submitted by Andrew Miller, Mrs. Edsall was excused but Miller was ordered to Newgate. Miller was a mezzotint engraver and printseller who had been selling pictures of Lucas bearing the inscription "An Exile for his Country, who, for seeking liberty lost."[89]

Lucas prepared his own version of the proceedings against him in the Irish parliament and published a long pamphlet, *The liberties and customs of Dublin asserted,* in London in February 1750. Weston

85. John Cope to Wilmot, October 21, 1749. Wilmot Mss., T.3019/1404.
86. *Commons Journal,* Ireland, V, 14.
87. Weston to Wilmot, October 17, 1749. Wilmot Mss., T.3019/1401.
88. *Commons Journal,* Ireland, V, 14.
89. A. Briton, *History of the Dublin Election with A Sketch of the Present State of Parties in the Kingdom of Ireland,* Dublin, 1753, 87.

requested that the English attorney general look into the matter and consider some sort of action.[90] The chief secretary set Sir Richard Cox to writing a response and arranged with Wilmot to have Cox's response published anonymously in London and then reprinted in Dublin.[91] The whole matter had to be done in complete secrecy and with utmost dispatch. In the meantime, at the Christmas assembly, the Dublin corporation disenfranchised Lucas, and for all practical purposes the affair was over, even though the *Censor* continued to appear until July 1750.

With Lucas gone and with most of his friends intimidated, the prospects for the popular party in the Dublin city election were much diminished. Harrington reported that the ferment within the city had ceased and that the election was proceeding well with all possible decency and quiet.[92] Once again Harrington was wrong. After an exciting poll, Latouche and Cooke were elected. Lucas was gone but Lucas' sometime colleague, Latouche, had won. However, almost before the popular party had finished celebrating their victory, Burton lodged a petition with the house of commons against the seating of Latouche, alleging undue influences in the election. Burton charged that Latouche had associated with Lucas and had influenced the poll with corruption and with seditious publications. Witnesses were called to appear and testify to the committee on disputed elections, and proceedings were protracted for eight days.[93] The vote went against Latouche in the committee, 110 to 54, and he lost again when the committee report, which took almost four hours to read, was presented to the house. In the end, Latouche was unseated and Burton was declared duly elected by a majority of 52. Pleased that the majority was so large, Waite expressed hope that the house had seen the last of Lucas and Lucasian principles.[94]

During all of the excitement and turmoil of late October and early November, a deep sense of helplessness ran through all of Harrington's official and private correspondence. He seemed to know that his situation was out of control, and yet he desperately

90. Weston to Wilmot, February 10, 1749/50. Wilmot Mss., C1827/42/80/67/207.
91. Weston to Wilmot, March 21, 1749/50. Wilmot Mss., C. 1827/42/80/67/222.
92. Harrington to Bedford, October 31, 1749. SP63/411/191.
93. Weston to Wilmot, December 16, 1749. Wilmot Mss., T.3019/1431.
94. Waite to Wilmot, December 18, 1749. Wilmot Mss., T.3019/1432.

sought assurances from England that it was not. Harrington's anxiety over losing credibility in London was genuine and well founded. The reasons why became very clear when the committee of supply reported the money bills to the house in mid-November. At that time, Harrington informed Bedford that there were "several variations in them from last session;"[95] and as the lord lieutenant feared, the English ministers viewed those variations as encroachments on his majesty's prerogative.

The simple fact of the matter was that once again the lord lieutenant had to confess that he had been misled. His advisors had insisted that the existence of a large surplus in the exchequer made demands for new taxes impolitic and unnecessary. They had persuaded him that the surplus and anticipated revenue increases in the course of the next two years ought to be sufficient to support the establishments and allow the government to proceed with the repair and reconstruction of certain strategic fortifications. However, on October 21, 1749, less than two weeks after informing the English ministers about the surplus and the impossibility of asking for new taxes, Harrington admitted that none of the surplus would be used for defense projects. The money would be used to pay off four-percent-government-bondholders and to retire some other five percent obligations, thereby discharging part of the national debt.[96] It was, insisted the lord lieutenant, "a thing earnestly desired by the King's servants and by both Houses of Parliament."[97]

It was also a thing that directly touched the majesty's undoubted prerogative to control the disposition of his own money. Since part of that surplus had been derived from the hereditary revenues— revenue sources belonging to the crown and not voted by parliament—one did not have to be an expert lawyer to predict that his majesty's English law officers would insist that the Irish parliament could not even discuss the disposition of such monies without the previous consent of the king. Weston admitted that the surplus was composed of balances from the hereditary revenues and from the

95. Harrington to Bedford, November 17, 1749. SP65/411/214.
96. *Historical Manuscripts Commission, Reports on the Manuscripts of . . . C. F. Weston, Esq., . . . Tenth Report Part I* (Printed by Eyre and Spottiswoode, London, 1885), 304. Hereafter cited as HMC Weston.
97. Harrington to Bedford, November 17, 1749. SP63/411/214.

additional duties. The former indisputably belonged to the crown, while authority over the latter was not clear.[98] However, "the whole is thrown into a Mass, and the Several Constituents of ye whole Balance remain undistinguishable when it is struck," the chief secretary concluded, "So the Parlt cannot be supposed to have a Share with ye Crown in disposing of the whole Ballance."[99] Harrington knew very well the nature of the constitutional thicket into which his Irish advisors were driving him, but he was powerless to resist them. To the English ministry, Harrington pleaded expediency and insisted that new language inserted into the Irish money bills would have the effect of strengthening, rather than weakening, the king's prerogative in this matter.

Because the time between final action by the appropriate parliamentary committees on the public accounts and introduction of the money bills was too short to apply for and receive his majesty's permission to dispose of the surplus, Harrington informed Bedford, "I determined to yield to the representations that were made to me on that subject which were indeed entirely agreeable to my own opinion." New language added to the preambles of the money bills, Harrington insisted, would leave no doubt in anyone's mind that the idea of applying the surplus to the national debt had originated with the king as a grace and favor to his subjects. This is, after all, he added, "the light in which the thing is seen and understood by everybody here."[100] Harrington hoped that his arguments would convince the English ministers that his majesty's prerogative to dispose of revenue surpluses had been strengthened by what had happened in Ireland, and he urged that the money bills be returned quickly without alterations or additions.[101]

Neither Bedford, Newcastle, Pelham, nor the king were convinced by Harrington's arguments. From their perspective, it appeared that the government of Ireland had passed entirely into the hands of the speaker and friends. Yet, nothing could be done at the moment. For all of his demonstrated weaknesses, Harrington was the lord lieutenant and the English ministry had to go with

98. Weston to Wilmot, November 17, 1749. Wilmot Mss., T.3019/1419.
99. *Idem.*
100. Harrington to Bedford, November 17, 1749. SP63/411/214.
101. *Idem.*

him. Pelham sent a carefully phrased, charitable private letter to Harrington on November 7, 1749, in an effort to revive the lord lieutenant's spirits and restore his self-confidence.

Harrington received Pelham's letter in the sense intended. The lord lieutenant was pleased and thanked Pelham profusely for sending it. He was hopeful that his explanations had fully obviated all apprehensions of any prejudices arising in the future over the necessity for the king's previous consent before parliament could discuss or act upon the disposition of future surpluses. Harrington also understood well that despite what Pelham had written, he was not much loved at St. James. Since there was no hope for redress or satisfaction in complaint, he would make none and would try to carry on as best he could.[102] However, carrying on at all depended on cooperation and support from the speaker and his friends; and by mid-November, bills for the payment of services already performed had been tendered. Because parliamentary business had been much greater than expected and the end of the session was several months distant, Harrington wanted the most important of those bills paid—particularly the ones presented by the speaker himself and by Sir Richard Cox.

In early November, the speaker applied to the lord lieutenant for a vacant regiment for his step-brother, Colonel Michael O'Brien Dilkes. Harrington approved the application and sent it off to London with a comment that Dilkes was "brother to the Speaker of the House of Commons who would be greatly obliged by such a mark of His Majesty's Royal favor."[103] However, he added a further observation that if the king were not pleased to approve Dilkes' promotion, there were four other lieutenant colonels equally qualified and anxious to succeed.[104] Another application on behalf of Henry Boyle Walsingham, the speaker's second son currently on active duty as a reduced captain, was sent off in early December for a vacant captaincy in another regiment. Both of these recommendations excited no controversy and were routinely approved. One debt for services performed during the present session was paid.

Harrington's obligation to Sir Richard Cox was not so easily dis-

102. Irish Official Papers, I, 73.
103. Harrington to Bedford, November 1, 1749. SP63/411/194.
104. Harrington to Bedford, December 2, 1749. SP63/411/220.

charged, and the chosen manner of rendering this political account involved the lord lieutenant in a bitter controversy with the three Englishmen serving on the Irish revenue board. Cox had taken the lead in the proceedings against Lucas and had consistently supported the government on other matters throughout the session. Sometime after the Christmas recess, Cox applied to Harrington for the post of collector of customs for Cork. However, the office was not vacant. It was presently occupied by Mr. John Love. Harrington proposed to satisfy Cox by working out an arrangement whereby Love would be offered a pension of £500 a year to resign in favor of Cox.[105] However, the three English revenue commissioners—William Bristowe, Frederick Frankland, and Henry Cavendish—opposed the exchange on the grounds that the revenue would suffer and persuaded Love to refuse to resign. Next, they presented Harrington with a memorial explaining in greater detail the reasons why they could not comply with the lord lieutenant's wishes and sent off a private letter explaining their position to Pelham.

Harrington became infuriated. He discussed the problem with the Irish commissioners—Ponsonby and Bourke—and after learning that they had no objection to the proposed exchange he met again with the English commissioners and wrote several strong letters to Pelham. Harrington argued that Cox's distinguished support of government in parliament merited reward. The objections laid against Cox and the whole proceeding were politically motivated and would give great satisfaction to Lucas' friends if not overruled. He insisted that in this matter the honor and dignity of the office of lord lieutenant was at stake and urged that one of the three recalcitrant English commissioners be dismissed as an example.[106]

Since virtually all of the business of the session was completed before this proposed exchange became a matter of viceregal honor, and since Harrington was due to depart for England shortly, Pelham proceeded very slowly in responding to Harrington's request. Pelham wrote first to Frankland, Bristowe, and Cavendish in order

105. Irish Official Papers, I, 72.
106. *Idem.*

to learn their side of the controversy. In particular, he wanted to know if the primate, Boyle, and Newport felt as strongly about the Cork collectorship as did the lord lieutenant. The commissioners replied that none of those persons had communicated anything to them about the exchange. For their part, the commissioners had not consulted with the lords justices about the exchange because, as they self-righteously asserted, it was their policy to stay out of politics and attend to their jobs. They did admit, however, that after they had refused to go along with the exchange, the primate and Ponsonby both recommended compliance with the lord lieutenant's wishes.[107] The commissioners explained further that they would of course approve the exchange if ordered to do so by the treasury or by a king's letter, but that it was against their better judgment to put Cox in that post. Bristowe—regarded by Harrington as the ringleader in this affair—complained bitterly about his treatment by the lord lieutenant and accused his lordship of making an absolutely disgraceful proposal to him.

Having heard self-serving arguments from both sides and a word or two on behalf of the commissioners from Henry Cavendish through Lord Hartington,[108] Pelham decided that the best course would be to end the controversy with as little pain as possible to all parties concerned. The minister delayed his decision until Harrington had left Ireland. After the lord lieutenant was safely ensconced at his country seat in Derbyshire, Pelham approved the exchange. Cox would get the Cork collectorship and Love would get his pension. The three English commissioners would be left in their employments but would be apprised of Pelham's disapprobation of their conduct toward Harrington and of his suggestion that they make proper apologies to the lord lieutenant. In Weston's mind, an end had been put to this very disagreeable affair.

This controversy between the English commissioners and the lord lieutenant was symptomatic of a general public discontent with Harrington during his last days in Ireland. The truth of the matter appeared to be that, except for the speaker and his friends, most Irish politicians were glad to see him go. Public confidence in the

107. *Ibid.*, 73.
108. Henry Cavendish to Hartington, April 7, 1750. Chatsworth Mss., T.3158/392.

government and parliament was minimal. Sir Edward O'Brien, an independent member for county Clare, expressed to a friend complete disgust with the way public affairs of the country had been conducted. O'Brien thought seriously about quitting parliament, not merely for the present session but possibly for the rest of his life. There was "so much villainy going forward in Dublin," he wrote, ". . . if I were my own master . . . I never wd spend . . . another week in a kingdom bought and sold where all confidence between man and man, and all public faith, is brought to an end."[109] Though O'Brien's reaction to the total domination of parliamentary politics by the speaker's party was extreme, he was by no means alone in his concern over what had been happening. There were other unattached members of the house no less disturbed by recent events than O'Brien, but unlike him these gentlemen were anxious to find some practical way of coping with the near-limitless power of the Boyle party. Among these persons were included some of the lesser Castle officials, many of the younger ambitious members of the house, and a few of the older, more cynical veterans of many sessions. During the latter part of the session, they began talking to one another and to Archbishop Stone. Here began the primate's celebrated displays of hospitality—the frequent drinking and dinner parties—whereby he began forming small groups of friends and followers into what would become a formidable parliamentary connection.

Whether Stone's socializing with members of parliament or Carter's constant insinuations to Boyle against Stone or both caused the speaker to turn against the primate is problematic; but whatever the cause, estrangement between these two future lords justices was a fact during Harrington's last months in Ireland. According to Stone, strange and unaccountable suspicions and jealousies were daily infused into the speaker's mind. The primate tried to dissemble and conceal all of the slights and ill treatment received from the speaker and his friends, foreseeing that an open difference between them would embarrass the lord lieutenant and delay completion of the king's business.[110] Stone discussed the developing situation with

109. John Ainsworth, ed., *The Inchiquin Manuscripts* (Irish Manuscripts Commission, Dublin, 1961), 162.
110. Irish Official Papers, I, 51.

the lord chancellor, who gave the primate sympathy but absolutely refused to get involved in his problems with the speaker. Meanwhile, Harrington was either totally unaware of what was happening between Boyle and Stone or he chose to ignore it. He sought permission to appoint the primate, speaker, and lord chancellor as lords justices in late February, recommended a follower of Bessborough and a friend of the speaker for peerages in March, and made preparations for a mid-April departure.[111]

The lord lieutenant did not embark for Parkgate until April 18, and his progress from the Castle to the waterside was a very unhappy one. According to Lord Chesterfield, bonfires were lit and a thousand insults were shouted at him. The people of Dublin had not forgotten what Harrington had done to their banished idol, Charles Lucas. At the time of his departure from Ireland, Harrington was certainly the most dominated and probably the most unpopular lord lieutenant of the century. Moreover, the extent of his unpopularity in Dublin was equaled and perhaps even exceeded at St. James. The king had decided that Harrington would not go back to Ireland even before the earl had boarded the yacht for Parkgate. Pelham reported to Newcastle in late April that the Duke of Dorset was telling everyone that he would be the next lord lieutenant of Ireland, and within two weeks everyone was telling Lord Harrington that he was out.[112]

When Harrington arrived in England, he met with Pelham and wanted to know if what he had been hearing was true. Specifically, the earl wanted to know the reasons why he was being turned out. Pelham parried the question as best as he could, telling his lordship that he knew of no new reasons for what was happening but did not disguise the fact that the king had no love for Lord Harrington. The earl asked next whether he was to be totally laid aside without any office or provision of any kind. Pelham responded by saying that it was not the wish of the ministry that Harrington should be turned out in such a fashion, but knowing the disposition of the king, he could not give the earl much hope that there would be

111. Harrington to Bedford, March 13, 1750. SP63/412/72.
112. William Coxe, *Memoirs of the Administration of . . . Henry Pelham . . .* (Longman, Rees, Orme, Brown, and Breen, London, 1829), II, 335, 337. Hereafter cited as Coxe Pelham.

Lord George Sackville. Engraving of c. 1800, after a
Joshua Reynolds portrait [c. 1755?]
Courtesy of A. P. W. Malcomson

anything for him. The best that Pelham could offer was the observation that nothing would be done until the king returned from Hanover six months hence and "nobody can tell what may happen before that time."[113]

During those six months Pelham worked manfully to try to persuade the king to give Harrington something. By mid-October Lord Harrington's future was firmly and finally decided. The king told Newcastle in no uncertain terms that nothing would be done because Lord Harrington deserved nothing.[114] Pelham was given the melancholy task of informing the earl of the king's determination, which he did with as much grace as the circumstances would allow. Harrington resigned forthwith, went into retirement, and took no further part in public affairs.

Dorset's appointment as lord lieutenant was announced on December 6, 1750, and that of his son, Lord George Sackville, as chief secretary was made public nine days later. Ireland had a new set of chief governors. As a former lord lieutenant, Dorset probably knew the country and its politicians as well as, if not better than, any other English candidates for the post. However, the duke knew Irish politics as it had been in 1736 when he was lord lieutenant. The realities of Irish politics had changed greatly in the course of fourteen years, and how Dorset and his talented and ambitious son would cope with those changes, time alone would tell.

113. *Ibid.*, 337.   114. *Ibid.*, 134.

CHAPTER IV

The Great Crisis in Irish Parliamentary Politics, 1750-1754

Personalities, Parties, and the Constitutional Doctrine of Previous Consent

Though Pelham and Newcastle at times had been distressed by Lord Harrington's inability to comply with ministerial instructions and agreements on specific issues during his lord lieutenancy, there is nothing to suggest that they perceived how weak Harrington's administration was or how much he had been under the direction of the speaker and his friends. Harrington was not forced out of office and out of all future public service because of what he had done or allowed to happen in Ireland. The earl was removed because the king despised him and because the Duke of Dorset wanted his office. Dorset had been reluctant to give up Ireland in 1737 and had wanted to return at first opportunity.

Generally, in English official circles, Harrington's disgrace was attributed to English causes only and not to his performance as lord lieutenant of Ireland. Among the Irish politicians, perceptions of the reasons for Harrington's disgrace were bound to be different. Few Irishmen were in a position to know either the intensity of royal prejudice against Harrington or the extent of Dorset's ambition to return to Ireland. Knowing for certain only that Harrington's last parliamentary session had been unlike any other in recent memory, many Irish politicians were able to persuade themselves that the earl had been removed because he had let control of public affairs fall in the hands of the speaker and his friends. For all Irish parties and connections, Dorset's reappointment as lord lieutenant signified a message, even though none appears to have been intended. The message was that the new chief governors of Ireland were charged to restore the direction of public affairs to Dublin Castle.

Certainly, in early 1751 the primate appears to have expected that changes were coming; and by May of that year he had matched those expectations with some action. With Boyle in Cork during much of the summer and with Lord Newport weakened by failing health, Stone spent most of his time in Dublin Castle attending to public affairs and acting as if he were the sole lord justice. The interests of Ireland were being looked after by a most industrious and resourceful man, who knew what power was and enjoyed using it.

However, in Ireland during the summer of 1751, knowing how to use power was not the same as possessing it. Power in Ireland was still very much in the hands of Henry Boyle and his friends; and before the summer was over, Stone and Lord Bessborough were given an object lesson in that fact. Sir Mathew Deane died in the spring, opening up a vacancy in the parliamentary representation for Cork city. Henry Cavendish announced his candidacy for it. Cavendish was a relative of the Duke of Devonshire, a member of the Irish revenue board, a former collector of customs in Cork, and a friend of John Ponsonby. According to Stone, Cavendish would have been chosen without much difficulty if Sir Richard Cox had not stirred up a violent opposition against him in Cork.[1] The prospect of Cavendish in the Irish parliament as a member for a Cork constituency was for Cox too horrendous to consider for even a moment. Cavendish was one of the three Englishmen serving on the Irish revenue board who had opposed Harrington's nomination of Cox for the post of collector of customs for Cork. Cox's campaign against Cavendish was bitter and personal, and was carried on with the frenetic zeal that most Irish public men had come to expect from Sir Richard. In particular, he worked very hard trying to persuade the speaker that Boyle's own interest as well as Cox's honor were involved in the outcome at Cork.

Boyle knew Cox as well as any man in Ireland, and at first attempted to stay out of what must have appeared to him as an intensely personal vendetta. Boyle met with Stone and raised ques-

1. *Irish Official Papers*, I, 52.

tions about the propriety of John Ponsonby soliciting votes in Cork for his near relation and colleague on the revenue board. Stone assured the speaker that Ponsonby had not used the influence of revenue board patronage on behalf of Cavendish and that whatever had been done was entirely proper. According to Stone, the speaker appeared to be convinced and gave the most solemn pledges that if Cavendish were able to poll a majority in the election, he would be returned. Thus, the matter appeared settled.

However, appearances were deceiving, and the speaker had a change of mind. He informed Stone that reports about customs house officials in Cork soliciting votes for Cavendish were true. Since a resolution of the house of commons prohibited such activities by revenue officers, he could no longer stand by the assurance given to Stone. The situation in Cork was now so altered, Boyle told Stone, that if a petition were lodged against Cavendish "he must fight it through."[2] The assurance given to Stone was withdrawn and Cavendish's prospects for an easy and inexpensive victory at Cork diminished. At this point, Dorset intervened, and by doing so he made a difficult situation worse.

Dorset's motives are easy to understand. Apprehensive about beginning the forthcoming session with a confrontation between the speaker's party and the Bessborough group over a disputed election petition, and wanting to display some public mark of regard for Boyle, Dorset prevailed on Cavendish to give up the election before the poll. When most Irish politicians learned about Boyle withdrawing his assurance about the Cork election from Stone, they must have been surprised. To risk offending Stone and Bessborough in order to gratify Sir Richard Cox was not good sense. Contests over disputed election petitions were notoriously unpredictable affairs, and the speaker's ability to manage their outcome was by no means a demonstrable fact.[3] Why Boyle and his friends chose to make this contest a test of their hegemony over the Irish house of commons is a mystery. The prize was not worth the risk of reaching for it.

2. *Ibid.*, 53.
3. A. P. W. Malcomson, "John Foster and the Speakership of the Irish House of Commons," *Proceedings of the Royal Irish Academy*, Vol. 77, Section C, no. 11, 1972, 291–292.

If most Irish gentlemen had been surprised by Boyle's decision to embarrass Stone and Bessborough in such a public way, they must have been shocked by Dorset's response to it. By persuading Cavendish to withdraw, the duke attributed a power to the speaker that no other Irish politician had ever enjoyed and that Boyle had rarely if ever exercised. Dorset attributed to Boyle a power of making the house as well as managing it. Cavendish's withdrawal signified that in effect Boyle had a right of nomination in by-elections. If a gentleman as well connected as Cavendish could be driven out of a poll, no man could stand for any constituency anywhere in the country without first obtaining an assurance from the speaker that after the poll no election petition would be carried against him.[4] Dorset's intended act of conciliation made Boyle and his friends appear much bigger and stronger than they actually were. It enhanced their prestige and probably increased their following in the house. Even more important, it encouraged Boyle's friends to think that they were all-powerful and that no reasonable patronage request would be refused. When Malone made such a request and had it denied, he persuaded himself and others in the Boyle party that those who had denied him needed to be taught the folly of their ways.

Malone's hopes for the post of master of the rolls were of long standing. However, as long as Carter's son was denied a reversion of that office and no one else advanced stronger claims for it than himself, Malone was content to wait until Carter vacated it one way or another. Though patient for himself, he was much less so for those who were dependent on him. Malone was extremely anxious to obtain a suitable place for his younger brother, Richard. Malone had approached Stone as early as 1746 about the prospect of Richard succeeding Warden Flood as solicitor general. At that time, Stone had promised to use his influence on behalf of Richard Malone whenever the office became available.[5] Stone's promise notwithstanding, Malone continued to press Lord Harrington for a job for Richard. In this instance, as in others when prominent members of the Boyle party were involved, Harrington did what he could.

4. For this argument, see pamphlet cited by A. P. W. Malcomson, *Ibid.*, 291.
5. HMC Emly, 176.

In 1750, Richard Malone was appointed second serjeant-at-law. Thus matters stood until the summer of 1751, when a retirement from the bench precipitated some promotions and changes among the law officers that left the post of solicitor general vacant.

At that moment, Richard Malone, present second serjeant-at-law, was the leading candidate to succeed Flood as solicitor general. His only serious rival was Philip Tisdale, a relative of old judge Singleton and third serjeant-at-law since 1741. Anxious to redeem what had been long ago promised, Malone approached Stone and asked that his brother be recommended for solicitor general. Still angry and embarrassed over the outcome of the Cavendish affair and unwilling to give another important office to the speaker's party, Stone refused to intercede on behalf of Richard Malone. Stone explained to the prime serjeant that his promise of support for Richard Malone's pretensions to be solicitor general had been made when he was bishop of Derry and in a private station. The promise had been made solely out of affection for the prime serjeant.[6] However, now Stone was primate and lord justice. He was at the head of the state and had to gauge all of his decisions by the standard of public good. In this case, as in all others arising while in his present station, Stone insisted, affection for the public rather than for individuals must govern all of his actions. Therefore, he believed himself "bound in conscience to break that promise which he had made without any view to the public." Thus it came to pass, concluded a contemporary, that "for conscience's sake Mr. Tisdale was made Solicitor General."[7]

As parliament's opening approached, relations between the principal person in the Irish executive, Stone, and the leadership in the house of commons—Boyle, Malone, and Carter — had become so strained that some sort of confrontation seemed unavoidable. Carter was totally alienated from Stone, and Malone and Boyle were rapidly becoming so. Malone and Boyle perceived the primate as an overly ambitious and untrustworthy man who had broken a promise to them once and would certainly do so again.

For his part, Stone insisted that Boyle was under the sole direction of the prime serjeant. As a lawyer Malone had no peer, and as an orator no one in the house of commons could be more persuasive.

6. *Idem.*   7. *Idem.*

Stone perceived Malone as being too talented and ambitious for the good of the country and represented him as such in conversations and in correspondence with friends after the parliamentary session began. Furthermore, in Stone's judgment even Malone's Protestantism was suspect.[8] Malone's mother had been a Catholic in her youth, and Stone argued that Malone was not sufficiently distant from popery and popish connections to be entrusted with the kind of power in the state which his talent, ability, and present circumstances seemed likely to obtain.

At some point in the late summer, it appears that the primate decided that some restraints ought to be imposed on the ambitions of Malone and on the power of the Boyle party. Perhaps Boyle's time to retire had come. Stone began talking with a select group of friends about such a prospect and with a wider group of other gentlemen about the virtue of committing themselves to support the new chief governors in the forthcoming session. In the course of these conversations, his speculations about Boyle were misinterpreted by some as a design to force the speaker into retirement, and his remarks to these other gentlemen were taken as a formal solicitation to become part of his personal parliamentary connection. In both sets of conversations, he appears to have said more than he intended.

Stone's personal following in the house of commons grew, but so did his reputation. In the long run, Stone's manner of suggesting more than he meant was damaging. Later, when what Stone had regarded as simple expressions of kindness were construed into promises and commitments that could not be honored, he paid dearly for uttering them. His enemies accused him of being devoid of all honor, and in the heat of political controversy many gentlemen proclaimed the primate a faithless man and personally attested that on some past occasions he had broken his word to them.[9]

Dorset's conversations with the king's English ministers before departing for Ireland were remarkably routine. The ministers were

8. C. Litton Falkiner, "Correspondence of Stone and Newcastle," *English Historical Review,* July 1905, 512. Hereafter cited as Falkiner Stone Correspondence.

9. *Eighth Report of the Royal Commission on Historical Manuscripts, Report and Appendix, Part I,* printed by Eyre and Spottiwoode for His Majesty's Stationery Office, London, 1881, 177. Hereafter cited as HMC Emly.

much concerned over the progress of Harrington's military reconstruction program and were a bit apprehensive that another apparent revenue surplus in the Irish treasury might be appropriated by
the Irish parliament to the national debt or to some other public
purpose without the prior consent of the crown. Unwilling to have
Dorset trapped, as had been Harrington, on the issue of protecting
the king's prerogative to dispose of his own money, they insisted
that the duke develop some strategy whereby the king's consent to
the application of any revenue surplus to useful public purposes
could be given before the Irish parliament actually appropriated
any such money. Thus instructed in what became known as the
constitutional doctrine of previous consent, Dorset was wished well
by Pelham and Newcastle and sent on his way, reaching Dublin on
September 19, 1751. Immediately, Stone began to educate Dorset
and Sackville about the present state of Irish parliamentary politics.

Dorset and Sackville learned from Stone how matters stood between himself and the Boyle party. The first effect of these conversations was a quiet exclusion of Boyle from important strategy
meetings at the Castle. This is not to say that the speaker was in any
way banished from the viceregal closet or that his advice on public
affairs was not sought. Boyle was consulted, but only for form's
sake and only after the major decisions had been made.[10]

The most important of these decisions was the manner of signifying the king's previous consent to the application of a revenue
surplus of £120,000 in the treasury to the national debt. After
discussing the matter with his principal servants, Dorset decided to
include a paragraph in his speech from the throne asserting that the
king would consent and graciously recommend that an appropriate
part of the surplus be applied to the national debt. By communicating his majesty's previous consent in the speech, Dorset and his
advisors believed that the house of commons would be obliged to
acknowledge the king's good will and generosity in their addresses.
Such an acknowledgement, in an address voted by the house of
commons, they assumed would stand as a formal and precedent-
setting recognition of the king's right to dispose of his own money.
In turn, this formal recognition would be reinforced by building

10. *Idem.*

on Harrington's precedent and adding language to the preamble of the money bill asserting that the king had graciously consented to an application of part of the surplus to the national debt.

Once decided, the duke sent off copies of his speech and an explanation of the intended strategy to Pelham. There was not time enough for Pelham to communicate his approval before the Irish parliament opened, but he was entirely pleased with what was intended. He congratulated Sackville and the lord lieutenant for their plan and even suggested that the language in the speech was so well turned that there was "not the least occasion for Lord George to signify the King's consent in the House of Commons." Pelham did not think that Harrington's precedent had been a good one and believed the "right of the Crown and his Majesty's prerogative better preserved without it."[11] The language in the speech and an acknowledgement in the address ought to be enough.

Prepared and confident, Dorset met his parliament on October 8, 1751, and delivered the speech from the throne as planned. Members were attentive, and from all appearances the speech was well received. However, the personal hostilities and political tensions of the last several months were not to be allayed by displays of viceregal pomp and ceremony. Absolute parliamentary decorum was maintained, but two days later, when the commons voted their customary addresses to the king and lord lieutenant, not a single word about previous consent could be found in either of them.

Dorset's strategy had gone awry. The addresses thanked the king for his "gracious recommendation, that a grant of the money now in the treasury should be applied toward reducing the National Debt." Nonetheless, neither address admitted or acknowledged any obligation by the Irish parliament to obtain royal consent before applying the revenue surplus in the treasury to the national debt. The omission was deliberate. It was also a fair warning to Dorset, Sackville, and Stone that the power of the Boyle party in the house of commons was undiminished and that thoughts about trying to govern without them were most unwise. For the present, however, the warning was ignored. Dorset and his intimates chose neither to recognize nor respond to it. They simply let the omission of any

11. HMC Stopford-Sackville, I, 176.

mention of previous consent in the addresses pass because a much more urgent and serious matter demanded their attention.

A few days after parliament opened, a report circulated throughout Dublin that the speaker intended to retire forthwith. Rumors alleged that Dorset had offered Boyle a peerage and a pension to give up the speaker's chair and that Boyle had accepted. Everything was supposed to be settled.

There is little doubt that Stone had discussed that prospect seriously with Bessborough and Ponsonby before the lord lieutenant and chief secretary arrived in Ireland. It is no less certain that the exclusion of the speaker from strategy meetings after Dorset and Sackville had installed themselves in the Castle was intended to make Boyle think about retiring. But spreading a rumor that Boyle had deserted his friends for money and a title was no way to facilitate the event desired. As a matter of fact, when Stone and Ponsonby first heard the story, they went immediately to the speaker's house on Henrietta street and denied that they had said or done anything to give rise to it.[12] Both assured Boyle that they wished him many more years in office and begged him to call in his son or anyone else to hear and be witnesses to what they had said. Stone wrote later that he thought his visit had made some impression, but it was slight and soon wore out. The speaker, Stone concluded, "was much heated at that time and has never since been cool."[13]

Under Malone's guidance in early November, the committee of supply reported a money bill that was significantly different from what the lord lieutenant had expected. Like the addresses lately voted, the preamble of the money bill, appropriating £120,000 of the revenue surplus, made no mention of royal consent. It simply stated that money was to be appropriated pursuant to his majesty's gracious recommendation communicated in Dorset's speech opening the session.[14] The full house quickly and easily approved the bill as reported and sent it on to the Irish privy council. Dorset decided against pressing for any remedial action in the Irish privy council and probably hoped that none would be attempted by the

12. Falkiner Stone Correspondence, 54.
13. *Idem.*
14. Dorset to Holdernesse, November 14, 1751. SP63/412/204. Council to the Lord Lieutenant, November 14, 1751. SP63/412/207.

privy council in England. When Dorset sent the money bills off to Lord Holdernesse, secretary of state, in mid-November, he said nothing about the omission of previous consent from the preamble. He pointed out that the bills "in general agree with those of last session" and hoped that they would be returned before Christmas.[15] In London, the king's English law officers were not persuaded that the language in the bill appropriating the surplus was specific enough to protect the king's right to dispose of his own money from encroachment by the Irish parliament. In the English privy council, the preamble of the bill was altered to include the word consent and returned to Ireland for final enactment before the Christmas recess.

When the amended money bill arrived, a public confrontation between the government and the speaker's party seemed unavoidable. Sackville regretted that the bill had been amended. He pointed out to Wilmot that omission of the word consent from the original bill was no accident, and he saw no useful purpose in debating the authority of the crown to dispose of the surplus in the present house of commons. Sackville did not believe that inserting the word consent strengthened the rights of the crown in this matter in any way. All that the amendment provided was another opportunity for the speaker and his friends to distress the Irish government.[16]

Stone's informants advised him that some of the speaker's friends viewed the return of an altered money bill "as a lucky occasion to bring the government under difficulties."[17] These same persons— possibly Malone and Sir Richard Cox—were insisting that an altered money bill could not be carried through the present house of commons. Boyle was in a quandary. He was deeply distressed by the behavior of the chief governors toward himself and his friends, but he also had no sympathy whatsoever for the arguments or for advocates of past or present constitutional independency doctrines. The speaker could neither bring himself to mouth the principles of Charles Lucas nor forgive those that he believed were trying to force him into retirement. Immobilized by this dilemma, Boyle seemed inclined to let events take charge.

15. Dorset to Holdernesse, November 14, 1751. SP63/412/204.
16. Sackville to Wilmot, November 28, 1751. Wilmot Mss., T.3019/6780/263.
17. Falkiner Stone Correspondence, 511.

Informants and advisors thoroughly convinced the lord lieutenant that the speaker and his party intended to embarrass his government on the issue of the altered money bill. Concerned over what
could be made of that issue in the Irish house of commons, Dorset
instructed Stone to meet with those members of the house generally
disposed to support the government and assure them that Ireland's
constitution had not been violated. The primate carried out Dorset's
instructions with dispatch and success. He explained why the money
bill had been altered and why the royal prerogative on this issue
had to be protected. Enough gentlemen were either convinced by
the primate's arguments or confused by the complexities of the
issue that a scenario prepared by Malone could not be played out.[18]
According to Stone, Malone had convinced the speaker that a
general rising would occur in the house of commons against an
altered money bill. However, Boyle soon discovered that outside of
his own party very few gentlemen in the house thought the alteration in the bill serious enough to justify voting against it.[19] Sufficient votes for rejecting a money bill were simply not to be found
in the house. Consequently, Boyle did not obstruct final passage of
the altered bill. He merely stated for the journals his dissatisfaction
with what the English privy council had done.[20] Those persons who
had leagued together to drive him from the speaker's chair would
have to be dealt with in another way.
To that end, Boyle lent a more willing ear to counsels from
Carter and Cox. Both of these gentlemen had grievances against the
primate and represented him to the speaker as a kind of resurrected
Wolsey, intent upon assuming the whole power of state unto himself. Carter and Cox denounced the primate in public and private
as the author of all present difficulties but never stopped insisting
that he was vulnerable. With a little luck and a lot of determination
any public man, no matter how popular or powerful, could be
destroyed. Carter and Cox convinced the speaker that, like Charles
Lucas two years earlier, the primate could be driven from Ireland.
They proposed to destroy the man by first destroying his reputation.[21]

18. *Irish Official Papers*, I, 54.   19. *Idem.*
20. McCracken , *op. cit.*, 164.   21. HMC Emly, 177.

Stone believed that such a plan had been concerted and was actually implemented by some of the speaker's more turbulent and mischievous friends. Moreover, this contention about a scheme to defame and libel Stone received strong corroboration from other sources. According to Edmund Sexton Pery, with great industry and in secrecy Carter spread libels about the primate and represented him as "not only devoid of all principles of religion and honour but even as a monster swayed by unnatural appetites."[22] Whether out of respect for his episcopal status or from a special sense of virtue or perhaps because of an evident coldness of character, Pery stated, Stone totally abstained from women. Yet, in a country and a social milieu where the quality and beauty of its women was dearly prized and much discussed, the primate's abstinence was a subject of general conversation. Carter and others "laid hold of this opportunity to blacken Stone's character with a vice the more easily credited the more abominable, and to which some of his connections, for which people could not account, did not a little contribute."[23] Simply stated, Carter libeled Stone as a notorious homosexual. The most scandalous pamphlets were daily published and circulated without the slightest fear of parliamentary scrutiny or punishment. By such means, Pery insisted, was the country inflamed and the primate "rendered the most odious man in the kingdom."[24]

Dorset and Sackville decided that the campaign could be most quickly put down by those who had taken it up. Though the evidence is far from being absolute, it appears that sometime between mid-December 1751 and early March 1752, Sackville may have called upon Henry Boyle and made the speaker a proposition about a peerage and a pension in exchange for retirement, which the old man scornfully rejected. Firm corroboration of this offer is not available. However, when writing to Dorset's successor six years later, Boyle referred to rumors in Dorset's time that he intended to give up the chair for a peerage and a pension of £3,000 a year and stated directly that buying him off was "the projected scheme of the ministers."[25]

22. *Idem.*   23. *Idem.*
24. *Idem.*
25. Boyle to Devonshire, February 12, 1757. Shannon Mss., D.2707/A/1/5.

In any case, not long after parliament reconvened in January, it was common knowledge that Boyle and Lord Sackville had become implacable enemies. As early as March 3, 1752, Stone felt obliged to assure Newcastle that reports about personal differences between Sackville and Boyle were false,[26] and he continued to justify his friend's conduct thereafter. Nonetheless, the great confrontation between the Boyle party and the government, so long in developing, was underway. When parliament rose after the Christmas recess, Boyle had finally found an issue on which to embarrass the government.

An inquiry into the monies expended for the building and reconstruction of military barracks under the direction of Arthur Jones Nevill, surveyor general, disclosed instances of gross mismanagement, inefficiency, and allegations of corruption. At last, the speaker had an issue that was simple, safe, popular, unrelated to independency doctrines or prerogative questions, and certain to attract allies. Moreover, in Nevill, the Boyle party had a perfect target. Nevill's abundant self-esteem and insufferable haughtiness had made enemies of several of the country's leading public men and of at least one very important nobleman. At the same time, his general ignorance of the construction business had made him the dupe of virtually every contractor engaged. Defense of Nevill would be difficult and unpopular.

The inquiry into barracks repair and reconstruction projects began quietly and proceeded slowly. A committee was appointed to examine job estimates and records of payments for work completed, and to hear complaints about the quality of materials and workmanship. The early meetings of the committee were carried on with great decency and temper—so decent, observed Stone, that "nobody seemed to think it worth their while to attend."[27] However, after the altered money bill had been approved, the character of the committee's proceedings changed. Decency and temper were replaced by ferocity.

According to Stone, Nevill was a gentleman of fair character— generally reputed as an honest man and possessor of a good estate.

26. Falkiner Stone Correspondence, 512.
27. *Irish Official Papers*, I, 55.

Part of his property happened to be in that part of a county where the Earl of Kildare was lord of the soil and simply did not tolerate interference or opposition. James Fitzgerald, twentieth Earl of Kildare, was Ireland's premier nobleman and an important influence in the Irish house of commons. Approximately nine members of the house took direction from the earl and followed his lead on most public issues. Kildare was also well connected in England. He was a brother-in-law of Henry Fox and was a frequent and welcome guest at Holland House. The earl understood very clearly his special position in society and in the politics of his county. He expected deference from social inferiors and was unforgiving when he did not get it. Stone contended that Nevill had said or done something at an assize or quarter session that offended Kildare and thereafter he became the object of his lordship's resentment.[28] It must be admitted that Nevill was probably an easy person to dislike and that Kildare's dislike of him was shared by many others. Nevertheless, Kildare's attitude toward Nevill had a special quality about it. Though his lordship never admitted that there was any personal reason for his animosity toward the surveyor general, he implied on a later occasion, when Stone had become his most hated enemy, that Nevill's politics was the source of the problem between them.[29]

Kildare alleged that in 1751 Nevill was a political creature of the primate and owed his parliamentary seat to his influence. Pery, an ally of Stone through all of these proceedings, agreed with Kildare about Nevill being in Stone's party and described him as being related to one of the primate's first favorites.[30] However, Stone emphatically denied any political or personal relationship with the surveyor general. In the primate's view then, Kildare's dislike of Nevill was personal and entirely of his own making. What was most important about Kildare's relationship with Nevill was not its cause but its consequence. Kildare's deep resentment of Nevill's management of the barracks repair and construction program became a furious and reckless persecution. Whatever the cause, after the character of the inquiry changed, Kildare's nine friends in the house of commons joined with the speaker's party and divided with them for the remainder of the session.

28. *Idem.*   29. *Ibid.*, 38.
30. HMC Emly, 177.

Once begun, the attack upon Nevill was pursued with great heat. Every defect, every bad roof or floor in any barracks anywhere in Ireland was blamed on Nevill.[31] Though Dorset himself admitted that Nevill had been negligent and inefficient in many particulars, the attacks upon him surpassed what evidence and justice allowed. According to Stone, the "sober parts of the House saw the tendency"[32] and soon became offended by the temper and methods of the inquiry. Some expressed their disgust to Stone that one of the king's servants should be singled out and hunted down as "a prey to private resentment."[33]

Crown servants in general were particularly distressed by the proceedings against Nevill. In several of his "private to yourself and to be burnt" letters to Wilmot, Thomas Waite was appalled by what was being done to Nevill. He insisted that every member of the house was convinced of Nevill's honesty and integrity. Alas, however, the utmost power of the speaker's party had been exerted against him.[34] The campaign against Nevill was nothing more or less than the "mere effect of violent power and of a party that meant to wound my Lord Primate."[35] Waite feared that if the present power of the party was not some how diminished he knew not what crown officer might be attacked next. This very nervous undersecretary was so concerned over "the injustice done [to] this poor Devil that I have not slept these three nights."[36]

It is not known whether or not Stone, Sackville, or Dorset lost any sleep over the Nevill business. As a matter of fact, it took the lord lieutenant and his principal advisers some time to perceive what was happening. However, when they realized that the real target was themselves, Dorset spoke out and let the world know that he would use all of his authority to resist violent measures from being voted against Nevill. In the end, Boyle and Malone pressed only for resolutions detailing Nevill's oversights and misdeeds, frauds committed by his agents, and favors shown to contractors, and for a requirement that he make good all known deficiencies at

31. *Irish Official Papers*, I, 55.
32. *Ibid.*, 74.   33. *Ibid.*, 55.
34. Waite to Wilmot, March 7, 1752. Wilmot Mss., T.3019/6781/274.
35. Waite to Wilmot, no date. Wilmot Mss., T.3019/6781/276.
36. Waite to Wilmot, March 10, 1752. Wilmot Mss., T.3019/6781/275.

his own expense.[37] While Dorset's intervention had some effect upon the campaign being waged in the house of commons, it had no influence whatsoever on the one being waged out of doors.

Outside of the house no restraints of any kind were applied. Even Boyle admitted that in forty years of public life he could not recall when party strife had been more intense.[38] The campaign of vilification against Stone continued and one against Lord George Sackville began. Boyle and his friends met nightly in taverns and toasted the damnation of the primate and the chief secretary. It was at these meetings that the special artistry of Thomas Carter attracted public attention. Pery attributed to Carter the ingenious invention of conveying libels in toasts. Once drink had united the company, Pery recalled, sharpened wit and malice were formed into toasts that were afterwards published in newspapers and circulated throughout the country.[39]

Recalling the state of affairs in March 1752 two years later, Stone denied that he personally had done or said anything to merit the defamation heaped on himself and positively exonerated Lord George of provocative language or action. In Stone's view, the hostility of the Boyle party toward Sackville was inexplicable. Dorset had denied Boyle nothing. Stone could not recall a single instance of rude or ungenerous behavior by Lord George cited by anyone in Ireland as offensive. He assured his correspondents in England repeatedly that whatever problems presently existed between the government and the speaker's party had resulted entirely from the machinations of Boyle, Malone, Cox, and Carter.

Almost from the day when the inquiry into Nevill's affairs had begun, Stone represented the issue presently at trial in Ireland as being constitutional rather than personal. It was not whether he or Sackville had said or done anything to antagonize the speaker. It was whether or not the lord lieutenant of Ireland "should have the *principal* or indeed any share in the direction of public affairs."[40] However, Stone's energy and articulation notwithstanding, few public men in Ireland or England in March 1752 saw the issue as

37. Resolutions of the Committee appointed to Inquire into the Barracks Accounts, March 6, 1752. SP63/412/263–273.
38. McCracken, *op. cit.*, 165.   39. HMC Emly, 177.
40. *Irish Official Papers*, I, 78.

the primate had defined it. Neither Dorset nor Sackville appear to have adopted Stone's interpretation of the Nevill inquiry and resolutions until the closing days of the session.

At first, Dorset and Sackville tried to minimize the significance of the inquiry. The lord lieutenant pointed out to Holdernesse that while the resolutions approved by the house of commons "generally censured" Nevill for his mismanagement of the barracks rebuilding program, neither the inquiry nor the resolutions should be perceived as a defeat for his government.[41] The inquiry, after all, had been concerned with transactions occurring during Lord Harrington's time and did not reflect upon the present chief governors in any way. As Dorset read the record in mid-March, nothing really serious had occurred, the government was still in control of public affairs, and matters were by no means as desperate as designing men would try to represent.

Sackville echoed his father's tempered optimism. Though the chief secretary admitted that the resolutions against Nevill were more severe than strict justice should have allowed, and that Nevill would have to be replaced, he insisted that, given the political circumstances of the moment, the entire affair had been well handled. Since the worst was over, and no votes had been in fact carried against the Irish government, Sackville hoped that the English ministers would recognize what had been accomplished in Ireland. Inheriting a very bad situation, the present chief governor had prevented it from becoming desperate. "I have had a good deal of trouble upon this occasion," concluded the chief secretary to Pelham, "but I shall be fully satisfied if I have the honour of your approbation."[42]

If the worst actually had been over, most likely Sackville would have obtained the kind of approbation from Pelham that he sought. However, the worst was not over; and when that fact became apparent, Pelham and Newcastle quickly lost confidence in their Irish ministers. The process took about two months. By the time Dorset's parliamentary session ended in early May, so much had happened in Ireland that both Pelham and Newcastle became convinced that the duke ought to be replaced.[43]

Between mid-March and early May 1752, Dorset, Sackville, and

41. Dorset to Holdernesse, March 10, 1752. SP63/412/266.
42. *Irish Official Papers*, I, 76.   43. Coxe Pelham, II, 425.

Stone lost control of the Irish house of commons. The barracks inquiry had given Boyle and his friends a majority in that body and they proceeded to make the most of their advantage. Boyle certainly acted as if the house of commons was his to command. He let pass no opportunity to harass the government and prolonged the duration of the session for over a month.

Outraged by what was happening, Sackville spoke out powerfully against the preposterous rumors circulating that all current funds in the Irish treasury were to be transported to Hanover and against the behavior of the Boyle party in the house of commons. He accused them of malicious mischief and branded them guilty of actions calculated "to disunite his Majesty and his subjects in Ireland."[44] Lord George did more than condemn irresponsible political rhetoric; he leveled the supreme insult at his political enemies by styling them as Irish patriots.

The mantles of Molyneux, King, Swift, and Lucas did not fit well upon the shoulders of Boyle, Malone, Carter, and Cox; and lengthy consultations among the speaker's friends followed Lord George's speech. Out of such meetings came two decisions. They would use their present majority in the Irish house of commons to repudiate formally all patriot doctrines and at the same time urge the king to replace Dorset and Sackville and ban Stone from further participation in the government of Ireland.

It happened then that shortly before the session ended Sir Arthur Gore moved and the house approved an address to the king wherein the house of commons proclaimed its steadfast loyalty to his majesty and their total abhorrence of independency doctrines. The chief secretary was at once greatly pleased and totally misled by Gore's address. He insisted that, no matter how persistently independency doctrines might be proclaimed in private, it was a fact that no one was "bold enough in public to avow himself the protector of them."[45] Despite all that had occurred in Ireland, Sackville reported to Pelham that all was well. He insisted that Gore's address was proof positive that the Irish government had routed its political enemies.

Whether Sackville was unable to recognize reality or had simply

44. *Irish Official Papers* I, 76, 78.   45. *Idem.*

decided to deny it in order to save the political reputations of himself and his father is difficult to ascertain. Gore's address was no Castle triumph; it was a carefully planned prelude to ultimate defiance. When the house voted its customary address of thanks to the king for wise and prudent government on May 1, the usual complimentary references to the lord lieutenant were omitted and replaced by a thinly veiled attack upon the primate. No other lord lieutenant in historic memory had been treated thus by an Irish house of commons, and even Sackville had great difficulty finding advantage for his father's government in what had happened. He simply collected the addresses from the house of commons and the house of lords and sent them off to London.

Clearly, Dorset's Irish government was in serious trouble. Even Ponsonby was fully aware of what had happened. He described the late session to his brother as "indeed a very unaccountable one." Almost from the first moment, Ponsonby wrote to Duncannon, "nothing was right, and every day produced some new pretended cause of quarrel, and every opportunity of lessening the figure of the administration here was taken."[46] The speaker had sent an unmistakable message to the king that the present chief governors of Ireland no longer enjoyed the confidence of the Irish house of commons and that one of the lord lieutenant's principal ministers ought to be removed.

Sackville and Stone quickly recovered from their surprise at the audacity of the house of commons' address, assessed what had happened, and in less than three weeks time, they devised and implemented a plan which they hoped would counter the effects of Boyle's defiance. Parliament ended on May 7, and Dorset and Sackville did not depart until May 24. The ministers worked very hard to ensure that the duke's progress from the Castle to the docks would turn out to be a demonstration of popularity and loyalty. By their own account they succeeded greatly.

According to Stone, "the whole city, both the better sort and the populace seemed to make a point of showing their regard . . . and expressing their satisfaction in his administration, and their wishes for the continuance of it, with a sort of public acclamation that I

46. Ponsonby to Duncannon, May 27, 1752. Chatsworth Mss., 7.3518/404/381/o.

never heard before."[47] In the primate's view, Dorset may have lost the house of commons but he had clearly won the hearts of the people.[48] Moreover, the people of Ireland, Stone insisted, would always be ready to support a government that would support itself. Thus fortified by such convictions and prepared to argue them in England, Dorset and Sackville boarded the yacht and set sail for Parkgate on May 24, 1752. As usual, the primate, the speaker, and the lord chancellor were sworn as lords justices. Thoughtful men in Dublin drawing rooms and in great houses throughout the country must have wondered what would happen next and probably made wagers on whether or not Dorset and Sackville would ever return to Ireland.

Preparing for Confrontation

After Dorset and Sackville had departed, the primate was determined that their interests would be protected. During May and June those interests seemed in greatest danger in England. Stone wrote to his brother, to Pelham, and to Newcastle during this period, urging them to support the duke and Lord George Sackville and to stand firm against those in Ireland who had striven so desperately to embarrass them. Stone insisted that the issues at stake in Ireland were far more important than the political reputations of the lord lieutenant and chief secretary. The heart of the matter was whether or not Englishmen would have any future roles in the government of Ireland.[49] Clearly there was a strong disposition on the part of many in Ireland to turn them out.

Stone did not think that Boyle and his friends were mad enough to entertain serious thoughts about separating Ireland from England. In that sense, when Malone, Carter, or Cox professed an abhorrence of setting up an independent interest, they should be believed. However, if they deny setting up in parliament and in the country an Irish interest, "in contra distinction to the English," the primate insisted, "they are lying." The constant language of the speaker's party had been "to proclaim the necessity of keeping up

47. Falkiner Stone Correspondence, 514.
48. HMC Stopford-Sackville, I, 185.
49. Irish Official Papers, I, 79.

such an interest in opposition to English governors who are always enemies."[50] The king's government and the king's English-born Irish ministers were daily damned out of the mouths of the king's Irish-born Irish ministers. If some sort of countermeasures were not undertaken, Stone warned, "the mischiefs to the interests of this country . . . and to the very being of an English government over it and the security and comfort of any Englishman in it, will be irreparable."[51]

To Newcastle on May 26, the primate stated that the government had the support of the best and more creditable men in the country. Moreover, the house of commons was not lost; it stood "at an equal balance."[52] It was a fact, however, that the votes of many persons holding public employments and pensions must be reckoned as being against the present Irish administration and that the political influence derived from such employment had been notoriously and consistently exerted against the government. This extraordinary state of affairs, Stone insisted, would change quickly "if his Majesty's pleasure could be fully known and manifested in some proper instances."[53] Later to Pelham, Stone argued, no action would more effectually secure the authority of the government of Ireland than a "full and entire removal of the worst servants a Government ever employed." Public men in Ireland were stating, in both private and public, that "forebearance of resentment is the effect of fear and not of moderation."[54]

What the primate wrote in letters, Sackville repeated in person to Pelham in a somewhat more subdued and temperate form. Lord George met with the minister in June and went through the events of the last session in great detail. Pelham was not yet ready to approve dismissals. The minister also questioned Sackville about the reports of his quarreling with the speaker and about measures that had been employed to try to get Boyle out of the speaker's chair. Sackville assured Pelham that such reports were totally without foundation, whereupon the minister lifted up "his hands and eyes with astonishment and then said that was most extraordinary."[55] It

50. HMC Stopford-Sackville, I, 185.   51. *Irish Official Papers*, I, 79.
52. Falkiner Stone Correspondence, 515.
53. *Idem.*   54. HMC Stopford-Sackville, I, 186.
55. Sackville to Stone, June 10, 1752. Wilmot Mss., T.3019/6781/281.

was clear enough that Pelham wished moderation would prevail, but if rougher measures were required, Sackville believed that Pelham would do whatever the situation required.

However, in June and July, another version of the recent events occurring in Ireland was being pressed upon the English ministry. The speaker wrote to Pelham in mid-June, urging him to discount reports circulated by "persons of the greatest distinction" that the gentlemen of Ireland entertained notions of "setting up for an independency."[56] Moreover, Boyle insisted, during the past ten sessions, wherein he had the honor of conducting the king's business in the Irish house of commons, there had not been a single occurrence upon which to found such a suspicion. The speaker assured Pelham that there was no basis whatsoever for suspecting his own conduct or that of his friends in the Irish house of commons. There was no group of gentlemen anywhere in the world, Boyle continued, more devoted to his majesty's interest and more zealous in supporting it than the gentlemen in the Irish house of commons who honored him with their friendship.[57]

It is clear that in June and July, 1752, Pelham and Newcastle were much concerned about Irish affairs, and that they were inclined to accept the Boyle version of what had happened. Newcastle believed that present governors of Ireland had misunderstood their political situation in that country and that the blame for the present difficulty must be laid upon the young ministers in Ireland. Dorset could not return to Ireland if matters remained as they were, and the present state of English politics made finding a successor impractical. Moreover, the king's growing interest in Irish affairs was still another reason for bringing the contending parties to an agreement as soon as possible. Dorset had to set himself aright in Ireland;[58] "the primate and Lord George must make up in reality with the Speaker, & c." The duke urged Pelham to persuade Andrew Stone to "see it in this light, and he will bring it about."[59]

However, in Ireland neither the primate nor Lord George showed little disposition to make up with the speaker. Almost from the moment when Dorset and Sackville left for Parkgate in late

56. Irish Official Papers, I, 81.   57. *Idem.*
58. Coxe Pelham, 426.   59. *Idem.*

May, the primate devoted much of his time and energy to conversations and dinners with members of the house of commons. On such
occasions Stone had no scruples about declaring his opinion that
the king had a right to dispose of his own revenues, that English
statutes were binding in Ireland, and that the lord lieutenant had
received no directions from the king to transport the contents of
the Irish treasury to Hanover.[60] Stone talked freely to whoever
would listen, and in mid-summer he was approached by a man
seeking political counsel of a more immediate and practical sort. A
vacancy had occurred in the parliamentary representation of the
borough of Athy. Though the Earl of Kildare was the traditional
patron of that borough, one of the burgesses came to Stone's house
in Dublin and sought advice about prospective candidates. Predictably, when Kildare learned of the visit, he became infuriated and
accused the primate of trying to overturn a long-standing interest.
Ironically, Stone made a powerful and unforgiving enemy by desperately trying to avoid doing so. Stone turned the man away and
refused to offer any advice about the parliamentary affairs of Athy.
Yet no matter how strenuously the primate denied involvement in
the affairs of Athy, the Earl of Kildare believed otherwise.

Moreover, by the end of the summer of 1752, the earl was ready
to believe any story, no matter how outrageous, about the primate.
In such a mood, Kildare was stunned when Charles Tisdale, a
relative of the present solicitor general, approached him in October
with a proposition about a political accommodation with the primate.[61] Kildare rejected Tisdale's proposition in the most public
way, and Stone denied that the young man had any authority to
make one.[62] It seems that Tisdale, as a relation of Kildare, had taken
the liberty of communicating his personal disapproval of the earl's
political conduct and advised him that if he would change his ways
and serve the government, favors appropriate to his rank and property would be forthcoming.[63] Tisdale denied that he had been com-
missioned by any person whatsoever in this matter and gave Stone
a letter wherein was stated explicitly that he had no authority, direct

60. Irish Official Papers, I, 93.
61. HMC Stopford-Sackville, I, 187.
62. HMC *Idem.*
63. Sackville to Wilmot, October 20, 1752. Wilmot Mss., T.3019/6781/295.

or indirect, to use the primate's name in making an approach to Kildare.[64] This affair confirmed whatever doubts Kildare may have entertained about the primate being a complete scoundrel. Hereafter, ordinary civilities and direct communication of any sort between these two powerful men ceased. For the next six years, Kildare's principal political objective was to drive George Stone out of the government of Ireland and to keep him out.

While relations between the primate and Kildare deteriorated, the necessities of office required that communications between Stone and Boyle remain open. In order to function as lords justices, Stone and Boyle did not have to be friendly or share confidences, but they had to meet and they had to be civil to one another. Yet in time, this civility became a polite mask for near-paranoiac mistrust. By January and February 1753, this mask of civility was dropped and the hopelessness of compromise or reconciliation became apparent. Newcastle and Pelham had to face the unpleasant fact that the principal servants of the crown in Ireland were determined to oppose the government and the policies of the king's lord lieutenant.

Boyle advised Pelham in late January 1753 that the union and harmony that had so characterized the conduct of the king's business in Ireland for so many years was now in danger of being interrupted. It was perfectly well understood in Ireland, Boyle asserted, that no man in friendship with him could hope for any favor no matter how inconsequential except by applying for it through the primate.[65] This unthinking rejection of capable and well-disposed men was the source of all present discontents, and no one could be certain what consequences would follow from the continuation of such a policy. Boyle insisted that he raised this matter at this particular time only with the greatest reluctance. However, the dangers were real and the English ministers must find some way of dealing with them.

The speaker's letter to Pelham did not remain confidential very long. It was passed immediately by Pelham to Sackville and Dorset, and then back to Dublin to Stone and Newport. As a matter of fact, the speaker's letter traversed the distance from Boyle's house at 10

64. *Irish Official Papers*, I, 92.   65. *Irish Official Papers*, I, 82.

Henrietta Street in Dublin to Pelham in Westminster and then back to the primate's house at 9 Henrietta Street in less than three weeks. According to Stone, the letter was a threat and revealed the real intentions of the speaker's party. They intended to force themselves upon the government.

In the weeks ahead both Stone and Boyle labored long and late to enlarge their respective parliamentary numbers. However, by mid-March, circumstances had changed. The uncommitted no longer responded to promises of jobs or commissions. Although no opportunity for recruiting should be overlooked, Stone advised Sackville, it was "hardly necessary any longer to angle for single votes." The small arms of viceregal patronage were as nothing when compared to the heavy guns of the Irish treasury that Boyle and friends were deploying throughout the county. The fire of those heavy guns was being directed by Nathaniel Clements, teller of the exchequer.

Connected to the Gores by marriage and a longtime friend of Henry Boyle, Clements as teller of the exchequer decided where treasury balances would be deposited. The country gentlemen, insisted Stone, were "subject to the bankers, and they are in the power of the Treasury."[66] For the moment, the power of the Irish treasury was in the hands of Clements and was being arrayed against the Irish government. This extraordinary circumstance, the primate contended, could be altered in a moment if only the English ministry would make clear its determination to support the duke of Dorset's government in Ireland.

In letters to England throughout the spring of 1753, Stone made the same point over and over again. Show the leaders of the present opposition that there is power to hurt them, Stone argued, and all will be quiet. Moreover, Boyle and his friends were ripe for such an experiment. The friends of the government made no secret of their attachments and were bold in declaring them.

Stone's confidence in the growing strength of what was now being called the lord lieutenant's party increased every week. A vacancy occurred in the parliamentary representation of county Armagh when old Robert Cope died in late March. Stone decided to employ

66. HMC Stopford-Sackville, I, 193.

his interest on behalf of young William Brownlow, scion of a distinguished Armagh family and son of a former member for the county. Stone chose Brownlow over Francis Caulfield, younger brother of Viscount Charlemont an absentee friend of Boyle. As a matter of fact, in mid-April Stone did not think that the Armagh election would even develop into a serious contest.

Stone's letters to Sackville during this period contained a great deal of political advice and an extraordinary amount of self-deception. That the next session would be a quiet one, he added, was the language in everyone's mouth. Some of the most judicious and careful gentlemen in the house, Stone concluded, had expressed amazement over how easily such a strong party had been broken in so short a time and own that it could not have been accomplished under any other government than that of the Duke of Dorset.[67] His grace's presence and authority was all that was "now requisite to make a Coup de Partie."[68]

Having assured his English correspondents that matters in Ireland were well in hand, Stone went off in late April to Leixlip, county Kildare, where his sister had a country house. Though the primate visited Dublin whenever official business required his presence, he remained at Leixlip for most of the spring and summer. However, Leixlip proved to be no refuge from the political strife of the last few months. About a month after Stone arrived there, his most implacable enemy, Lord Kildare—only a few miles away at Carton—went off to England to present a long memorial to the king on the discontent and political divisions presently existing in the Irish house of commons and among Irish Protestants. Somehow Stone learned of Kildare's intention and took immediate steps to counter it. In mid-May the primate wrote a long letter to Pelham advising the minister that a "sort of complaint of me" would be soon directed to him. Stone announced himself ready to justify his own conduct and proceeded to do so. Opposition in Ireland, he insisted, arose entirely from the servants of the crown—"it cannot but be some clog up[on] any government to have the Chancellor of the Exchequer, the Treasury, and the Master of the Rolls acting openly against it."[69]

67. *Ibid.*, 195.   68. *Ibid.*, 196.
69. *Irish Official Papers*, I, 93.

At this time, Stone came very close to admitting that his own conduct, well-intentioned as it had been, might have contributed something to the present discontents. If it happened, he concluded, "that I am become the point of objection, and if by giving up all share in civil business things can go on quietly, I shall be ready to withdraw myself from it with much more cheerfulness then I entered into it."[70] Most likely, Stone truly believed what he wrote to Pelham and would have withdrawn from the Irish government if asked to do so. Nonetheless, the primate does not appear to have expected for a single moment that such a prospect was possible. He could not imagine that anything written or said by Kildare, Boyle, or any other Irish politician in London would seriously damage the credibility of the present chief governors of Ireland.

Clearly, Lord Kildare was of another mind. The purpose of the memorial presented to the king on May 26, 1753, was to urge his majesty to replace the Duke of Dorset with someone else before the opening of the next session of the Irish parliament. The earl believed that his majesty was misinformed about the present state of Irish politics. The earl assumed that if the king only knew the truth, he would act upon it. Kildare appears to have had an unfounded faith in the efficacy of written words from Ireland's premier nobleman to change policy, and he proceeded to give the king a version of truth to consider. It was a version of the truth very different indeed from what his majesty had been hearing from his Irish and English ministers.

In his memorial Kildare made much of the Nevill affair, the alleged assumption of the entire power of the state by the primate, and Lord George Sackville's arrogance and mistreatment of Boyle. The earl insisted that each day divisions among Irish politicians grew wider and that he would be wanting in duty and attachment to his majesty's royal person if he did not lay these unhappy transactions before the best of kings. He regretted the necessity for this memorial, but at the present time Ireland's loyal Protestant subjects were so unfortunately circumstanced that they had no means of communicating with the king except through the lord "who has the opportunity of representing your Majesty's faithful people in what light he thinks most proper for his purposes."[71]

70. *Idem.*   71. *Ibid.,* 40.

Kildare's memorial was intended to shock the king and his English ministers, and shock them it did, but not into the kind of actions that the earl expected. It is doubtful whether even Sackville appreciated how determined the opposition of the speaker and men such as Kildare had become since the lord lieutenant had left Ireland. Stone's letters to Sackville during the interval between sessions had been full of assurances that Boyle's party had been broken and that the next session would be far more tranquil than the last. Consequently, the English ministers were psychologically unprepared and possibly even temporarily unnerved by Kildare's audacious appeal to the king to replace the Duke of Dorset. After several discussions among themselves and with Dorset, the English ministers recommended preparation of a rejoinder which would declare in very clear language the king's great confidence and firm support of the Duke of Dorset.

The task of drafting such a rejoinder was given to Lord Holdernesse. The secretary of state did not proceed hastily. He cast it in the form of a letter from himself to the Irish lord chancellor, who was instructed to communicate its contents to Kildare and to such other persons thought appropriate to receive it. Although the whole process from receipt of the memorial to dispatch of the rejoinder to Ireland took about a month, both Kildare's memorial and Holdernesse's rejoinder were immediately printed in pamphlet form and widely circulated throughout Ireland.

In the rejoinder, Holdernesse described the Kildare memorial as "an account of supposed discontents and divisions among his Majesty's faithful subjects in Ireland" and as "an uncommon and extraordinary application."[72] He expressed the king's great surprise at receiving such a document because he knew well the ability and fidelity of the Duke of Dorset and for that reason had twice appointed him chief governor of Ireland. In this station, the duke deserved his majesty's support and would continue to receive it. With respect to Kildare himself, Holdernesse repeated the king's resentment that any particular person, however respectable, would presume "to speak in the name of a great body of his people, much less one of his Houses of Parliament there, and to put an

72. *Ibid.*, 40–41.

interpretation upon their proceedings and resolutions, which they have not thought fit to express."[73] He concluded his letter by observing how unpersuasive were representations of the kind made by Kildare when contrasted with "daily proofs of fidelity and zeal in his service." The premier nobleman of Ireland had been put in his place and very soon everyone knew it.

The severity of Holdernesse's rejoinder notwithstanding, Kildare's memorial had a profound if not openly admitted impact on the king's English ministers. As Lord Hardwicke explained to his old friend Lord Newport, Kildare was "a peer of great quality, estate, and consequence in Ireland" and was much respected in England. No matter how easily refuted were many of the points contained in Kildare's memorial, the fact that such a memorial had been written and presented was highly damaging to the Duke of Dorset and to the present government of Ireland. Hardwicke believed that it would be "impossible for his Grace, or any other Lord Lieutenant to administer the government there, with any service to the Crown or reputation to himself, if such improper representations continued."[74] By no means had Lord Holdernesse's rejoinder closed the matter in English ministerial circles.

Reactions to the Holdernesse rejoinder in Dublin were swift in coming and generally satisfying to the English ministry. Lord Newport received the rejoinder in early July and immediately presented copies of it to Kildare, Boyle, Stone, and others. In Newport's judgment the rejoinder was appropriate and timely. By rejecting the allegations in the memorial and by denying Kildare's presumption to speak for the Irish parliament the king and the English ministry had given the Irish government the kind of public support it needed.

Stone's reaction to the memorial and rejoinder was predictable. He described the memorial as indecent to the king, false in substance, mean and illiterate in composition, and reprobated by all who had seen it.[75] He prepared a point-by-point refutation of each of the allegations in the memorial for Holdernesse and made a promise to try to discover and report the speaker's attitude toward

73. *Ibid.*, 44.
74. Hardwicke to Newport, July 5, 1753. Add. Mss. 35, 592, 100.
75. *Irish Official Papers*, I, 95–96.

it as soon as possible. Stone had to rely on informants for knowledge of Boyle's thinking and was unable to report anything until late August. According to one informant who had asked the speaker about the memorial, the old man was supposed to have responded with some quickness, "What have we to do with Lord Kildare's memorial?" Stone believed that Boyle saw the memorial as "material either for opposition or accommodation, and is considering to which of the two it will be most advisable to apply it."[76]

Stone's reference to the possibility of an accommodation between himself and the speaker, even in the context of a letter reporting on Boyle's attitude about the memorial, has to be taken seriously. There is a strong suggestion that despite all of the bravado of earlier months, Stone himself had started thinking about the idea of an accommodation. There was a good and substantial reason why Stone and possibly even Boyle would consider the possibility of accommodation and be initially receptive to efforts by a third party to work one out. The reason was the state of the country during the summer of 1753.

There was a new and dangerous spirit abroad in Ireland. Pamphlets damning the government and describing the present Irish constitution as a grievance were printed in large numbers and circulated throughout the country. The English ministry and the entire English nation were represented as being the most determined enemies of all Irishmen. Present and past lords lieutenants were treated with contempt; and if Stone can be believed, even the king's good intentions toward Ireland were questioned.[77] As had happened so often in the past in Ireland, once again in the spring and summer of 1753 violent words were accompanied by violent acts.

In Ireland as elsewhere, violent words did not of themselves beget violent acts. Other circumstances were necessary. Violent words were only one part of the complicated social context that riot and disorder required. In the summer of 1753, the most important other circumstance contributing to the outbreak of popular violence was hunger. Harvests had been bad in the early 1750s and contin-

76. Falkiner Stone Correspondence, 516.
77. *Irish Official Papers*, I, 57.

ued to be poor for almost the entire decade culminating in near famine conditions during the summer of 1753. Bread prices had risen steadily since 1750 and reached exorbitant levels in May and June 1753. Disturbances occurred in Dublin in April 1753,[78] and a more serious one erupted near Kilcock, county Kildare, in June.[79] The country seemed on the verge of a major social crisis.

Made desperate by food shortages and soaring food prices, and perhaps encouraged by the spate of pamphlets attacking the Irish government and by the Earl of Kildare's public denunciation of the primate's alleged unlimited power, many of the small farmers and laborers of county Kildare turned to direct action. Finding a leader in one James Deering, these farmers and laborers—many of whom must have been tenants of Lord Kildare—tried to strike down what they perceived as causes of their present misery. A mob temporarily took over the town of Kilcock. They posted proclamations in that town and elsewhere inviting discontented farmers and laborers to come into Kilcock and join them. Consequently, the Kilcock mob grew to about 1,600 persons. Groups sallied out into the country-side, filling ditches recently dug to enclose lands hitherto thought to be common. Others laid waste to some of the finest parks in the county, which according to one account had "not been common in the memory of any person living."[80] Still others pulled down hedges and piers, burned gates, and marched with drums, trumpets, and colors flying. For about two weeks this mob terrorized much of north Kildare, extorting money and threatening death to anyone brave enough to resist or give information against them.

Thus matters remained until late June when the lords justices and privy council issued a proclamation "for the suppression of rioting in Kildare caused by the alleged enclosure of Commons" and Colonel Folliot marched five companies of foot and two squad-rons of horse from Dublin into Kildare to disperse the rioters. The march turned out to be a parade. Upon hearing that troops were on the way, the mob vanished, proclamations disappeared, and order was restored.[81] The timely arrival of troops in Kildare was

78. *Calendar of Ancient Records of Dublin*, ed. Lady Gilbert (Joseph Dollard, Dublin, 1903), Vol. X, 104.

79. *The Gentleman's Magazine*, 1753, 295.

80. *Idem*.   81. *Ibid.*, 343.

matched by the fortuitous arrival shortly thereafter in Dublin of two grain ships from Danzig. Dublin bread prices immediately dropped to reasonable levels and once again the streets were safe.

In the 1750s, grain was an extremely important staple in the diet of most of Ireland's people. Unless some mechanism for increasing Irish grain production could be devised or until some other crop replaced oats and wheat as the principal food of the people, scarcities would continue, dependence on food imports would increase, and popular disturbances would multiply. Echoing the sentiments of a few politicians, some Dublin journalists urged the establishment of a system of bounties to stimulate tillage and ensure adequate grain supplies for domestic consumption.[82] Both Stone and Boyle gave the idea of a tillage promotion scheme serious thought, but political cooperation between these two men in the forthcoming parliamentary session on any issue short of repressing rebellion or repelling foreign invasion was extremely unlikely. Apart from issuing a proclamation calling for the apprehension of James Deering and others for causing riots in Kildare, nothing was done to avert future problems arising from food scarcities. The minds of the lords justices were preoccupied with other concerns.

Stone complained to Newcastle about the difficulty of trying to settle political disputes that had arisen without just cause.[83] As parliament's opening approached Stone became increasingly fearful about the effect a political confrontation between the Irish government and the speaker's party would have on the state of the country. After some reflection, he decided to give accommodation a try. According to Stone, Luke Gardiner—deputy vice treasurer, wealthy contractor, and builder—approached him and, after lamenting the differences presently dividing the king's principal servants, offered several good reasons why those differences should and could be amicably composed. The primate listened to Gardiner's argument and then agreed to allow him to go to the speaker and offer in Stone's name an overture toward accommodation.[84]

According to a memorandum prepared by Gardiner, the deputy vice treasurer went directly to Boyle and spoke to him in the same

82. *Idem.*
83. Falkiner Stone Correspondence, 515.
84. Irish Official Papers, I, 57.

open and frank manner as he had done with the primate about the present state of political affairs. Boyle responded by complaining about slights and contemptuous treatment of himself and of his friends by the primate. However, Boyle was very careful to exonerate Dorset from any role in what had been done to himself and his friends. Boyle professed the highest regard and honor for the duke, "who had it not in his nature to do a wrong thing."[85] All present difficulties arose from misrepresentations by the primate.

Gardiner returned to the primate forthwith and reported the substance of his conversation with the speaker. Stone affected surprise that Boyle had attributed all present disagreements to himself. At no time, Stone insisted to Gardiner, had he the slightest inclination to lessen the power of any part of the government or enter into any man's province. Furthermore, Stone declared, if the lord lieutenant and speaker were disposed to live in harmony he "would do everything in his power to improve and cement it."[86] Stone authorized Gardiner to go back to the speaker and communicate fully and completely what he had said.

By all accounts Gardiner's second meeting with Boyle was a disaster. The deputy vice treasurer went to the speaker's house and related to him what the primate had said. According to Gardiner, the speaker replied at great length touching on many subjects but concluded with the observation that he would not suffer the primate to stand between himself and the lord lieutenant.[87] Gardiner was surprised and completely unnerved by Boyle's response. He was so distraught by the speaker's unexpected intransigence that the primate described him upon returning from Boyle as "angry and ashamed" and his report of the meeting as "very confused and indirect."[88] At this point, Stone gave up all hope of effecting an accommodation. He simply could not believe that compromise or reconciliation was possible.[89] Nevertheless, Stone instructed Gardi-

---

85. Memorandum on a series of conversations between L[uke] Gardiner and the Primate [George Stone], and L[uke] Gardiner and the Speaker [Henry Boyle], about the animosity existing between the Speaker and the Primate, and the need for reconciliation before the meeting of Parliament. Shannon Mss. 707/A/12/4. Hereafter cited as Gardiner Memorandum.

86. *Idem.*   87. *Idem.*

88. Falkiner Stone Correspondence, 517.

89. Irish Official Papers, I, 94.

ner once again to go back to the speaker and tell the man that he had never had any thoughts whatsoever about standing between him and the lord lieutenant. On the contrary, if the speaker and lord lieutenant "were inclined to be well together, he would do everything in his power to cultivate a good understanding between them."[90]

Anxious to extricate himself from a difficult and embarrassing situation, Gardiner wrote a memorandum on all that had transpired between himself and the primate and himself and the speaker and delivered it to Boyle's house. Boyle's impatience with Gardiner can be imagined; his reaction to the memorandum is recorded. Written in Boyle's own hand at the end of the memorandum is the endorsement: the "S[peaker] was greatly astonished at G[ardiner]'s giving him this narrative in which there is not contained any one particular circumstance of truth, as far as it related to the conversation between G[ardiner] and [the] S[peaker]."[91] So much for the credibility of peacemakers.

Thus matters stood at the end of August 1753. Gardiner's initiative toward accommodation had failed. Confrontation of some sort between the Boyle party and the Irish government seemed inevitable. Stone did not enjoy being "made the single mark of jealousy and obloquy" and offered to step aside or undertake any part that might be assigned to him.[92] Since neither Dorset nor the English ministers were disposed to give him up as part of a price for accommodation, the primate began preparations for the opening of the session.

Stone and Lord Newport had kept Dorset and Newcastle apprised of the progress of events in Ireland. Both were vitally concerned about what was happening there during the summer of 1753, but neither of them began to appreciate fully how alienated and determined the Boyle party had become until late August. In mid-July, when Newcastle reported to Dorset the king's negative reaction to the memorial, the minister made a special effort to assure the lord lieutenant that no one in the present English administration was more zealous in supporting Dorset's credit, reputation, and author-

90. Gardiner Memorandum, Shannon Mss., D. 2707/A/12/4.
91. *Idem.*
92. Falkiner Stone Correspondence, 517–518.

ity than himself.[93] The duke was heartened by Newcastle's expression of confidence; and during August he made several recommendations for Irish peerages and a few appointments to the Irish privy council, and distributed some patronage posts and sinecures to persons with parliamentary interests. One indicator of the viceregal mood at the end of August 1753 was the fact that Dorset gave away the office and emoluments of the second serjeant-at-arms which had been granted to Thomas Carter and son in Carteret's time to a prospective supporter.[94]

Confrontation and Defeat

Sometime in early September, on the road from Knole Park to Holyhead, Dorset and Sackville changed their minds about the wisdom of standing fast against the Boyle party. They began thinking seriously and favorably about an accommodation initiative of their own. Even if an accommodation could not be arranged, nothing would be lost by trying. Stone had assured his grace repeatedly that no matter what the Boyle party did, the king's business in the forthcoming session would be carried out. Boyle and his friends did not have the power to prevent the Irish government from doing so.

Dorset's progress from the waterside to the city was stately and traditional. Once installed in the Castle, the duke quickly discovered that the Boyle party was of no mind to cooperate with the present Irish government. Sackville reported to Holdernesse that the speaker's friends were representing Boyle as the protector of liberty in Ireland. One case seemed absolutely settled. Waite reported that Nevill was to be expelled whether or not he fulfilled the resolutions of the house of commons.[95]

With the intentions of the Boyle party becoming clearer every day, and already disposed to make one last effort toward accommodation, Dorset held several meetings with Boyle during the week preceding the opening of the session. The duke asked Boyle to explain what he believed were the causes of their present discontents and then offered an accommodation on the basis of forgetting

93. HMC Stopford-Sackville, I, 197.
94. Dorset to Holdernesse, August 30, 1753. SP63/413/29.
95. Waite to Wilmot, July 31, 1752. Wilmot Mss., T.3019/6781/311.

past conduct and of an equitable allocation of places and rewards for present and future services. For his part, Boyle made great professions of duty to the king and of personal respect for the lord lieutenant. However, Boyle insisted that his friends were so exasperated with the primate that they could not be brought to a proper temper without an assurance that Stone would never again serve as lord justice.[96] Dorset told Boyle that he would not give up the primate and the meeting ended. Accommodation was impossible; both sides prepared for a trial of strength when the session began on October 9, 1753.

In the week before parliament opened, the intended strategy of the Boyle party was widely known. Since it was customary for the speaker to appoint the persons who would move the addresses which followed the lord lieutenant's speech from the throne, Boyle and his friends had an opportunity to embarrass Dorset on the first day of the session. Reports from all parts of the city indicated that they intended to show disrespect to the lord lieutenant and the present government of Ireland by omitting from the customary addresses to the king the usual paragraph of thanks for continuing the duke as lord lieutenant of Ireland. If Boyle's friends succeeded in carrying their addresses without this compliment to the lord lieutenant, they planned to move a resolution calling for the removal of the primate from any role in the government of the country.[97]

Dorset reacted to the reports of the speaker's intentions by instructing Sackville to be certain that all friends of government were very exact in their attendance on the first day of the session and by pressing Boyle on a daily basis for information about the proposed addresses. Both Sackville and Boyle responded to the duke's requests as one would expect. Sackville was diligent about soliciting his friends, and Boyle was evasive about the addresses as long as possible. Finally, on Sunday evening, three days before parliament was scheduled to open, Boyle brought his choice for mover of the address to the king to meet with the lord lieutenant. Boyle's choice turned out to be none other than Thomas Packenham, member for

96. HMC Stopford-Sackville, I, 198.
97. Ibid., 200.

county Longford, and a close relative of Lord Kildare.[98] Though neither Boyle nor Packenham would reveal to the duke the substance of their proposed motion, it was very clear what was intended. The compliment was to be omitted. At this point, the success of Sackville's solicitations became critical.

As events were quick to show, the chief secretary had done his work very well. In the course of four or five extremely busy days, Sackville obtained assurances of support from dozens of prominent gentlemen and developed a strategy to counter Boyle's plan for the addresses. Two gentlemen—Hercules Langford Rowley, member for county Londonderry, and William Conolly, nephew and heir to the late speaker Conolly—distinguished by their fortunes and by being generally free from party engagements, agreed to introduce and second amendments to the addresses which would restore the compliment.[99] Within a few days, the extent of Sackville's success in getting support for the Rowley amendment became widely known.

Within an hour of departure time for the opening of parliament, Boyle called at the Castle on his way to the College Green. The speaker requested an audience with the lord lieutenant, wherein he told the duke that after much persuasion he had prevailed upon his friends to give his grace all possible honors in the address. The address to the king would include a proper thanks to his majesty for continuing Dorset in the government of Ireland.[100] Dorset was delighted with the prospect of a victory without fighting and treated the speaker cordially.

The house that rose for Dorset's speech was very full. Stone reported that "never was such an attendance known."[101] The duke complimented the lords and gentlemen for their demonstrated zeal on behalf of the king's service and saw in that zeal the strongest assurances that the business of the session would be carried on with candor, temper, and unanimity. He asked only for the usual supplies. Next, in words carefully chosen to protect the crown's right to dispose of revenue surpluses, Dorset reported that the king had commanded him to acquaint the members that "His Majesty

98. Falkiner Stone Correspondence, 517.
99. HMC Stopford-Sackville, I, 199.
100. *Ibid.*, 200.
101. Falkiner Stone Correspondence, 519.

would graciously consent, and recommend it to you, that so much of the money remaining in the treasury or as shall be necessary, be applied to the discharge of the national debt."[102] With the doctrine of previous consent formally asserted, the duke then promised in the name of the king to direct an inquiry into the condition of several fortifications. He concluded by urging all those present "to let the true interest of Ireland be ever your great object" and assured the members that he would do the same.[103]

On the following day, October 10, 1753, the speaker brought the addresses to the house and met with Sackville for about a half hour in a private room to discuss them before taking the chair and opening the session for that day.[104] To be sure, as promised, the compliment for continuing Dorset as lord lieutenant was included in both addresses. However, the address to the lord lieutenant did not contain a single word of thanks to the duke for having faithfully represented the loyalty of the house to the king. The chief secretary insisted that words acknowledging the duke's faithful representation of the loyalty of the Irish parliament to the king be inserted in the address to the lord lieutenant. At first Boyle resisted, but he yielded quickly after Sackville threatened that if proper words were not added he most certainly would divide the house on the address.[105] Aware of the promises and commitments Sackville had obtained, Boyle agreed to accept the words "your faithful representation of our inviolable attachment to his Sacred Person, Royal Family, and government."[106] In the address to the lord lieutenant, Sackville agreed that no further changes would be required. Thereupon, the chief secretary and the speaker took polite leave of one another and hurried off to their respective places in the Irish house of commons.

Paradoxically, both Sackville and Boyle must have gone away from their brief meeting greatly satisfied. The chief secretary saw this meeting with Boyle as a complete victory for the present administration. All efforts to embarrass the lord lieutenant in the ad-

102. Dorset to Holdernesse, October 10, 1753. SP63/413/43–46.
103. *Idem.*
104. Falkiner Stone Correspondence, 519.
105. *Idem.*
106. Dorset to Holdernesse, October 10, 1753, SP63/413/59.

dresses had been stopped. By his actions in this meeting, the speaker had virtually admitted that for the moment the government could command a majority in the house of commons. For his part, Boyle had even greater cause than Sackville to be satisfied with the outcome of their short meeting. Most likely in concert with Malone, Carter, and Cox, the speaker had set a trap into which Sackville had freely run. Boyle knew his opponents well and thoroughly distracted them from what were to be his party's principal points of attack by affecting an intention to insult and embarrass the lord lieutenant in the addresses. Certainly, Malone and Carter could count heads in the house of commons as well as Sackville and Stone. They knew that their party did not yet have an issue that would turn the votes of the unattached gentlemen in the house against the government. Consequently, the decision to spare the duke in the addresses was a strategic one. The speaker and his friends decided to shift their attack to a person more vulnerable than Dorset and to think seriously about the possibility of driving the duke out of the government of Ireland by reviving the controversy over the constitutional issue of previous consent. Nevill was both available and far more vulnerable than Dorset, Sackville, or Stone. That the Irish government would try to protect Nevill was fairly certain. The speaker was cautious enough to know that raising a constitutional conflict between the prerogative of the crown and the rights of the Irish parliament was a very risky business and should not be undertaken without a fair prospect of success. Obtaining such a prospect would require an extensive campaign in the public prints and private salons, but no such campaign would be possible during the present session if the house of commons gave any measure of formal acceptance to the doctrine of previous consent in their addresses.

The words in the lord lieutenant's speech dealing with previous consent had been carefully chosen, and the language in the addresses on this issue had to be no less so. The strategy of the Boyle party appears to have been to harass and distract the government on the compliment and on the matter of faithful viceregal representation of the sentiments of the Irish parliament to the crown, in order to keep language out of the addresses that would commit the Irish house of commons to a formal acceptance of the doctrine of previous consent. This strategy worked perfectly. Sackville was so preoccupied with those parts of the addresses purporting to reflect on Dorset that he completely ignored the absence of language in them touching on previous consent. By giving up on the compliment and on the matter of faithful viceregal representations, Boyle obtained unanimous approval by the Irish house of commons of language which took no notice whatsoever of the previous consent of the crown to the disposition of surplus revenues in the Irish treasury. Neither Dorset, Sackville, nor Stone appear to have been aware of what Boyle and his friends had done to them. They all affected genuine surprise when the issue of disposing of a revenue surplus was raised by Malone in the committee on supply a month later.[107]

After the events of October 9 and 10, 1753, Stone and Sackville were convinced that the worst was over. They both believed that public affairs had taken a much more agreeable turn and advised Newcastle and Pelham accordingly. The primate would not say that the speaker and his friends had given up for the session. However, he did say that the change in the outward appearance of things in these last few days was surprising. Stone expected some disagreement on what he called "subaltern points, such as the Armagh election," but he hoped that the eclat of this signal victory on the addresses would affect all other proceedings.[108]

The English ministers were pleased by the reports from Ireland but were cautious about forecasting the future behavior of the Boyle party from them. Clearly, Newcastle was very worried about the future. He advised Dorset to be on his guard because the opponents of government in Ireland most likely would try again on another issue. To Stone, Newcastle was even more cautious. Experience has shown, he wrote, that once the spirit of opposition is raised it is not so easily put down. The lord lieutenant and all of his friends in the house of commons should be on their guard, he concluded, "by the continuance of that attendance which alone defeated the designs of the first day of the session."[109]

If these English ministerial warnings were intended to promote

107. HMC Stopford-Sackville, I, 201.
108. Falkiner Stone Correspondence, 520.
109. *Ibid.*, 521–522.

sobriety and caution in dealing with the Boyle party, they had little effect. Sackville saw only what he wanted to see and heard only what he wanted to hear. He informed Pelham at the end of October that "we are going on with the public business without the least apparent intention of its being obstructed." Boyle, Malone, and Carter of late had been acting responsibly and seemed to have resolved to concur with the lord lieutenant in whatever he proposed for the king's immediate service. In all probability, Sackville wrote, "our money bills will be despatched [sic] from hence by the middle of next month."[110]

According to Sackville's informants, the Nevill matter and the Armagh election seemed to be the questions by which the speaker's friends hoped to rally unattached members to their party.[111] Malone and Carter were trying to persuade members that such questions did not really relate to government. Men could vote against Nevill or against the primate on the Armagh election petition and not be voting against the king.

Sackville did not think this new strategy would work. If Nevill had behaved ill, the government would not try to protect him. If the opposition tried to expel this unfortunate man in order to demonstrate their power, then the government would respond with a spirited defense.[112] The Armagh election was another matter. Treachery was at work there. The Armagh mail had been robbed by two men dressed as gentlemen and the writ to the sheriff taken out in order to delay the election.[113] Brownlow had headed the poll, and in Sackville's judgment, he should be supported with all of government's strength. In character with his military profession, Sackville seemed to be anticipating, actually hoping for, the one great battle wherein the enemies of the crown could be put to flight and political tranquility restored to Ireland. Whatever their source, the chief secretary's fantasies were short-lived. The world as it was crashed upon him when the house of commons took up the money bill.

Paradoxically, the greatest political crisis occurring in the Irish parliament since 1724 actually began in early November 1753 with

110. *Irish Official Papers*, I, 43.   111. *Ibid.*, 85.
112. *Idem.*
113. Falkiner Stone Correspondence, 521.

a small victory for the government. Resistance to dropping the tax of four shillings levied on every pound paid to absentee office holders and absentee pensioners faded quickly before a few good words, a little flattery, and some stern warnings.

After reporting success on the absentee tax matter to Pelham, Sackville noted the general good progress of the king's business in the house of commons and observed that "in a few days the money bills will be prepared and I shall do myself the honour of acquainting you if anything new arises."[114] To be sure, Sackville had uttered a self-fulfilling prophesy. In a few days' time, something new did arise, and to Pelham he had much to communicate.

Sometime between November 12 and 14, the lord lieutenant and chief secretary learned that the Boyle party intended to revive and contest the issue of previous consent. Malone announced in the committee on supply that no consideration would persuade him to agree to accept the inclusion of language in any of the money bills signifying the king's previous consent to the appropriation of surplus treasury funds by the Irish parliament to the national debt.[115] The trap Boyle, Malone, Carter, and Cox had set—by threatening to embarrass Dorset in the addresses and thereby to avoid including the word consent in the addresses—was about to be sprung. Stone admitted that Malone had been consistent in his continuing opposition to previous consent as constitutional doctrine but affected great surprise, as did Dorset and Sackville, that this issue had been revived. None of these men seemed aware of what Boyle and his friends had done to them on October 10, when they agreed to accept the address of the house of commons without further amendment once the compliments to the duke had been restored.

As soon as Dorset heard of Malone's statement in the committee on supply, he summoned Boyle and Carter, chairman of the committee, to attend him at once. Both gentlemen arrived promptly and proceeded to inform the duke that they had been converted to Malone's point of view. When Dorset asked whether they would support the government's position in a vote, Boyle responded by

114. *Irish Official Papers*, I, 85.
115. HMC Stopford-Sackville, I, 201, 202.

asking the question: how could his grace expect any aid from me when all power had been taken away? I am, Boyle declared, disabled from giving any assistance. Carter's conversion to Malone's position on the issue of previous consent was so complete that, as chairman of the committee, he absolutely refused to insert the words added to the bill last session into the present one.

Having gotten nowhere with Boyle and Carter, Dorset met next with Malone and tried to reason with him. The prime serjeant remained intransigent. He contended that if the notion of previous consent was insisted upon and carried it would be fatal to his majesty's prerogative because hereafter there would be no future treasury surpluses to worry about. No future supplies would be granted to the crown, Malone argued, except under strict and specific appropriations whereby future surpluses and future disputes over this point would be prevented.[116] Malone asserted that the prerogative would be better preserved by dropping previous consent from the money bills than by including it. Severely pressed for time because the money bills were scheduled for presentation to the house on November 14, 1753, Dorset called those of the king's servants that he could trust to the Castle on the morning of that day in order to decide upon a course of action.

Stone, Sackville, Newport, and Singleton were among those present at what turned out to be an extremely depressing meeting. Stone developed an elaborate political explanation of Boyle's decision to oppose the government on the issue of previous consent which he later communicated to the Duke of Newcastle.[117] The primate saw Boyle's decision to attack the king's prerogative as an act of desperation intended to keep his political connection with the Earl of Kildare from disintegrating.

While Stone's analysis of the present situation was perceptive and probably accurate, it was also irrelevant to the problem at hand. All of the persons at the meeting advised the duke to let the money bills, as introduced by Carter, pass the house without any attempt to amend them.[118] The principal reason favoring this strategy was

116. HMC Stopford-Sackville, I, 201; William Yorke to Hardwicke, November 16, 1753. Add. Mss., 35,592, 198.
117. Falkiner Stone Correspondence, 523.
118. HMC Stopford-Sackville, I, 201.

the ill wisdom of trusting so tender a point of the prerogative to a hasty decision in the house of commons when the attack was to be made by the king's principal servants.[119] Having thus decided on a course of action, the ministers took their leave of the lord lieutenant and went off to the house to watch happen what they could not prevent.

Carter introduced a bill for the application of £77,500 in the treasury to the national debt without a preamble reciting the king's previous consent to the transaction. The bill was accepted from the committee without amendment, passed by the house, and sent to the lord lieutenant for transmittal. Notice was taken of the omission by the Irish privy council in a letter sent to Lord Holdernesse, but the bill was sent off to England in exactly the same form as Carter had brought it in. Surprised and unnerved by the experiences of the past few days, the lord lieutenant explained to Newcastle on November 16, 1753, that in an affair of this delicate nature he could not venture to take any other steps without the king's express command. Dorset assured Newcastle that every day the necessity for putting some stop to the power that had grown up in Ireland became clearer. Moreover, the longer the attempt to do so was delayed, the more violent would be the inevitable confrontation.[120]

Dorset hoped for some strong expression of support from the English ministry and would have preferred to have taken no further actions until he knew the minds of Newcastle and Pelham on the recent events. However, his opponents in the house of commons would not allow the government any respite. The speaker's friends let it be known that they intended to move against Arthur Jones Nevill. The move came on November 16, on an immaterial question relating to Nevill's affairs, which all of the principals in the house understood to be a test of strength between the government and the Boyle party. The debate was heated and lengthy, but when the question was called, the government carried it by a majority three votes. Stone observed that the parliamentary attendance of 239 members for this division was the greatest of the century. In his mind, this division was proof positive that there was a strength in the

119. Falkiner Stone Correspondence, 524.
120. HMC Stopford-Sackville, I, 202.

country ready to stand with the government against an imperious faction, and he hoped that the king and his English ministers would act quickly to mobilize it.[121] This victory also meant that the Irish government had committed itself to defend Nevill—a difficult task in the best of circumstances, and with a majority of three on an immaterial question the circumstances were not the best.

The chief secretary advised Nevill that no help would be forthcoming if he had done wrong and that nothing would be said in his favor if the former surveyor general did not offer to the house to deposit any sum with any person they should so designate. Upon that basis only, insisted Sackville, did the government agree to support him.[122] Moreover, Sackville did not support him in everything. The chief secretary joined in passing censures when deserved and expected that when the examinations were over this unfortunate man's pocket would be punished rather than his person. However, Sackville's expectations in this affair were not to be realized. The Earl of Kildare insisted upon expulsion, and after the vote of November 16, the speaker decided to make a maximum effort. According to Sackville, Boyle declared that he would give up the speaker's chair if Nevill were not expelled.[123] The speaker's declaration had its intended effect. Persons with past obligation to Boyle simply would not forsake him on a matter in which he had declared such a direct and personal interest. Arthur Jones Nevill's public career came to an end on November 23, 1753. His offer to the house of commons was rejected. He was voted in noncompliance with the resolutions of last session 124 to 116 and was expelled from the house of commons by a vote of 123 to 116. Appropriately, the tellers for the majority were Malone and Walter Weldon, member for Lord Kildare's sometime rebellious borough of Athy.

When Newcastle learned that language signifying previous consent had been omitted from the Irish money bills he acted with immediate dispatch. The duke discussed the implications of this omission with Pelham, and because the first minister's health was so poor Newcastle himself agreed to bring the matter to the attention of the king at once. Newcastle met with the king on November

121. Falkiner Stone Correspondence, 524.
122. *Irish Official Papers*, I, 87.   123. *Idem.*

21, and his majesty reacted as the brothers had anticipated. The king was outraged that gentlemen in his service would behave as did the leaders of the Boyle party. To George II, the assault on the prerogative seemed clear and deliberate. The king agreed with Newcastle's suggestion that some proper marks of royal displeasure were in order.[124]

Newcastle left the king, conferred briefly with Pelham, and then on November 22, 1753, sent Dorset an account of his meetings and some advice about what to do next. Newcastle assured Dorset that language signifying previous consent would be added to the money bill by the English privy council. He wanted to know who ought to be dismissed if opposition to the amended bill from office holders persisted and what persons ought to succeed those dismissed? Newcastle reported the general opinion in English ministerial circles that Malone and Carter were the leaders of the opposition and the most likely candidates for removal. Nonetheless, he cautioned that no steps could be taken "till we see what part they will act upon the return of the bills, I would only wish to know your Grace's thoughts provisionally."[125] In effect, this letter of November 21, 1753, from Newcastle provided the lord lieutenant with the expression of confidence and support for which he had hoped. Believing himself secure enough in royal and ministerial favor to proceed against his enemies in the Irish house of commons, Dorset began to compile a dismissal list. However, before he had a chance to complete it, the confidence so recently and generously given was partially withdrawn. Newcastle and Pelham were shocked by the news of Dorset's defeat on the expulsion of Nevill.

When Newcastle learned of the vote on the Nevill matter, he conferred with his brother, and then went directly to the king. His majesty and two chief ministers seemed to have concluded that Dorset had lost control of the Irish situation. In their minds, the lord lieutenant no longer seemed capable of distinguishing between what was important and what was not. The tone of Newcastle's letter to Dorset, written on November 30, was much changed. It was critical and patronizing. In Newcastle's view, Dorset had aban-

124. Falkiner Stone Correspondence, 526.
125. *Ibid.*, 527.

doned the very strong position of defending the prerogative for the hopeless one of trying to protect Nevill and "thereby gave a great cause of triumph to their opposers."[126] We think, Newcastle continued, that you should have let all other matters go and reserved yourself for the great question. Instead you have suffered yourselves to be beaten on an insignificant one and find yourselves now less able to stand the great question when it comes.

About the future, Newcastle was most explicit. What has passed is over, he wrote, "the present attention must be to carry the money bill thro' with as great a majority as possible; but, in all events, to carry it."[127] The minister concluded his letter by observing that the governors of Ireland must strive to "keep upon public points— there you are strong—and avoid as much as possible, all private personal considerations."

Knowing well the minds and dispositions of Pelham and Newcastle, and anxious to exonerate himself and Sackville from allegations of poor judgment, Stone expanded in his correspondence with Newcastle an idea Sackville had suggested in his letters to Pelham. According to Stone, the cause of the present state of affairs was one of very long standing. The ghosts of Molyneux and Swift were abroad once again. The old independency doctrine had been resurrected by Malone. Stone insisted that "[t]he constitutional dependency upon England is the object upon which the prime serjeant's eye is constantly fixed."[128] In Stone's judgment, assertions that amending the Irish money bill in the English privy council would end liberty in Ireland were proof enough that the real issue in this conflict was the constitutional dependence of Ireland upon England.

By representing Malone as an independency man Stone conveniently forgot Sir Arthur Gore's address, moved at the end of the last session. By stretching the truth in letters to Newcastle, the primate hoped to frighten the duke and turn ministerial minds away from the notion that he and Sackville were responsible for the present difficulties. Though the independency doctrine was an absolute anathema to Newcastle, and while he was ready to believe

126. *Idem.*   127. *Idem.*
128. Falkiner Stone Correspondence, 530.

almost anything about Malone or Carter, the duke could never be persuaded that a man such as Boyle would ever espouse it. Stone did not even try to convince him. The primate described the speaker as being dragged unwillingly along by Malone and doing "many things contrary to his inclinations and principles, rather than suffer any abatement of power while he can with any means preserve it."[129] If Malone was a doctrinaire independency man, Boyle was hardened and corrupted by long-unrivaled possession of power.

Recurring self-justifications notwithstanding, Stone tried desperately to communicate to Newcastle the nature of the present extraordinary political situation in Ireland. Nevill could not have been given up without a defense any more than Brownlow could be abandoned in the forthcoming confrontation with the Boyle party over the Armagh election. The present political situation was unique. The chief opponents of the lord lieutenant were office holders; his principal supporters were the unattached country gentlemen. This circumstance, Stone argued, profoundly affected Sackville's decision to defend Nevill. Most of the country gentlemen were convinced that Nevill's prosecution was founded on malice and resentment and that the extent to which it had been carried was grossly unfair. It was they who demanded that Nevill be defended. If Nevill had been given up without a defense, the primate continued, "I am satisfied we should not this time have been sure of thirty votes in the House of Commons."[130] What was undertaken on behalf of this man, Stone concluded, was begun only after he had promised his private fortune as security for all uncompleted and faulty construction work attributable to him and because the friends of government insisted that something be done for him.[131]

The same circumstances prevailed with regard to disputed elections. There were important reasons why Brownlow had to be supported in the Armagh election dispute. There were two other gentlemen—Daly and French—lately returned from Galway whose elections were similarly challenged. According to Stone, all three had been challenged because they were reputed as friends of the government. In the case of Daly and French, the motives for trying

129. *Idem.*
131. *Idem.*

130. *Ibid.*, 529.

to unseat them were absolutely clear. As soon as these men had taken their seats, wrote Stone, they received messages in the house that if they voted with the government, petitions alleging improper elections would be lodged against them. The gentlemen voted with the government and petitions were so lodged.[132] In the minds of both Stone and Sackville, the issue to be tried when the Armagh petition came before the house was whether or not the Boyle party could succeed in expelling three more government supporters from that body. If the lord lieutenant did not use all of his resources to save the seats of gentlemen who were "persecuted only on account of their attachment to the government," Stone insisted to Newcastle, "[w]e should very soon be destitute of all support."[133] When the Armagh petition was presented to the committee on disputed elections on December 6, 1753, everyone knew that it had become a trial of strength between the Boyle party and government.

This election had been a sharply contested struggle between two prominent county families—the Brownlows and the Caulfields. A Brownlow had represented county Armagh in every Irish parliament since 1692. When young Francis Caulfield challenged young William Brownlow for the vacant seat in 1753, his prospects were not good. When the polling ended, the sheriff returned Brownlow as the winner. However, encouraged by Boyle, Caulfield and his friends alleged that Brownlow's majority was made up of improperly registered freeholders and that the sheriff's return was illegal. This was the issue the members of the Irish house of commons meeting as a committee of the whole had to decide after two days of hearings on December 8.

It was understood by everyone that the trial of the Armagh petition would be a test of strength between the Castle and the Boyle party; extraordinary preparations were made by both sides. When the committee of the whole divided on whether or not the sheriff's return was legal, Caulfield lost by a vote of 122 to 118. However, the speaker and his friends would not accept this defeat as final. They worked tirelessly to improve their numbers when the committee's report would be acted upon by the whole house. The Boyle party had two days in which to change one vote and secure

132. *Idem.*   133. *Idem.*

two abstentions from the Brownlow majority while holding their own 118 votes steady. If such were done, the numbers on each side would be equal and then the speaker could himself break the tie.

On the morning of December 10, it appeared that the Boyle party had succeeded in getting the needed commitments. But by the evening they had lost one of them. John Preston, member for Navan, had supported Brownlow on December 8, but had been persuaded to abstain on December 10. Yet at eight o'clock in the evening, Preston responded to a summons from Lord George Sackville by leaving a dinner party and Mrs. Caulfield's presence to go to the house and once again vote for Brownlow.[134] Preston's vote made the difference. Caulfield's petition was rejected by a vote of 120 to 119 and Brownlow continued in place as a member for county Armagh. The reaction of the Boyle party to their loss of Caulfield and to Preston's breach of honor was predictable. They withdrew the petitions against Daily and French,[135] found some pleasure in Preston's sudden death two weeks later, and decided to risk all and fight the government on the issue of previous consent.

The Irish money bill had been received by the English privy council on November 28, 1753, whereupon language signifying the king's previous consent to the application of surplus Irish treasury funds to Irish national debt had been added to it. A letter from the English privy council to the Irish privy council was prepared in which the issue of previous consent was stated to be a point of prerogative from which his majesty would never depart.[136] Together, the money bill and letter from the English privy council were sent off to Ireland forthwith, arriving in Dublin on December 6.

The money bill was presented to the house of commons, and on December 14, a committee was appointed to examine the bill for alterations. On Saturday afternoon alterations were reported. After some discussion, Monday, December 17, was set for house action on the altered bill. As arranged, in the evening of December 15, the speaker, Carter, Malone, Tisdale, Warden Flood, John Gore, John Ponsonby, John Bourke, William Bristowe, Luke Gardiner,

---

134. HMC Charlemont, I, 188. 135. *Ibid.*, 203.
136. HMC Emly, 178.

and Nathaniel Clements gathered at the Castle to meet with the lord lieutenant. The invitations, as Stone observed, had been offered because of regard for offices, not for persons.[137] Dorset greeted the group with cordiality and then read the letter from the English privy council to them. After reading the letter, he remarked on the importance of the issue raised by it and "called upon them all, in his majesty's name, to use their utmost influence in their respective stations to support the just prerogative of the king."[138] The speaker and those of his friends at the meeting listened politely and said nothing. After a few minutes of silence they simply left the lord lieutenant's presence without having uttered a word. Stone summed up the situation in a letter to his brother by saying that "[a]ccording to all appearances, and all reports, they are determined to throw out the bill."[139]

In the short time remaining there was little that the government could do except see to its numbers. Dorset expected no surprises from the country gentlemen. At this moment of crisis a few defected, but most remained steadfast and supported the government. The real problem was with the king's Irish ministers. The example of crown officers standing against the prerogative and the government was very difficult to counter. According to Stone, the ferocity of the attack by the king's servants upon the king's government confounded the minds of ignorant and uninformed people. They were told that the issue before the house of commons was the last struggle for Ireland and that the men in office were ready to sacrifice their employments for the preservation of the country.[140] Stone feared that if the Boyle party succeeded in rejecting the bill by these means, they would proceed to other violences. "If this faction is not broke," wrote the primate to his brother, "all government is at an end."[141]

The debates on the money bill began at two o'clock in the afternoon of December 17 and lasted until past midnight.[142] Carter began the proceedings by moving rejection of the bill. He was followed by a succession of speakers—each being more strident

137. Falkiner Stone Correspondence, 531.
138. Idem.   139. Idem.
140. Ibid., 531–532.   141. Ibid., 532.
142. HMC Charlemont, I, 191.

than the last. The most inflammatory of all was William Harward, member for the Cork borough of Doneraile, who declared that if these alterations were allowed to stand, the surplus in the Irish treasury would be carried off to Hanover. The burden of responding to Harward and to most of the gentlemen arguing for rejection fell to Lord George Sackville. He spoke well, with great emotion, and often, but finally in the early hours of Tuesday morning, December 18, 1753, when the division was called, the Boyle party had a clear majority. The Irish house of commons rejected the altered money bill by a vote of 122 to 117.

Outside of parliament the victory of the Boyle party was celebrated as the people's victory. On the night of the debate, bonfires burned in several parts of the city, and when parliament adjourned after the division, about 1,000 Dubliners escorted Boyle and Kildare from the College Green to their respective townhouses. Lord George Sackville left the house by a back door and made his way to the viceregal apartments without injury or unusual insult. Other government supporters were not so fortunate. Several endured affronts and indignities; a few suffered property damage.[143] The primate escaped insult, but the sight of a large mob invading Henrietta street and cheering the speaker as the savior of the country could not be forgotten.

Sackville reported the results of the division on the money bill to Pelham on December 18, and Dorset followed with a longer explanation to Newcastle three days later. The lord lieutenant described the event as so unexpected, surprising, and full of bad consequences that he wanted the king's express commands about what he should do next. The idea that gentlemen ought to be dismissed from office because of how they voted in parliament was so novel in Irish politics that Dorset wanted unqualified backing from the English ministers before he acted upon it.

Nevertheless, the present situation was so dangerous that something had to be done. The house of commons was so balanced that neither the government nor the Boyle party could command a dependable majority. Dorset feared that violence and extreme measures by persons in and out of parliament would be attempted in

143. *Idem.*

order to gain such a majority. He recommended that the linen and supply bills now depending be quickly enacted and that an end be put to the session as soon as possible thereafter.[144]

In a detailed analysis of the division on the money bill, Stone argued that a combination of bad luck and treachery accounted for the defeat. Six promised government supporters were prevented from attending by sickness; three other abstained. Of those three, two were bankers —John Mccarrell, a Dublin alderman and member for Carlingford, and Henry Mitchell, member for Castlebar. Mccarrell and Mitchell were receivers of government deposits and for this reason were most amenable to Nathaniel Clements' influence. One word from the teller of the exchequer would have ensured the presence and votes of these two bankers.[145] The word was not given. Clements gave his own silent vote to the government, but all of his friends and connections voted with the Boyle party. The primate concluded that on this most important issue the weight of the treasury had been actually cast against the government.[146] Like Dorset, Stone insisted that something had to be done.

While Dorset awaited the king's pleasure on what to do next, he kept the house of commons in session only long enough to enact the supply and linen bills. On December 23, those bills were approved, and on the following day the lord lieutenant adjourned parliament for three weeks. Neither Dorset nor Boyle anticipated a quiet Christmas holiday. The lord lieutenant and the speaker were both extremely anxious that their respective groups of friends in England understood what had happened in Ireland. Dorset dispatched his private secretary, John Maxwell, to England on December 21, and for the Boyle party Lord Kildare embarked shortly thereafter.

While Dorset worried, the primate planned and wrote. In a letter to his brother, written on December 24, the primate addressed directly the question of whether or not office holders should be dismissed for their votes in parliament and argued for a strategy he believed would ensure comfortable parliamentary majorities for the Irish government in the years ahead. Stone insisted that the

---

144. Falkiner Stone Correspondence, 534.
145. *Ibid.*, 736.   146. *Ibid.*, 737.

honor of the crown and the interest of the king's service in Ireland required that, as soon as the present session ended, those leaders of the late opposition holding office ought to be dismissed.

On December 28, two letters—an official one from Holdernesse and a private one from Newcastle—were dispatched to Dorset. Holdernesse asked for additional information about the state of parties in the Irish house of commons and instructed the lord lieutenant to keep the house out of session by a series of short adjournments until the proper moment for prorogation. For his role in expunging the previous consent clause from the money bill, Carter was to be dismissed from his post as master of the rolls, turned out of the Irish privy council, and deprived of all pensions. Malone was to be replaced as prime serjeant, Dilkes removed as quartermaster general, and Bellingham Boyle stripped of his pension.

Newcastle's letter was both supportive and candid. He reported the king's deep dissatisfaction with those gentlemen in his service who had voted for rejection of the money bill and his decision that "some few examples should be forthwith made."[147] However, his majesty wanted to know Dorset's mind on how a substantial number of those well-meaning but misled gentlemen that had voted with the majority could be brought back to a proper submission to royal authority. Great efforts had been made to alienate the minds of loyal and faithful Irishmen from a proper subordination and dependence upon England. The king wanted an end put to these efforts and he wanted to know how it might be best done.

In Newcastle's view, some plan of government had to be laid down and steadily pursued. He did not believe that two or three removals would change anything. An overall plan had to be developed that would include commitments from persons of credit and ability to carry on the king's business in the present house of commons because on no account did the king want to be forced to dissolve this Irish parliament. In all things, the king's interest and authority had to be supported. "The constitution of Ireland," declared Newcastle, "as connected with and dependent upon, this kingdom, must be maintained. All personal considerations must

147. Falkiner Stone Correspondence, 540.

yield to these two great and cardinal points, which I hope will never be departed from."[148]

The question of the moment was whether or not the speaker should be dismissed from his post as chancellor of the exchequer. If Boyle were removed, who would lead in the house? Singleton was able but old. Bowes was able but, like Singleton, he was on the bench and not in the house of commons. Any decision about Boyle's employment had to await resolution of this other question.

Also, Newcastle stated that he would not be acting the part of a faithful friend if he concealed from Dorset the fact that in official circles there was an opinion that the opposition in Ireland "(tho' in appearance upon great public points) have their rise from private pique, and resentment, and are not designed to be carried further."[149] Newcastle himself denied any agreement with that opinion, but advised Dorset to make allowances for it in whatever recommendations he might make about the future government of Ireland.

Dorset received the long-awaited letters from Holdernesse and Newcastle in the second week of January. He was delighted with their contents and immediately shared them with Sackville and Stone. On January 14, 1754, Dorset assured Holdernesse that his majesty's commands relating to the dismissal of Carter, Malone, and Dilkes and the stopping of Bellingham Boyle's pension would be carried out.[150] He also promised to prepare an account of the present state of parties in the Irish parliament and to send it to the secretary of state as soon as possible. Next, Dorset drafted a message and delivered it to the house of commons on January 15, wherein that body was adjourned for another three weeks, by which time he hoped to have received instructions from the king about the most expeditious way of ending the session.

In less than ten days, the king and his English ministers had settled on a scheme for proroguing the Irish parliament. A search of the House of Commons Journals revealed that more than once the parliament had been prorogued by proclamation while the houses were under adjournment. Holdernesse directed Dorset to pursue this method in the present case as soon as convenient.[151]

148. *Ibid.*, 541.   149. *Ibid.*, 242.
150. Dorset to Holdernesse, January 14, 1754. SP63/413/103.
151. Holdernesse to Dorset, January 24, 1754, SP63/413/111.

Consequently, on January 31, 1754, the lord lieutenant issued such a proclamation and thereby formally ended what had been to date the most heated and controversial session of the century. One task still remained. A mechanism had to be found whereby the revenue surplus could be appropriated. Newcastle insisted that some "signal reassertion of the royal prerogative should be made so that there would never again be any doubt about the need for the king's previous consent."[152] Dorset met with his law officers, and unanimously they recommended that the king should order under his sign manual the application of the money to the same purposes intended by the rejected bill. Thus would Newcastle have his full assertion of the crown's right to dispose of such surpluses now and for all time. Furthermore, because the basis for rejecting the bill had been disagreement with words in the preamble and not with anything in body of the bill, there was no obligation for the crown to take any formal notice of what had happened.[153] Pelham reached the same conclusion after consultation with English law officers, and at the end of February the king signed the appropriate instrument applying £77,500 of the revenue surplus to the national debt.[154]

With all of the administrative and fiscal details of the late session settled, Dorset, Sackville, and Stone turned their attention to the political ones. Before dismissing Carter, Malone, and Dilkes from their employment and depriving Bellingham Boyle of his pension, the lord lieutenant met with the speaker "to inform him of the orders he had received; and of the lenity that had been shown personally to him."[155] Dorset expressed the hope that perhaps Boyle had been forced into some of the late measures against his better judgment and then asked directly whether he was not disposed to support the king's business and act in concert with whomever his majesty had appointed or should appoint for such purposes.

The speaker answered with strong professions of duty and loyalty to the king. Dorset responded by declaring that Boyle's loyalty was not in question. The issue was whether or not in the future the speaker would be a "useful servant which he must allow had not

152. Irish Official Papers, I, 44.
153. Falkiner Stone Correspondence, 740–741.
154. HMC Stopford-Sackville, I, 208.
155. Ibid., 206.

been of late the case."[156] The lord lieutenant then insisted that a clear and explicit answer must be made to that point. Boyle answered slowly and deliberately, mentioning how some of his present difficulties followed from connections and engagements but not offering any justification for the behavior of himself or of his friends in rejecting the money bill. All that Dorset could get out of the speaker was a request for more time to think about his answer before delivering it.[157] The duke agreed and did not press him any further. However, Dorset admitted to Newcastle that the symptoms and circumstances were not promising.

Next, Dorset summoned Malone, Dilkes, and Bellingham Boyle to the Castle. The duke communicated to them his majesty's displeasure and then gave formal notice of their respective dismissals and loss of pension. According to Sackville, each of these gentlemen received their notice of dismissal from the king's service with great propriety and decency. At the same time, Carter had been similarly summoned but begged to be excused because of a severe seizure of gout in one of his hands. Thereupon, Sackville went directly to Carter's house and had long and cordial conversation with his sometime tutor, now become political adversary.

Carter was not surprised by the visit, as the speaker had already acquainted him with its purpose. Carter admitted disappointment at being dismissed from the king's service, but observed that he could not have acted otherwise without quitting friends to whom he had been attached for more than thirty years. He asked Sackville to assure the lord lieutenant that being out of employment would not alter his conduct in the least. If any business should come into parliament upon which he would have assisted the government while in office, he would be equally ready to do the same in his present situation. It was very plain, observed Sackville, after departing from Henrietta Street that the objections to the previous consent "had been first undertaken and afterwards pursued in complyance with the opinion of the Prime Sergeant Malone."[158]

The decorum exhibited by the gentlemen dismissed and the genuine cordiality that existed between Sackville and Carter should not

156. Falkiner Stone Correspondence, 741.
157. *Idem.*
158. HMC Stopford-Sackville, I, 206.

be surprising. Nor should Carter's explanation of how and why he had taken a stand on the issue of previous consent be doubted. To be sure, the decorum exhibited in the lord lieutenant's presence contrasted sharply with what was happening in the streets, what was being toasted in the public houses, and what was written in the public prints. These gentlemen, after all, were gentlemen and simply returned decency for decency. As Sackville explained to Pelham, he had been particularly careful to keep himself upon as familiar footing as possible with all of the chief persons in the opposition. The chief secretary had succeeded very well in all of this except with Lord Kildare. The earl simply refused to take any notice of him. With Boyle, Malone, and Carter, a social relationship had been maintained. "We have occasionally been at each other's house," Sackville wrote to Pelham, "and have every day conversed in the house of commons."[159] The chief secretary's determination to remain on good terms with his political enemies followed in part from the fact that Carter and Malone were very interesting people and from the hope that if some sort of accommodation were possible, he would be in a situation to arrange it.[160]

Sackville believed that in one sense Carter and Boyle had been trapped by their respective situations, but he insisted that the situations that had trapped them derived from present political realities and not from long political or social association or from past favors. In Sackville's mind, an analysis of parties in the Irish house of commons told the whole story. Boyle was by no means the absolute leader of the party that carried his name. The house was so divided that defection by any one of the principal men in opposition with any sort of following would give the government a clear majority. For common safety then, the chiefs of the opposition "have been obliged to flatter and support the passions and absurd propositions of each other."[161]

If Sir Richard Cox were turned out, and if the offices already vacated by the dismissal of Carter, Malone, and Dilkes were wisely distributed, then the present balance of the house could be broken and a settled government majority obtained. To that end, Cox

159. *Ibid.*, 205.
160. *Idem.*   161. *Idem.*

was dismissed and replaced by James O'Brien, present collector of customs of Drogheda and uncle to the Earl of Kildare, who had remained loyal to the government throughout the entire session. Similarly, Carter was replaced by old Henry Singleton, Malone by Eaton Stannard, and Dilkes by Lord Forbes. Finally, after giving Boyle sufficient time to think about his situation and reconcile himself to the government, the lord lieutenant pressed the speaker for assurances of future loyal behavior. None were forthcoming, and in April Boyle lost his sinecure as chancellor of the exchequer to Arthur Hill. For the moment, no action was taken against Clements.

The king had agreed to dismiss Boyle because Dorset, Sackville, and Stone has persuaded him and the English ministers that there were men attached to the government who could manage the Irish house of commons. After lengthy conversations with members and a careful counting of heads, Stone believed that in future sessions the government could get the numbers required by facilitating the attachment of independent country gentlemen to the Bessborough party.

Stone explained that in the Irish house of commons "there must be some gentlemen of Ireland set up with a contenance and authority from the government. . . . That must ever be the case."[162] Stone proposed that John Ponsonby, Lord Bessborough's second son, be set up as such a gentleman. Some one man had to stand out from all others in the house so that country members could resort to him as a person with "particular credit and support from the government."[163] When any man, regardless of abilities, was marked in that way, the primate insisted, advantages would soon appear. Such indeed had been the history of Henry Boyle.

Neither Stone nor anyone else who knew Ponsonby pretended that he could speak as well as Malone or manage as successfully as Carter. As a matter of fact, Lady Kildare saw Ponsonby as a man of mean ability at best and a threat to no one.[164] Stone admitted as much when he described Ponsonby as a man with "no qualities that

162. Falkiner Stone Correspondence, 737.
163. *Idem.*
164. Brian Fitzgerald, *Correspondence of Emily Duchess of Leinster 1731–1814* (Irish Manuscript Commission, Dublin, 1949), Vol. I, 17. Hereafter cited as Fitzgerald Leinster Correspondence.

can make him dangerous."[165] In Stone's view, if English principles were ever to be introduced into the Irish house of commons, they would have to be imported in Irish bottoms. Ponsonby was admirably equipped to function as such an Irish bottom. "I see no person so proper," wrote Stone. Ponsonby may be used "for very good purposes, and I think will never suffer himself to be used to bad ones."[166] Stone's plan for the future was simple. If Clements were removed, and if Ponsonby could be put forward as the spokesman for the government in the house of commons, then that body would be manageable.[167]

Stone had argued consistently that the confrontation between the government and the Boyle party over previous consent had been unavoidable. In order to support his contention that personal ambition had played no part in recent events, and to increase the credibility of his explanation of those events, on January 14, 1754, Stone offered to retire from further participation in the government of Ireland. He asked Newcastle whether it might not be better for the king's service "that my name may be left out of the next commission for appointing lords justices."[168]

Stone's offer to resign had a powerful impact on Newcastle. He showed it to the king forthwith and then reported to the primate that "I never in my whole life saw the King more really pleased with a letter than yours." Every part of it, the duke continued, carried conviction. "It is great work and will have its weight everywhere."[169] Speaking for himself and his brother, Newcastle rejected completely any consideration of the primate's retirement from public life. This letter sent off by Newcastle to Stone on January 24, 1754, is very important. It reflects both the precise moment in time at which the primate's influence over Irish affairs in English ministerial circles reached its highest point, and the one at which that influence began to decline. With regard to Stone's argument and recommendation that Clements should be dismissed, Newcastle praised the primate's reasoning and reported the king's agreement that the man should be turned out, but observed that "you should not be surprised that we have deferred it a little."[170] Though neither Newcastle, Stone,

165. Falkiner Stone Correspondence, 737.
166. *Idem.*   167. *Idem.*
168. *Ibid.,* 739.   169. *Ibid.,* 740.
170. *Idem.*

nor anyone else perceived that the tide of events had turned, it had. Two circumstances transformed Newcastle's little deferral of Clement's dismissal into an indefinite postponement. The first of these circumstances was Henry Pelham's death on March 6, 1754; the second was the utter failure of the dismissals of Malone, Carter, and Dilkes to intimidate the Boyle party or to quiet Irish politics.

The death of the minister who had managed English affairs for twelve years affected Irish politics in two ways. First of all, in spite of Pelham's reputation for moderation and accommodation in English politics, in the present Irish controversy he was convinced that firmness was the only viable policy. Less than a week before he died, Pelham despaired of all past and any further efforts to reconcile Boyle to the government. The minister declared to Dorset that "if a proper stand is not now made the dependency of Ireland on this country is over."[171] Dorset, Sackville, and Stone had lost a faithful friend; Boyle and Kildare found themselves providentially delivered from a powerful and unforgiving enemy. Second, after Pelham's death, decisions affecting Ireland during the next three years were made within a context of ministerial instability and weakness in England and against a background of deteriorating international relations.

Newcastle's accession to his deceased brother's place as first lord of the treasury and head of the ministry was unchallenged, but once installed, the duke found that his new eminence was far more difficult to maintain than it had been to reach. Driven by international events which he could neither understand nor control and harassed almost daily by men whose genius for mischief seemed exceeded only by their passion for causing it, the duke's perspective on Irish affairs changed. For Newcastle, the urgency of Dorset's problems in that country diminished. Making a proper stand appeared much less important than ending an unwanted controversy. As first minister, Newcastle came to this position surely if not quickly.

The more Newcastle thought about Ireland in the spring of 1754 the more seriously he considered the possibility of an accommodation with the Boyle party. What turned his mind in this direction was the state of law and order in Dublin during February and March. Mob action in Dublin intensified, culminating in the Smock

171. HMC Stopford-Sackville, I, 208.

Alley theatre riot in early March, wherein the stage was wrecked and the house was reduced to a shell because an actor refused to repeat lines from Voltaire's *Mahomet* considered insulting to the lord lieutenant and his supporters:

> . . . crush, crush these vipers,
> who, singled out by a community
> to guard their rights, shall, for a grasp of ore,
> Or paltry office, sell them to the foe.

The Smock Alley riot all but exhausted the lord lieutenant's patience. For the moment, he had enough of Irish politics and needed a respite. On March 9, 1754, Dorset wrote to Holdernesse requesting permission to leave Ireland and to appoint the primate, Lord Newport, and Lord Bessborough as lords justices.[172] For the first time in twenty years, Henry Boyle's name had been omitted from a viceregal recommendation for that commission. When Newcastle received Dorset's recommendation he had reservations about dropping Boyle while keeping Stone. He gave some consideration to the idea of not appointing any lords justices and instead sending out from England the Earl of Hertford as lord deputy to govern the country in the lord lieutenant's absence. Friends of Sackville close to Newcastle informed the chief secretary of this prospect, and forthwith Dorset wrote to Newcastle to stop it.

As Dorset's departure time approached, Stone became more optimistic about the state of the country. The temper of the people seemed to be changing every day for the better. To be sure, the primate observed, the poison still remained among the very lowest and most dissolute parts of the population; but the riotous and insolent spirit of the last several months had visibly abated. When the last point—Clement's dismissal—was settled and carried out, Stone insisted, "there can be no doubt that his majesty's government will be successfully and creditably supported." However, one must expect, he added by way of a proviso, that "some difficulties must be looked for on the first setting out in the face of so violent and obstinate an opposition."[173]

Ever since early March, Dorset had been extremely anxious to

172. Dorset to Holdernesse, March 9, 1754. SP63/413/43.
173. Falkiner Stone Correspondence, 746.

leave Ireland, and at long last his time came on May 10, 1754. Preparations for the departure had been very thorough and Dorset's passage from the Castle gate through the streets to the north wall was spectacular. Gentlemen appeared outside of the Castle in their most elegant coaches and formed a lengthy train to attend his grace as he passed through the city. An eyewitness described the viceregal procession as unmatched by any of his predecessors. Moreover, "among the prodigious number of people who assembled to see him pass, there was no sign of ill humor, but all the decency and respect imaginable."[174] The crowds cheered and Dorset smiled in grateful appreciation. Our eyewitness concluded that "[t]his behavior of the people in general must have proceeded from good will, and it may certainly be concluded from it that attempts to poison and enflame them have by no means had the desired effect."[175]

Good will toward Dorset on that day there was, but the display of it was not altogether spontaneous. A follower of Stone writing three years after the event described Dorset's departure as orchestrated by a person skilled in such matters and aided by a mob made drunk for the occasion.[176] In any case, a few days after the lord lieutenant had sailed, the lord mayor of Dublin took examinations and issued a warrant for the apprehension of one Drury for inciting a riot. Drury, a justice of the peace, was alleged to have given money and drink to several persons "to knock down all those who speak disrespectfully of my Lord Lieutenant."[177]

Dorset was gone; and despite Stone's assurances, much bitterness remained. At the moment when the duke and Sackville boarded the yacht for Parkgate, there appeared to be great uncertainty in both Westminster and Dublin about how to deal with it. Accommodation had been tried in Lord Harrington's time and had failed. Yet, Dorset's policy of trying to win new friends by making examples of old enemies had not fared much better. The dismissed office holders had not exhibited proper contrition, private or public, for their behavior during the last session, and whether or not an Irish government could manage the house of commons without them or

174. HMC Stopford-Sackville, I, 209.
175. *Idem.*   176. HMC Emly, 179.
177. HMC Stopford-Sackville, I, 210.

against them was yet to be determined. Most men assumed that Dorset's policies would be continued if he returned and that some sort of accommodation was probable if he did not.

However, the issue of Dorset's return, upon which the prospects and ambitions of so many Irish politicans depended, would not be determined by Irish men or Irish events. English politics and the exigencies of a great war would be controlling. The unstable condition of the former and the unavoidable realities of the latter must have made many Dubliners think, while reading about Dorset's well-reported progress to the waterside, that Ireland had seen the last of their present lord lieutenant and chief secretary.

CHAPTER V

The Great Crisis Resolved, 1755-1756

Preparing for Change

Three days after Dorset and Sackville had left the country, Boyle's friends organized a public display of popular affection for the speaker and dissatisfaction with the lords justices. Sir Samuel Cook, seven or eight other gentlemen, and perhaps forty merchants, backed up by a mob of about three hundred, presented Boyle with a complimentary address from the city of Cork. After presenting the address the mob went to different parts of Dublin cheering or groaning before the houses of the principal people. Each of the lords justices was appropriately groaned. They paid a special visit to Lord Kildare's house, intending to assure his lordship that they had had no part in the lord lieutenant's recent triumphant progress to the north wall. Alas, Kildare was not in town to receive them, but a near neighbor, Lord Molesworth, was annoyed by the din. Molesworth dispatched a party of men to disperse the mob, who obliged the viscount by breaking up and going their separate ways without further insult or violence.[1]

For the moment, Irish politics was in a dead calm. Not even the import from England of a virulent seventy-page invective against Stone and Sackville, entitled *The State of Ireland laid open to the view of his Majesty's subjects,* ruffled the calm. In effect, this calm was really maturing anxiety. The question on the mind of most public men was whether or not Clements would be continued or dismissed. Because there was so much uncertainty about that question, it grew rapidly in importance and acquired the character of a portent. A correspondent of Sackville advised the chief secretary that several of Clements' nearest relatives were saying publicly that he had made

1. HMC Stopford-Sackville, I, 209.

peace with Dorset and would be continued in office. Such reports made the friends of the government uneasy, he wrote, and "the conclusion drawn from this is that the Lord Lieutenant must have resolved not to honour us any more with his presence here."[2]

Not until the end of June was there any reliable information about Clements' prospects. Hill arrived from England with a letter from Dorset for the lords justices directing them to meet with Clements, discuss the assurances he had given about his future behavior, and then make recommendations about continuing him in office.[3] The meaning of this charge was clear to Stone. It was very plain, the primate wrote to Sackville, that "the Lord Lieutenant wished Mr. Clements to be kept in his command."[4] For whatever reasons, Dorset had changed his mind about Clements and wanted the lords justices to develop arguments justifying that change. A series of meetings between the lords justices and Clements were scheduled for late July, and perhaps the most indicative action following Hill's arrival in Dublin was the quiet preparations under-taken by Waite to pack and ship Sackville's plate and linen off to London.[5]

The lords justices met twice with Clements. At the first meeting, they communicated the content of Dorset's letter to Clements and asked him for assurances about his future conduct. He affected surprise that his past conduct had offended the government, in-sisted that such had not been intended, and promised that his future endeavors would make all possible amends for what had happened in the past. When pressed for specifics about how he would employ the influence of his office or private connections on behalf of the government in the next session of the Irish parliament, he re-sponded with assurances that the bankers Mitchell and Macarell would support the government and that he would try to bring two of his sons into parliament to do the same. At the second meeting, Clements seemed a bit more expansive. He repeated his assurances about Mitchell and Macarell and hoped that he might be able to prevail on other persons now serving in parliament to support the government.

2. *Ibid.*, 213.   3. *Ibid.*, 214, 215.
4. *Ibid.*, 221.   5. *Ibid.*, 217.

The lords justices dutifully reported what had transpired during their meetings with Clements to Dorset. They were impressed by his earnest manner and by his obvious concern over the possibility of being dismissed from a post of such great advantage. Their lordships all believed that henceforth Clements sincerely intended "to act up to his professions."[6] The problem for the lords justices was not what Clements would do if kept on, but how the friends of the government during the last two sessions would react to his not being turned out. On this issue, as a group, the lords justices refused to offer an opinion and thereby declined to make a recommendation for continuing or dismissing Clements.

Stone's private letters to Sackville written during August show the lords justices as being much less pusillanimous than their formal reply to Dorset would suggest. He advised Sackville that, in spite of the lord lieutenant's obvious preference at this time to continue Clements in office or of what the lords justices had written in their reply, after actually hearing Clements "not even the most moderate of the lords justices could take it upon himself to say it would be well to continue him in his employment."[7] While the inquiry was underway, Sir Richard Cox and others made the treasury their daily resort. Certainly, the primate insisted, their anxiety for Clements' safety shows that some advantage must be expected from him. The calm in Irish affairs Stone had observed in June had disappeared. The spirit of patriotism was never higher and abuse of government never more reckless. Dorset's failure to settle the Clements matter had led to all sorts of speculation and rumor. Stone pleaded for some public expression of support by the king for the conduct of the lords justices and his majesty's other servants in Ireland.[8] Even though their friends had remained steadfast so far, the primate warned Sackville, there was "an apprehension that the Government is falling off from itself."[9]

By the end of August, what Stone and Newport called the "trumpets of sedition and falsehood" were blowing so loud and often in Dublin that both of these gentlemen wondered whether they should apply for permission to leave the country. It was now past contro-

6. *Ibid.*, 220.   7. *Ibid.*, 221.
8. *Ibid.*, 224.   9. *Idem.*

versy, Stone insisted, that the discontents in Ireland were fomented and encouraged from England.[10] Kildare and Boyle were openly assisted by persons of no small name in the king's English administration, he added, giving color to the report that the present ministry intended to ditch the Irish chief governors. Whenever an active ministry was established in England, Stone concluded, government would be strong in Ireland. At the moment, however, government in Ireland was faltering because "it is not believed that the present system is to subsist."[11]

By the end of August, Sackville and Dorset had heard enough from their friends in Ireland on the Clements matter and recommended to Newcastle that the man be dismissed.[12] Newcastle listened to Dorset's arguments attentively and agreed with virtually all of them. Newcastle then advised Dorset to go alone to the king and make his arguments to his majesty direct and in person. On the day following his meeting with Newcastle, Dorset went to the king alone and presented his case against Nathaniel Clements.

Dorset began his audience by describing the efforts undertaken to get assurances from Clements about his future conduct. The duke believed that the declarations given by Clements to date were unsatisfactory, and that continuing him in his present situation would discourage the friends of government in Ireland and raise the spirits of their enemies. After hearing Dorset's case against continuing Clements in office, the king asked Dorset, "[W]ill you and those in my service in Ireland say the turning of him out will secure a majority in the House of Commons next session of Parliament?" If they will, he added, "I am ready to do it immediately, but I do not yet hear whether the dismissing the others has brought any accession of strength."[13]

Dorset responded to the king as best he could. He pointed out that, although neither he nor anyone else could control future events with certainty, he would say that, in the opinion of those entrusted with managing the king's affairs in Ireland, dismissing Clements would "most probably secure a majority in the House of Commons." Thereupon, the king said, "If they are ready to answer

10. *Ibid.* , 225.
11. *Idem.*
12. *Ibid.*, 228.
13. *Ibid.*, 229.

for that, I am ready to turn him out."[14] With that observation, the audience ended and Dorset went directly to Newcastle to report what had transpired. Newcastle listened carefully to Dorset's report and then promised to write private letters to Stone, Bessborough, and Arthur Hill asking for information about the true state of affairs in Ireland and whether they thought dismissing Clements would secure a majority in the next session.

Sackville had been privy to everything that had happened, and he communicated a detailed account of the royal interview to Stone. The chief secretary also offered an opinion about the meaning of the interview and what to expect in the future. The ferment in Ireland had alarmed both the English ministry and the king. His majesty had rather not turn out Clements but would do so if given the most positive and explicit assurances that it would make a difference. Everything would depend on having a majority in the next session and "no means should be neglected to procure it if possible."[15] If they succeeded, Sackville continued, all would be right. If they failed, explanations and reasonings would go for nothing. They would be condemned and their failure would be attributed to rashness and ill management.

After receiving Sackville's account of Dorset's audience with the king, the primate reflected on the present state of affairs and then agreed to call together all of his friends and "come to an explicit account of the strength that can be depended upon, making ourselves answerable for our undertakings if we think it practicable; if we do not, we must declare so in time and strike our sails."[16] Stone believed that at that moment the Irish government had a majority in the house of commons but was chagrined by the prospect of being answerable if disappointments should happen. It is the same thing as fighting with a halter about your neck, he wrote to Sackville, "and is not a pleasant hearing, considering the cause that we are engaged in."[17]

As the events of the next four months were to show, the primate's figure of speech was most appropriate. During this time it often seemed that Stone and the other two lords justices were fighting

14. *Idem.*   15. *Ibid.*, 230.
16. *Idem.*   17. *Ibid.*, 231.

battles with halters around their necks. For them, however, the most frustrating aspect of their situation was uncertainty. The lords justices did not know whose hands held the rope or when the noose would be tightened. They did not know what the present English government would do or how long it would last.

The indecision exhibited by Newcastle in the Clements matter cannot be attributed to oversight or to impatience with a small problem needlessly complicated. Indecision was the dominant characteristic of Newcastle's entire administration. Within the broad spectrum of ministerial concerns during the last half of 1754, the future of Nathaniel Clements might appear to be a very small one indeed; but the provocations occurring daily in America and the apparent determination of the French to extend their real control into the Ohio valley were not. Yet Newcastle did not discriminate large problems from small ones. The duke could act no more decisively against the threat of a French presence on the Ohio than he had been able to decide whether to continue or dismiss a politically influential Irish office holder.

Under the pressure of deteriorating foreign affairs and incessant criticism from Pitt and Fox in the British house of commons, Newcastle's government had reached the brink of collapse by December 1754. In order to silence some of his critics and add both resolve and confidence to his administration, Newcastle made an accommodation with Fox and gave him a seat in the cabinet. Newcastle's accommodation with Fox affected Irish affairs in two ways. It set an obvious precedent for some sort of accommodation between the Irish government and the Boyle party, and it provided a direct conduit into the English cabinet for the views of the Earl of Kildare. Most likely, while Stone and the other two lords justices were collecting their response to the latest requests for information about the true state of affairs in Ireland, Fox had already received a much different version of Irish affairs from his sister-in-law and frequent visitor at Holland House, the Countess of Kildare.

By early November, the lords justices had collected information about the possible effect of Clements' dismissal upon the Irish house of commons and sent it on to Newcastle. These latest dispatches contained little that was new. Stone reported that the animosity of the principal persons engaged in the late opposition continued in full vigor, but efforts to excite the lower orders to tumultuous and violent behavior on behalf of the dismissed persons or to demonstrate popular support for their attack on the prerogative had been disappointing.

According to Stone, all of the lords justices agreed that Clements ought to be dismissed, and the majority of persons of first rank, fortune, and character in Ireland were of the same mind. Although "it is a hard task to speak with certainty before hand of the effect of any measure," Stone added, "if Mr. Clements were removed the government would at least have all the strength that he has yet produced, in whatever hands the treasury should be put."[18]

However, the lords justices were realists and, prompted by still another request from Sackville in mid-January for information about the probable effects of Clements' dismissal,[19] they recognized the necessity for compromise. On January 21, 1755, Stone proposed as a last expedient that Clements' office be divided and shared with another more trustworthy person. Though the primate viewed this proposal as one that had been "extorted from me as in the last extremity," he believed that implementation of it would "be attended by some good effects."[20] It would abate the triumph of one side and relieve the disappointment of the other. When Stone first broached this idea, he recommended Benjamin Burton, Bessborough's son-in-law, as the person most suited for appointment as Clements' associate.[21]

In offering this scheme, Stone had several objectives in mind. He was well aware of how ambitious Bessborough was for the advancement of his family. Stone also may have suspected that the way those ambitions were satisfied would determine how the earl disposed of his considerable political interests in the next session. To date, those ambitions had received virtually no satisfaction at all. Though the primate took every opportunity to deny rumors of dissension among the lords justices, he knew that Bessborough's loyalty to him rested on the fragile ground of convenience.

At one time, Bessborough had entertained hopes that Burton

18. Falkiner Stone Correspondence, 749.
19. HMC Stopford-Sackville, I, 235–236.
20. Falkiner Stone Correspondence, 758.
21. *Ibid.*, 757.

would replace Clements. Yet the earl was fearful that his own role in pressing for Clements' dismissal would be misrepresented as that of one intent upon sacrificing an experienced public servant in order to make way for a relative. For Bessborough, those same objections seemed equally applicable to Stone's scheme for dividing Clements' office and then appointing Burton as an associate. The earl told the primate that he would rather lose Burton's friendship than live under "the load of public clamor" either of these arrangements would create.[22] However, ideas and schemes came easily to Stone and while discussing this one with Bessborough he thought of another. Stone suggested that a place on the revenue board might be found for Burton by offering a pension to the person promised the next vacancy; and then William Richardson, member for county Armagh and a man knowledgeable in financial affairs, could be joined with Clements in the treasury.[23] Bessborough was delighted by this proposal and the more he thought about it, the more delighted he became. The more delighted Bessborough became, the more single-minded became the lords justices.

Stone apprised Sackville of his latest proposal at the end of January and asked him to discuss it with Dorset and then with Newcastle. In any case, this proposal was to be his last. If it is rejected, Stone wrote, "we must take down our standard, and everything must take a new turn."[24] In Stone's mind the critical moment had arrived. With this scheme Clements would be little hurt, he concluded, "and possibly something like good will and friendly communications (as things in this country come by starts) may arise out of it." By the end of January, however, none of Stone's schemes could affect the course of events. The time for decision had arrived and passed.

The last act of the Clements affairs, which also turned out to be the finale of the Dorset administration, began on January 14, 1755. On that day Dorset and Sackville met with Newcastle and Hardwicke to discuss the present situation in Ireland and to make some decisions about future policy. Dorset declared himself anxious to do whatever would be most acceptable to the king and whatever would most effectively promote his service. For himself, Dorset cared not

22. *Ibid.*, 758–759.   23. *Ibid.*, 759.
24. *Idem.*

whether he returned to Ireland as lord lieutenant or gave up that office to someone else. Having thus set a tone of complete openness in their discussion, they proceeded to talk at length about the temper of the Irish parliament, the views of particular members, and what methods ought to be pursued to support the authority of the government and restore quiet and good order among the people. In due course a consensus was reached. As reported by Sackville, all of those present agreed that Dorset should return to Ireland and that some means should be found for a public expression by the king of his confidence in the lord lieutenant and in the rest of his majesty's servants in Ireland.[25]

Neither Hardwicke nor Newcastle hesitated a moment in acknowledging the necessity of having the Irish treasury under the immediate direction of the government. However, Sackville found Newcastle to be unclear in his opinion of what Clements' future behavior might be. Newcastle wanted to believe that Clements had seen the error of his ways and would conduct himself accordingly in the next session. Dorset and Sackville simply could not agree. The weight of contrary testimony from their friends in Ireland was overpowering. Sackville pressed Newcastle for an explanation of his seeming partiality for Clements. The minister assured Dorset and Sackville that he had no partiality for the man, but it was very clear that he feared the consequences of turning him out.

Dorset and Sackville tried to counter one set of Newcastle's fears by raising others. They argued that continuing Clements in the treasury would be seen by the Boyle party and by Kildare as a triumph and would occasion an alarm and perhaps even desertion among their friends. Both Newcastle and Hardwicke were visibly shaken by this riposte, and the consensus reached earlier began to disintegrate. At this point in the meeting, Newcastle decided to try to salvage as much agreement and good will as he could. He resorted to delay. The minister decided that more information was needed. He instructed Sackville to write to his friends in Ireland and obtain their final sentiments on the Clements matter. Though neither Dorset nor Sackville realized what had happened, the decision to defer the Clements matter once again was in fact a decision to send

25. HMC Stopford-Sackville, I, 235–236.

a new set of chief governors to Ireland. When Sackville and Dorset were unmoved by Newcastle's argument about the risks all of them invited if they recommended Clements' dismissal, they became a burden Newcastle was no longer willing to bear.

The change came quickly and was a complete surprise. In early February, Stone learned that at a social gathering Abraham Creighton, member for Lifford borough, spoke of the Irish government in a way no more or less disparagingly than had become customary for the speaker's friends during the last two years. However, on this occasion Lord Carrick, Boyle's son-in-law, silenced Creighton with the observation that he hoped never to hear a word again on such subjects. Shortly thereafter, the primate met with Lord Carrick, Sir Arthur Gore, and Malone at the board of navigation and talked separately with utmost ease and civility with all of them. Furthermore, Ralph Gore told a friend of Stone that the Boyle party "had gone a great way too far, and he hoped the people would soon see their mistake, and that all would be quiet."[26] The open language of the entire Boyle party seemed to be that there should be no more fighting.

The primate was astounded by this new behavior and did not know what to make of it. He wrote hurriedly to Sackville inquiring whether the opposition knew more of the true state of things than he did. Rumors circulated all over Dublin that the Duke of Dorset had given up the government of Ireland and had asked to serve the king as Groom of the Stole. Stone did not want to believe such rumors because he could not imagine that this information about "so capital an alteration" would have to be picked up in the streets of Dublin.[27] However, by the beginning of March, Stone knew that the rumors were true. Boyle had received a letter which he read to anyone who would listen assuring him that Dorset had been dismissed and that the cabinet would meet in a few days' time to choose a successor. The struggle was over, and Stone had to think about the future.

Stone wrote to Sackville and to his brother in early March. To Sackville, the primate complained bitterly about the present disor-

---

26. Falkiner Stone Correspondence, 760.
27. *Idem.*

dered state of public affairs in Ireland and urged that something be done quickly before the last remaining spark of authority vanished. Stone offered to come to London himself and speak directly to the ministers there if Sackville could arrange such a meeting. The primate believed that only such a trip by him would quiet the minds of their friends in Ireland, who "are now full of apprehension that their case is not understood, and therefore . . . that it has even been fairly represented."[28]

To Andrew Stone, the primate urged that the selection of a new lord lieutenant be carefully done. The nobleman chosen must be a person of great credit and authority, otherwise he would be obliged to submit to those in Ireland whose late conduct the king had disapproved. As a matter of fact, Stone had such a person in mind— William Cavendish, Marquis of Hartington. Hartington was an attractive candidate to succeed Dorset for both English and Irish reasons. He was thirty-five years old and extraordinarily well connected. Hartington was the eldest son of the Duke of Devonshire, a close friend of Henry Fox, a brother-in-law of John Ponsonby, and through his late wife's inheritance owner of large properties in Waterford and Cork. Moreover, his wife was a niece of Henry Boyle. Stone did not mention Hartington by name, but his description—a person "whose name and character, built upon his father's reputation, with the strength of his own property here"—leaves no doubt about who he had in mind. The primate asked his brother to communicate this recommendation confidentially to Newcastle and even offered to come to London to argue the case.[29]

The primate's motives in making this recommendation are not crystal clear. To be sure, connected as he was in both England and Ireland, Hartington was an obvious candidate. Whether the primate knew at the time of this writing, March 4, 1755, that Newcastle was already disposed to choose Hartington for English political reasons is uncertain. On the one hand, Stone was well aware of the weaknesses of the English government, and he may have hypothesized that after Newcastle's arrangement with Fox an approach to the Devonshire family was a logical next step. On the other hand, the

28. Stone to Sackville, March 4, 1755. Chatsworth Mss., T.3158/634 (163/49).
29. Falkiner Stone Correspondence, 761.

primate had reason to remember the Duke of Devonshire's years in Ireland with mixed feelings. It was a fact that Devonshire had recommended Stone for the Bishopric of Ferns in 1740 and then approved his translation to Kildare in 1743. Yet the primate could not have forgotten how utterly dependent on Boyle and Carter Devonshire had become during this last parliamentary session, 1743–1744. In any case, whether knowingly or not, by recommending Hartington, Stone told Newcastle exactly what the minister wanted to hear.

However, a fortnight later, when everyone in Dublin knew that Lord Hartington was the new lord lieutenant designate, Stone joined with Bessborough to make a request no one in or close to the present English ministry wanted to hear. Once again the two lords justices returned to the Clements matter. They wrote joint letters to Devonshire and to Newcastle. The lords justices urged Devonshire to help them persuade his son, Lord Hartington, to dismiss Clements.

Devonshire received the lords justices' letter on March 25, 1755, and on the following day responded to them jointly with the most formal and routine sort of acknowledgement promising nothing.[30] At the same time that Devonshire sent off his response to the lords justices, he also wrote a private letter to Lord Bessborough, assuring him of his continuing friendship and great satisfaction with the alliances between their two families. He then proceeded to marvel at the ignorances of the primate about the real state of affairs. There was nothing in the lords justices' letter that would be approved. Once the decision to replace Dorset had been made, Clements was secure in his employment. The king had come to the opinion that existing animosities in Ireland might be more easily composed by a new chief governor who had not been in the country when they had arisen. Moreover, as the possibility of a break with France increased, the ministers decided that good policy required a serious effort to quiet Ireland while "at the same time assert the King's just prerogative and government." The simple meaning of all this was that if Ireland was to be quieted Clements would stay

30. Devonshire to Lords Justices, March 25, 1755. Chatsworth Mss., T.3158/634 (163/49).

and most likely the primate would have to go. By early April, Bessborough knew the true state of things, but Stone did not.[31]

To Newcastle, the lords justices had been a bit more circumspect. They expressed their complete satisfaction with the expediency and wisdom of changing chief governors of Ireland at this time. Stone and Bessborough declared themselves confident that this exchange had been undertaken because it was in the best interest of the king's government "and of those gentlemen who have steadily attached themselves to it" to do so.[32] They hastened to add that many of their friends would not regard the change in this light unless there were some tangible evidence that it was. The most creditable evidence to this effect would be action on the Clements matter. Dismissal would be the most positive and sensible way of proceeding, but in the present circumstances appointing an associate might be more practical. This arrangement, the two lords justices concluded, "would effectually put a stop to the triumphs which must be expected among the followers of those who are, or pretend to be, elated with having obliged the government of England to remove a Lord Lieutenant."[33] It would also put a stop to current rumors that Stone and Bessborough had quarreled with one another and had become personal and political enemies.

Newcastle's reaction to this latest scheme for settling the Clements situation is unknown. Boyle contended that the decision to appoint Hartington was made precisely when it was in order to forstall further applications from Dorset in the Clements case.[34] However much Newcastle wanted to be rid of this most difficult matter, he was genuinely concerned about the rumor of a falling out between the primate and Bessborough. If true, the consequences of such a situation would be entirely unpredictable and could immeasurably complicate an already difficult problem for the new lord lieutenant. Newcastle heard what politicians in both Dublin and London had heard. The story was that the primate either had written or intended to write to Newcastle claiming that Jemmet Brown, Bishop of Cork,

31. Draft of Letter Devonshire to Bessborough, March 25, 1755. Chatsworth Mss., T.3158/645 (205/6).
32. Falkiner Stone Correspondence, 761.
33. Ibid., 762.
34. Boyle to Robert Pratt, April 1755. Chatsworth Mss., T.3158/645 (205/6).

had come from Boyle to offer terms of accommodation. If he, Stone, would separate himself from the Bessborough interest, Boyle would join with him and act under his advice.[35] Though Boyle disavowed making such an offer, Brown denied delivering one, and Stone wrote a letter to Brown swearing that none had ever been received, the willingness of Irish politicians to accept such a development as a possibility must have given Newcastle pause. It probably influenced his thinking about the next step for Ireland after Hartington's appointment had been formalized.

The decision to replace Dorset had been made primarily for Irish reasons. The duke's dismissal policy had not intimidated or quieted anyone. His hopes for obtaining a secure majority in the next session by turning out still more office-holders struck all of the English ministers as being extremely ill-founded. Moreover, Kildare had been present in London while the decisions on Dorset and Hartington were being made. The earl's principal concerns were retirement of the primate from the government of Ireland and restoration or some form of compensation for the dismissed. On the matter of previous consent, Kildare seemed reasonable; and on the selection of Hartington he had an open mind. If the earl spoke for all or most of the Irish opposition, then Newcastle had reason to believe that the intended change of governors in Ireland would be popular.

Once the decision to appoint Hartington had been made, Newcastle directed all Irish correspondence to the marquis and immediately involved him in Irish affairs. What he learned from this correspondence was disturbing. The political uncertainties of the past few months in Ireland had combined with the prospect of a new war with France to produce a major crisis of confidence. Two Dublin banks stopped payment in early March, and severe runs were expected on the other five. Some merchants, gentlemen, and noblemen associated to assist the bankers, and a few businessmen urged that treasury funds be used to help threatened financial houses meet their calls. Though this prompt action was sufficient to ease people's minds and the runs quickly abated,[36] the lords justices were perceived in both Dublin and London as being divided and

35. HMC Charlemont, I. 213–215.
36. HMC Charlemont, I, 208; HMC Stopford-Sackville, I, 238; Waite to Wilmot, March 4, 1755. Wilmot Mss., T.3019/6781/379.

ineffective. Something had to be done quickly and Newcastle did it. Hartington's appointment received royal approval on April 2, 1755, and the marquis was ordered to proceed to Dublin as soon as possible and take over the government of Ireland.

The new lord lieutenant acted with commendable dispatch. He appointed Colonel Henry Seymour Conway as chief secretary on April 9, met with the Earl of Kildare and Henry Fox several times, completed all of his personal arrangements, and set out for Holyhead in the second week of April. Hartington reached Dublin on May 5, 1755, and proceeded directly to the Castle to be sworn and to discover what awaited him.

Conciliation and Reconstruction

Insofar as the Boyle party was concerned, the prospect of a new lord lieutenant had been long anticipated. Sometime after Dorset's departure in May 1754, the speaker had written in his own hand a general plan detailing how his friends ought to behave in the next session of the Irish parliament if the chief governors of Ireland were continued or changed. Whatever happened, Boyle insisted in the summer of 1754, his group should make the strongest professions of duty and attachment to the king's person and government, but at the same time they should be equally assertive of the right of the house of commons to propose to the king an application of surplus treasury funds without his majesty's previous consent.

If Dorset returned, the duke should not be given an easy moment. Opposition should begin with the addresses—the king should not be thanked "for sending him in whom we can have no confidence." A short money bill might be necessary, but violent opposition ought to be avoided except when absolutely required. Temper and moderation on all accounts would be advantageous and provide fewer opportunities for viceregal misrepresentation of their intentions and actions.[37] If Ireland received a new lord lieutenant, he should be properly received and accommodated in the addresses if not disposed to insist on previous consent. If he were so disposed, then means ought to be considered whereby the surplus in the treasury could be reduced.

37. Boyle's Notes, Spring 1755. Shannon Mss., D.2707/A/1/12/5.

In the year between Dorset's departure and Hartington's appointment, Boyle's determination to justify the position of the parliamentary majority on the issue of previous consent weakened. When the prospects for a change in chief governors became favorable at the beginning of 1755, Boyle began to think more about the causes of the divisions in the Irish house of commons than of their effects. In early April 1755, after Hartington's nomination had become known, Boyle prepared a set of notes and instructions for his son Richard, who was in London. Boyle wanted Richard to meet with the new lord lieutenant and prepare the ground for formal communication and later personal meetings between himself and Hartington.

Boyle advised his son to insist to the new lord lieutenant that the primate "was the principal incendiary and cause of all divisions and disturbances this hour subsisting amongst us." There would be no peace so long as the primate continued to hold any degree of power. If, in the course of discussing Irish affairs with the new lord lieutenant, questions relating to the prerogative should be raised, Richard Boyle was admonished to steer clear of them. The controversy in the late session of the Irish parliament should be represented, Boyle continued, as having been a consequence of a scheme devised by the primate and Sackville. In concert with Andrew Stone and others in England, the primate and Sackville intended to distress any gentlemen in Ireland who resisted their efforts to become absolute governors of this kingdom. Having made those points, Boyle next urged Richard to remind Hartington that the much-misrepresented gentlemen comprising the late opposition were the true old whig interest of the kingdom whose families had distinguished themselves so noticeably in support of the Hanoverian succession during the later years of Queen Anne's reign. Since that time, these families had never deviated from their support of the present monarchy or from a steadfast devotion to the liberty of their country.

Boyle concluded his advice to his son by touching upon a price for reconciliation. Reinstatement of the dismissed gentlemen in their respective employments and emoluments was the minimum acceptable compensation, along with a public and formal correction of past misrepresented facts during the next session of the Irish parliament.[38] The substance of the message Boyle wanted his son to deliver to Hartington was very clear. If some redress for the dismissed gentlemen was not forthcoming, the new lord lieutenant should prepare himself for recriminatory addresses when the house of commons opened in October.

Richard Boyle met with Hartington in April[39] and delivered his father's message. Following that meeting there were rumors enough in Dublin that a treaty of sorts had been struck in London between the new lord lieutenant and an agent of the speaker and Malone. Hartington was supposed to have agreed to give up previous consent, vindicate the Boyle party, and disgrace the primate.[40] Another rumor alleged that Bessborough was privy to the treaty and had secretly consented to it,[41] while yet another contended that the "Bessberonians" were "quite down and gone" because of what had been promised.[42] Hartington himself denied all rumors of a treaty but admitted that conversations with friends of the speaker had taken place in England in April. He advised his brother-in-law, John Ponsonby, that a broad-bottomed willingness to act with well-disposed individuals was to be offered to both sides.[43]

In May, Boyle wrote a letter congratulating Hartington on being appointed lord lieutenant and observed that his own situation was "somewhat different from that in which your noble father found and left me." He complimented Hartington by stating that his excellency's known qualities of mind and talents were precisely what the government of Ireland needed at this critical juncture. When the lord lieutenant had an opportunity to meet and talk with Boyle and his friends, and fair allowances had been made for involuntary errors, he hoped that his excellency "will not think us unworthy of His Majesty's royal favour and countenance." With an unmistakable reference to the Duke of Dorset, Boyle

38. Boyle's Notes, April 1755. Shannon Mss., D.2707/A/1/12/6.
39. HMC Charlemont, I, 215.
40. Clark, op. cit., 285.
41. HMC Emly, 179.
42. Letter from Boyle, May 8, 1755, endorsed by Shapland Carew, MacCartney Mss., D.572/2–78.
43. Clark, op. cit., 285; Hartington to Ponsonby, April 8, 1755. Chatsworth Mss., T.3158/646 (260/130).

concluded his letter with the observation that "one thing we are absolutely secure of, we shall not suffer by misrepresentation."[44]

The approaches made to Hartington in London on Boyle's behalf, as well as the speaker's own letter to him, succeeded. Hartington was disposed to be patient with the speaker, and Boyle seemed anxious to do his excellency some service. Boyle met with the lord lieutenant on Tuesday, May 6, and attended all of the formal levees for the rest of the week. According to Kildare, Boyle and Hartington had a long conversation and seemed to like one another very much.[45] As a matter of fact, everything at that moment was very well indeed. Hartington described his meetings with Boyle and Malone as friendly and open. Boyle pressed the lord lieutenant to promise not to bring up the issue of previous consent and to assure him that the primate would not have the sole direction of public affairs and continue in the government of the country.[46]

Hartington assured Boyle that, if his party would support the government properly, they would have no cause to be fearful of him. On the issue of previous consent, the lord lieutenant refused to promise that he would not bring it up, but declared that he had no intention of doing so during the forthcoming session. While Hartington stated unequivocally that he would proscribe no one— meaning the primate—he was "determined to judge for myself, and wd be govern'd by no one person."[47] For their parts, Boyle and Malone declared themselves perfectly satisfied with the lord lieutenant's conditions and promised to support the government, make no mention of the issue of previous consent, refrain from censures and retrospective resolutions, and do whatever they could to restore peace and tranquility to the country.[48]

Anxious to demonstrate good faith, Boyle agreed to present all of the dismissed gentlemen at a levee on May 8. Except for Malone, none of these gentlemen were of mind to go. However, Boyle managed to persuade all but Cox to attend the levee and exchange

44. Boyle to Hartington, May 1755. Shannon Mss., D.2707/A/1/4/31c.
45. Fitzgerald Leinster Correspondence, I, 9.
46. Earl of Ilchester, ed., *Letters to Henry Fox, Lord Holland with a Few Addressed to His Brother Stephen, Early Ilchester*. Privately printed for presentation to the members of the Roxburghe Club, London, 1915, 63.) Hereafter cited as Ilchester Letters.
47. *Idem.*   48. *Idem.*

courtesies with the lord lieutenant. The speaker and Kildare were both determined to see that the new chief governors had a fair beginning, and both hoped that everything would be done to make Hartington's government easy and happy if he went on well.

Boyle and Kildare were pleased by the change in chief governors and acted accordingly. Other Irish politicians active in the late opposition were delighted that Dorset was gone but were distressed that Hartington had come over. The reluctance of Carter, Dilkes, Cox and others to attend Hartington's levee was one measure of that distress. Some of Boyle's friends would have been better pleased if any other nobleman in England had succeeded Dorset. They were suspicious of Hartington's close connection with the Bessboroughs and feared that he would favor the interests of that family over all others.[49] Lady Kildare recognized the problem but did not think it serious. She believed that the Bessboroughs would have to be taken into the administration because of their close connection with the lord lieutenant. Bessborough was old and "everybody, you know, agrees that party will never subsist whenever he dies, for there is nobody to keep it up as he has done."[50] Neither of his sons, she continued, were capable of doing so. Jack Ponsonby was ridiculous and Lord Duncannon did not trouble his head about anything in Ireland—"so that party must fall necessarily in a year or so."[51]

In this matter, however, Kildare was more impressed by what he saw and heard in Dublin than by his wife's opinion of the Ponsonbys. Hartington seemed to be acting as if he were a partisan of the Bessboroughs. The lord lieutenant announced his intention to travel with John Ponsonby into the south to inspect barracks and fortifications in county Cork. The stated purpose of this trip was not believed for a minute by anyone. Kildare informed his wife that the affair was not much liked and that its real purpose seemed to be to intrude into and otherwise disturb the great political interest of the speaker in that country. Ponsonby wanted to be seen in Cork with the lord lieutenant and trade upon the influence of Cavendish property in that country. As you know, Kildare concluded, Ponsonby was vain enough to believe his excellency's estates might be

49. HMC Charlemont, I, 211, 213.
50. Fitzgerald Leinster Correspondence, I, 17.
51. *Idem.*

sufficient to undermine the speaker in the county constituency and perhaps in a borough or two.[52]

Despite promises made or implied in London to Irish leaders or whatever instructions were received from Newcastle, Hartington and Conway found themselves in a situation in Dublin that a false step could turn into disaster. The lord lieutenant had gotten on well with Boyle and he expected no difficulties from Stone. The primate's much-stated disposition to serve the king in office or by retiring from it was known to Hartington;[53] and in any case, Stone himself made firm promises of support directly to the lord lieutenant shortly after his excellency arrived at the Castle.[54] It was doubtful whether Hartington had made up his mind about what to do with Stone before meeting with Boyle and Kildare in Dublin. The lord lieutenant's original intentions were to come to Ireland to establish a presence for his administration, meet personally with the principal men from all parties, make as few concessions as possible, and then go back to England in five or six weeks' time. He was prepared to offer Arthur Hill a place on the revenue board, thereby vacating Boyle's old office of chancellor of the exchequer. The lord lieutenant could restore Boyle to his sinecure as evidence of the good will of the new governors, reappoint the same lords justices, and then return to London. This was the scenario intended and the one Newcastle had accepted and approved.

However, Hartington quickly discovered that this scenario would have to be changed. In a conversation with the lord lieutenant on May 24, 1755, Kildare had told Hartington in no uncertain terms that the primate had to be given up. The gentlemen of Ireland expected it, the earl insisted "and it was a point that I would never give up." Hartington replied to Kildare in language no less insistent than that which his lordship had used toward him. As the king's representative, he would take advice from everyone but dictation from no one. Hartington told Kildare to his face that in the present state of affairs his lordship's support was not essential to the survival or success of his administration. As lord lieutenant and a friend of Fox, he wanted to have Kildare's support and to show him all of

52. Fitzgerald Leinster Correspondence, I, 19.
53. *Ibid.*, 23.   54. McCracken, *op. cit.*, 175.

the regard in the world, but he also wanted Kildare to know that he could go on without him. Hartington suspected that Kildare might find himself the "dupe to some hot headed People," and urged Fox to give him good advice.[55]

Kildare's reaction to this exchange with Hartington was disappointment but not despair. "I don't think he was pleased with my last conversation," he reported to his wife on May 27, 1755, "I know that he did not look as if he was."[56] Kildare attributed the lord lieutenant's testiness to youth and inexperience and urged Lady Kildare to persuade Fox to send him some good advice. If Hartington did not give up the primate with a good grace, the earl insisted, he would "have as disagreeable a session as the Duke of Dorset ever had." Moreover, if Hartington did have a disagreeable session, it would be his own fault because he knew more about the true state of affairs than had any of his predecessors. Fox seems to have responded to Kildare's request for good advice with precisely what the situation required. In any case, after this straightforward exchange of views, relations between Hartington and Kildare did not get any worse. The lord lieutenant could never understand the earl's willingness to preach reason to his friends and then stand with them when they refused to accept it.[57] Kildare suspected Hartington's attachment to the Bessboroughs and therefore never entirely trusted him. Because of their respective connections with Fox, relations between the lord lieutenant and the earl remained frank and proper but never cordial.

Despite the fact that Hartington reported to Fox that "if there is any faith in men, I cannot fail of success;"[58] for the moment, however, he must have thought himself between a hammer and an anvil. The lord lieutenant could not reappoint Stone as a lord justice because of the uproar certain to follow, but at the same time he could not exclude him because of a necessity to preserve the king's right to choose his own ministers. Hartington's only option was to remain in Ireland and thereby avoid appointing any lords justices at all.

When Newcastle learned of Hartington's decision to remain in

55. Ilchester Letters, 67.
56. Fitzgerald Leinster Correspondence, I, 28.
57. Ilchester Letters, 73.   58. Ibid., 67.

Ireland, he became annoyed. The duke feared that the lord lieutenant intended to restore the speaker to his old sinecure and perhaps
the other dismissed gentlemen as well while staying in Ireland to
avoid appointing lords justices. Newcastle opposed this strategy
because it distributed rewards before proof of altered behavior by
the Boyle party had been received. However, as Hartington's time
in Ireland increased, Newcastle accepted his decision to remain
there and became much less directive about Irish affairs.

Hartington continued meeting with persons from all parties during June, but by mid-summer he had moved closer to the Bessborough party and exhibited an ever-increasing dependence on them.
Increasingly, he tended to view the Boyle party from a distinct
Bessboroughian perspective. To Fox, Hartington wrote, "I have
seen enough of the Speaker and his Friends never to trust them or
put myself in their power."[59] In his view, the balance of parties
in Ireland must be controlled by the lord lieutenant or orderly
government could be impossible. The lord lieutenant knew that
obtaining such a balance would be difficult, but he did not despair
of doing it. By July, Hartington believed he knew what had to be
done to ensure a reliable majority in October, and he proceeded to
do it.

Conway was sent to London to communicate in person to Newcastle the lord lieutenant's recommendation that the demands of Boyle
and Kildare respecting the primate be met. Hartington insisted
that the present state of affairs in Ireland required that Stone be
excluded from the commission of lords justices whenever they
might be next appointed. After discussing the Irish situation with
Hardwicke and Conway, Newcastle agreed to deal with the primate
from his side of the water. He authorized Hartington to assure
the speaker and his friends that the primate would be out of the
government and that the lord lieutenant had been given discretion-
ary authority to restore the speaker to his sinecure. However, Hartington was not given authority to install Boyle as a lord justice if
and when the occasion arose for appointing one.

Next, Newcastle asked Andrew Stone to write to his brother
requesting that he fulfill earlier promises to withdraw his name

59. Ilchester Letters, 71.

from consideration as a lord justice if the king's service required that it be done. In early September, the primate complied; he called upon Hartington and asked to be excused from future service as a lord justice. Though Hartington was gracious, it was not an easy thing for Stone to do, and later he described his feelings in a letter to Newcastle as those of a person who had been forced to swallow a very bitter pill.[60]

Once Hartington had decided to remain in Ireland, he soon discovered that party politics was not his only concern. In Ireland there always seemed to be law and order problems somewhere, and the summer and fall of 1755 were no exception. Often enough, Stone had insisted that irresponsible language and behavior by the Boyle party invited others less fortunately circumstanced than themselves to behave irresponsibly, but the outbreak of violence in the north and in Dublin sprang from other causes. Violence was reported in the Belfast area as early as December 1754. On that occasion, ditches were destroyed and sixty trees cut down.[61] Elsewhere in Antrim and Down, houses were entered or fired upon, stables burned, and horses and cattle maimed. Much of the trouble seemed centered around properties belonging to or recently sold by the notorious absentee Earl of Donegal, where leases had fallen in and heavy fines were being exacted for renewals. Threatening letters signed Captain Burner and Captain Cutter circulated, and rewards were offered for information about those responsible for writing and printing them.[62]

Frightening as these incidents in Antrim and Down were, the magistrates in those counties managed to contain the spread of violence during 1755. Such would not be the case a few years hence. However, for the moment extraordinary measures were not required. Troops were not dispatched to Down in 1755 as they had been sent to Kildare two years earlier. The lord lieutenant seemed intent upon reassuring the English ministers that the reports of violence in Ireland were overstated. Hartington said virtually nothing in his official dispatches about violence in the north and tried to minimize the size and importance of disorders in Dublin. The

60. McCracken, *op. cit.*, 175.
61. *Belfast News Letter*, January 31, 1755.
62. *Belfast News Letter*, October 31, 1755.

lord lieutenant admitted that Dublin had been riotous for some time. In late August a particularly demonstrative mob had decorated one another with white cockades and made nuisances of themselves in different parts of the city. However, beyond disturbing the peace they did not go. Hartington believed that sufficient precautions had been taken and that once the ring leaders were apprehended, Dubliners would see no more of white cockades or posturing bullies.[63]

With Stone excluded from the government, the prospect of political peace in Ireland turned out to be a very reasonable one. It was Kildare's insistence that Boyle accept what the lord lieutenant had been authorized to offer that helped to make it so. On his part, Hartington restored Boyle to his old office of chancellor of the exchequer. The lord lieutenant also promised restoration or suitable compensation for the other dismissed gentlemen, to make no mention of previous consent, and to allow Boyle to insert words in the address disavowing any past intention of encroaching upon the king's prerogative.[64] For their parts, Boyle and his friends agreed to support the government and to forego retrospective resolutions or other recriminatory actions against their opponents of last session.

Hartington was proud of his settlement and represented it to Newcastle as the first step in a new system of governing Ireland without a party and of making those seeking favors look to the lord lieutenant for them instead of to powerful men with large followings in the house of commons.[65] Lady Kildare was less sanguine about Hartington's achievement. She did not think that Boyle and his friends had been given enough to ensure that they would keep their promises and was distressed that nothing had been done for her husband. She observed that the speaker was always fond of promising and complained that neither Fox nor Hartington knew "our friends as well as we do" and therefore had no doubts about them.

Before Hartington left Ireland, he would come to know Boyle and his friends very much better and after leaving Ireland would agree with Lady Kildare's judgment that those men would always

63. Hartington to Robinson, August 25, 1755. SP63/413/287.
64. Clark, *op. cit.,* 290; McCracken, *op. cit.,* 175–176.
65. Clark, *op. cit.,* 282; McCracken, *op. cit.,* 176.

be sure to take care of themselves.[66] Before parliament opened
Hartington attended to one more matter. Lord Newport had recently married as his second wife Frances, widow of the Earl of
Rosse. Newport asked for a rise in the Irish peerage as a reward
for his many years of loyal service and commensurate with the social
status of his new wife. Hartington recommended a viscountcy and
before the year was out Baron Newport had become Viscount Jocelyn. In late September, Hartington believed that his preparations
for his first and only session of the Irish parliament were thorough
and complete.

Hartington's Settlement

Hartington went to the parliament house on October 7, 1755,
and delivered a speech calculated to offend no one and to put an
end to past differences. He alluded to his early arrival in Dublin by
explaining that the king had judged it necessary in so critical a
juncture "for him to come over to Ireland early and to meet with
Parliament in order to concert proper measures for securing the
tranquility and promoting the interests and happiness of Ireland."
To the gentlemen of the house of commons, Hartington addressed
a request for supplies sufficient to support the establishments and to
meet current security needs. Defense and security were mentioned
several times in the speech, which concluded with an observation
that "union among the King's subjects was the best form of security"
and an exhortation that "we must all have the same interest."[67]

The speech was well received but occasioned little in the way
of reactions or comments. It was what most people expected.
After delivering the speech Hartington must have gone straight
back to the Castle and did what Boyle's friends were waiting for
him to do. The lord lieutenant set off to London a request that
Carter be added to the Irish privy council and that Malone be
granted "precedence of his Majesty's Prime Serjeant, Attorney
General, Solicitor General and all other of His Majesty's counsel
learned in law in this kingdom during His Majesty's pleasure."[68]

66. Fitzgerald Leinster Correspondence, I, 31.
67. Hartington's Speech, October 7, 1755. SP63/413/308–309.
68. Hartington to Robinson, October 8, 1755. SP63/413/311,313.

Hartington had clearly indicated how far he was willing to go to get cooperation from Boyle's friends, and he waited to see some signs of accommodation from them. If such signs were to appear, they would appear in the addresses.

The addresses introduced on October 9, 1755, were appropriately servile. The gentlemen of the house of commons declared themselves willing to continue to support the king's prerogative and all other just rights of the crown with the same steadiness and zeal given to the defense of the just rights and privileges of the people. They expressed concern over not having had an opportunity during last session to put their proceedings before the king in a proper light, but believed that Lord Hartington would make a just and impartial representation of the state of affairs. Most important, the address promised to grant cheerfully whatever supplies were necessary to support the establishments and to concur in every measure that would contribute to the healing of the unhappy divisions existing among Irish Protestants.[69]

With the addresses approved without opposition and with the money bills proceeding quietly in the appropriate committees, Hartington fulfilled the rest of his bargain. Carter was recommended for a secretaryship of state with an additional salary of £1,000 per year. Clements gave up his place as teller of the exchequer to Sir Henry Cavendish for an appointment as deputy vice treasurer,[70] and Benjamin Burton, Bessborough's son-in-law, was put on the revenue board. Though nothing except precedence at the bar had been given to Malone, the former prime serjeant was a frequent companion of the lord lieutenant and, in the judgment of Lady Kildare, was rapidly becoming an intimate friend.[71] Of the dismissed gentlemen, by early November only Cox remained unreconciled; and by the end of the month even that most difficult of men was persuaded to cooperate with the lord lieutenant. Moreover, Hartington had nothing to fear from Stone. The primate promised no opposition and asked his friends to continue their support of the government.[72] By mid-November all causes for political anxiety by Hartington had disappeared. He dispatched the money bills

69. *Idem.*   70. McCracken, *op. cit.,* 176.
71. Fitzgerald Leinster Correspondence, I, 29.
72. McCracken, *op. cit.,* 176.

to England with the usual request that they be returned before Christmas.

As tensions between England and France increased in early December, personal tragedy visited Hartington. The lord lieutenant learned that his father, William, third Duke of Devonshire, had died at the age of fifty-seven on December 5th. Hartington, now William, fourth Duke of Devonshire, did not return to England for his father's interment. He remained at his post in Ireland, tending to the defenses of the country and to the political needs of his government. In early January, 1756, Devonshire received an important letter from Fox, advising him that war with France was unavoidable and that he should make all preparations necessary to meet this eventuality. In that spirit, the lord lieutenant obtained an address from the house of commons urging him to put the fortifications of the country into a better state of defense, sent a list of artillery needs to London,[73] ordered the preparation of embargo proclamations, and entered into private and secret conversations with the Earl of Bessborough and Henry Boyle about the present and future state of Irish politics.

Ever since coming to Ireland, Devonshire had been determined to find a way of balancing political factions in the country and governing without dependence on any single party. The lord lieutenant's first inclination was to put power into Kildare's hands because he believed that the earl would make proper use of it and through him "be able to turn the balance against either party that shall be unreasonable."[74] Yet the more Devonshire got to know Kildare, the less certain he became that the earl ought to play that role. If not Kildare then, the question was who could? In mid-December, Devonshire confided to Sir Robert Wilmot that "something must be done for it is impossible to leave this country in the state it is now in with two parties nearly equal in a state of warfare."[75] At this point if not earlier, Devonshire began to consider seriously his Ponsonby relatives as an alternative to Kildare. To be sure, there were genuine problems in fixing too great a dependence upon the political wisdom of John Ponsonby. He was still greatly under the

73. Devonshire to Fox, February 23, 1755/56. SP63/414/67.
74. Clark, op. cit., 292.   75. idem.

influence of the primate and he was one of those persons who simply could not be trusted to keep confidences. However, Ponsonby was a relative and he was available.[76]

During November and December 1755, several trials of disputed election petitions suggested that the speaker's party was in fact disintegrating. In Devonshire's mind, this circumstance followed from the fact that the men attached to Boyle had finally realized that their party could not dictate to the lord lieutenant through Boyle. At the same time, Boyle appeared to Devonshire as having become visibly tired of remaining in the chair now that it was clear that he could not govern in the manner of former times. The duke had been told that many of the speaker's friends had advised him to make an arrangement and take care of his family before it became too late to do so.

In early January 1756, the lord lieutenant received intelligence that Boyle might be willing to discuss terms for resigning the speakership in favor of John Ponsonby. It is not clear who initiated this idea, but Bessborough is certainly a prime candidate. Devonshire claimed that the idea of Boyle resigning had been brought to him. Later, Boyle stated that he had been persuaded to resign the chair by Devonshire out of a kind regard to his own family, to another family, or perhaps to both families.[77] In any case, negotiations began in late November and were completed by the end of February.

Reverend George Chinnery, Dean of Cork, reported gossip among gentlemen in that city in early December that Boyle would retire with a pension and peerage before the end of the session. Though it was treason even to hint of this here, wrote Chinnery, "I wish it for his sake to be true; he hitherto has done nothing for his family."[78] It was true. Boyle demanded generous compensation for himself and for his closest friends. He asked for himself an earldom and £2,000 a year for thirty-one years, charged to the Irish establishment—the same financial reward given to Sir Thomas Robinson for giving up the office of secretary of state and the position of leader in the English house of commons. Malone was to receive

76. Conway to Hartington, August 17, 1755, and Conway to Devonshire, August 17, 1755. Chatsworth Mss., T.3518/825 (416/9–10).
77. Boyle to Devonshire, February 12, 1756/57. Shannon Mss., D.2707/A/1/5/18.
78. Chinnery to Midleton, December 2, 1755. Midleton Mss., 1248/20/80.

Boyle's old sinecure of chancellor of the exchequer, augmented by £700 a year and an appointment to the Irish privy council. At least ten others in Boyle's party expected to be rewarded with peerages, appointments, jobs, salary increases, or pensions.[79] By any standard these terms were high. Devonshire justified a settlement of this magnitude to Newcastle in mid-January on the grounds that it would be lasting, "all parties would be reconciled, none of them left powerful to dictate, and the authority of government restored."[80]

In this context, Devonshire's notion of reconciling the parties was that of separating the principal leaders from one another—Bessborough from Stone and Kildare from Boyle—and separating the leaders of Boyle party from their followers. The lord lieutenant was absolutely convinced that an extraordinary opportunity to free the government of Ireland from party domination was at hand. Certainly the prospect of tranquil politics in Ireland at a time when that condition seemed to have disappeared from the rest of the world must have touched Newcastle. He accepted Devonshire's recommendations and joined with Fox to try to persuade the king to accept them. This task was extremely difficult. His majesty would suffer no arguments about rewarding people who had opposed him. He insisted upon severe measures and damned virtually everyone in the Irish public life including John Ponsonby. However, Newcastle was very much up to the challenge of changing his royal master's mind. Ultimately the duke succeeded, though it took two stormy meetings. The argument that won the case appears to have been that by granting a large pension to the speaker the king would be enabled in Ireland "to do what he might think proper with pensions, which they then could not complain."[81]

Devonshire advised Boyle on February 26, 1756, that a peerage and pension for himself and the arrangement for Malone has been approved.[82] He also agreed to do what he could when he could for the others in Boyle's party expecting rewards. For his part, Boyle gave the strongest assurances that all of his people would support

79. *Idem.*
80. McCracken, *op. cit.,* 177; Clark, *op. cit.,* 293.
81. Newcastle to Devonshire, January 8, 1755/56. Chatsworth Mss., T.3158/1099 (186/68).
82. Clark, *op. cit.,* 292.

the government and belong absolutely to the lord lieutenant. He could not promise that all of his people would vote for John Ponsonby, but he was certain enough of them would do so that Bessborough's son would win the chair by at least sixty votes.[83] On March 6, 1756, Devonshire formally requested a grant of the dignities of Earl of Shannon, Viscount Bandon, and Baron of Castlemartyr for Henry Boyle.[84]

Up to the moment of agreement, the intentions of Boyle, Malone, and the others had been kept secret. When the terms became public, most of Boyle's friends were shocked; others were infuriated. One group of dissidents was so outraged that they met in a Dublin tavern to dine "on a roasted speaker."[85] Devonshire described the Boyle party to Fox as prodigiously soured with one another. Not far from the College Green, a mob of about a thousand demonstrated against Boyle's apparent defection from popularity by hanging him in effigy and insulting Malone, and all of the sometime patriots were loudly groaned in Dublin playhouses. Malone was so shaken by the experience that he asked Devonshire to postpone his appointment as chancellor of the exchequer for two terms.[86] One contemporary contended that Malone requested and obtained from Devonshire an arrangement whereby the office of chancellor of exchequer remained in the possession of Boyle but the salary was secretly diverted to him.[87]

In any case, popular indignation against Boyle and Malone was shortlived. Ponsonby succeeded to the speaker's chair without opposition, and Devonshire truly believed he had managed a political coup of near-monumental proportions. The lord lieutenant boasted to Newcastle and to Fox of having put an end to party spirit in Ireland. Conway asserted that at long last the government was again vested in the hands of the governor,[88] and the lord lieutenant proceeded to act as if it were to demonstrate the point. He issued an embargo proclamation on March 12 and then took it off on April

83. *Ibid.*, 293.
84. Devonshire to Fox, March 6, 1756. SP63/414/88.
85. A. P. W. Malcomson "John Foster and the Speakership of the Irish House of Commons," *Proceedings of the Royal/Irish Academy*, Vol. 72, Section C, No. 11, 277.
86. *Op. cit.*, 178.   87. HMC Emly, 181.
88. McCracken, *op. cit.*, 178.

3. Whatever might happen in Ireland thereafter, Devonshire had won a strong reputation in England for himself as a successful crisis manager. Establishment of such a reputation was perhaps the most significant short term consequence of the duke's tour in Ireland. Moreover, Devonshire himself probably sensed that such was the case and wanted to take advantage of it. Once the uproar over Boyle's resignation began to dissipate, the lord lieutenant turned all of his energies to completing the session and returning to England as soon as possible.

There was a matter dealing with religion which gave Devonshire concern but did not require action. A bill was introduced into the Irish house of lords by James Hamilton, Lord Clanbrassil, intended to break what he described as the close connection between popery and Jacobitism. According to Clanbrassil, the attachment of Irish Catholics to the cause of the pretender was self-evident, and the zeal of Irish priests for Jacobitism was notorious. Proscribed by the legislature and living under the severest penalties for every exercise of their religious functions, Irish priests had no reason for affection toward the government of Ireland. It was a fact that very few Irish priests exhibited gratitude for the lenity several administrations had extended by allowing them, contrary to law, to perform their functions openly in every parish in Ireland. Clanbrassil contended that the priests attributed this lenity by the government to fear rather than to humanity—fear of driving three-fourths of the people into despair. The earl proposed to begin the dissolution of this connection between popery and Jacobitism by bringing the priests under the protection of the government and obliging them to give security for good behavior in order to obtain that protection.[89]

The heart of Clanbrassil's proposal was renovation of the old registration system. By such means, the number, names, and places of abodes of all the priests in Ireland would be publicly known and thereby be a valuable check upon them. However, once these priests had tasted the comfort of a legal protection "which would give them a kind of property in their parishes," they should be ready enough to give information against the itinerant friars ("these restless emissaries of France and the Pretender"), who swarmed into Ireland

89. Russell Correspondence, II, 264.

and devoured many small emoluments that otherwise would fall to the parish priests.[90] Clanbrassil assured the members of the Irish house of lords that, once thus indulged, Irish priests would be as good subjects to the king of Great Britain as the German priests were in Hanover to the elector. Many of the lay lords listened and were persuaded that the experiment ought to be tried. The law lords and all of the bishops except three saw the scheme as recognition and near-establishment of popery in Ireland. Nevertheless, the bill went through three readings and was not defeated directly. Further consideration of the bill was postponed to an impossible day by a vote of 18 to 16.[91] Heartened by this narrow defeat, Clanbrassil made clear his determination to try again in the next session.

Though war was not formally declared until the French began their attack upon Minorca in mid-May, war had been a fact of life in Ireland since the end of January. Devonshire received intelligence of Marshal Belleisle's plans to assemble three expeditionary forces between Dunkirk and Cherbourg for possible descents upon Scotland, the west of England, or Ireland. Belleisle had no thought of conquest; the most that the marshal could hope for was a campaign, in one or all three areas, sufficiently damaging to the English to force a quick and favorable peace. French America might well be secured in Moray or Devon or Cork. The lord lieutenant took such intelligence reports seriously, and on April 1 he sent messages to both houses of the parliament warning them about the prospect of an invasion and the need for increasing the country's military forces.[92] The lords and commons responded with promises of cooperation and support for whatever was needed to meet the present emergency, and loyal addresses from all parts of the country flooded into Dublin Castle.

In the end, Belleisle's bold stroke was never delivered. Instead, on April 10, 1756, Marquis de la Galissoniere departed from Toulon for Minorca with twelve ships of the line and 15,000 men. Nevertheless, throughout the very tense month of April, Devonshire gave the government of Ireland firm direction and must

90. *Idem.*   91. *Ibid.*, 265.
92. Devonshire to Fox, April 1, 1756. SP63/414/137.

receive credit for the fact that serious anxieties over security did not escalate into panic.

In mid-April, the lord lieutenant made final preparations for an early May departure. He decided upon Jocelyn, Kildare, and Bessborough as lords justices.[93] Boyle was excluded because Newcastle and the king would have it no other way. Devonshire chose Bessborough over Ponsonby because, as he claimed, there was great virtue in reducing the power of the speaker's office.[94] Surely a major step toward that end would be to deny the holder of that office routine appointment as a lord justice—a policy recommended as long ago as 1733 by Archbishop Boulter. However, Devonshire's argument had a disingenuous ring to it. Denying the new speaker—Ponsonby—the opportunity of serving in the commission of lords justices and then appointing the speaker's own father—Bessborough—did not strike contemporaries as much diminution of anyone's power.

In the waning days of the session, the viability of Devonshire's settlement was mildly tested. On a motion to present papers to the house of commons relating to the powers of the Irish privy council to suppress bills, Malone made one of the strongest defenses of the prerogative ever heard in that body. If contemporaries are to be believed, Malone was carried away by the logic of his own rhetoric, insisting that all those persons inclined to limit such powers deserved the severest penalties the state could prescribe. Those gentlemen in the house at the time took fire at hearing such doctrine uttered by the late opponent of previous consent. The new speaker terminated discussion by putting the question and declaring the motion defeated. An observer reported that no more than eight members supported the motion and that even Malone, totally unnerved by the uproar against his speech, actually cast his aye for the motion he had spoken against.[95] Sharp words were also spoken when Pery's motion to consider a place bill requiring members accepting pensions or offices of profit under the crown to vacate their seats and stand for reelection was rejected 85 to 59.

Alarmed at these indications of a rising storm, Conway prevailed

93. Devonshire to Fox, April 13, 1756. SP63/414/14B.
94. Clark, *op. cit.*, 282.   95. HMC Emly, 181.

upon his new friends in the house of commons to put extravagant praises into the customary address thanking the lord lieutenant for his administration of the country. However, wiser counsels prevailed and some of the more fulsome expressions were excised before the address was presented. Even with such changes, one member spoke bitterly against the address and "expressed himself against the Lord Lieutenant."[96] In the Irish house of commons, such liberties with the character of lords lieutenants were rarely ever taken. Moreover, the affront was allowed to pass without rebuke or censure. The lord lieutenant thought ending the session to be the better course, which he did on May 8, 1756. Anxious to reach London before the English parliament rose, Devonshire left for Parkgate on the following day.[97]

Soon after the lord lieutenant left Ireland, the primate began a series of letters to friends in England explaining how patiently his present disgrace had been born and how condescending the Ponsonbys had become. During the past session Stone had kept his word completely about serving the government as best and in whatever capacity he could.[98] Even if the Duke of Dorset had been lord lieutenant, Stone claimed, more could not have been done. It was a fact, however, that Devonshire had kept him at a distance, exhibiting minimal courtesy and no confidence. When the settlement with Boyle became public and when Ponsonby's succession had taken place, Stone assumed that his persecution would cease. It did not. A condition of support for the new speaker from opponents of the previous government was that Ponsonby should have no sort of communication in business with the primate. Stone believed that in the general pacification following Pononsby's succession only he was excluded.[99]

Lord Duncannon told Stone to his face that his banishment from public affairs had been absolutely commanded by the king before Devonshire had left England. Stone may have been pushed aside, but he did not perceive himself as being defeated or driven out of Irish politics. Before Devonshire reached London, the primate had

96. *Idem.*
97. Lords Justices to Fox, May 11, 1756. SP63/414/195.
98. HMC Stopford-Sackville, I, 239.
99. *Idem.*

resolved to go to England, meet with Sackville, and perhaps discuss a range of public questions with some of his lordship's new political friends—George Townshend, Henry Bilson Legge, and William Pitt.

Though Devonshire's settlement of Irish affairs in 1756 fell far short of being the kind of permanent system for governing Ireland the duke had hoped to obtain, it was an important event in Irish political history. The settlement was important because of the political attitudes and developments it encouraged. First, as Lord Charlemont suggested in memoirs written thirty years after the event, Devonshire's bargain with Boyle demonstrated to Irish politicians that the Irish government could be opposed with success. After all, the lord lieutenant had agreed to put aside the doctrine of previous consent, and the dismissed gentlemen were restored or compensated. What had happened once could happen again.

Second, this settlement established the Ponsonby family as a major political force in Irish politics. Indeed, the fourth Duke of Devonshire as lord lieutenant in 1756 only completed a process his father, the third Duke, had begun in 1739. The Cavendish connection and paternal guidance carried John Ponsonby to an eminence in Irish politics that natural ability alone could never have effected. Nonetheless, John Ponsonby wielded a political power in Ireland after 1756 that no future lord lieutenant dared discount and a few strove to break.

Third, by raising up the Ponsonbys to a position of relative parity with the Boyle party, the Kildare connection, and Stone's group, Devonshire established the very balance among Irish parties that he had wanted so desperately to upset. Moreover, after 1756 the idea of employing party leaders as undertakers proposed by Lord Midleton and Thomas Carter to Lord Carteret as long ago as 1725 and rejected by him at that time became practical. Devonshire's successors had to face not one dominant party or even two closely balanced ones in the Irish house of commons; they were forced to seek parliamentary support from changing combinations of groups with ever-escalating patronage demands. In the years ahead, wartime pressures or simple convenience require that such demands be met.

Fourth, Devonshire's settlement encouraged the involvement of prominent English politicians in Irish affairs. Not since Queen Anne's time were Irish political leaders so closely connected with principals in the government of England. Fox was both advocate and adviser to his brother-in-law, Kildare. At times, Stone's relationships with Newcastle and Pitt was similar. The ties between the Ponsonbys and the Devonshire interest were close and strong. Consequently, in the years after 1756 there were periods when Irish parliamentary leaders had representation in English ministerial circles which rivaled that of some of the serving lords lieutenants. There were also times in the future when Irish trumps were played in English politics for English reasons by those who held them. After Devonshire's settlement, politicians in the two countries tended to interact in ways that had not been usual before 1756. Persons and groups in Ireland identified with persons and groups in England, correspondence was regularly maintained, and on occasions careers were advanced and partisan interests on both sides of the Irish sea were served.

Fifth, Devonshire's settlement also provided English ministers with an object lesson and an enduring perception of the nature of eighteenth-century Irish Protestant patriotism. Boyle had been a patriot and became a courier because it suited the interests of himself and his friends to do so. Boyle's example was a powerful inspiration to a generation of ambitious aspiring politicians. Moreover, in the years ahead many English ministers perceived the advocacy and agitation of patriot causes in the Irish house of commons as little more than calculated rhetoric. Agitation of constitutional issues in Ireland simply lacked high credibility at Westminster. Ministers had to be persuaded that opposition in Ireland could not be quieted with a place, a pension, or a peerage. This too-easy assumption was perhaps the most pernicious and enduring consequence of Devonshire's settlement.

CHAPTER VI

War and the Transformation of Irish Parliamentary Politics, 1757-1758

The Duke of Bedford Takes Charge

When Devonshire reached Westminster in mid-May great events were underway. In the house of commons, Pitt's attacks upon Newcastle's proscrastination intensified with every new report of bad news from America or the Mediterranean. Admiral Byng's desertion of the Minorca garrison in late May and the subsequent surrender of that island to the French at the end of June made ministerial changes inevitable at Westminster. After furious and complicated negotiations, Newcastle resigned and Pitt entered the ministry as a secretary of state with Devonshire as the nominal head of the government as first lord of the treasury. Devonshire had agreed to serve with Pitt as a patriotic duty. He saw himself as the only protection for the king from complete domination by Pitt and his friends. One of the first tasks of the new government was to find a new chief governor for Ireland.

Pitt had no one specifically in mind for Ireland, and rumors circulated throughout Dublin that the new lord Lieutenant would be Pitt's relative, Lord Temple.[1] However, Devonshire did have someone in mind. As soon as the principals in the new government had been chosen, Devonshire approached the Duke of Bedford about going to Ireland. Bedford was friendly but noncommittal. After repeated solicitations, John Russell, fourth Duke of Bedford, obliged Devonshire and accepted the post. He was appointed on

---

1. Waite to Wilmot, November 9, 1756. Wilmot Mss., T.3019/6782/479.

January 3, 1757, and immediately chose a longtime friend and political ally, Richard Rigby, to be chief secretary.

Bedford was forty-six years old in 1757 and had taken office for the first time in Pelham's administration as first lord of admiralty in late 1744. He had succeeded Chesterfield as a secretary of state in 1748, but he had never gotten along with Newcastle and was disliked by George II. Bedford was perceived by contemporaries as a proud, over-assured man of strong temper, devoted to his friends and frequently ruled by them.

Richard Rigby was the duke's choice for chief secretary. A grandson of a prosperous London linen draper who had obtained property in Essex once held by the Earls of Oxford, Rigby made politics his calling and became one of the most celebrated placemen and wire-pullers of his day. He was a good speaker, possessed a quick mind, and made friends easily. After Sackville, Rigby was one of the most able chief secretaries of the century. He was also a posturer, a garish dresser, and by any standards a confirmed alcoholic. It was said that Rigby used brandy as the rest of the world used small beer; he described himself as "a good four-bottle man."[2] Untroubled by principles, Rigby was also generally untouched by prejudices. One of the most unusual characteristics of both Rigby and his patron was disdain of religious persecution and a strong disposition to consider the practicality of some degree of legal toleration for Irish Catholics.

Given the personalities and character of Bedford and Rigby and their attitudes toward persecution and toleration, plus the facts that harvests in England and Ireland in 1756 had been very thin and the war was going badly, the probability of a tranquil and easy session of the Irish parliament at its next sitting was not high. Whatever the future might be, business in Ireland had to go on. Among the first decisions that Bedford had to make was selection of new lord chancellor for Ireland. Lord Jocelyn had died in December 1756 and a choice of a successor from among sitting judges in Ireland proved to be noncontroversial. The qualification of English birth for this office virtually limited the appointment to John Bowes, Chief Baron of the Exchequer. Moreover, Bowes had received some promises from Devonshire, and Bedford assured the chief baron

2. Russell Bedford Correspondence, II, 257.

The Right Hon.ble RICHARD RIGBY, Esqr.

Richard Rigby, Esq. Courtesy of A. P. W. Malcomson

that those promises would be honored. Bowes was appointed in early 1757 and assumed the position of speaker of the house of lords when parliament convened in October, but he did not receive a peerage until the summer of 1758.

Because Bedford and Rigby did not set out for Ireland until September 1757, Devonshire and Pitt found themselves dependent on the lords justices for action and support. Additional troops were needed in America, and Ireland turned out to be the principal source from whence they could come. Six regiments on the Irish establishments were chosen for American service in early January. Pitt ordered that these regiments be recruited up to full strength immediately. For reasons of both inability and infirmity, many of the officers in these regiments were unfit for overseas service. The lords justices transmitted dozens of memorials and recommendations about who should go and who should not.[3] Marching orders for Cork and Kinsale were issued to the designated regiments on January 28, 1757, and twelve ships of the line under the command of Admiral Francis Holburne were ordered to rendezvous with transports at Cork for a February embarkation.

With the business of the embarkation underway, Bedford and Rigby had to turn their attention to a problem of serious food shortages in the north of Ireland. The summer of 1756 had been one of the wettest in memory throughout the British Isles. Large quantities of grain had been ruined by wind and rain and most of what remained was defective in both quantity and quality. Food prices soared, and there were extensive food riots in different parts of England throughout the fall and winter of 1756. In Ireland, the situation was aggravated by an intense frost during the winter of 1756–57. Food shortages were acute in the north, especially in Belfast and Londonderry, and according to reports received by Rigby, "famine is almost at their door."[4] Bedford obtained from the king a promise of funds for a corn importation bounty in February and, despite confusion about the legality of this commitment, he proceeded to act on his own in order to get supplies of barley and oats shipped into the north of Ireland. Bedford spent more than

3. Russell Bedford Correspondence, II, 228.
4. Ibid., 232.

£5,000 of his own money to bring supplies of food to Belfast and Londonderry during the winter.[5] The situation continued serious throughout the country during spring and summer. In June and July, cargoes of grain were shipped to Newry, Dublin, and Waterford as well as Londonderry and Belfast. The shortages and near-famine conditions in Ireland during 1757 provided the inspiration and motivations for the enactment of legislation by the Irish parliament in 1758 to encourage grain production in rural Ireland by paying bounties on the transport of grain grown in inland counties to Dublin.

While trying to facilitate the embarkation at Cork and relieve food shortages in the north of Ireland from Woburn Abbey and Leicester Fields, Bedford and Rigby had to devote much of their time to English politics. In February, Lord Temple, Pitt's brother-in-law and recently installed First Lord of the Admiralty, had a terrible scene with the king over a pardon for Admiral Byng, presently awaiting execution under sentence by court-martial for his conduct at Minorca. Byng went to his death bravely before a firing party on the quarterdeck of his former flagship *Monarque* at Portsmouth. Within a fortnight of this unforgettable event, the king sent dismissal notices to both Temple and Pitt.

Henry Legge, George and James Grenville, and a few others resigned after the dismissals; and Devonshire, Holdernesse, Mansfield, and a caretaker administration managed the affairs of the country until a new ministry could be chosen. Thereupon followed three months of complicated and protracted negotiations among English political leaders that was extraordinary by both English and Irish standards. There were clandestine conferences, letters written to be read and then burned, accusations of broken understandings, and disputes between faction leaders and followers. At the center of these intrigues was Archbishop George Stone, working to bring Newcastle and Pitt together.

In the end, Newcastle and Pitt were brought together. Newcastle explained the situation clearly and succinctly in a memorandum sent to the king on June 6.[6] "I cannot come in without bringing my enemy, Mr. Pitt," wrote Newcastle. "[H]e turned me out, but I can't

5. *Ibid.*, 248.   6. Ayling, *op. cit.*, 206–207.

serve without my enemy." The truth was that Newcastle had been persuaded, in large part by Archbishop Stone, that an administration with Pitt in it was what the whole nation called for and the only one that could give the king public tranquility and domestic happiness.[7] On June 18, Hardwicke brought the king a list of ministers upon which all the principals had agreed.

Stone's role during the interministerium negotiations was carefully observed by Lady Kildare and duly reported to her husband. Living in London from mid-May to late July, the countess informed the earl in mid-May that "[o]ur Primate has it seems done a great deal of mischief; he and Pitt are hand in glove."[8] The primate was "the person that cabals between Pitt and the Duke of Newcastle, and has brought them well together."[9] In the process of so doing, Lady Kildare insisted, Stone had "undone himself with the Duke of Bedford. This outcome was, she added, "a good thing for us; for by what I find he was before this extremely well with them."[10] Even more important in Lady Kildare's view was the fact that the king himself now clearly saw Stone for what he was. His majesty was very angry over the primate's role in bringing Pitt and Newcastle together and described Stone as a meddling fellow properly detested by all who had been obliged to endure him. One could not help being glad of the king's new awareness of Stone's true character, concluded Lady Kildare, "though it would not hinder his being put in the Government tomorrow if the Ministry settled it so."[11]

The intrigues of late May and early June fascinated Lady Kildare, and she tried to keep her husband apprised of what the politicians were doing and what informed people were saying. From her point of view, political affairs were all changed. The Duke of Bedford had left London vexed and angry. Lady Kildare feared that his grace would give up Ireland; and if that happened, she wrote to her husband, "we are undone too, for the Primate is all powerful with these people."[12] However, Bedford's anger quickly abated, and

7. Basil Williams, *The Life of William Pitt, Earl of Chatham* (Longmans, Green, and Co., New York, 1913), Vol. 1, 321.
8. Fitzgerald Correspondence, I, 33.
9. *Ibid.*, 34.   10. *Ibid.*, 35.
11. *Ibid.*, 36.   12. *Ibid.*, 47.

for the sake of the king and of several of his friends the duke agreed to serve with Pitt. Neither Bedford nor Rigby expected that Pitt would be an amiable colleague—Rigby referred to him frequently as "our impenetrable minister"—but when asked to stay in office they accepted and made preparations for a September departure. Lady Kildare was much relieved that Bedford had decided to go to Ireland. "I am sure you will agree with me in rejoicing that the Duke of Bedford certainly comes to us," she wrote, "for at this time there is really none but himself that wou'd not be extremely disagreeable to us."[13]

Lady Kildare's anxieties were finally put to rest at the end of June when all of the appointments to the new ministry were made public. Pitt returned to his old office of secretary of state for the southern department and Newcastle went back to the treasury. Devonshire became lord chamberlain. As events were to show, this ministry was to be a great war ministry. It was broadly based and virtually all of the English factions and parties were represented, but Pitt was clearly in charge. However, unlike the previous ministry wherein Pitt had been also clearly in charge, now, with Newcastle's obedient majority behind him, he had an excellent prospect of remaining in charge long enough to make a difference in the way the war was being waged.

With political affairs settled in England, Bedford and Rigby could now give full attention to Ireland. One of the first issues directed to them was Lord Clanbrassil's proposed revival of the old registration system for Irish Catholic parish priests. In a letter written to Bedford on July 17, 1757, Clanbrassil described the history of his bill in the Irish house of lords during the previous session[14] and repeated the arguments that he had made at that time.[15] The earl explained that he now had in hand a new version of the bill that had been so narrowly defeated in last session. This new version had been altered in a few points to meet past objections; and knowing Bedford's views on toleration, the earl took this opportunity to present a copy of it to his grace so he could consider it thoroughly

13. *Ibid.*, 50.
14. Russell Bedford Correspondence, II, 265.
15. *Ibid.*, 263–264.

before the session began. Clanbrassil concluded by urging the duke to throw his support behind a measure long overdue.[16]

Bedford read Clanbrassil's letter very carefully and responded in a generally favorable way to the earl in early August. The duke pointed out that his sentiments with regard to persecution and toleration corresponded exactly with those of Clanbrassil. Any measure consistent with the laws of religion and humanity that had the effect of making the papists of Ireland good subjects of the king and useful members of the commonwealth deserved serious consideration. He had some doubts whether the priests could in conscience take the oaths prescribed in Clanbrassil's bill but assured him that these doubts should not be construed as opposition to the bill. He entirely approved the spirit of this measure, but could say no more until the king had an opportunity to consider it.[17] Clanbrassil was much encouraged by Bedford's response and was strengthened in his determination to proceed.

Of even more immediate concern to Bedford than some sort of rapprochement with Catholic parish priests in Ireland was his stance toward the country's political factions and parties. Bedford sought advice about Irish politics from his friends in England; and according to Lady Kildare, the duke had two different strategies recommended to him. The first, coming most likely from Devonshire or Lord Hillsborough, was to determine which of the three principal active parties—Bessborough's, Kildare's, or the primate's—was strongest and then govern through it while trying to reconcile one of the other two to it as a form of insurance. The other strategy, most persistently advocated by Rigby, was to keep good relations with them all and not become dependent on any one party.[18] Bedford himself preferred the latter but found himself increasingly driven by friends and events toward the former.

Of the same mind as Devonshire, neither Bedford nor Rigby trusted the primate. They simply could not believe that Stone would not direct Ponsonby and stir up an opposition in the next session. Unlike Devonshire, however, they had no confidence in Ponsonby.

16. *Ibid.*, 265.   17. *Ibid.*, 266–267.
18. Fitzgerald Correspondence, I, 35.

Lady Kildare described the new speaker as being reputed in England "in still more insignificant a light than in Ireland." Ponsonby was, she wrote, thought of here as "a mighty dull, as well as a very empty foolish fellow,"[19] but one that the new chief governors would have to deal with. Devonshire had been very busy frightening both Bedford and Rigby about the primate and arguing the necessity of making friends with the Ponsonbys.[20] For his part, Stone appears to have had minimal contact with the new lord lieutenant. By mid-June, the primate had returned to Dublin, made some pronouncements about withdrawing from politics that few Irish politicians believed, and then retired to Leixslip for the summer.[21]

During the summer the education of Bedford and Rigby into Irish affairs proceeded. They learned that one of the great voices in the Irish house of commons had been muted if not stilled. Thomas Carter had been struck by palsy with attendant losses of speech and mobility.[22] He appeared near death in the summer of 1757 but, much to the chagrin of Lady Kildare, who coveted his employment for her husband,[23] Carter recovered sufficiently to remain in parliament and enjoy that employment for six more years. The chief secretary had an unforgettable visit from a Mrs. Humphry, the housekeeper at Dublin Castle for the past twenty years. This "termagant brimstone" spent an entire morning with Rigby, abusing past lords lieutenants for nonpayment for services and making demands for a personal apartment in the Castle sufficient to her station.[24] Rigby managed to divert Mrs. Humphry from an intended descent upon Bedford at Woburn Abbey, and Bedford was able to complete travel preparations uninterrupted by her.

When Bedford traveled to Holyhead in mid-September, he was supremely confident of his own ability to succeed in an office where so many had failed. The Admiralty provided a suitable convoy for the crossing, and Bedford arrived in Dublin on September 25, whereupon he proceeded directly to the Castle to be sworn and to begin preparations for the opening of the Irish parliament a fortnight hence.

19. *Ibid.*, 36.   20. *Ibid.*, 57.
21. Bowes to Wilmot, June 14, 1757. Wilmot Mss., T. 3019/6761/570.
22. *Idem.*   23. Fitzgerald Correspondence, I, 60.
24. Russell Bedford Correspondence, II, 262.

Primate Stone's Most Unusual Proposition

Bedford and Rigby held meetings with officials and prominent politicians and were told that the primate still talked about withdrawing from politics, Ponsonby and his friends intended to support the new administration, and a general political calm prevailed throughout the country. However, there were rumors about a stir being made in the house of commons about pensions granted during and after the last session and that Ponsonby's hold on the speaker's chair might be challenged.[25]

The principal source of this stir and uneasiness appeared to be located among some of Lord Shannon's unforgiving and unrequited friends. In part, to appeal to what remained of the old Boyle party, and in accord with his declared policy of distributing government favors impartially, Bedford recommended Malone for the Irish privy council.[26] This recommendation pleased Malone and perhaps Shannon but not many others. Malone was still much abused by his former friends for the salary rise Devonshire had obtained before leaving the treasury, and Stone's friends interpreted this appointment as signifying a role of first minister for Malone in the new Irish government. Rigby repeatedly assured these former courtiers that nothing of the sort was intended and that a just share of patronage and favors would come their way. The chief secretary tried to quiet all parties by urging patience and insisting that the duke was not disposed to trample on anyone.[27] Thus matters stood when the session began on October 11.

However, the first shock to the Bedford administration came not from the College Green but from Newcastle. On behalf of the king, Newcastle sought Bedford's views on the possibility of charging a pension of £6,000 a year for his daughter, Mary, Princess of Hesse, and her children, to the Irish establishment for the life of the princess and for her children until any of them succeeded to the Landgravate of Hesse Cassel. The Landgrave of Hesse Cassel had been driven from his own country by the French, and the princess had appealed to George II for protection and support during their present distressed situation.

25. Waite to Wilmot, September 18, 1757. Wilmot Mss., T.19/6761/582.
26. Bedford to Holdernesse, October 1, 1757. SP63/415/59.
27. Rigby to Wilmot, September 29, 1757. Wilmot Mss., T. 3019/6761/584–585.

Bedford responded quickly and forthrightly. He described the state of the pension list and of the civil establishment from 1727 to the present. The pension list had increased by more than £7,000 since that year and the whole civil establishment by almost £12,000. The lord lieutenant asserted that once his majesty considered all of the facts of the present state of Ireland, he would be the best judge of how well this country could stand an additional burden of £6,000. Bedford wondered whether the parliament of Great Britain might not be prevailed upon to grant such a sum to the princess on the grounds that their distressed situation was a direct consequence of the Landgrave's alliance with England.

On the wisdom and propriety of this pension Bedford had given his opinion and now he awaited orders about what to do. Yet, before those orders arrived, events took charge. As rumored before the season began, several gentlemen in the house of commons proceeded to speak at length about the pensions and salary increases granted during the last two years. The duke found himself in a very difficult position. Not only did he feel obliged to defend Devonshire's conduct with respect to pensions and salary increases, but he also had to respond to severe parliamentary criticism of the Irish pension list knowing full well his majesty's intention to add substantially to it and the deep personal reasons why he wanted to do so. However, on the eve of the opening of the session, such difficulties were in the future and entirely unanticipated.

In general the opening went well. The duke's speech was well received. In the house of commons, the only untoward behavior was some hostile observations by Robert French, member for Galway, about the peremptory manner in which the last session had been ended.[28] For his part, Bedford tried very hard to maintain his policy of impartiality. After recommending Malone for the privy council, the lord lieutenant gave a deanery and a place on the linen board to friends of Ponsonby. In the case of the latter appointment, the recipient, a Mr. Stratford, gave Rigby a solemn and unsolicited honor-bound promise that he would forever support his grace's administration in all things.[29] No wonder then with all of the feast-

---

28. Rigby to Wilmot, October 11, 1757. Wilmot Mss., T.3019/6761/586.
29. Rigby to Wilmot, November 22, 1757. Wilmot Mss., T.3019/6761/5B8.

ing, drinking, and good fellowship that accompanied the opening of the session the lord lieutenant and chief secretary were surprised by what happened in the house of commons on November 1.

On that day John Bourke, put on the revenue board by Lord Harrington in 1747 as favor to Boyle, reported that the committee appointed to inspect the public accounts had directed him to introduce several resolutions of utmost importance to the country. The committee had resolved that annual pensions and salary changes added to the civil establishment since March 1755 amounted to £28,000, that several of these pensions had been awarded to persons who did not reside in Ireland, that several of these pension were granted for long and unusual terms, and that an improvident disposition of the revenue was an injury to the crown and to the public.[30] When discussion of Bourke's report ended, the full house resolved *nemine contradicente* that the granting of pensions to nonresidents of Ireland was a prejudice to the country, the increase of pensions was a national grievance that demanded redress, and alienation of so much of the public revenue in pensions for long periods of time injured the crown and the kingdom and was detrimental to the public. In addition, the members present ended the proceedings for the day by resolving unanimously that the house with its speaker attend the lord lieutenant with these resolutions and desire him to present them to the king as the sense of this body. Rigby tried to respond but was called to order by the whole house.[31] When Bedford learned what had transpired in the house, he became angry and very determined to disassociate himself completely from the resolutions, which he perceived as being outrageous and founded on serious arithmetical miscalculations.[32] With this end in mind, the duke summoned the principal servants of the crown to a meeting at the Castle on November 6 and received another surprise.

Bedford told his ministers that the resolutions appeared to him to be so derogatory to his majesty's prerogative and so indecently expressed that he could not think of returning the usual promise of transmitting them to the king without expressing some negative.

30. Martis I Die, November, 1757. SP63/415/113.
31. Martis I Die, November, 1757. Sp63/415/114; Rigby to Wilmot, November 18, 1757. Wilmot Mss., T.3019/6782/509.
32. Russell Bedford Correspondence, II, 299.

He wanted advice about the most appropriate strategy to pursue when the resolutions were presented to him, and he got admonitions to comply with the desires of the house of commons. Ponsonby's remarks on this occasion were most unusual. The speaker expressed personal disapproval of the resolutions, denied any knowledge of them until reported from the committee, and disavowed any political connection with the primate.[33] Up to this point, Bedford had not attributed any role to Stone in what had happened in the house of commons. For the moment, Bedford let Ponsonby's remarks pass and returned to the subject at hand. The duke insisted that as a servant of the king he was obliged to register some form of dissent to these resolutions.

In the end, on Saturday, November 12, Bedford adopted what he believed was the very gentle tactic of receiving the resolutions from the house but expressing his disapprobation of them. What the duke perceived as a moderate gesture was interpreted by the house as something quite different. Members were outraged. The leadership of the house refused to enter the lord lieutenant's answer in their journals, and several prominent members threatened to stop all consideration of the money bills until the resolutions were transmitted as desired. By the end of the day, Bedford knew that he was confronted by a major parliamentary crisis.[34]

In a letter written in the evening of November 12, the duke complained that the violence and intensity of party animosities in Ireland had so divided the king's principal servants that little dependence could be placed on them. He asked for trust and support from the English ministers; specifically, he wanted authority to dispense rewards and punishments in a manner that would enable him to get a dependable majority in the Irish house of commons.

On Sunday, November 13, the lord lieutenant summoned to the Castle those crown officers whose steadiness on the matter of the resolutions he had reason to doubt. He was most concerned over the possible defection of speaker, John Ponsonby; the solicitor general, Philip Tisdale; the attorney general, Warden Flood; and the postmaster general, Sir Thomas Prendergast. The lord lieutenant put

33. *Ibid.*, 289n.   34. *Ibid.*, 286.

to each of these gentlemen three questions, to which he tried to get yes or no answers. Bedford wanted to know whether each of these crown office-holders would support or oppose an adjournment motion to delay action on the money bills, whether each would use all of his influence to get a money bill transmitted to England in time to get it approved and returned before the present one expired, and whether each believed that stopping the money bills or otherwise disrupting the king's business was a proper way of proceeding against a lord lieutenant whom he believed had done wrong. As one might expect, the duke did not get the yes or no answers that he sought. However, by the time the meeting had ended, Bedford knew that Ponsonby and Tisdale would not go on with the money bills until an absolute promise to transmit the resolutions had been given, that Prendergast would support an adjournment for a short period, and that Warden Flood stated his intention to oppose any such adjournment motion.[35] For his part, Bedford assured each of these gentlemen that on the next day, Monday, November 14, he would send an answer to the house with a promise to transmit the resolutions.[36]

However, after reflecting upon the events of the last few days on Sunday evening, the lord lieutenant claims to have decided against sending any sort of message to the house of commons on Monday. His reasons for breaking the assurances given at the Sunday meeting are unclear. Bedford may just not have made up his mind what to do or he may have been hopeful that some instructions would arrive from England. In any case, the reasons stated to Pitt in a letter dated November 17 were that in view of all that had happened in the house when his last message had been delivered to the house on November 12, he wanted to give members time to cool, and that allowing the money bills to come in as scheduled on Monday, November 14, would be the best way to persuade those who wished well to the government to demonstrate their good intentions. The lord lieutenant explained also that only by a division in the house on postponing the money bills would he know for certain which gentlemen could be trusted in any future exigency.[37] On Monday,

35. *Ibid.*, 288.   36. *Ibid.*, 290.
37. *Idem.*

Bedford let events take charge and the results were embarrassing. On a motion to postpone consideration of the money bill, eighty-five members divided for postponement and only sixty-four voted for proceeding. Losing the question by a majority of twenty-one votes was for Bedford and Rigby an object lesson in Irish politics that they would not forget. Moreover, wanting no more such lessons the lord lieutenant and chief secretary reluctantly decided that some sort of compliance was their only practical course.

Bedford and Rigby had been surprised and were angered by their defeat, but they did not panic. They met at the Castle on Tuesday morning with the leaders of the minority that had supported them in order to prepare a proper message for delivery to the house in the afternoon. Bedford was told directly that the slightest suggestion of disapproval of the resolution in the message would prejudice the money bills. Finally, the duke capitulated completely. On Tuesday afternoon in the house, Rigby delivered a simple message from the lord lieutenant that the resolutions would be transmitted to the king.

The house responded to Bedford's message by taking up the money bills and completing all discussion of them in two days. After the money bills had been approved, he enumerated for Pitt in several long letters the revenue officers, army officers, office-holders, and pensioners in the house who had voted for postponing the money bills. Among this group was the same Stratford, Ponsonby's friend, who had promised never to vote against Bedford's government, and several close friends of the primate. The state of parties in the house was so evenly balanced that a small group of gentlemen headed by Pery and French could disrupt proceedings and bring government to a standstill by joining whichever of the two predominant parties happened to be discontented. Though Pery and French had been courtiers in Dorset's time, Bedford described them as "determined against all government, in whatever hands it may be placed."[38] In Bedford's judgment, the situation in the house of commons was so bad that he could not continue in office if he were not authorized to quell the spirit of faction. As lord lieutenant, the

38. Russell Correspondence, II, 292; Rigby to Wilmot, November 22, 1757. Wilmot Mss., T.3019/6761/588.

duke had tried to remain independent of the factions; now he wanted authority to break them.

Bedford insisted that neither ambition or thirst for power induced him to seek the authority requested, only a thorough persuasion that he could not do his duty otherwise prompted him to seek it. The present parliament had sat for so long. The country had been visited by so many different chief governors since 1727 and had endured such dissonant plans of policy, Bedford declared, that it can be readily understood why such violent parties and factions presently exist in Ireland. Threats made daily about attacking the prerogative by attempting an alteration of Poyning's law should be taken seriously.[39]

Rigby's analysis of recent events was at once simpler and more optimistic than that of Bedford. According to the chief secretary, reports of the primate's retirement to Leixslip and Ponsonby's intention to support the government were false intelligence. "The mask is now thrown off, and they are avowedly one," Rigby wrote, and old Bessborough had come up from the country from where he had assured the duke he would never stir to be a party to their treaty.[40] Whatever they do, he concluded, we are not intimated. Whether or not Rigby appreciated the irony in the present situation is uncertain, but ironic it truly was. George Stone, Archbishop of Armagh, sometime lord justice, influential advisor to the Duke of Newcastle, friend of Pitt, and often styled by himself and by political opponents as the head of the English interest in Ireland, was now leagued against his majesty's governors. If Rigby thought about this remarkable circumstance, he most likely would have explained it with observations about the durability of political principles and their well-known extraordinary fragility in Ireland.

The chief secretary admired good work, and he had a deep appreciation of the primate's ability to influence the Irish parliament. Rigby respected Stone for what the man was able to do, whereas he found Ponsonby uninteresting and ineffective. For others in the house of commons, the chief secretary had undisguised contempt. In Rigby's judgment, the behavior of some gentlemen

39. Russell Correspondence, II, 296–297.
40. Rigby to Wilmot, November 24, 1757. Wilmot Mss., T.3019/6761/591.

had become bizarre, and he did not mince words when describing it. He told friends in England that he lived in a world populated by blockheads and spent far too much time on trivialities. The chief secretary cited one example when he and the lord lieutenant spent more than five hours in a privy council meeting hearing arguments about the selection of a sheriff at Carrickfeargus. The parties at the meeting had become deadlocked and the lord lieutenant had to decide.[41] "If I had any feeling for the honor and credit of the Irish parliament," Rigby concluded, "I should be ashamed to write of such utterly ridiculous stuff."[42]

Pitt's first reaction to Bedford's difficulties with the Irish parliament was a temperate one. First, Pitt assured the duke in the most extravagant terms of his majesty's countenance and support so long as Bedford remained chief governor of Ireland. Next, he suggested that the present majority in the house of commons was the product of widespread apprehension that the privileges of parliament were being attacked, implying that the majority would vanish as this apprehension diminished. Furthermore, the balance of parties and the irresponsible behavior of the small group styled by Bedford as "determined against all government," Pitt contended, virtually dictated a conciliatory policy—"all softening and healing arts of government consistent with its dignity and as far as maybe practical." Pitt did not specifically deny Bedford the authority to punish and reward as he saw fit, but strongly urged him to try to recoup the strength of the Irish government by "allaying and compromising animosities."[43]

The duke had serious doubts about the practicality of the conciliation policy recommended by Pitt, but believing himself for the moment at least secure in London, he and Rigby agreed to give it a fair trial. However, a fair trial did not prove to be easy. The only conciliation strategy which seemed workable at the time was to try to bring together the Kildares and the Ponsonbys. After several meetings and discussions with friends of the principals, Bedford confessed to Pitt that there was little reason to expect success.[44]

41. Rigby to Wilmot, November 24, 1757. Wilmot Mss., T.3019/6761/591.
42. Rigby to Wilmot, November 29, 1757. Wilmot Mss., T.3019/6761/595.
43. Pitt to Bedford, November 26, 1757. SP63/415/122–127.
44. *Ibid.*, 311.

One of the reasons for his pessimism was the widespread report so industriously circulated throughout Dublin by the primate's friends that Bedford's last dispatches from England had tied his hands from taking whatever measures might be required to bring the king's Irish servants back to a proper sense of duty. The duke complained about the shameful misrepresentations of designing men in Ireland abetted by a very considerable person in England. He could be of no service to the king in Ireland if secret dispatches from the English ministry to him were not secure and inviolate. Bedford entreated Pitt not to send the contents of any secret letters to anyone in Ireland except himself, and positively asserted that the same messenger who had brought the recent dispatches to the Castle also carried a letter to the primate that was the source of the misinformation. The duke specifically accused Sir Thomas Prendergast, Postmaster General, of propagating these unfounded rumors about the city. In Bedford's mind, this latest incident only confirmed what he had been urging since the vote on postponing the money bills. In the present factious and unsettled state of Irish politics, no lord lieutenant could govern Ireland without "that power which can alone enable him to make that reformation, as well in men as in things, which appears to be absolutely necessary at present."[45]

From whatever causes, contention continued after the money bills were approved and transmitted. On November 29, French and Pery served notice that they intended to attack the power of the Irish privy council and requested an account of all bills approved by the Irish house of commons during the last session that had not been transmitted by the Irish privy council to England. The house obliged by approving production of this account and by agreeing to listen to French and Pery deal with the intricacies of Poyning's law.

At first, in early December, Pery seemed determined to begin proceedings that would lead to repeal of Poyning's law. When that effort was stopped by a vote of 127 to 38,[46] he moderated his tone and adopted a different strategy. In mid-December, Pery sought leave to introduce a bill that would touch nothing "whatsoever in

45. *Ibid.*, 313–314.
46. Rigby to Wilmot, December 5, 1757. Wilmot Mss., T.3019/6761/590.

the material part of Poyning's Act which related to Great Britain."[47] What needed reform was the Irish privy council, not the privy council in England. In Pery's mind, the assumption of altering and suppressive authority by the Irish privy council had no basis in law and sometime or other would have to be given up.[48] That time, however, was not to be now. Rigby reported that on December 12, 1757, the house denied Pery leave to bring in this bill by a vote of 102 to 75.[49]

Having disposed of one attack on the Irish privy council, the lord lieutenant and chief secretary had to decide how to react to another on the management of the Irish revenue. On December 5, 1757, Sir Archibald Acheson moved for the appointment of a secret committee to inquire into the state of Irish revenue during the past twenty years. This motion, offered by a longtime friend of Lords Shannon and Kildare, was directed against the primate and Ponsonby. After some soul-searching, Bedford and Rigby decided to go along with it. As a matter of fact, both Rigby and Pery acted as tellers for the majority when the motion carried 98 to 60. The primate and the speaker were shocked by the chief secretary's behavior and put out the report that he and Bedford had joined Kildare's party. Rigby explained in the house that nothing of the sort had happened. If public benefit arose from this inquiry, Rigby stated, he would play a role in it. However, if the proceedings of this committee appeared to be one party running at another, he promised to withdraw. After the motion had passed both the primate and the speaker stopped coming to the Castle.[50]

Whatever anxiety Stone and Ponsonby may have had over the inquiry must have dissipated quickly after the balloting for the secret committee was over. Virtually everyone in the house wanted a place on the committee; and according to Rigby, the friends of Stone and Ponsonby succeeded in winning most of them. The results were bruited as a triumph over Kildare. The chief secretary was not pleased with the final choices, but thought them much better than the gentlemen supported by Kildare. The earl's friends

47. HMC Emly, 182.   48. *Idem.*
49. Rigby to Wilmot, December 13, 1757. Wilmot Mss., T.3019/6761/601–602.
50. Rigby to Wilmot, December 5, 1757. Wilmot Mss., T.3014/6761/590.

were so impractical, Rigby observed, "that they would have hanged all of the commissioners" had they been in the majority.[51] Despite the outcome of the balloting, the revenue commissioners were fearful of the inquiry and several of them, including Ponsonby, requested an audience with the duke to discuss their situation. All lamented having earned Bedford's displeasure and complained bitterly about Rigby's role in the inquiry. The duke responded with strong approval of his chief secretary's conduct and concluded by assuring the commissioners that he would not interfere in the inquiry one way or the other.[52]

On the matter of noninterference Bedford could be absolutely truthful because he had virtually no influence over the committee. The primate's friends had come to dominate the proceedings so completely that it ceased to be a threat to anyone. As early as December 18, Rigby admitted as much. After noting the inquiry was moving ever so slowly, the chief secretary observed, "nor will it nor is it intended to come to anything."[53] In Rigby's mind the pointless activity of the secret committee was being replicated by the house of commons in all of its activities as the Christmas recess approached. He complained often about working in the house until six or seven o'clock every night "on one nonsensical resolution after another and suffering abuse from all parties."[54] Even more discouraging was the prospect that this distressing state of affairs would continue after the recess.

Bedford was extremely candid when he wrote to Pitt during the recess about the present state of Irish politics. The simple facts of the situation were that the lord lieutenant could scarcely count twenty certain votes in the house of commons. Party and faction had proceeded so far that not even the principal servants of the crown in that body were dependable. The duke admitted an absolute inability to prevent the combined parties of Stone and Ponsonby from doing almost whatever they pleased when parliament reopened. These two parties had joined hands "to distress govern-

51. Rigby to Wilmot, December 10, 1757. Wilmot Mss., T.3014/6761/595.
52. *Idem.*
53. Rigby to Wilmot, December 18, 1757. Wilmot Mss., T.3019/6761/603.
54. Rigby to Wilmot, December 10, 1757. Wilmot Mss., T.3019/6761/595.

ment in order to force themselves into it." At the same time, the Kildare party, by which alone these other two could be kept at bay, stood aloof and would not risk its popularity unless Bedford would "put the whole weight and power" into the hands of the earl and his friends.[55] The country had gone mad over politics.

In Bedford's judgment the immediate future was extremely uncertain. Points touching the prerogative or tending to lessen the dependence of Ireland upon England were daily threatened and found willing advocates. Already there were bills pending before the privy council that would limit the duration of parliaments in Ireland and require more frequent general elections.[56] Moreover, rumors indicated that the government could expect a full-scale parliamentary attack by Pery and his friends, supported by the combined forces of the primate and the speaker. Pery had made known his intention to reopen the committee of supply in order to appropriate funds for a variety of projects, including payment of bounties for the inland carriage of corn from the producing counties to Dublin and for the water transport of coal from Irish collieries to Dublin.

Funds for these socially desirable projects Bedford reported were to come from a tax of 2s. on the pound on all pensions paid to absentees and from a tax on dogs.[57] The truth of the matter was that no one in the house of commons seriously expected that either absentee pensioners or dogs would be taxed. It was a way of saying that the corn and coal bills ought to be funded directly out of the hereditary revenues and not from new taxes of any sort. Bedford understood fully what was intended and believed that promoters of the corn and coal bills were inspired more by a passion for popularity than for the good of the country. Indeed, requiring the crown rather than the gentlemen in Ireland to pay for socially desirable projects was one certain way to cultivate popularity. Moreover, by burdening the hereditary revenues with a load that should be born by new taxes, a small but determined group in the house of commons intended to weaken the prerogative and otherwise distress government in Ireland.[58]

55. Bedford to Pitt, January 4, 1758. SP63/415/178–182.
56. *Idem.*   57. *Idem.*
58. *Idem.*

Bedford suspected that even more hostile measures were intended in order to exhaust his patience and force him to accept whatever terms the primate and speaker chose to offer. In order to prevail over faction and ensure success, the duke needed full discretion to use all of the powers of his office whenever he saw fit to do so. Bedford asked specifically, for permission to dissolve the Irish parliament if it became too refractory. With the money bill safely enacted, he argued, government may go on until "the minds of the people may be brought to such a temper that a general election might be held with success." The duke sought such authority provisionally and would exercise it only if the house of commons went to extremities. He did not think that a dissolution would be necessary but that option had to be quickly available to him.[59]

At this point, Bedford was not sanguine about lasting solutions and dreaded what might happen when he returned to England. He simply did not know who to recommend as lords justices. Because all parties feared that the powers of government would be put into the hands of antagonists, Bedford confessed himself unable "to frame a regency of those who could be supposed to act cordially together." The only practical remedies appeared to him to be appointment of future lords lieutenants who would reside continually in Ireland during their respective tenures or dispatch of a lord deputy from England during the parliamentary intervals who was entirely free by birth and attachments from all Irish connections. He urged Pitt to consider the possibility of sending out a lord deputy and pressed him to send instructions of some sort on the matter of provisional authority to dissolve the parliament as quickly as possible.[60]

When Pitt's instructions arrived in early February, they were neither encouraging nor helpful. Pitt reminded Bedford of previous instructions about using the healing and softening arts of government and in spite of all that duke had written about Irish politics the ministers asked for more information. Pitt did not find the idea of lord deputy appealing and described it as "an inaccustomed and ill tempered expedient."[61] He thought the strategy of dissolving

59. *Idem.*   60. *Idem.*
61. Pitt to Bedford, February 2, 1758. SP63/415/203–207.

parliament if matters got out of hand to be inadvisable and dangerous. Once again Pitt urged Bedford to a policy of conciliation and
union and to report specifically the names and connections of all
those persons who were incurably irreconcilable to government.

However exasperated Bedford might have been in private after
reading Pitt's instructions, he responded politely and promptly on
February 8, 1758, to the minister. The duke insisted that he had
gone as far with the softening and healing arts as anyone might
reasonably expect. His policy of firmness and fairness, Bedford
argued, had stopped the progress of several disrespectful and unconstitutional measures in the house of commons, and he believed
that no more serious trouble was likely except that of loading the
money bills with large sums for a variety of public purposes through
parliamentary addresses. He reiterated the near-paranoiac fear of
the different factions that political enemies would be installed as
lords justices and named the speaker and his friends as the most
obnoxious and irresponsible group. At the same time, Bedford
described the speaker as a cipher and totally under the influence
of the primate. He was convinced that Kildare would never agree
to serve in any government with the primate and asked Pitt to
determine who should be put into power when he left. The duke
concluded by promising that the will of the king and his English
ministers would be carried out without further complaint and that
he would say or write nothing more on the causes of the present
state of affairs or about remedies for it.[62]

Indeed, Bedford had exhausted his patience and almost reached
the point of not caring what Pitt thought of him. The duke may
have heard of the criticisms that Walpole and others were circulating about him, namely, that he had involved himself so much with
Kildare and was so unwilling to disoblige Fox by affronting the earl
that the Irish government had come to a standstill. It is unlikely
that Bedford knew at this time—but he most certainly learned
later—that John Bowes, Irish lord chancellor, was perhaps even
more negative about his performance in Ireland than was Walpole.
According to Bowes, neither Bedford nor Rigby were equal to
the tasks before them. Right intentions by the lord lieutenant and

62. Bedford to Pitt, February 9, 1758. SP63/415/242–245.

openness in business by the secretary might improve things, but in Bowes' judgment the attention of both Irish chief governors to either was shameful.[63] In this instance what Bowes really may have been saying was that the attention of the chief governors to the lord chancellor was shameful. In any case, Bedford reached his lowest point on February 9. However, almost moments after the duke's most recent letter had been dispatched to Pitt, the political situation in Ireland changed quickly and completely. The primate came to the lord lieutenant with a most unusual proposition.

Stone offered to do all in his power to put an end to the present contention of factions by placing himself and his party at the disposal of the Irish government. The primate indicated also that his union with the speaker was so firm that all of the Bessboroughians would most likely do the same. The terms Stone offered for his accommodation were reasonable. The primate wanted assurances that no prescriptions for the past would be laid upon himself or his friends and that future favors should be dealt out to them on an equal basis with whatever might be given to "the adverse faction."[64] Stone did not insist upon superiority; he asked only for an equal share of patronage.

The primate made this approach to the lord lieutenant because he feared what might happen to the country if current rumors that Bedford had put himself entirely in the hands of the Earl of Kildare proved true. The earl's party was a minority, and many influential gentlemen in the house of commons were prepared to go to great lengths to prove that point if he were established as the sole power in the state. However, Stone assured Bedford that the prejudice against Kildare among his own friends and among those of the speaker was by no means invincible. Neither he nor the speaker would object to acting conjointly as lords justices with any persons from the other party so long as there was "an equal balance, without a superiority being given to either side."[65] Stone and Ponsonby were willing to serve in the government with Kildare or with anyone else the lord lieutenant and the king chose to appoint. The essence of the primate's proposal was to secure peace among the parties and

63. Bowes to Wilmot, January 5, 1758. Wilmot Mss., T.3019/6761/606–607.
64. Bedford to Pitt, February 10, 1758. SP63/415/246–248.
65. *Idem.*

parity in the government by appointing four lords justices instead of three.

For Bedford, the primate's offer was heaven-sent. The primate's scheme for balancing the lords justices effectively removed the all-pervasive fear that one faction would dominate the other. This idea was so promising and so simple that Bedford embraced it at once. As the duke wrote to Pitt, "I left nothing unsaid that might confirm him in his good intentions, with an assurance that I would do everything in my power that might conduce towards bringing the other party into like terms of union and compliance."[66]

Bedford was very serious about trying to persuade the Earl of Kildare to accept the idea of coalition and equality. He arranged a private meeting with the earl for the morning of February 13. At this meeting, Bedford used every argument founded on both private and public advantage to persuade Kildare to make peace with the primate and agree with him in the government of Ireland. Kildare would not be moved and absolutely refused to depart from his long-standing determination of never coming to terms with the primate.[67] At subsequent meetings with Kildare, Bedford went so far as to offer to pay out of his own pocket all costs incurred by the appointment of a fourth lord justice in order to assure the earl that the public would not suffer any additional expenses because of his new arrangement.[68] Kildare thanked the duke for his generosity but refused to reconsider. Rigby approached Malone and Gore, and both of those gentlemen argued eloquently with Kildare about the necessity of forgetting the past and effecting a union of all parties for the good of the country.[69] Even though Malone's oratorical magic could not turn his lordship's head completely, it was turned somewhat and compromise of a sort became possible.

On March 7, 1758, Kildare gave his absolute and final refusal about joining with the primate to the lord lieutenant. However, Kildare told the duke that, as a private man, he was "perfectly well disposed to promote peace and a submission to government" under Bedford's administration.[70] In other words, Kildare would not join

66. Russell Correspondence, II, 328.
67. Rigby to Wilmot, March 9, 1758. Wilmot Mss., T.3019/6761/619–620.
68. Rigby to Wilmot, March 9, 1758. Wilmot Mss., T.3019/6761/619–620.
69. Rigby to Wilmot, March 9, 1758. Wilmot Mss., T.3019/6761/619–620.
70. Bedford to Pitt, March 8, 1758. SP63/415/262.

with the primate, but he would not oppose the government of Ireland because George Stone was in it so long as the Duke of Bedford continued as lord lieutenant. Bedford was absolutely elated by Kildare's concession and saw a quick resolution of his problem. The duke had held several conversations with the Earl of Shannon about coming into the government with Kildare as counterweights to the primate and speaker, and the old man had responded favorably. When Kildare gave his absolute and final refusal on March 8, Bedford went directly to Shannon to find out whether or not he would come in without Kildare. Shannon raised no difficulties and wanted only time enough to explain his decision to the earl personally.[71] According to Rigby, the meeting between Shannon and Kildare did not go well. Shannon told Kildare that he was ready to serve with the primate. Kildare's precise response is unrecorded, but later Shannon told Rigby that he had parted from Kildare "in a way not very likely to meet again."[72] Except for Kildare, the old enemies of 1751 had joined hands to bring peace to Irish politics. Bedford reported the agreement of all parties to the new arrangement to Pitt on March 8, and in the same dispatch requested permission to return to England as soon as parliamentary business could be completed.[73]

Rigby was as pleased with the new arrangement as Bedford. The chief secretary wrote to friends in early March, exclaiming, "It is at an end. It is done."[74] Rigby thought Kildare's obstinacy regrettable and his withdrawal from the government of Ireland a great loss. "It is too bad," Rigby wrote. Kildare was "as agreeable a man to do business with as I ever met in my life."[75] As the negotiations about the new arrangement progressed, the primate's friends in the house of commons became more supportive. Rigby reported that Stone seemed to be everywhere. He attended the house of commons every day, arranged dinners almost every evening for one group or another, and lately had sent "his Speaker" to the Castle to inquire when the lord lieutenant might be pleased to end the session.[76]

71. *Idem.*
72. Rigby to Wilmot, March 9, 1758. Wilmot Mss., T.3019/6761/619–620.
73. Bedford to Pitt, March 8, 1758. SP63/415/262.
74. Rigby to Wilmot, March 9, 1758. Wilmot Mss., T.3019/6761/619–620.
75. Rigby to Wilmot, February 16, 1758. Wilmot Mss., T.3019/6761/615.
76. Rigby to Wilmot, February 19, 1758. Wilmot Mss., T.3019/6761/615.

There was at least one important member of the Irish house of commons who did not view the new arrangement as desirable. Pery had been a supporter of the primate in 1753 and had published a pamphlet on the great crisis of that year in 1757. He knew the primate and Ponsonby very well and expected that the new arrangement would in effect put paramount influence and power into the hands of Stone. Also, Pery had designs on the speaker's chair himself and must have resented a man of Ponsonby's mean abilities obtaining such an easy access to it. For whatever reasons, Pery made clear his disapproval of what had happened and indicated that he would not be part of the new system. The primate must have communicated Pery's dissatisfaction to Sackville because on March 24, 1758, Lord George wrote Pery a flattering letter urging him to support the primate's effort to settle Irish affairs on a lasting foundation. Pery was moved by Sackville's letter, certainly, but not very far. He wanted to wait and see how well the new system would work and what sorts of measures the new Irish ministers could persuade the lord lieutenant and chief secretary to support.

Of the accomplished speakers and influentials in the house of commons, Pery's reservations about the primate, the speaker, and Shannon assuming formal roles as undertakers and managers were exceptional. By the first week in March, Rigby reported the temper of the house greatly moderated and its mood turned cooperative. Indeed, between January and mid-March, something extraordinary had happened in Irish politics. Though not a sitting member of the Irish house of commons, George Stone demonstrated that he was master of it. English birth, past political controversies and failures, and clerical vocation notwithstanding, George Stone had suddenly become the most powerful Irish politician of his day. Furthermore, Stone's new position in Irish politics rested upon the most substantial of all foundations. The primate was powerful because he was indispensable. Stone was indispensable to the chief governors because he could manage the parliamentary factions, and he was indispensable to the factions because he could manage the chief governors. For the former, Stone put an end to the turmoil and the legislative absurdities of December and January.[77] For the latter,

77. Rigby to Wilmot, March 9, 1758. Wilmot Mss., T.3019/6761/619–620.

Stone promised a fair share of patronage and official acceptance of a limited number of popular measures.

It was this last point that distinguished the harassed and despised George Stone of 1753 from the powerful politician of 1758. He had always displayed intelligence, mastery of political detail, and unlimited energy. However, the failures of Dorset's time and veritable proscription during Hartington's tenure had taught Stone patience and the importance of popularity. The rejection of the altered money bill in 1753 was an object lesson for the future. What happened once could happen again. There was a public opinion outside of the house of commons that, when mobilized around issues of perceived national importance, could not be ignored. Furthermore, there were in the house an increasing number of younger members who were intent upon building political careers as advocates of popular measures, and several of them were friends of George Stone. In any case, part of the new arrangement was viceregal acceptance of a popular measure such as the corn bill.

The corn bill was a popular measure. By paying bounties for the land carriage of corn from Irish-producing areas to Dublin, the promoters hoped to relieve corn scarcities in Dublin, reduce the sums spent out of the country for food imports, and generally improve domestic tillage. Pery had introduced and carried such a bill in the waning days of Hartington's session only to have it suppressed in England. When he reintroduced the measure in 1757, political conditions were much altered. Bedford's position in the house of commons was weaker than had been that of Hartington. The present lord lieutenant could not command a majority in the house; and in spite of the absurd tax on dogs that Pery attached to the measure, a strong majority for enactment was certain. Initially, Rigby and a few others spoke against the corn bill, with little effect, as special interest legislation intended to enrich a few promoters and contractors. A more serious objection was the fact that the bill authorized payment of bounties—5d. every five miles for every forty stone of grain or flour brought from a greater distance than ten miles from Dublin by inland carriage—without providing new taxes to pay them. Funds for the bounties would have to come from the hereditary revenues and the governors of Ireland would have no practical control over how much was paid out. The constitutional

and political implications of this proposed mutilation of the hereditary revenues were serious and went far beyond delivering grain to
Dublin or enriching a few Kilkenny and Tipperary contractors.
Depletion of the hereditary revenues in any substantial way would
increase the dependence of the Irish government upon the Irish
parliament for additional supplies and perhaps even lead to the
necessity for annual parliamentary sessions.

Bedford was well aware of the dangers inherent in the corn bill,
but he simply did not have the votes to defeat this measure in the
house of commons. Suppression of the bill again in either the Irish
or English privy councils was a possibility, but Bedford and Rigby
persuaded themselves and the English ministers that it would be
unwise. If popularity had to be appeased, better to do it with the
corn bill rather than with a new modeling of Poyning's law, shorter
parliaments and more frequent general elections, reform of judicial
tenure, or a habeus corpus act. Some concessions were unavoidable
and at the moment the corn bill seemed least dangerous. Moreover,
in the context of the new arrangement under negotiation with the
primate and Shannon in February, acceptance of the corn bill by
the government was a clear sign of good faith. In any case, Bedford
changed the minds in England that needed to be changed, and once
royal assent for the corn bill had been obtained, Pery publicly
thanked Bedford "through whose mediation it has been returned
to us."[78]

All of Bedford's concerns during this session were not directly
related to partisan politics. As a matter of fact, an important issue
affecting the state of religion in the country was taken up by the
duke and his advisors in an absolutely nonpartisan manner. Clanbrassil's registration bill cleared the house of lords with a favorable
vote and was taken up in Irish privy council in mid-January. As had
been the case in the previous session virtually all of the law lords
and the bishops opposed the bill in the house and in the council.
True to his word given to Clanbrassil in August, Bedford strongly
supported the bill in the council. The duke spoke for more than
three quarters of an hour, arguing that it was time enough that
"another mode be tried, in closer consonance with the principle

78. HMC Emly, 183.

that persecution is not the proper method of putting a stop to religious prejudices."[79] There could be little danger, he concluded, in giving this new registration system a fair trial "when the experience of half a century had demonstrated the inefficacy of the present system."[80] The discussion went on for five hours and was completely abstracted from partisan politics. The primate and the chancellor both opposed the bill, but for different reasons. Chief Justice Caulfield and Chief Baron Willes were also hostile to it—the latter denounced the bill "because it would approve a toleration of that religion which it had been the general policy of England and of Ireland to persecute and to depress."[81] When the council voted, the bill was rejected by a count of 14 to 12.

Of the principal politicians present, it appears that Shannon opposed the measure but did not carry his friends on the council with him[82] and that Kildare voted with the lord lieutenant and for the measure. The recently formed group of Catholic landlords and merchants known as the Catholic Committee watched these proceedings with great attention. Dr. Charles O'Connor prepared an address to the lord lieutenant, which was approved at a meeting in Dublin and delivered to the speaker of the house of commons for presentation to Bedford. In this address, O'Connor prayed for a future relaxation of the popery laws, professed profound loyalty to the king, and thanked the lord lieutenant for his wisdom, justice, and moderation.[83] Thus ended the most serious effort to reform the popery law system since the accession of King William.

In mid-March, Bedford believed that most of his problems were behind him. The lord chancellor had been piqued by his exclusion from appointment as a lord justice, but a long meeting with Bedford and the promise of a baronetcy and salary increase of £500 left him in what Rigby described as "good temper and satisfaction."[84] Bedford had reason for some anxiety over Pitt's reaction to his new arrangement. The minister had not been receptive to Bedford's earlier suggestions about coping with the factions in the Irish house

79. Russell Correspondence, ii, xvi.
80. Ibid., xvii.   81. Ibid., xv.
82. Rigby to Wilmot, January 9, 1758. Wilmot Mss., T.3019/6761/609–611.
83. Russell Correspondence, II, xviii; James, op. cit., 257.
84. Waite to Wilmot, May 10, 1758. Wilmot Mss., T.3019/6761/624.

of commons, but the duke hoped for the best this time. Bedford's hopes in this instance were fulfilled. On April 3, 1758, Pitt agreed to the new arrangement, approved Bedford's recommendations for the lords justices, and authorized the duke to return to England as soon as parliamentary business was completed. Bedford lost no time in trying to bring the session to an end. The duke had one or two nuisance divisions on popular questions called by Pery, who managed to muster no one except Richard Harwood, an angry old gentleman of strong patriot tendencies who had been recently denied viceregal support for a judicial post. With matters thus in hand, Bedford could afford to be gracious. He spoke to both houses, thanking the lords and gentlemen for their generosity and support, and then specifically mentioned the unprecedented circumstance of his majesty giving royal assent to the corn and coal bills even though no provisions had been made for the payments authorized by them. The speech was well received, and in a mood of unusual goodwill Bedford closed the session on April 29, 1758.

The change in the mood and temper of Irish politics between February and April was extraordinary. Rigby observed shortly before boarding the yacht for Parkgate that his grace would leave behind nothing but harmony. Both Kildare and the primate publicly expressed great satisfaction with Bedford's administration.[85] Kildare was himself so satisfied with Bedford's accomplishments in the short time that he had been in Ireland that he promised to attend the levee and personally witness the swearing of the new lords justices. Kildare did this, Rigby added, to let the world know that he was "not displeased at the persons appointed" and that only a personal point of honor prevented him from being among them.[86]

Bedford and Rigby departed for Parkgate on May 7, and the lord chancellor swore the primate, the speaker, and Lord Shannon as lords justices. The harmony Rigby had noted seemed likely to continue. The first formal act of the new lords justices reflected Shannon's presence among them and the principle of equal distribution of employments and favors. The three lords justices signed a warrant authorizing the appointment of Sir Richard Cox to the revenue

85. Rigby to Wilmot, May 4, 1758. Wilmot Mss., T.3014/6761/622.
86. *Idem.*

board.[87] Even more than Kildare's presence at the swearing of the
lords justice, the primate's acceptance of Cox for the revenue board
signified that the events of 1753 were now history and that he was
absolutely determined to make the new arrangement work.

Preparing for Invasion

When Bedford arrived in England, he went first to London to
report to the ministers and to the king and then to Woburn Abbey.
The duke's time in Ireland had been difficult but he had learned a
great deal about Irish politicians and popular political issues. Part
of what the duke learned, he put into his diary as a guide for the
future. "As things are circumstanced," the duke wrote, "business
may be easily carried on the next session; but the leading people
must have *douceurs,* a great many of which I must at a proper time
lay before his Majesty." By these means, Bedford concluded, the
king "may do what he pleases with that country."[88]

In effect, Bedford came away from Ireland with the same message that had been taken away by his predecessors. Political opposition in Ireland was usually a means to an end and invariably could
be quieted with a place, a pension, or a peerage. Derived as it was
from the experience of two very prominent and respected English
noblemen, this perception of Irish politics as an issueless scramble
for patronage became widely accepted in official circles and profoundly affected the way English ministers thought about and acted
upon Irish problems. English ministers feared popular agitation in
Ireland, especially of constitutional issues, but at the same time
found themselves hard put to take such agitation seriously. It was
a dilemma from which the English government could not escape.

Bedford's reflections on his time in Ireland were different from
those of his predecessor in one very important respect. Bedford
had to go back to Ireland, and he proceeded to lay before the king
those recommendations he hoped would make his next session a
quiet one. In addition to a peerage and a salary increase for John
Bowes, the duke requested three promotions to earl, two new vis-

---

87. Waite to Wilmot, May 10, 1758. Wilmot Mss., T.3019/6761/624.
88. Russell Correspondence, II, 335.

counts, and the creation of six barons. Also, the duke proposed four new appointments to the Irish privy council and six persons as being worthy of pensions of £200 a year. Bedford assured the king that all of the persons recommended were "either very considerable in themselves, or by their connections with others" influential in the house of commons.[89] Next, Bedford turned to the matter of pensions for the Princess of Hesse—the king's daughter—and her children. He believed that, given the present tranquil state of the kingdom and the fact that several recipients of large pension payments had recently died, the present time was opportune for the king to place a provision of £5,000 a year for his royal daughter and her family on the Irish establishment. The combination of a pension for the Princess of Hesse and six pensions for persons resident in Ireland, Bedford insisted, would enable him to carry on the king's business in the next session and quiet people's minds about the prospect of £5,000 a year being carried out of the country.[90]

Meanwhile in Ireland, management of the affairs of the country fell more and more into the capable hands of the primate. Shannon spent most of his time at Castlemartyr and the speaker was preoccupied with the failing health of his father. In early July, the old Earl of Bessborough died. Some politicians saw the passing of Bessborough more as a political event than as a sad familial loss. John Bowes expected that the Bessborough political connection would break up. The new earl was nonresident and the present union between Ponsonby and Stone was not one of equals. Bowes believed that the primate would take advantage of his ally and enlarge his own personal political interest.[91] However, nothing of this sort happened. Stone remained close to Ponsonby and on good terms with Shannon while trying to make himself indispensable to the lord lieutenant.

The primate was determined to keep party and faction under control and succeeded grandly in doing so. There were no divisions among the lords justices, and the business of government proceeded efficiently and expeditiously. Stone himself was specifically gratified

89. *Ibid.*, 339.   90. *Ibid.*, 337–338.
91. Bowes to Wilmot, July 21, 1758. Wilmot Mss., T.3019/6761/628.

by the performance of Sir Richard Cox at the revenue board. He described his former enemy as "both useful and acceptable to those who were most averse to the thought of his coming amongst them."[92] All in all, Stone kept Bedford informed about the state of the country and constantly counseled fiscal prudence.

In particular, the primate did not want the lord lieutenant or the English ministry to be deceived by outward appearances. In his view, Ireland was poor, desperately poor. The substance of the country, he wrote, should not be estimated by the splendor and luxury of a few families. The bulk of the people were regularly neither lodged, clothed, nor fed. Even though the value of estates had almost doubled during the last thirty years, Stone continued, the condition of the occupiers of the land was no better now than before that increase. Stone's letters to Bedford during the summer of 1758 were always interesting. He gave advice and seemed to be using the giving of advice as a mechanism for developing his relationship with both Rigby and Bedford. The tone of the primate's letters varied. At times, he seems to have assumed the role of a contrite sinner seeking forgiveness. On other occasions, he is a voice of experience, a political sage, and a wire-puller. But whatever the tone or the persona, George Stone was always in control.

Drafts for expeditions to the different theaters of the war were regularly taken from battalions stationed in Ireland during most of 1758. The removal of three regiments of dragoons in June prompted Bedford to alert Pitt to the fact that the size of the forces in Ireland had been reduced to dangerous levels.[93] He asked Pitt to send replacements, especially cavalry, to Ireland as soon as possible. However, the eyes of the first minister were directed elsewhere. Pitt had hopes of conquests in West Africa and advised Rigby in late August of his intention to withdraw troops from Ireland for service in Senegal.

Pitt sympathized with the lord lieutenant's military problem in Ireland but refused to allow them to influence imperial strategy. Pitt was convinced that the war would be won only by defeating the enemy. As first minister he had determined to defeat the enemy

92. Russell Correspondence, II, 351.
93. Bedford to Pitt, July 2, 1758. SP63/415/333.

as often and as thoroughly as possible whenever and wherever opportunities arose. At present, there were such opportunities in Germany, North America, India, the West Indies, and Senegal, but not in Ireland. For this reason, Pitt took troops from Ireland and deployed them where needed. Altogether the equivalent of a battalion was embarked at Cork in November and joined Captain Augustus Keppel's squadron bound for Goree, a French held island south of Senegal. The drafts from Ireland certainly helped lieutenant Colonel Richard Worge capture Goree in late December 1758 and secure English commercial and slave-trading interests in that area. However, once those drafts had embarked from Cork, Pitt did what he could to remedy the military deficiencies of Ireland.

The first minister authorized intensified recruitment of Protestants in Ulster for all understrength regiments in Ireland. He also allowed those regiments to send recruiting parties to England and Scotland. Moreover, in order to encourage Irish Protestants to take the king's shilling, the recruits were assured that service outside of Ireland would not be required. Also, the ministry directed several regiments returning from the East Indies in fall of 1758 and spring of 1759 to proceed to northern Ireland for service and rehabilitation. To be sure, three of these regiments—Aldercorn's arriving in October and Strode's and Brown's landing in July—were much more in need of the latter than capable of doing much of the former when disembarked, but they were replacements of a sort and Bedford was grateful to receive them. In addition, Pitt also obtained quick royal approval in October of Bedford's recommendation of Lord Kildare to succeed the deceased Viscount Molesworth as master general of his majesty's ordnance in Ireland.[94] This appointment brought the earl back into public life and provided him with £1,500 a year.

Of all the measures taken by Pitt and Bedford to increase military strength and efficiency in Ireland, the appointment of Kildare as master general of ordnance produced the most immediate controversy. The earl attended to his official duties with a dispatch that had been unknown in that office for many years. There was scarcely an aspect of defense preparations that the earl did not think re-

94. Bedford to Pitt, October 17, 1758. SP63/415/380.

quired his personal approval. In military matters, as in most of life's activities, Kildare gave advice more willingly than he received it. Consequently, by the early spring of 1759 the earl found himself embroiled with Lord Rothes, commander-in-chief in Ireland.[95] Kildare disagreed sharply with Rothes over troop dispositions. When the commander-in-chief refused to change them, Kildare responded as one might expect. He drafted a memorial to the Duke of Bedford and set out for London in early April to deliver it personally to the lord lieutenant.

Kildare arrived at Holland House on April 18 but was unable to reach either Rigby or Bedford because both were out of the city. Within a fortnight, Kildare had his conversation with Bedford and it turned out to be a disaster. "Nothing I said had any weight," Kildare wrote to his wife, "and all the papers I had to show him he said he should look upon them as waste paper."[96] Thoroughly crushed for the moment and persuaded that his honor had been damaged, Kildare resolved to present his memorial to the king and then resign. "All I want to do," he concluded to Lady Kildare, "is to put him in the wrong which will not be difficult to do."[97] Henry Fox advised Kildare to do whatever he thought was right, but urged him not to give up his employment.[98]

Lady Kildare was of the same mind. She was very sorry about losing the income from the ordnance post, telling her husband that "for one man to sacrifice £1,500 a year to the obstinacy of another would be very wrong."[99] The prospect of such a sacrifice, she reported, would delight Kildare's enemies in Ireland and certainly bring an end to the renovations and landscaping presently underway at Carton. It was a fact, Lady Kildare concluded, that one year's income from a job that was "perfect for you would pay all the expenses we are at here."[100] The countess' letters had an effect. Kildare presented his memorial to the king, who received it without comment on May 25. Pleased by his majesty's quiet courtesy, he put all thoughts of resignation out of his head. For the sake of Carton and Lady Kildare, the earl decided this time he would try to forgive

95. Fitzgerald Correspondence, I, 72.
96. *Ibid.*, 73–74.   97. *Idem.*
98. *Ibid.*, 77.   99. *Ibid.*, 92.
100. *Ibid.*, 98.

and forget. There were moments when, even for the premier noble-man of all Ireland, honor and dignity had to be put aside for the sake of wall hangings and new furniture. He left London and set out for Ireland immediately.

When Kildare arrived in Ireland in early June, he found the lords justices preoccupied with military preparations. They had received intelligence from England that the French planned to invade "either Great Britain or Ireland or possible both at the same time."[101] Ac-cording to one source, the Earls of Clare and Clancarty had been named to command an expedition which intended to put 5,000 men ashore in the southwest of Ireland. Strategic and tactical deci-sions made months earlier in London and Paris were being imple-mented on three continents. Such decisions would change the course of the war and make Englishmen of this generation remem-ber 1759 as the *annus mirabilis.*

If English church bells were worn thin with the ringing of victories during this extraordinary year, there were also moments of great anxiety over the prospect of invasion. The French were determined to bring the war they had been unable to win in other parts of the world directly to the British Isles. The overall plan for an invasion of England was an elaborate one. The fleet at Brest under Admiral Hubert de Conflans, consisting of twenty-one ships of the line and several frigates, was to be reinforced in early August by twelve ships of the line from the Toulon squadron under the command of Commodore de la Clue. The Toulon ships were expected to elude English patrols at Gibraltar and reach Brest by September.

Next, this combined fleet would break out of Brest and escort the Duc d'Aiguillon's force of 20,000 men from Brittany to Scotland, where they would make a diversionary landing and occupy Edin-burgh. At the same time, a fleet of five frigates and a small landing force under the command of Francois Thurot, an experienced smuggler in Manx waters and a man of Irish extraction—his father's name was Farrell—now turned privateer, would penetrate the Irish sea and attempt diversionary descents along the northeastern coast of Ireland. Meanwhile, the main invasion force of 50,000 men in Flanders was to await the return of Conflan's fleet from Scotland

101. Russell Correspondence, II, 373.

and then be convoyed in 200 flat-bottomed barges from Flemish ports to the northern shore of the Thames estuary. An additional hundred small vessels were to transport supplies and stores for this invasion force in sufficient quantities to make further cross-channel reinforcement unnecessary.

A plan as elaborate as this one could not be kept secret. Throughout the first half of 1759, Pitt and the cabinet were kept informed of French preparations through Newcastle's excellent intelligence sources in Europe. That the French were planning to come, the English ministers could not doubt. They did not know when or where. The prospect of invasion was so serious in early May that the principal English ministers, including the Duke of Bedford, held an emergency meeting in Lord Holdernesse's house in London on May 8 to devise an appropriate defense strategy.[102]

At this meeting, there was some discussion by Bedford of the general condition of law and order in Ireland, but most attention was directed to the state of military preparations there. The forces at the king's disposal in Ireland were at once too dispersed and too few to prevent an enemy from landing in the distant southern and southwestern parts of the country. Bedford feared that if the French could put 5,000 men ashore in the south or west the most optimistic scenario would be to prevent them from reaching Leinster or Ulster. The best defense strategy for Ireland appeared to be that of defeating the French at sea and thereby prevent them from ever reaching Ireland.[103] The ministers approved this strategy and ordered the admiralty to rendezvous as many warships as possible at Torbay for patrols and action along the French coast. At the same time, the ministers ordered a large force of infantry to be encamped in the Isle of Wight with transports in readiness to carry them wherever needed. In the event that accidents of wind or weather allowed a French invasion force to reach England or Ireland, this force on the Isle of Wight could be quickly transported to the point of danger. Because no one could be certain when or where the French would strike, no additional troops could be sent to Ireland.[104] For the present, Ireland would have to improvise and provide for her own defenses.

102. *Ibid.*, 374.   103. *Idem.*
104. *Ibid.*, 375.

Bedford sent a long dispatch to Ireland warning the lords justices about French intentions and ordering them to array the Ulster militia and recall all absent officers on the Irish military establishment to duty. He also recommended that application be made to the Ulster nobility and gentry to recruit among their friends and Protestant tenants two or three thousand men to complete Aldercorn's regiment and two weak battalions presently serving in the north. Bedford concluded his dispatch with a strong expression of concern over accounts of what he called "the unbridled licentiousness of the lower class of people in Ireland, as well in town as country."[105] He was particularly disturbed by the riotous behavior of a mob in Dublin that lately had attacked English cattle buyers who had been given leave by the Irish parliament to purchase livestock in the city cattle market. Bedford wanted Stone to look into this matter and wondered how long such mob interference could be tolerated by a civilized country.

Bedford's dispatch reached Stone at Leixslip on May 27, and he immediately communicated the contents of it to the speaker who happened to be visiting with him. Shannon was in Cork and learned of the invasion threat as soon as messengers could reach him. Lord Rothes received the same orders in the same report that had been sent to Stone, and he journeyed at once to Leixslip to confer with the primate and the speaker. After a discussion of several hours at Leixslip about appropriate measures, Stone and Ponsonby proceeded to Dublin in the evening of May 27 in order to put what had been decided into immediate execution. The lords justices ordered all regiments of cavalry and foot to several predetermined strategic locations.

When considering the probable strength of enemy forces that might be engaged, the primate and the speaker had to think about more than just intelligence estimates of troops ready for embarkation in Brittany and Flanders. The lords justices also had to consider what the majority of Irish Catholics would do if a French force actually landed in the country. After discussions with several of the most prominent Catholic landlords and merchants, Stone was convinced that little or no danger should be expected from that

105. *Ibid.*, 376–377.

quarter. The primate did not doubt that if a French army were to land in Ireland "many single vagabonds would be ready for hire to take arms with them."[106] However, Stone had absolute confidence that propertied Catholics, whether landed or monied, feared such an attempt by the French and that many more would assist the king than aid the enemy. Moreover, Stone believed, the long-experienced equity and lenity of his majesty's government in Ireland had given Catholics something to lose. In any case, the lords justices decided to deploy available troops "with a view to the invading enemy only, without laying equal stress upon any particular places of supposed disaffection."[107]

With regard to the other points raised in Bedford's dispatch, Stone promised to assist the Ulster nobility and gentry to recruit for the understrength battalions serving in the north and then addressed the problems of mob violence in Dublin. The fact that Bedford had raised this matter in the manner that he did in his dispatch persuaded Stone that the English ministers had been displeased by the way the Irish government had handled the situation. In this instance, troops had not been used to restore order and protect the English cattle buyers. What the magistrates were able to handle was handled and what they could not do was not done. Stone assured Bedford that all of the lords justices were well aware of the licentiousness of the Dublin mob and deplored it, but if troops had been used to protect the English cattle buyers it would have been impossible to undertake the troop dispositions presently in progress. Once the present dangers subsided, promised Stone, proper measures for ensuring the peace and quiet of the city would have to be taken up for consideration.[108]

Meanwhile, as defense measures proceeded apace in Ireland during June, French invasion preparations intensified. English agents reported from Brest that officers freely and openly stated in cafes that when the Toulon squadron arrived the combined force would depart as quickly as possible for a major assault upon the British Isles. However, the Toulon squadron never arrived. It was overwhelmed by Admiral Boscawen near Lagos Bay in late August.

106. *Ibid.*, 379.   107. *Ibid.*, 380.
108. *Ibid.*, 382.

Reports of the destruction of the Toulon squadron did not reach London until September. Consequently, Boscawen's heroics had virtually no effect on the state of Ireland's military preparedness during August and September. The French had been expected in July and when they did not come in August, the lords justices began to doubt whether they would come at all. Forage and supply contracts for the troops in encampments expired on September 17, and Stone and Shannon did not believe there was a necessity to make new ones. Unless contrary orders were sent forthwith from Bedford, the lords justices intended to return the troops to their regular quarters once the present contracts had run out. When Pitt learned of the lords justices' intentions about the encampments and the forage contracts, he exploded. What upset Pitt most was the assumption of the lords justices that the approach of winter lessened the prospect of invasion. Utmost vigilance was indispensable at this critical juncture,[109] and the troops were kept in their encampments.

While Pitt, perhaps unfairly, admonished the lords justices for lack of vigilance, he also made organization of an effective defense in Ireland extremely difficult by making frequent demands for drafts from regiments serving in that country. In August, Pitt requested drafts of two privates from every company of foot in Ireland to reinforce the British forces in Germany. There simply were no soldiers in Ireland to spare. Four regiments were greatly understrength. Aldercorn's regiment had arrived from the East Indies in October 1758 with only seventy-six rank and file soldiers. Strode's and Brown's had landed in July 1759 with respective complements of 102 and 189. Sebright's regiment, after strenuous recruiting efforts, was only up to battalion strength.[110] Drafting out of these regiments was unwise for two reasons. Not only were these regiments too weak to draft but taking drafts out of them would put an end to recruiting. All of these regiments had availed themselves of the king's directive allowing them to guarantee that recruits would not be obliged to serve out of the country.

Though Bedford was preparing to leave for Ireland, he found time to argue strenuously with Pitt against any September drafts.

109. Pitt to Bedford, September 7, 1759. SP63/416/67–68.
110. Bedford to Pitt, September 2, 1759. SP63/416/59.

The duke's argument had some effect. Pitt relaxed his demands. The drafts from Aldercorn's, Strode's, and Brown's regiments were reduced from two privates a company to one. Other regiments had to suffer drafts as directed in the same manner as regiments serving in England, and the lords justices were urged to proceed with embarking the drafts with as much expedition as possible.[111] With this matter settled, Bedford and Rigby had a final meeting with Pitt wherein all agreed that the Irish parliament should meet on October 16, 1759. The lord lieutenant and chief secretary spent about ten days attending to personal business and then proceeded to Holyhead. They embarked in the early evening of October 6 and arrived in Dublin at noon on the following day, full of anxiety about what might happen if the French actually did come.

111. Pitt to Bedford, September 4, 1759. SP63/416/61.

CHAPTER VII

A Most Unusual and Extraordinary Session, 1759-1760

The Great Dublin Riot

During the ten days between Bedford's arrival in Dublin and the opening of parliament, he devoted most of his time to military and recruiting matters. The army had been so weakened by frequent drafts, and recruiting had proceeded so slowly and unsatisfactorily, that virtually every battalion in the country was understrength. Bedford estimated that at least two battalions of foot and a regiment of cavalry or dragoons had to be kept in Dublin for the security of the Protestants in the capital. Given all of these circumstances, there simply was not much of a force available to march against the French if they should attempt a landing. Bedford believed that recruiting would improve if the principal people of the country could be persuaded that a descent was actually intended against Ireland.

Bedford began his campaign slowly. The speech from the throne delivered on October 16 to a very thin house was temperate and free of any special anxiety about the possibility of invasion. It mentioned the victories occurring in different parts of the world, expressed the lord lieutenant's hope for union and harmony among the king's loyal Irish subjects, and asked only for the usual supplies plus the costs of preparedness.[1] The addresses voted were similarly temperate and anxiety-free. Rigby described the mood of the house as one of perfect serenity, with members being disposed to hobnob with one another and do little else.[2]

---

1. Bedford to Pitt, October 16, 1759. SP63/416/87–90.
2. Rigby to Wilmot, October 17, 1759. Wilmot Mss., T.3019/6762/560.

The king and the English ministry were disappointed by the apparent complacency of the Irish parliament and particularly by the failure of recruiting efforts in Ireland. Pitt stated in a letter to Bedford that the city of London alone had raised and equipped more men that had the entire kingdom of Ireland.[3] Pitt also warned the lord lieutenant that in the present emergency Irish Protestants must act now on their own behalf. The dangers of the moment were real enough. Pitt had authentic intelligence that the French were going to come and that some might already be on their way.

Intelligence sources in France revealed that, far from abandoning invasion plans because of the disaster to the Toulon fleet, the French ministers were more determined than ever to proceed. In a dispatch received by Bedford on October 19, 1759, Pitt represented the French ministers as driven by despair to risk all by an assault upon England. Specifically, Pitt warned the lord lieutenant that at Vannes the Duc d'Aiguillon had assembled 18,000 men with more than sufficient transport to move them anywhere. A few days later, the lord lieutenant learned also that François Thurot had broken out of Dunkirk with three frigates and escaped into the North sea. Most likely Thurot's destination was northern Ireland.[4]

The content of Pitt's dispatches to Bedford about French intentions was almost instantly and universally known. To allay exaggeration and minimize rumor the lord lieutenant immediately called a meeting of Irish officials and principal politicians and communicated to them the substance of Pitt's intelligence. Bedford was elated by the zeal of those at the meeting and believed that at last he had found a means of exciting the loyal people of Ireland to commit some of their own resources for the defense of the kingdom.[5] Rigby was much less sanguine about getting the Irish to do anything to save themselves, but did not think the situation was as serious as Pitt had represented it to be. Rigby did not believe that the French could put enough men ashore in Ireland to make a difference. Intentions were one thing, successful execution of such an enterprise was another.

Nevertheless, on October 29, 1759, Rigby went into the house of

3. Russell Correspondence II, 392.
4. Rigby to Wilmot, October 24, 1759. Wilmot Mss., T.3019/6762/502.
5. Russell Correspondence, II, 387–388.

commons and informed the members about the prospect of invasion. Lord Hillsborough did the same in the house of lords on the following day. The effect of both speeches was as Bedford had expected. The house of commons responded with loyal speeches and unanimous approval of Malone's motion authorizing unlimited credit for the government during the present emergency.[6] Noblemen, gentlemen, and even serving officers offered to raise and equip regiments at their own expense. The noblemen and gentlemen making such offers requested military rank appropriate to the size of the units raised, but the war office was reluctant to give it to them. Rigby recognized what such new commissions and promotions did to the seniority system, but urged that those public-spirited noblemen and gentlemen be indulged with a little rank, otherwise there would be much discontent at a time when none was needed.[7]

The dangers of Ireland were perceived by the lord lieutenant and chief secretary as being real and immediate. They had received information from Edinburgh that Thurot's present location was unknown. The duke issued orders to the customs commissioners to instruct their officers to keep a sharp lookout all around the coasts. The worst possible situation would be for Thurot to land a force in the north of Ireland and then have the Duc d'Aiguillon's force elude Sir Edward Hawke's patrols off Brest and effect a second landing in the south. With only 7,200 infantry and 2,800 horses available for marching orders, the army in Ireland could ill afford a division of its forces.[8] For the moment, the Irish government waited for news of Thurot and prayed that Hawke would contain the Brest fleet.

During this time of crisis, Bedford was very active and purposefully visible throughout the city of Dublin. One example was his organization of an association of noblemen, gentry, and merchants to support the credit of the banks by promising to accept notes and negotiable drafts in all payments. The principal objectives of this association were to secure public credit, ensure a sufficient supply of specie to pay the troops, and prevent the hoarding of cash in private hands.[9] While Pitt and the king applauded Bedford's efforts

6. Rigby to Wilmot, October 30, 1759. Wilmot Mss., T.3019/6762/641.
7. Rigby to Wilmot, November 1, 1759. Wilmot Mss., T.3019/6762/643.
8. *Idem.*   9. Russell Correspondence, II, 389.

to secure public credit, many in Dublin saw them as a warning and acted accordingly. A serious run on the banking house of Mitchel, Clements, and Whitelock began in early November, forcing that establishment to close its doors on November 6. the firm of Malone, Clements, and Gore suffered the same fate shortly thereafter. Rigby believed that there were other reasons besides the dread of invasion and the prospect of heavy cash demands operative in the collapse of the Mitchel and Malone banks.[10] Rapid and over-ambitious expansion were certainly contributing causes.

These two bank failures also promised to be politically damaging to the Irish government. After all, both Malone and Clements were longtime office holders and very prominent politicians. "What will be said in England," questioned Rigby, "to a bankrupt chancellor of the exchequer and deputy vice treasurer?" The chief secretary feared that Clements would be attacked in the house of commons as unfit to continue as one of the heads of the treasury and did not know how the man could defend himself.[11] However, the public reputations of Clements and Malone were not the primary concerns of the governors of Ireland at the moment. The availability of sufficient cash to pay for the deployment of troops in strategic locations in Ireland was.

Defending the entire south coast was impossible. There were not sufficient troops to do so. Bedford intended to assemble the main army at Clonmel, whence it could proceed quickly to any of several potential landing sites on the south coast. He also dispatched several small advance parties to Cork and Kerry. The mission of these advance parties was to harass French landing operations if attempted in those counties and to impede their progress from the coasts inland. If successful in their mission, these advance parties would gain time so that the duke could march the main army from Clonmel to Cork city. In the end, the defense of Ireland did not depend on the luck and courage of the advance parties in Kerry and Cork, the mobility of the main force at Clonmel, or the ability of the English government to transport troops from encampments on the Isle of Wight to Ireland. If a battle for Ireland was to be

10. Rigby to Wilmot, November 7, 1759. Wilmot Mss., T.3019/6762/644.
11. Rigby to Wilmot, November 12, 1759. Wilmot Mss., T.3019/6762/648.

fought, the best place to wage it was at sea. Such a battle was to be fought in mid-November.

Admiral Sir Edward Hawke's great victory over Conflans' force of twenty-one ships of the line occurred on November 20, 1759, in Quiberon Bay. The entire Brest squadron was annihilated as a fighting force. All possibility of an invasion of England or Ireland ended in Quiberon Bay. Official news of Hawke's victory did not arrive in Dublin until early December.[12] Therefore, the great events transpiring off the French coast had no effect whatsoever on Irish politics during November.

The prospect of invasion and the patriotic behavior danger inspired did not make Irish politicians more tractable or less ambitious. This session was distinguished by the appearance in the Irish house of commons of a brilliant young orator who was absolutely bereft of tractability and totally possessed by unbounded ambition. John Hely Hutchinson was a new experience for the men charged with managing the Irish house of commons. Lord Chancellor Bowes described Hely Hutchinson as not speaking before he was sworn, but a few minutes thereafter and not stopping since.[13] What Bowes meant was that this supremely self-confident thirty-five-year-old man was a superb debater and knew it. He was a master of polished sarcasm and loved to use it. Perhaps even more important was the fact that he would not wait. If there were no occasions in the house of commons for Hely Hutchinson to display his great talents, he would create some.

Though well-connected in Cork and happily married to a fine lady blessed with intelligence and money, Hely Hutchinson rejected connection politics and had little use for Stone, Ponsonby, Boyle, or Kildare. In the years ahead, he neither led nor followed well, but the Irish house of commons was his arena and he made the most of it. Hely Hutchinson spoke beautifully the rhetoric of patriotism, but in the course of the next thirty years he collected offices and emoluments as avidly as other gentlemen collected horses and dogs. No matter what he said or when he said it, Hely Hutchinson was at all time vitiated by an intense and inordinate desire to aggran-

12. Pitt to Bedford, November 30, 1759. SP63/416/179–180.
13. HMC Various Collections, VI, 71.

dize his family. In 1759, the way to begin such a career was to attack the Duke of Bedford's government. Hely Hutchinson began well and at once.

In Rigby's view, Hely Hutchinson was himself the only significant opposition encountered by the government during the present session. "Do not be alarmed at our late sitting," he wrote to Wilmot, "our opposition consists of but one man, who had either sense, speech, or understanding, and about seventeen or eighteen others who have none of these qualities."[14] In Rigby's judgment, Hely Hutchinson was a clever young lawyer who was extremely jealous of Pery and intended to overtake him at the bar and in politics by following the trail Pery had blazed, only doing so faster and better. Hely Hutchinson took the popular side on every question. Rigby recognized ambition when he saw it in Hely Hutchinson and was convinced that the young man would unsay tomorrow what he had said today if the price was right.

In any case, in spite of Hely Hutchinson's eloquence and persistence, the government had little trouble completing the king's business. A loan authorization for £150,000 at four percent was approved and a proposal to tax absentee placemen and pensioners was defeated. The money bills were sent off by November 25, and some conversations occurred in the house on a bill Rigby sought leave to introduce that would enable the Crown, in case of invasion, to call a parliament during prorogation. However, the major political concern among Irish public men during November was not money bills or loan approvals, it was patronage. The aged Henry Singleton died on Friday, November 9, 1759, and the lucrative office of master of the rolls became vacant.

On Saturday, November 20, 1759, Rigby applied to the lord lieutenant and shortly thereafter to Fox, Pitt, and Newcastle, for the vacated sinecure. There were no rivals for this place in England, but there was a very influential one in the person of Philip Tisdale, attorney general, and legal heir to the estates and other properties of the deceased Singleton. Tisdale wanted it, expected it, and threatened to go into opposition if he did not get it. Rigby recognized that the prospect of transferring such a handsome Irish sine-

14. Rigby to Wilmot, November 20, 1759. Wilmot Mss., T.3019/6762/570.

cure to an Englishman would be regarded as a national crime by many gentlemen inside and outside the Irish house of commons. Bedford proposed to quiet Tisdale by offering him the reversion of Carter's present post as secretary of state.[15]

This proposal worked wonders and all breaches were healed. According to Rigby, all of the lawyers who on Saturday morning had thought the country undone if a secretary were suffered to carry the place of master of the rolls out of the kingdom had changed their minds by Monday and now believed the chief secretary to be the most proper person to have the office. Only two or three persons knew about the bargain with Tisdale, but everyone knew that within seventy-two hours, for whatever reason, the attorney general had become marvelously satisfied. Newcastle presented the recommendation to the king for approval on November 16, 1759, and the formal instrument of appointment was issued forthwith and received in Dublin on November 28.

The transfer of this lucrative sinecure from an Irish politician to an English chief secretary was viewed at the time as an interesting fact, not as a national outrage. It was simply too small a fact to be outrageous. There were too many other larger facts for Irish politicians to worry about. The sometime smuggler Thurot was loose somewhere with his squadron and no one knew where or when he might appear. The prospect of a French invasion or of at least a descent upon the coast was very strong. Two Dublin banks had failed, disgracing several prominent politicians in the process, and there were rumors about the security of at least two others. Fear and uncertainty touched Dubliners of all classes. Only a proper catalyst was required to transform that fear and uncertainty into mistrust and violence. Given the state of the city in the third week of November, a proper catalyst turned out to be Rigby's bill enabling the Crown, whenever an invasion threatened, to call a parliament during prorogation. The introduction of this measure was widely and deliberately misinterpreted as the first step toward abolition of the Irish parliament and legislative union with England. On the day when the bill was to be introduced, Saturday, November 24, a large mob gathered at the College Green and threatened to invade

15. Rigby to Wilmot, November 12, 1759. Wilmot Mss., T.3019/6762/567.

the house of commons. For most of the next ten days in Dublin, mobs broke the peace and brought public affairs to a standstill.

Rigby's proposed bill to enable the crown to call a parliament during prorogation was a consequence of a similar measure added as an amendment to the English militia bill in 1756. In England, this special authority was considered a legitimate security measure in a time of national emergency and passed without opposition. Rigby opposed consideration of a clause in the British house of commons that would bind Ireland on the grounds that it would be very unpopular in that country. Rigby strongly urged that the consent of Ireland to this measure be obtained through its own parliament and promised that he would propose such a clause in the Irish parliament at first opportunity.[16] Rigby did not see this measure as an important one and simply wanted to discharge the promise he had made to the British house of commons. Thereupon, the measure was introduced and when several members opposed Ribgy's motion, the chief secretary agreed to delay further proceedings until a later time, when fuller consideration of reasons for or against it could be taken up. The later time was November 24, 1759.

Preparations for the intended discussion of Rigby's bill on November 24 were well made. Printed papers insisting this measure was a prelude to ending the Irish parliament through a legislative union with England were circulated through the city.[17] At least one member of the Irish parliament—old Richard Harwood—was suspected of giving time and energy to organizing resistance to what was represented as an English ministerial plan to effect a union. On Saturday, November 24, when members began approaching the College Green, they encountered a mob of several hundred shouting insulting Protestant slogans and demanding that the Irish parliament be saved. Such incidents prompted the speaker to send for the lord mayor and to direct him to keep the peace. Insofar as the measure that inspired these outrages was concerned, Rigby advised the house that he was indifferent to the bill and withdrew his motion.[18] Outside of the house, magistrates appeared and the mob dispersed.

16. *Gentleman's Magazine*, XXX, 1760, 638–639.
17. Rigby to Wilmot, November 26, 1759. Wilmot Mss., T.3019/6762/572.
18. *Idem.*

For the next three or four days, rumors of the direst sort could be heard in all parts of Dublin. Now identified as being primarily Protestant weavers from the Liberties, the mob was expected to break the peace again. Sporadic disturbances continued for two or three days. The house of commons appointed a committee to inquire into the causes of the disorder and to discover the names of the ringleaders. On November 28, Rigby reported the late commotions ended and peace and quiet restored. However, the chief secretary's optimism was premature.

On Monday, December 3, a mob of approximately three thousand people, many armed with bludgeons and swords, gathered in front of the parliament house by mid-day. According to eyewitnesses, a large part of that mob had been led into the College Green from Dame Street around 10:00 a. m. by a man in a brown coat who was loudly beating a large drum. When members approached the house, one part of the mob abused and obstructed those who tried to enter the building. At the same time, another part of the mob seized control of the streets and lanes leading to the parliament house, while others actually entered the house of commons and took possession of the chamber.

As speaker of the house, Ponsonby was allowed to enter the chamber without molestation; and after a brief discussion with the few members allowed in the building, he adjourned proceedings forthwith. Next, Ponsonby spoke with some of the leaders of the mob and managed to persuade them to allow himself and those members who had been able to enter the house to leave. John Bowes, lord chancellor and speaker of the house of lords, was not so fortunate. The mob stopped the chancellor's coach and demanded that he and his companion, Chief Justice Caulfield, alight and swear that they were for the country and against a union. After being detained for about a half-hour both men were allowed to leave in the chancellor's coach.[19]

Bowes and Caulfield went straightaway to Dublin Castle and reported the state of affairs to the lord lieutenant, who immediately sent for the lord mayor and sheriffs and then convened a meeting of the privy council to deal with the situation. At this meeting, the

19. HMC Various Manuscripts, VI, 71–72.

lord mayor and sheriffs declared that they had done everything in their power as civil magistrates to disperse the mob. John Tew, the lord mayor, in the presence of Lord Chancellor Bowes, told the lord lieutenant that there was no serious disorder. Bowes sharply contradicted the lord mayor, and later Rigby accused Tew of gross insolence, cowardice, or both.[20] Convinced that the time for talk was over, the lord lieutenant ordered a captain and fifty foot soldiers to march to the parliament house and clear the streets. The soldiers, unaccompanied by civil magistrates, marched quickly to the scene, whereupon the mob retreated some distance but failed to disperse and threatened to overwhelm the small force arrayed before it.

Upon receiving reports of this development, the lord lieutenant and council decided to dispatch a large detachment of cavalry to the area with the commanding officer charged in writing to disperse the mob. The sight of cavalry had the effect of intimidating the rioters, who retreated from the parliament house and College Green into nearby streets and lanes and began pelting the horses and men with stones. The troopers responded by advancing against the mob at full trot with swords drawn, wounding several, and taking some prisoners. During the rest of the night parties of horse and foot patrolled different parts of the city, restoring order and keeping the peace. It turned out that virtually all of the prisoners taken had been spectators rather than participants in the riot and that most of the latter were alleged to be dissenters.[21]

On the day following the riot, the lord lieutenant assembled the privy council and discussed the events of the previous twenty-four hours in great detail. Everyone present agreed that the disorder might have been earlier and easier suppressed if the lord major and sheriffs had exerted themselves with proper spirit. The council severely reprimanded these gentlemen for neglect of their duty and applauded the speaker of the house of commons when he summoned them to the bar of the house to be charged anew to take care of the peace of the city.[22] In addition to denouncing the lord mayor and sheriffs, the house passed several resolutions declaring the behavior of the late mob to be a most outrageous and dangerous

20. Rigby to Wilmot, December 23, 1759. Wilmot Mss., T.3019/6762/579.
21. Bedford to Pitt, December 5, 1759. SP63/416/217–219.
22. *Idem.*

violation of the rights of parliament and a high crime and misdemeanor.

The lord lieutenant issued a proclamation, posted a reward, and even obtained the assistance of the Catholic clergy in Dublin and elsewhere in seeking information and quieting the people. Insofar as encouraging informers or apprehending suspects, these actions by the Irish government, house of commons, and Catholic clergy produced poor results. About a half-dozen persons were arrested and charged with obstructing and insulting members of parliament. Trials were held six months after the event in the Court of King's Bench and all were acquitted. The Crown had been unable to prove the presence of the accused at the riot. Though the accused were discharged, the court obliged them to give security for good behavior for seven years.[23]

Thus ended a series of events which few present would ever forget. One could argue that the twelve hours between noon and midnight, December 3, 1759, had changed forever the direction of Irish politics. Anti-popery had been the primary political force affecting the majority of Irish Protestants for a very long time and would continue to be so for many of them a longer time still. However, a new political cause had been born that night in streets and alleys leading to the College Green. The popularity and power of constitutional issues had been demonstrated for all to see. There was an Irish Protestant nation in being with interests to protect, and there were formally unrepresented constituencies of that nation that henceforth had to be served.

Looking for Answers and Finding Remedies

Once all appropriate countermeasures had been taken in the immediate aftermath of the riots, analysis and explanation began. The most important of these explanations was the one prepared by Bedford for Pitt. The lord lieutenant sent off to London a long account of the riot and a short statement about its probable causes on December 5, 1759. When Bedford dispatched the messenger with this account, he knew that Hawke had defeated Conflans and

23. *Gentleman's Magazine*, XXX, 1760, 344.

that all immediate danger of a French invasion of Ireland had passed. Nevertheless, the possible role of French emissaries in promoting the late disturbances was a question the English ministers were certain to ask, so he dealt with it straightaway. He admitted great anxiety over the fact that the recent disorders occurred when a French invasion force was at sea. However, the strictest inquiry into the cause of the riots of November 24 and December 3, Bedford concluded, revealed that they took their rise from a most industriously propagated report that "a motion was to be made in the house of commons here this session, for uniting this Kingdom to Great Britain and that in consequence thereof no more Parliaments would be held in Ireland."[24]

When Bedford's account reached Whitehall on December 27, it was immediately laid before the king. However, the king and his ministers found Bedford's reasons why the disturbances occurred difficult to accept. As Pitt explained, "an idle report alone, however industriously propagated, of a motion to be made in the House of Commons for uniting the two kingdoms does by no means appear here to be an adequate solution to the strange distemper of the people."[25] Pitt accepted as a possibility that on this occasion the French may not have been involved, but in the country with such a large Catholic population that possibility had to be investigated. The minister questioned how far "unwarrantable money dealings by persons in places of high trust in his Majesty's service in Ireland" might not have contributed to this apparent extraordinary loss of respect for government by the people.[26] In the minds of the king and his ministers, scandal was more creditable as cause of what happened in Dublin than popular anxiety over the future of the Irish parliament.

Whatever the cause of the late riots, both punitive and preventative actions had to be taken. The king had been appalled by the conduct of the magistrates during the riot and directed that their conduct should be strictly inquired into in order to ascertain whether there was a basis for criminal prosecution. If such a basis could be found, then those magistrates should be prosecuted for

24. Bedford to Pitt, December 5, 1759. SP63/416/219.
25. Pitt to Bedford, December 20, 1759. SP63/416/234–235.
26. *Idem.*

criminal negligence. Finally, his majesty was gratified by the actions of the parliament after the riot and was pleased by the duke's leadership during the disturbance.

The duke received Pitt's dispatch on December 23, when parliament was in recess for the holidays, and spent much of Christmas day responding to it. He assured the ministers that nothing would be left untried or undone to rectify the evils that persecuted this unhappy country. Bedford was not content to rely only on rewards and proclamations to discover the identities of the principal rioters; he employed "more private and secure ways" to try to bring some of the guilty to proper punishment. Extraordinary efforts of some sort were necessary because Ireland had no riot act and because the "ill judged popularity of the great men seems to give little prospect of obtaining one in this Parliament."[27] In his own mind, the duke was not optimistic about apprehending and punishing many of the rioters. He simply did not believe that Dubliners would step forward and denounce their neighbors to the government, and not very many did.

With regard to the business of the lord mayor and sheriffs, Bedford stated unequivocally that he could not and would not try to proceed against them on his own authority. He counseled waiting until parliament ended its recess on January 14, 1760, and then to charge the house of commons in a special message to undertake a formal inquiry. On the question of Catholic participation in the riots, the lord lieutenant had no doubts that large numbers of them were in the mob on December 3, but the place where that mob took its rise was in the Earl of Meath's Liberty. That area, Bedford pointed out, was "chiefly inhabited by weavers, many of whom were Protestants, and of those called the New Light Presbyterians or Swadlers."[28] The tenets of this sect, both in Dublin and in the north of Ireland, were reputed to be "totally republican and averse to English government." Even though many Catholics were present in the mob, Bedford did not see Catholics as organizers or as being responsible for what had occurred.

Bedford also denied that the financial dealings of Malone and

27. Bedford to Pitt, December 25, 1759. SP63/416/257–263.
28. *Idem.*

Clements contributed much to setting the mob to attack the houses of parliament. The participation of persons in places of high trust in his majesty's service in Ireland in the banking business was not new. Neither Malone, Clements, nor any of their partners should be considered as dishonest men or in any sense as having gambled with public money. They defaulted because the mortgage market collapsed, and no popular acrimony had been directed toward them as members of parliament or as bankers.[29]

On one subject, however, Bedford's response to Pitt's dispatch of December 20 was disingenuous. He really did not know how to deal with the minister's doubts about reports of an intended union being the principal cause of the riots. In the end, the duke decided to agree with Pitt but not give up his main point. Bedford stated that reports of a union were probably more of a handle than a cause. Reports of a union had been confidentially talked of during last summer, long before a word of giving the Crown a power of assembling the parliament during a prorogation had been mentioned in Ireland. Therefore, the duke continued, "I may with truth assume, that this report of an intended union was industriously propagated by emissaries of France to stir up the people with a jealousy of England and to be ready to break forth at proper juncture."[30] Stung by ministerial criticism of his analysis of why the riots occurred, Bedford seems to have come to the opinion that if French agents or gold were the source of the rumors about a union, then those same rumors somehow would appear more credible to the English ministry as the principal cause of the late disturbances. For the moment, the duke stopped trying to explain to ministers who could not comprehend his meaning of what had happened to Irish politics during the last decade. He would leave that task to others who might be able to do it better.

Rigby was such a person. His message to friends in England was simple and direct. There was hardly a man from any party in the present Irish parliament who would support the government on an unpopular question. In Rigby's judgment, no one in the house of commons dared speak an opinion freely in that body if he thought the gallery would object to it. Even Ponsonby and Stone, though

29. *Idem.*   30. *Idem.*

generally willing to support the lord lieutenant, would not sacrifice popularity to do so.[31]

John Bowes, Lord Chancellor, and John Ryder, Archbishop of Tuam, reiterated much of what the chief secretary had said about the effects of popularity upon Irish politicians but also added insights of their own. Bowes attributed the failure of law enforcement and the general disrespect of authority in Ireland evidenced by the late riots to the events of 1753. The wicked insinuations, the many verbal and bitter attacks upon government made at that time effectively altered that disposition of the people in this country. According to Bowes, the people will believe anything prejudicial to English rule in Ireland. What possibly can be in the minds of leading men here, questioned Bowes, when a few days after one of the longest and worst riots in memory, a motion was made in the house of commons by Hely Hutchinson and supported by Anthony Malone, chancellor of the exchequer and ruined banker, for a committee to inquire into what laws may be necessary to support the liberties of the people. To be sure, the lord chancellor admitted, the motion was lost, but raising such issues at this time was totally irresponsible. It was also indicative of what had happened to Irish politics in the last seven years.[32]

Though born in Ireland and on the episcopal bench since 1742, Archbishop Ryder shared completely the views of his English-born friends Rigby and Bowes on the present state of Irish politics. He agreed that there was a general indisposition toward the people of England and a strong determination not to acknowledge the dependency of Ireland upon the British legislation. "We are all bred up," he wrote, "in a steeled antipathy to the superiority of the parliament of England." Ryder knew of no plan for asserting an independency, but to be uneasy over the present state of things and to express this uneasiness among themselves had become the turn and fashion of the upper sort of people and from them it had passed downwards. Moreover, from what had passed in recent sessions of parliament, it was clear that the way to achieve popularity was to touch upon those constitutional points that implied a subordi-

31. Rigby to Wilmot, December 10, 1759. Wilmot Mss., T.3019/6762/575.
32. Bowes to Wilmot, December 27, 1759. Wilmot Mss., T.3019/6762/581.

nation of Ireland to England. All disappointments, difficulties, and hardships were attributed to this subordination. According to the archbishop's informants, "What happened lately in Dublin is applauded on all hands; it is considered as an event which will have its effect in the preventing any new laws, or in the exercise of any power, but with the general approbation of all without doors."[33]

About remedies, the Archbishop was very clear. The English riot act should be extended to Ireland along with the provision for summoning a parliament during prorogation by the authority of the English parliament. In Ryder's mind, the failure of the British government and parliament to exercise their authority over Ireland had been a major cause of the present state of affairs. In short, the archbishop concluded, "the too seldom use of the legislative powers of Britain relative to matters in Ireland, makes us think you *dare* not use it." To the English ministers in receipt of Ryder's analysis, the archbishop added, "This you will regard as waste paper or make whatever use you think proper.[34] It would appear that if Pitt ever read His Grace of Tuam's recommendations, he must have judged them in the manner that the archbishop suspected they would be judged. The English ministers simply did not believe what they were hearing from Ireland and were not disposed to act upon it.

For example, Pitt simply denied the possibility that Presbyterians of any sort would be opposed to the English government in Ireland. Historically, he insisted, this sect had been ever and always against the Church of Rome and zealous supporters of King William and the Hanoverian succession. The fact that the riot took its rise among such people was proof positive to Pitt that the money transactions of Malone and Clements constituted the most fatal ingredient among those mentioned by the lord lieutenant as causes of the late disturbances.

About the magistrates, Pitt was ready to believe almost anything. He described Tew and the sheriffs as having totally lost all sense of fidelity and duty and urged that if proper grounds could be found, they should be prosecuted. However, Pitt insisted that the inquiry into the behavior of the magistrates should be directed by the execu-

33. Archibishop of Tuam to Wilmot, January 1, 1760. Wilmot Mss., T.3019/6762/582.

34. *Idem.*

tive power of the Irish government and not by the house of commons. If the house was involved directly in such proceedings, Pitt
feared that the result might be a further relaxation of the authority
of the king's government in Ireland. Since the riots were over and
the war was continuing, Ireland would have to provide a fair share
of the troops required to wage it. Pitt asked Bedford to increase
recruiting efforts and to release two regiments of horse for service
in Germany.[35]

Bedford's problems meeting Pitt's escalating military demands
were twofold. There were too few Protestants available to meet
existing army needs and no funds had been authorized by the Irish
parliament to pay for future augmentations. The lord lieutenant
agreed to prepare the two regiments of horse for embarkation
but insisted that recruiting Protestant private soldiers to make up
deficiencies in them would not be easy. Even more difficult than
finding Protestants to enlist for German service would be the task
of persuading the Irish parliament to increase the size of the military
establishment. He suspected that present requests for funds would
encounter some objections in the Irish parliament but in the end
all of them would be approved. About the prospect for additional
requests Bedford was not sanguine. However, Bedford had in
mind a plan whereby additional forces, in this instance marines,
could be raised for the fleet at minimal cost.

Within the last two years, about 1,200 recruits for the marines
had been raised in the predominately Catholic parts of the country.
Moreover, many more could have been obtained if proper methods
and suitable officers had been used. The proper methods were to
employ gentlemen with estates in heavily Catholic area as recruiters
and offer them commissions in the marines for doing so. Rank
would be dependent upon the number of recruits raised. Prospective captains would have to enlist 150 men whereas lieutenants
would need obtain only 75. The costs of recruitment, pay, provisions, and equipment would be born by the admiralty, commencing
as soon as the men were delivered to a naval tender for transporta-
tion to the fleet. Bedford believed that 2,000 marines could be
recruited in less than four months' time if the religion of the recruits

35. Pitt to Bedford, January 5, 1760. SP63/417/149–155.

was "out of the case." The duke's plan was approved quickly by the king, and by early February Bedford reported that more than 300 men had been raised in county Carlow alone. This group awaited inspection and approval by a field officer and arrival of a tender.[36] Henceforth, there would be places in his majesty's naval service for Irish Catholics and generally there would be recruits enough to fill them. Under the press of wartime necessity an important change in social policy had occurred almost unnoticed.

Bedford's misgivings about possible opposition to additional army increases in Ireland were well founded. On January 18, 1759, when Rigby publicly complimented Lord Drogheda and several other lords and gentlemen in the house of commons for their public service and generosity in raising troops, he was answered sharply by Hely Hutchinson and Pery. Hely Hutchinson introduced a motion attacking the raising of regiments without a previous communication of that intention to the house of commons. Whether Hely Hutchinson referred only to the efforts of Lord Drogheda and others or whether he knew about or alluded to the government's scheme to recruit Catholics for the marines is uncertain, but what astonished Rigby was the fact that Hely Hutchinson carried thirty-six members with him.

During the debates on Hely Hutchinson's motion, Pery made some observations that had no effect on the outcome of the motion but that created a great stir on the following day. During the debates of January 18, 1759, Pery stated that the motives behind the recruiting efforts of Lord Drogheda and the other gentlemen attempting to raise new regiments were not strictly those of public service and generosity. Pery suspected the real motives were greediness for rank and an expectation of being continued in place beyond the end of the war. The house adjourned immediately after Hely Hutchinson's motion was rejected and no notice was taken of Pery's remarks. When the house convened on January 19, Lord Drogheda, the speaker's nephew, was present and sitting two rows behind Pery and Brownlow. His lordship reached over to Pery across Brownlow and asked for an explanation of what had been said last night in the house concerning himself. Pery answered in effect that

36. Bedford to Pitt, February 10, 1760. SP63/418/163.

nothing had been said last night that he would not say again today. If that were so, responded Lord Drogheda, "then you and I must have some further explanation." Thereupon, Brownlow jumped up in his place and complained to the speaker that a breach of privilege had been committed by a peer then in the house.

Near pandemonium followed. The speaker cleared the house of all strangers, giving time for tempers to cool. Pery delivered a long speech urging members to take no notice on his account of what had transpired. Others insisted that Lord Drogheda's behavior had been an affront to the house of commons rather than to Pery. For this reason, Pery should not feel any necessity to give or seek satisfaction out of doors. The proceedings came to an end when the speaker apologized for his nephew's conduct in the house and gave assurances that Lord Drogheda would not call upon Pery in private. Rigby was at once disgusted and amused by the incident. He suspected that it would probably be widely exaggerated in England and tried to persuade his correspondents that indeed the affair had been a small matter and that it was over. "Though there is no longer a mob without doors," the chief secretary joked, "we are all fighting within."[37]

Two other disputes in the house of commons found no such easy resolution. The cases against the lord mayor and sheriffs for misconduct during the riot and against Malone and Clements for their financial transactions were not developing as hoped. In the former case, it appeared that nothing could be done and in the latter that too much would be attempted. There were two special problems in moving against the lord mayor and sheriffs that had to be overcome. First, the difficulty of finding persons in the general population who would come forward and give evidence to a jury about the conduct of the lord mayor and sheriffs during the riot. Second, the impropriety of most of those members of the privy council present when the lord lieutenant offered military assistance to the lord mayor appearing in a court as witnesses against him. To which must be added the absolute impossibility of Bedford himself appearing in court in this matter.[38] Though the lord lieutenant

37. Rigby to Wood, January 19, 1760. Wilmot Mss., T.3019/6762/584.
38. Russell Correspondence, II, 405–406.

continued to assure the English ministers that his law officers were diligently pursuing leads in this matter, the longer action was delayed, the less likely it became that any would be taken.

In sharp contrast to the progress of the case against the lord mayor and sheriffs, proceedings during January and February against Malone and Clements were rapid and becoming increasingly severe. A bill had been introduced that would require the setting of charges on the estates of these two unfortunate gentlemen for the benefit of their creditors. The storm against Malone and Clements in Dublin blew stronger than ever. Many members of the house of commons had declared that nothing less than their entire property, real and personal, should be pledged against the losses of the people who had trusted them. Some few went so far as to state publicly that their very plate and furniture should be sold to make up the security required. Malone tried very hard to raise money but had enormous difficulty finding purchasers. He was reluctant to advertise the sale of some of his properties for fear of driving down the price because his desperation was so widely known. Instead, Malone offered an agent three hundred guineas if he could find purchasers either in Ireland or England for properties in Meath and Roscommon.[39] At the heart of the problem for Malone and Clements was the attitude and behavior of their debtors. The many persons owing money to the firm of Malone, Clements, and Gore, Malone complained, had not the "least solicitude about what difficulties we are layed under, we are in their power as well as in that of our creditors which is a situation so disagreeable in it that I will try everyway I can think of to get out of it as fast as possible."[40]

Rigby heard the speeches and statements in the house of commons about Malone and Clements with regret. It was impossible to avoid pitying them now as it was to defend their past conduct, wrote the chief secretary. Both men were totally dejected and expected some sort of parliamentary action to remove them from their employments. Rigby hoped to be able to parry that blow because he

39. Malone to Clements, July 27, 1760. Clements Correspondence, TC 1741–43, Vol. II, Trinity College Library.
40. Malone to Clements, October 17, 1760, TC 1741–43, Vol. II, Trinity College Library.

knew what the disposition toward them would be in England if such an action were taken by the Irish parliament.[41] There would be neither sympathy nor protection. The chief secretary's compassion for Malone and Clements was shared by the lord lieutenant. Both Bedford and Rigby saw these gentlemen as honest men brought down by circumstances they could not control. Certainly some poor judgment may have contributed to their plight, but the collapse of the mortgage market and widespread cash flow problems were general causes damaging conservative and adventurous bankers alike.

In any case, the compassion extended to Malone and Clements by the chief governors was genuine. However, if genuine this compassion was also in very short supply, and as the session progressed not much of it was extended to others. The bickering in the house of commons over military needs tended to make the lord lieutenant and chief secretary impatient and unforgiving. The Irish government had majority enough to deal with these matters, but many of those whom Rigby called the "most obliged people" divided with the minority. "Favors received," complained the chief secretary, "are not reasons for supporting government and gratitude is wholly out of the question, but we shall do the King's business and that will satisfy very well."[42] However, a frightening new dimension was suddenly added to the king's business. On February 21, 1760, three French ships entered Belfast Lough and put about one thousand men ashore near Carrickfeargus. François Thurot, so long expected, had arrived.

The Invasion Crisis and After

Thurot's squadron of three ships—*Mareschal Belleisle* of 40 guns, *Le Blond* of 30 guns, and *Le Terpsicore* of 30 guns—carrying about 1,500 troops, had left Bergen before Christmas and had spent the last two months at sea. Suffering from a severe shortage of provisions and driven by violent gales, Thurot's squadron appeared off the Scottish island of Islay, Argyleshire, on February 17. In search

41. Rigby to Wilmot, January 14, 1760. Wilmot Mss. T.3019/6762/583.
42. Rigby to Wood, February 1, 1760. Wilmot Mss., T.3019/6762/585.

of provisions, the squadron made its way to Belfast Lough by February 20 and landed about 1,000 men near Carrickfeargus on the following day.

Engaging about 300 men of the 62nd regiment under the command of Lieutenant Colonel John Jennings, the French captured and occupied the town of Carrickfeargus. French objectives went no further than obtaining provisions and leaving Ireland as soon as possible. Provisions were obtained from both Carrickfeargus and Belfast. Before reembarking on February 25 and departing the next morning on an easterly course, the French burned and plundered most of Carrickfeargus.

When the news of the French landing first reached Belfast, Stephen Haven, Sovereign of the town, sent off a frightened message to Pitt dated "half an hour past three o'clock in the morning" February 23. He reported the fact of the landing and the occupation of Carrickfeargus, and warned the minister that if the French appeared before Belfast, surrender was his only option. Haven protested the neglect of defense preparations in his area, claiming that the inhabitants were spirited and anxious to defend their property but had no arms with which to fight. Furthermore, Haven contended, the king's troops in the area were insufficient and untrained, consisting "of no more than one hundred and fifty new levies."[43]

The most pressing problem, as Haven indicated, was the lack of arms and ammunition, especially the latter. Arms for 1,400 men had been delivered to depots in Down and another 1,200 had been sent to Armagh. Requests for arms had been received by the lord lieutenant from Cavan and Londonderry. However, no requests for arms had been sent from Belfast[44] and apparently none had been delivered. It would also appear that when arms had been delivered to places in the north, sufficient stocks of ammunition had not accompanied them. In any case, when militia men began arriving in Belfast on February 22 from the county they had some arms but very little ammunition.[45]

Throughout the entire five days of the French occupation of

43. Haven to Pitt, February 22, 1760. SP63/418/173.
44. Russell Correspondence, II, 411–412.
45. Strode to Bedford, February 22, 1760. SP63/418/168.

Carrickfeargus, the behavior of military authorities in Belfast and Dublin was intelligent and professional. General Strode in Belfast had forces under his command in numbers suitable for guarding prisoners of war but not for repelling a landing force of the size the French had put ashore. Strode made the most of what he had. The general took no unnecessary risks, secure in the belief that time was on his side and that reinforcements would come. Most important, Strode kept his lines of communication with Dublin open. The flow of information between Belfast and Dublin during this period was constant and fast. In addition, coordination between Belfast and military and naval units elsewhere in the country was excellent.

For example, the French appeared off Carrickfeargus at 11 o'clock in the morning of February 21, 1760. Strode's first dispatch to Bedford about the situation was dated twenty-five minutes past five o'clock in the afternoon of February 21. Strode's dispatch reached Dublin Castle a little before eleven o'clock in the morning of February 22.[46] A copy of Strode's dispatch, along with a message from the lord lieutenant, was sent off immediately to Captain John Elliott of his majesty's frigate *Aeolus* at Kinsale, ordering him to depart for Carrickfeargus as soon as possible. Bedford's message reached *Aeolus* on February 24,[47] and Elliott wasted no time issuing sailing orders to the captains of *Pallas* and *Brilliant*. Elliott's squadron of *Aeolus*, 32 guns, *Brilliant*, 36 guns, and *Pallas*, 36 guns, cleared Kinsale Roads on February 24 and made excellent progress through St. George's Channel, reaching Malahide on February 26,[48] only a few hours after the French had left Carrickfeargus. This extraordinary combination of excellent communication between Belfast, Dublin, and Kinsale, ship readiness at Kinsale, and favorable weather put Elliott's squadron in position to make an interception in the north channel before Thurot had an option of choosing an easterly or westerly passage of the Isle of Man into the Irish sea.

If the performance of the military and naval authorities in Ireland during the invasion crisis was intelligent and professional, the initial responses of the public in Dublin were otherwise. The first public reaction to the news of the landing at Carrickfeargus was a run

---

46. Russell Correspondence, II, 405.
47. Elliott to Bedford, February 24, 1760. SP63/418/150.
48. Elliott to Bedford, February 29, 1760. SP63/418/166.

upon the four remaining banking houses in the city. Parliament responded with a flood of patriotic speeches and then voted the government a credit of £300,000 for military preparations.[49] Rigby seemed almost to enjoy the escalating fear and intense anxieties exhibited by many in the house of commons. "Most of the Patriots," Rigby wrote to a friend on February 27, "are gone to do this country as little service with their hands and their militias, as they do with their heads at the College Green."[50] Almost at the very moment when the chief secretary scoffed at the behavior of lords and gentlemen with property in the north, a more proper service which even Rigby would never mock was being performed in the seas between the Mull of Galloway and the Isle of Man. Captain Elliott's frigates made contact with the French squadron at first light on February 28. Thurot's remarkable escapade had come to an end.

Elliott's force chased the French squadron for about four hours until *Aeolus* came abreast of *Mareschal Belleisle* at about nine o'clock in the morning, whereupon Elliott ordered his first broadside. The engagement became general among all six ships and continued briskly for an hour and a half until all three French ships struck their colors. Captain Thurot had been killed in the second or third broadside. Elliott estimated that French losses amounted to upwards of 300 men killed and wounded. He reported only 5 killed and 31 wounded in his entire squadron.[51] Though both sides were evenly matched in numbers of guns, Elliott's ship handling had been extraordinary and the marksmanship of his gunners was superb. It was a great victory and church bells in Belfast and Dublin rang out the news.

Bedford knew that questions would be asked by Pitt and by the king and he wanted to have answers ready for them. One such question would touch upon Jennings' behavior at Carrickfeargus. Bedford sent an officer to the actual battle site to prepare a plan of the French attack and Jennings' dispositions for defense. The officer questioned both French and English participants in the battle and reported that in his judgment Jennings had done everything possible with a handful of men at a place that was virtually indefensi-

49. Rigby to Wilmot, February 23, 1760. Wilmot Mss., T.3019/6762/586.
50. Rigby to Wilmot, February 27, 1760. Wilmot Mss., T.3019/6762/592.
51. Elliott to Bedford, February 29, 1760. SP63/418/166.

ble.[52] Bedford conveyed the substance of this report to Pitt and recommended that at a future time Jennings should be offered a commission in an older and more fashionable regiment.[53] The Irish house of commons agreed heartily with the duke's evaluation of Jennings' leadership and said so in a public vote of thanks.

Another question would be one relating to the lack of arms in the north for the Protestant militia. Pitt asked such a question directly as early as March 13. The minister sent the lord lieutenant a copy of Stephen Haven's discouraging dispatch of February 22 intimating that surrender of Belfast was unavoidable and complaining about the failure of the Irish government to provide Belfast Protestants with arms and ammunition. Bedford was outraged that Haven had sent such a letter and pronounced the man's assertions patently false. The duke insisted that the government had denied arms to no Protestant gentlemen who had asked for them. In the case of Belfast, not only had no application for arms ever been submitted, but Haven was absolutely unknown even by name to the duke. The first time that Bedford ever saw the name of the man was in the letters transmitted by Pitt. This accusation of neglect of duty probably angered the duke more than any other incident during his entire time in Ireland. He wanted Haven disciplined in some way, and asked Pitt directly whether such an insolent and unprovoked attack upon the lord lieutenant of Ireland "shall not receive from you such a check, as may prevent like impertinences to me, and trouble to you for the future."[54] Insofar as is known, Pitt did not pursue this matter any further.

In Ireland, however, there were a few men very anxious to pursue further this matter or any other that would have the effect of embarrassing the duke's government. The issue of shortages of militia arms in the northern counties was taken up by George Lowther, member for Ratoath and a friend of Hely Hutchinson. Lowther sought leave to move an address to the lord lieutenant requesting that more arms be sent to the north. The motion was badly presented and got nowhere. Rigby described the effort as

52. Bedford to Pitt, March 6, 1760. SP63/418/180.
53. Russell Correspondence, II, 411.
54. Russell Correspondence, II, 412.

pathetic and the last gasp of the opposition during the present session. Lowther was a man, wrote Rigby, "who had just learning enough to read one of Hely Hutchinson's motions when he puts it into his hand."[55] Not only did Lowther withdraw his motion but the government carried a vote thanking the northern counties of Down, Armagh, and Antrim for "their zeal, activity, and courage in defending themselves."

Rigby's observation that Lowther's motion was the last gasp of opposition in the present sitting of parliament was almost true. Until the final weeks of the session, when Pery and Hely Hutchinson recommenced what the lord chancellor styled as their "oratorical malady," the chief governors of Ireland gave little of their time to affairs at the College Green. Not much happened in the Irish parliament during March and early April except routine approvals of bills returned from England. The lord lieutenant gave most of his attention to military matters occurring in Ireland and elsewhere.

Recruitment and training of new levies was of utmost importance, and Bedford found himself without directions from the war office about what to do and without resources to enable him to do anything. Therefore, the duke prepared his own plans for maneuvers and encampments during the summer and submitted them to Pitt for approval.[56] Not only did Pitt approve Bedford's plan, but the tone of the approval was noticeably different. It was almost friendly, or as friendly as Pitt could be at this stage of his career. Perhaps feeling a bit guilty over the way the Haven message had been handled, Pitt advised Bedford that the king relied entirely upon the lord lieutenant's judgment in these matters, but reminded him politely that the enemy had not yet laid aside all thoughts and plans of invasion.[57] The other pressing military problem was preparing the cavalry units selected for German service for embarkation, but in late March all such preparation had to stop. The country had been struck by a severe epidemic of horse distemper. It was everywhere and no one dared lead a horse out of a stable. No horse guards were mounted at Dublin Castle and not a hackney coach or

55. Rigby to Wilmot, March 6, 1760. Wilmot Mss., T.3019/6762/594.
56. Bedford to Pitt, April 8, 1760. SP63/418/234.
57. Pitt to Bedford, May 3, 1760. SP63/418/250.

horse car was anywhere to be seen. There would be no embarkation until the epidemic had run its course.[58]

There was one other as yet undetermined military matter of great interest to many Irish politicians. In August 1759, Prince Ferdinand of Brunswick had won a major victory over the French at Minden. At a critical moment during the course of that battle, Ferdinand had ordered a charge by five regiments of British cavalry under the command of Lord George Sackville in order to turn a victory into a rout. Sackville questioned what he believed were confusing and conflicting orders and three times refused to advance. The French, having lost 10,000 men and 115 guns, were allowed to retire from the field relatively unhindered to regroup.

Ferdinand was appalled by Sackville's conduct and said so publicly. Enraged and insulted, Sackville asked to be recalled, and upon arriving in London three weeks after the battle he learned that he had been dismissed from the army. Sackville immediately applied for a court martial, which, after much procrastination by the government, was convened at the Horse Guards in London on March 25, 1760. The proceedings of the court martial were closely followed by Sackville's friends in Ireland. When the court martial reported its findings on April 5, 1760, that Sackville was guilty of having disobeyed Prince Ferdinand's orders and then judged him unfit to serve the king in any military capacity whatever, those Irish friends were shocked. In particular, Stone was absolutely distraught. The primate had received daily accounts of the proceedings, which he relayed to Rigby and Bedford.[59] Although neither Bedford nor Rigby felt as strongly about Lord George as did those in Ireland who had known and worked with him, they had to deal with the consequences of the court martial's judgment.

The king, whose earlier dislike and distrust of Sackville when in Ireland had grown into a positive detestation, confirmed the sentence of the court martial and required that it be recorded in order books, then given out in the public orders of every regiment, wherever stationed. Bedford lost no time in executing the king's commands in this regard, and when the king struck Lord George's name

58. Rigby to Wilmot, April 3, 1760. Wilmot Mss., T.3019/6762/600.
59. *Idem.*

from list of English privy councillors, Bedford did the same in Ireland.[60] With the business of the session virtually finished, Bedford requested leave to return to England and to appoint the primate, speaker, and Lord Shannon as lords justices. The request for leave to return and the appointment of lords justices was quickly approved in London on April 15 and received back in Dublin on April 24.[61]

Anticipating no difficulties about the appointment of the lords justices, Bedford made plans for a mid-May departure. However, during the last half of April the practicality of such a departure date became very much in doubt. On April 10, Dawson's bank closed its door. A very short run had forced Dawson to stop all payments. Of the other three functioning Dublin Banks—Finlay, Gleadowe, and LaTouche—only LaTouche seemed out of danger.[62] Moreover, circulation of paper currency of any sort in the city had come to a total stop. The cause of the present crisis was of long standing. There simply was not enough cash in Ireland to fuel an expanding economy. Until there was a paper currency that people would accept with confidence, cash flow problems would continue to be endemic in the commercial life of the country. When banks failed for whatever reason, credit became uncertain, merchants reduced stocks, imports and exports declined, and public revenues suffered. By 1760, this pattern was familiar enough, but the failure of Dawson's bank added a new dimension to it. Dawson publicly blamed the Irish government for his failure and a great many people believed him.

According to Rigby, Dawson and his friends attributed the cause of their disaster to the government loan offered by the Irish treasury. In their view, the cash of the country was being drawn into the treasury through loan subscriptions. Both Rigby and Sir Henry Cavendish, cashier for the loan, denied that such was the case, insisting that no more than 18,000 guineas had been received. The rest of the money subscribed was in banker's bills. Moreover, increased military expenses required that at least 18,000 guineas in

60. Bedford to Pitt, May 1, 1760. SP63/418/254. Bedford to Pitt, May 3, 1760. SP63/418/256.

61. Pitt to Bedford, April 15, 1760. SP63/418/244.

62. Rigby to Newcastle, April 10, 1760. Wilmot Mss., T.3019/6762/602.

specie be kept in hand.[63] Despite the statements of Rigby and Cavendish about the amount of cash actually in the treasury, Dawson's argument was accepted by the Dublin business community to the extent that a petition setting forth the low state of public and private credit, desiring the interposition of the government in the present crisis, and urging that some means be found to circulate a paper currency was presented to the house of commons. The petition was introduced by Dunn, member for the city, and seconded and principally supported by Pery.[64]

Bedford summoned the principal crown servants to the Castle on April 14 in order to determine how to deal with the petition. The report that large amounts of money were lying in the treasury was widely credited throughout the city, and the memory of December 3 was in everyone's mind at the lord lieutenant's meeting. The discussions were extremely heated. Some of those present were violent against Dawson. Rigby pointed out that when Dawson discovered that his bank was in danger, he applied to the duke for money; and when refused, the man brazenly began propagating atrocious lies in order to create a crisis he hoped somehow would save him.[65] Another insisted that Dawson was an utter rascal. There was strong sentiment among those who spoke first for rejecting the petition. In the end, however, after considering the heat and temper of the people in the city, the consensus of Bedford's advisers was to receive the petition, but to do so a week hence, April 21, rather than on April 15 as Pery had demanded.[66]

On April 19, Rigby was approached by a committee of merchants who wanted to present to him their plan for restoring credit and public confidence in paper currency. After assuring the chief secretary that they had no intention of attacking the government, he agreed to see them and examine their plan. Rigby was not at all disarmed by their deference. The chief secretary was ready for a difficult time, but it did not happen. He suspected that the merchants knew that the government had parliament tight in hand and

63. *Idem.*
64. Rigby to Wilmot, April 15, 1760. Wilmot Mss., T.3019/6762/603.
65. *Idem.*
66. Rigby to Wilmot, April 15, 1760. Wilmot Mss., T.3019/6762/603.

that for the sake of their cause it was best to be civil.[67] In any case, when the house of commons took up the business of the merchant's petition in a committee of the whole on April 21, the chamber was full to capacity, so full that Rigby described the sitting of April 21 as more like a committee of the whole nation than of the whole house.[68]

The proceedings began with an examination by the committee, lasting several hours, of three of the most prominent merchants on the present state of credit and paper currency. When the examination was over, the merchants were dismissed by the committee and asked to reduce to writing whatever scheme they had in mind and to present it to the committee for consideration later in the day. The merchants did their work quickly and returned with a scheme wherein the Irish parliament would become security for the three remaining banks in Dublin to the extent of £150,000 for two years. This sum would be equally distributed among the three financial houses.[69]

The merchant's scheme was received by the committee, and resolutions intended to implement it were prepared and scheduled for introduction and presentation to the house on April 23. In the evening of April 22, the lord lieutenant, chief secretary, and principal crown servants met at the Castle to decide what the government position on the merchants' scheme ought to be. After a very long meeting, those present agreed neither to adopt nor to oppose the scheme. If the house of commons approved the resolutions and became security for the Dublin banks, which appeared to be the prevailing disposition, then the house of commons would bear the burden of the scheme and be answerable for the efficacy of it. Rigby believed that if the scheme worked, the government would benefit directly because an improved circulation of paper currency would prevent a further diminution of trade and thereby keep up the revenue. He was willing to give the scheme a try.[70] The resolutions implementing the merchants' scheme were introduced on April 23 and approved unanimously.

67. Rigby to Wilmot, April 19, 1760. Wilmot Mss., T.3019/6762/604.
68. Rigby to Wilmot, April 22, 1760. Wilmot Mss., T.3019/6762/605.
69. *Idem.*   70. *Idem.*

Hopeful that the resolutions would help restore the credit of the remaining banks to the extent that people would again deposit money with them, and admitting to friends that he had grown weary of Irish politicians and Irish problems, Bedford began final departure preparations. Rigby expressed the states of mind of himself and the lord lieutenant by complaining to a friend that he had spent all day in the house and all night in the council, and then written himself blind until morning.[71] This impossible regimen came to an end when Bedford went to the house on May 17 to deliver the customary speech and to prorogue the session. However, in spite of Bedford's complimentary speech and the polite addresses from the commons urging the duke to return and continue in the government of Ireland, the session ended almost as it had begun, with Hely Hutchinson speaking.

Indeed, this man had risen in the world since October. Excellent preparation characterized his performances in the house of commons, and on the final day of the session, he disappointed no one. As he had spoken earlier for a committee to inquire into what laws might be necessary to support the liberties of the people a few days after the riot of December 3, and as he had supported Lowther's proposed address on the shortage of militia arms in the north shortly after the defeat of Thurot, he spoke on May 17 about the large sums of money allegedly lying in the treasury while banks failed and credit disappeared. Hely Hutchinson had a resolution to offer, but before any action could be taken on it, the usher of the black rod interrupted his speech in order to allow members to hear from the lord lieutenant. The duke thanked the house of commons for their support and generosity during the session and, much to the satisfaction of all those present save one, he brought the session to an end.[72]

Bedford and Rigby wasted little time thereafter. The lord lieutenant and chief secretary boarded the yacht *Dorset* on May 19 and departed for Parkgate at one o'clock,[73] anxious to leave but expecting to return. Bedford and Rigby had served the king in Ireland

71. *Idem.*
72. Henry Cavendish to Wilmot, May 17, 1760. Wilmot Mss., T.3019/6762/609.
73. Lords Justices to Pitt, May 20, 1760. SP63/418/252.

under very difficult circumstances. They had managed parliament well and coped successfully with financial panic, public disorders, and the threat and reality of invasion. The duke was respected if not loved. Rigby's abilities as chief secretary were much admired. He was after Lord George Sackville, the brightest man of the century so far to serve as chief secretary, and he certainly wrote the most informative and entertaining official letters. Those in Ireland who knew him well liked him. Thomas Waite, secretary to the lords justices, described Rigby as the most agreeable master a man could have, treating his subordinates with the openness and affection of a brother, and "to the latest hours of my life, I shall love, honor, and esteem him."[74] There were others within and without the Irish parliament who disliked the chief secretary intensely, particularly those who had been the objects of his wit and sarcasm; and there was at least one Irish nobleman who made public his intention to meet Rigby on the field of honor. However much the abilities of Bedford and Rigby were appreciated or the two men as persons respected or disliked, their time in Ireland was a critical turning point in the history of Irish parliamentary politics.

Bedford and Rigby were midwives to the birth of a new political system in Ireland. The basis of this new system was the agreement with Stone made in February 1758 to represent the principal Irish political factions in the appointment of lords justices, the increased popularity of constitutional issues inside and outside of the Irish parliament, and the growing perception by members of the house of commons that there was an Irish Protestant national interest that needed to be protected and served. Indeed, the true dimensions of this new system were not to be altogether clear for about a year and a half, and it would take a general election to make them so. Bedford and Rigby had worked out the basis for a great change in Irish politics, but under the existing Irish constitution only God could provide the general election that would bring that change about.

Most likely none of this was in the minds of the lord lieutenant and chief secretary as the *Dorset* approached the Chester coast mak-

74. Waite to Wilmot, January 30, 1761. Wilmot Mss., T.3019/6762/629.

ing for Parkgate. Bedford and Rigby were most concerned about discovering the true nature of ministerial and royal opinion about their performance while in Ireland. In matters of this sort, no one could ever be sure that what had been said in public was what was being said in private. Both were extremely anxious to find out where they stood.

CHAPTER VIII

The End of an Era

A Matter of Honor

When the *Dorset* reached Holyhead, Bedford went off to his country house and Ribgy proceeded directly to London. The chief secretary was extremely anxious to discover what sort of reception Bedford could expect when he journeyed to St. James. Rigby had to get his sense of the state of things from second- and third-level people because there was not a minister connected with Irish affairs to be seen. Nonetheless, Ribgy presented himself at court and was received warmly by the king, who inquired about the duke and duchess and gave every appearance of complete satisfaction with the duke's administration of Irish affairs. The king's attitude seemed to be generally shared by others and Rigby reported to Bedford that he would be graciously received at St. James and "it is hoped that you will be as well pleased with the ministers as they with you."[1]

Part of the reason for the pleasant mood of the king and the court was the good news from Canada. French efforts to retake Quebec had been thoroughly defeated. General Murray's letters proclaimed that French affairs were quite over in that part of the world.[2] Rigby enjoyed the news from Canada and the celebrations that news inspired as much as anyone, but he longed to be quit of pending Irish business as soon as possible and be off to his beloved Mistley Park. Consequently, the chief secretary pressed Pitt and Newcastle with four categories of recommendations for honors, pensions, and jobs. There were recommendations that came from the lord lieutenant and there were those that emanated from the speaker, from the pri-

1. Russell Correspondence, II, 414–415.
2. *Ibid.*, 415.

mate, and from Lord Shannon. The new political system Bedford
and Rigby had established in Ireland in February 1758 had to be
implemented. The lords justices had successfully undertaken the
king's business during the late session and now their followers expected that promises made would be kept.

Ponsonby reminded Rigby of the new arrangements for managing the Irish parliament by recalling the several favors that the chief
secretary "had been so kind to promise his friends."[3] Those favors
included a deanry, a small church living, the reversion of a small
employment in the customs, an employment worth £400 a year, two
small pensions, a law appointment, one military commission, and
two changes of military assignment. The primate's requests were
more formidable. Stone sought three small pensions, three military
appointments, and several small church matters. He also asked that
Lord Drogheda be made a colonel and that his lordship, along with
Benjamin Burton, be added to the privy council. On the matter of
major church appointments, the primate would not presume to
deter the lord lieutenant from commitments already made; but
when future vacancies occurred and if the duke had no particular
person in mind, Stone hoped he would consider Dr. Benjamin
Barrington, present rector of Armagh, as a candidate for an Irish
bishopric.[4] Lord Shannon's needs were relatively modest. He asked
only for two new baronets and reminded the lord lieutenant about
a promise made to Jemmett Browne, Bishop of Cork and Ross,
to succeed to the Archbishopric of Cashel when the incumbent
archbishop died.[5]

By mid-August virtually all of the post-session Irish business was
completed. Rigby took his leave of the Duke of Newcastle and at
long last sent out for Mistley Park. Though the war was going badly
in the east and the French had once again invaded Hanover, the
mood of the court remained cheerful. Rigby reported that, despite
his near seventy-seven years, the king appeared to be in good health
and that business both at court and in the ministry proceeded
expeditiously. The chief secretary hoped to have a few weeks'
respite among his own people in Essex from the demands and

3. Ponsonby to Rigby, May 14–18, 1760. Bedford Mss., T.2915/9/47.
4. Memorandum from Stone, May 19, 1760. Bedford Mss., T.2915/9/52.
5. Jemmet Brown to Bedford, June 10, 1760. Bedford Mss., T.2915/9/58.

sensitivities of Irish politicians and the problems of Ireland. Such was not to be the case. Irish problems followed Rigby all the way to Mistley Park. The Earl of Clanricarde sent a letter to the Duke of Bedford on August 22, 1760, wherein he threatened him with bodily harm at their next meeting. The lord lieutenant rebuked Clanricarde in the strongest possible terms, questioning whether his lordship had actually labored under some indisposition when he wrote the letter. In Bedford's judgment, the letter was "false, impertinent, and unworthy of a gentleman to write."[6]

Rigby learned of Clanricarde's behavior in October and could not account for it. However, he advised a friend that if the earl did not "make good his words of breaking my bones the first time we meet, I certainly shall break his."[7] The chief secretary was not content with private jokes at Clanricarde's expense. He wanted to protect the character and reputation of the Duke of Bedford and took immediate steps to do so. Rigby delivered Clanricarde's letter to the Duke of Devonshire, who in turn brought it to the attention of the principal ministers. Devonshire was outraged by the letter and demanded that Clanricarde be put under immediate arrest.[8] Pitt was unwilling to go that far at this moment, but he agreed with the other ministers that the letter must be viewed as an affront to the king and to his government and that a solemn proceedings upon it should be held before the whole cabinet, wherein Crown lawyers could consider what legal actions were appropriate. In this meeting, Lord Mansfield urged Rigby to prevail upon Bedford not to publish anything that had passed between himself and Clanricarde until the lawyers had time to determine a proper legal strategy.[9]

Rigby advised Bedford that Clanricarde's reputation as an irresponsible fool and scoundrel was well known to several of the ministers. The chief secretary also assured the duke that protection of his grace's honor and character was uppermost in the minds of all of the ministers. What Rigby did not say to the duke or to any of the ministers was that he, Richard Rigby, had no intention of waiting

6. Draft of a letter from Bedford to Clanricarde, August 31, 1760. Bedford Mss., T.2915/10/27.
7. Rigby to Wilmot, October 19, 1760. Wilmot Mss., T.3019/6762/616.
8. Devonshire to Wilmot, October 25, 1760. Wilmot Mss., T. 3019/6762/617.
9. Rigby to Bedford, October 22, 1760. Bedford Mss., T.2915/10/44.

for the wheels of justice to turn. His patron had been injured and satisfaction would be demanded forthwith. On October 18, 1760, two days before Lord Mansfield took the Clanricarde matter under advisement, Rigby dispatched a messenger to Ireland with a challenge to his lordship to come to Holyhead with a friend at his own time and disavow what he had written or face the consequences.[10]

The challenge was delivered but the duel did not occur. The attorney general of England intervened by ordering a prosecution of Clanricarde for libel and the earl could not come to England without risk of arrest. Rigby subsequently published his challenge declaring Clanricarde no gentlemen for failing to accept it. The earl published his version of the challenge in January 1761, explaining that because of the pending prosecution England was no proper place for a meeting with Rigby. Clanricarde implied that Rigby knew about the prosecution and that was why the chief secretary had chosen Holyhead. The earl insisted that he was ready to meet Rigby at some other place at any time or for that matter to meet any man who thought there were reasons to call upon him. Clanricarde declared himself ready to defend his honor against anyone no matter how high born or well circumstanced. If not, he would be "very unworthy to bear the names most dear to me, Irishman, and gentleman."[11] Thus was the Clanricarde affair put to rest. This case along with every other matter of political and administrative business was suddenly eclipsed by an event that most people expected sooner or later but not at the present moment. On October 25, 1760, King George II died. Every active politician in England, Scotland, Wales, and Ireland had to wonder about the future. The mood at the court and in Leicester House was clear enough. One era had ended and a new and different one was about to begin.

The Hegemony of Primate Stone

Accounts of the royal demise did not reach Dublin until October 29. When the news arrived, the primate and Lord Shannon were in the city but the speaker was in distant county Kerry. Because the

10. Rigby to Clanricarde, October 18, 1760. Wilmot Mss., T.3019/6762/626.
11. Clanricarde to the Public, January 21, 1761. Wilmot Mss., T.3019/6762/626.

roads were so excessively bad, Ponsonby did not get back to Dublin
until November 4. He discovered, as did the other two lords justices
in Dublin, that grief for the deceased monarch was genuine and
spontaneously expressed by all classes of Protestants and Catholics.[12] However, principals in the Irish government and public men
in and out of Dublin could not afford much time for public or
private mourning. They had to turn their attention to politics. The
first issue to be determined was whether or not the Irish parliament
had been dissolved by the king's death. A search of the statutes in
England and Ireland revealed that such was not the case. By law
the present parliament was continued for six months after the death
of the sovereign.[13] There would have to be a general election soon
but not as quickly as many had feared.

The intensity of the election fever that swept over the country
was beyond anything that most members of parliament could remember. Not very many sitting members had been in their places
when the first session of the present parliament had opened thirty-
three years ago. The change in Dublin was astonishing. Before the
news of the king's death arrived, official Dublin had been preoccupied with the behavior of an over-zealous Scot assigned to the coastal
revenue patrol.[14] Accusations against Captain Dalrymple ranged
from theft to piracy, but all his escapades, real and alleged, were
forgotten in the excitement of preparing for a general election.
Electioneering actually began before Ponsonby returned from
Kerry. Thereafter, it became the principal business of the lords
justices. Their houses were filled from morning to night with
candidates and agents. However, there was little disagreement
among themselves or between themselves and Lord Kildare about
candidates. They appear to have agreed not to compete.[15]

Though there were reports of great activity by the lords justices
and much discussion about the election in the city, canvassing in
the counties and in the few other relatively open constituencies did
not begin in earnest until late November. One observer reported

12. Waite to Wilmot, November 6, 1760; Bowes to Wilmot, November 18, 1760.
Wilmot Mss., T.3019/6762/620, 621.
13. Rigby to Wilmot, September 28, 1760. Wilmot Mss., T.3019/6762/615.
14. *Idem.*
15. Waite to Wilmot, November 6, 1760. Wilmot Mss., T.3019/6762/620.

to Bedford that not more than six county elections and very few constituencies in the large towns and boroughs would be seriously contested. What surprised everyone was the strength and apparent durability of the union of parties Bedford had established. Agreement seemed to be everywhere and friends of Bedford were predicting that not even a single disputed election petition would divide the governing group the duke had put in place.[16] Yet by the end of November, Lord Chancellor Bowes reported that electioneering had emptied the city and that the best guesses were that seventy to one hundred new members would be present in the new parliament. Some old members appeared to be in difficulty. Malone had to look elsewhere than county Westmeath for a safe seat. Venality reached new heights. As much as £2,000 for a seat had been offered and rejected in several instances, and the fiscal arrangements of prominent men in quest of seats was the basis of much gossip in great houses throughout the country.[17]

The lords justices persuaded Bedford that the welfare of the country required a prompt dissolution of the present parliament and a swift issuance of writs calling for the election of a new one. They wanted the elections to begin no later than December 20, 1760, and to be completed by mid-February 1761, all within the year of the present sheriffs because, in the judgment of their lordships, delay of the election would have the effect of increasing party animosities and occasion idleness and riot in many parts of the country.[18] The lord lieutenant was willing to comply, but actions by the lords justices and a majority of the Irish privy council made it extremely difficult for him to do so.

Bedford responded to the lords justices' request for a prompt dissolution and election on November 18, 1760, by formally ordering their lordships to dissolve the Irish parliament and instructing them to prepare and transmit to the English privy council a bill as a cause for the summoning of a new parliament.[19] Because contrary winds delayed arrival of packets from England, the lords justices de-

16. W. H. Fortescue to Bedford, December 2, 1760. Bedford Mss., T.2915/10/60.

17. Bowes to Wilmot, November 18, 1760. Wilmot Mss., T.3019/6762/621.

18. Russell Correspondence, II, 422.

19. Bedford to the Lords Justices, November 18, 1760. Shannon Mss., D.2207/A/1/6/2.

cided to take up the matters of the dissolution and bill preparation
with the Irish privy council at a meeting scheduled to deal with routine business on November 22, 1760, before the lord lieutenant's response to their request had actually arrived. The lords justices anticipated that Bedford's approval of a prompt dissolution and early
elections would be forthcoming, so in the interest of saving time they
put these matters to the privy council without apprising the members
that new and important business had been added to the agenda of
what was supposed to be an ordinary meeting of the council.[20] Lord
Chancellor Bowes knew nothing about the nature of the new business
until he took his seat at the council table on November 22.[21]

At this council meeting, Stone approached Bowes and in the
presence of Tisdale asked for advice about what sort of bills ought
to be prepared for transmittal to England as a cause for calling a
new parliament. Bowes responded by complaining that instant
answers to questions as complex as this one were inappropriate, but
he presumed that the lords justices should try to discover what had
been done in the past and then follow precedents. Insofar as Bowes
could remember, a money bill had always been transmitted for this
purpose. When this matter was put to the council, Malone objected
strenuously to transmitting a money bill. He argued that there
would be sufficient time after parliament opened to prepare a
proper supply bill because the present duties would not expire until
December 25, 1761. Malone insisted that if a supply bill were
transmitted most likely it would be rejected when returned and
would probably produce heats which should be avoided in a new
parliament.[22] Others at both ends of the council board took up
Malone's argument and added to it. One member contended that
in 1727 at the accession of his late majesty, the necessity for transmitting a money bill as a cause for calling a new parliament was vigorously opposed. However, at that time arguments of expediency,
such as the lateness of the season and the risk of allowing the duties
to expire, prevailed and a money bill was in fact transmitted.[23]

20. Lords Justices to Bedford, November 23, 1760. Shannon Mss., D.2207/A/1/
6/3A and B.
21. HMC Various Collections, VI, 75.
22. *Idem.*
23. Lords Justices to Bedford, November 23, 1760. Shannon Mss., D.2207/A/1/
6/3A and B.

As the discussion continued, Bowes suspected that each speaker on the matter of transmitting a money bill had become convinced that this issue would be a popular point in the forthcoming election and strove to appear very strong against it. The principal problem facing those at the council board appeared to be how to oppose transmittal of a money bill without encountering strong opposition and resentment from the English side of the water. They persuaded themselves that Bedford could prevail upon Pitt and the other English ministers that their arguments against transmitting a money bill were constitutionally sound and politically expedient. To this end, the lords justices were charged to make the case for the Irish privy council to the lord lieutenant as firmly and as quickly as possible.[24]

On the day following this council meeting the lords justices wrote a long and closely argued letter to the duke. The purpose of this letter was to forestall resentment and explain in detail the apprehensions of the privy council, and to urge that only "such bills as can be liable to no exception be transmitted."[25] If the duke agreed with their proposed method of proceeding, the lords justices continued, they saw themselves, the parliament, and the whole kingdom freed from a great impending distress. However, if the duke misunderstood or otherwise disagreed with their recommendations, they hoped that all proceedings would be postponed and the calling of a new parliament delayed until a more distant time. Anxiety about this matter would surely remain high until the lord lieutenant's determination was known, and a lengthy delay of the election might transform what was now a spring of discontent into a torrent that could not be withstood.[26]

Before the lords justices' letter reached London, Bedford's instruction of November 18, ordering a dissolution and preparation of bills for transmittal, was received at Dublin. The lords justices acted with dispatch by dissolving parliament and immediately sending off on November 26 a routine amendment to a popery act and an amendment to a judicial procedure act as bills to serve as causes

24. HMC Various Collections, VI, 75.
25. Lords Justices to Bedford, November 23, 1760. Shannon Mss., D.2207/A/1/6/3A and B.
26. *Idem.*

for summoning a new parliament. These two bills were presented to the English privy council on December 3, whereupon that body declared that the bills were not according to the usual legal and customary form and therefore were insufficient causes for summoning a new Irish parliament.[27] Their lordships of the English privy council communicated their sentiments to the Irish lords justices in a letter which reached Dublin by mid-December. The English privy councilors did not find the bills sent agreeable to former precedents and instructed the lords justices to prepare some bills that were.[28]

The lords justices studied the letter from England very carefully and prepared a strategy to deal with it when the Irish privy council assembled on December 18. The letter from England was read to the Irish councilors and was followed immediately by a reading of the letter sent by the lords justices to the duke of Bedford before the frivolous bills had been certified by the Irish privy council and dispatched to England.[29] According to Lord Kildare, the bills that had been sent were admitted to be of no consequence. However, the impropriety of sending over a money bill was urged from all sides of the council table. Delay seemed the only viable course and several schemes were offered. Finally, the primate proposed a plan he believed would clarify the present situation and perhaps resolve it. Stone recommended that a committee be appointed to draw up a bill or bills that would be of real use to the country. The primate argued that only by sending useful bills would the councilors ever know whether nothing would do except the dispatch of a money bill.[30]

Stone's proposal was suggested by an ambiguity he and others had perceived in the letter from the English privy council. In that letter the necessity for sending over a money bill as a cause for holding an Irish parliament was implied throughout but nowhere explicitly mentioned. The relevant words in the letter were *agreeable*

27. English Privy Council to Lords Justices, December 3, 1760. Shannon Mss., D.2207/A/1/6/5A and B; Kildare to Fox, December 18, 1760. Bedford Mss., T.2915/110/66.
28. English Privy Council to Lords Justices, December 3, 1760. Shannon Mss., D.2207/A/1/6/5A and B.
29. Kildare to Fox, December 18, 1760. Bedford Mss., T.2915/110/66.
30. *Idem.*

to former precedents.[31] This ambiguity, however slight, plus the fact
that Pitt's name did not appear among the signatories of the letter
gave Stone and others hope that perhaps the English privy councilors were not as firm as their letter indicated. Stone's argument in
this instance was at best problematic, and there was some hesitation
about accepting it. Kildare sensed the mood of the council and
strove to conclude the discussion by moving that the proposed
committee should be instructed to draw up a bill granting a supply
to his majesty. This motion threw matters into a confused silence
with councilors looking at one another but not speaking. Kildare
dispelled the confusion and brought business to an end by moving
an adjournment until the next day whereupon his motion would
be considered. Adjournment carried. The lords of the council
dispersed for dinner and private discussions. Though no division
had been taken on the specific issue of preparing a money bill,
Kildare estimated that only Lord Chancellor Bowes, Chief Justice
Yorke, Chief Baron Willes, and himself were supportive.[32]

When the council reassembled on Friday, December 19, Kildare
was persuaded to withdraw his motion of the previous day. The
earl agreed to withdraw his motion on the condition that when the
committee met he would offer a supply bill for consideration. After
Kildare withdrew his motion, the committee met forthwith. The
earl immediately moved for adjournment to the next day in order
to get a supply bill drafted. Efforts were made to postpone consideration to a farther day on the grounds that councilors needed time
to satisfy the minds of the people in the constituencies. Kildare
reminded those present that they were members of his majesty's
privy council and chided the councilors who had offered such an
argument for being too much under the influence of the mob. He
urged the other lords and gentlemen present to obey the king's
commands before heeding those of the rabble. Kildare's outburst
succeeded. The tactic of a farther day was given up and consideration of the earl's supply bill was set for Monday, December 22.[33]

The weekend must have been an occasion of frenetic activity by
the lords justices because when the council met on Monday the

31 . *Idem.*   32. *Idem.*
33. Kildare to Fox, December 20, 1760. Bedford Mss., T.2915/110/66.

lords justices were ready to cope with Kildare and the four judges. Kildare offered his supply bill but no action was taken. A motion was made and carried putting off consideration until January 12, 1761. Stone made much of the fact that the Duke of Bedford had not yet responded to the long letter sent to his grace by the lords justices on November 23. However, the truth of the matter appeared to be that most of the lords and gentlemen councilors wanted time to extricate themselves from a difficult situation. They did not want to vote against a supply bill, but needed time to unsay publicly what so many of them had said or had been represented as saying on the money bill issue. In any case, Bowes prevailed upon Kildare to be reasonable and nonobstructive, insisting that delay would improve the chances of carrying the bill. Kildare accepted Bowes' argument, left the council, and made plans to embark for Parkgate as soon as the yacht arrived.[34]

All in all, Kildare was pleased with his own performance. One might wonder whether or not the great patriot of 1753 had changed principles in 1760. With Kildare one could never be certain which principles inspired what behavior. What is certain is that Kildare's enemy in 1753 and 1760 was the same. He had despised and opposed the primate in 1753 and did so again in 1760. In the present situation, however, Kildare did not believe that the clamor about approving a money bill was as loud as Malone and the lords justices had insisted. He believed that great pains had been taken to raise a clamor, but success had been minimal. This was the message that he sent to Henry Fox in England and repeated to others when he arrived there after Christmas.[35]

With matters postponed in the Irish privy council until January 12, 1761, the lords and gentlemen went their separate ways for the holidays and the recess. Yet politics took no holiday. Bowes, the lords justices together, and Ponsonby on his own put pen to paper to try to explain to English friends what was happening in the Irish privy council and why. In Bowes' view, the prospect of the first general election in thirty-three years had created a situation in which all of the leading parties were determined to secure their

34. Kildare to Fox, December 22, 1760. Bedford Mss., T.2915/10/66.
35. *Idem.*

parliamentary interests. Popular questions were taken up to secure political advantage, and once taken up no party dared put them down. Each of the lords justices, as well as virtually every other party leader except Kildare, was determined to demonstrate that on popular issues his patriotism was as pure or purer than any other public man's. The effect was for all of the party leaders to stand together on such issues. Bowes concluded by declaring the events of 1753 as the cause of present difficulties, urging sympathy for the Duke of Bedford, and wishing him "a quieter situation more suited to his principles and years."[36] Bowes agreed with Lord Kildare and others that the present Irish government could not appease the heats of the moment and that the duke was very unpopular and suspected of harboring evil designs against the country.[37]

The lords justices offered the most detailed and lengthy explanation of the present crisis in a long letter to Bedford sent off on December 27, 1760. They began by complaining that their letter to Bedford of November 23, 1760, had never been answered. Total silence in this instance, their lordships asserted, was undeserved and unfair. They described the proceedings of the privy council on the money bill issue and insisted that delay beyond January 12, 1761, in resolving this matter could have serious consequences. Next, the lords justices argued that they had not been wanting in their duty to the king and denied that they were "attempting to innovate on the constitution of this country."[38] Their lordships categorically denied as had been rumored that they had conspired together and had a plan to exploit this issue for political advantage. They professed deep shame over the necessity of clearing themselves from this widespread imputation and asked the duke to consider whether their conduct while serving the crown tallied "with this disingenuity of which we are told we stand suspected."[39] The lords justices feared the most serious consequences in the parliament and in the country if a money bill was certified by the Irish privy council and transmitted to England. This advice was their

36. HMC Various Collections, VI, 77.
37. Russell Correspondence, II, 428–429.
38. Lords Justices to Bedford, December 27, 1760. Bedford Mss., D.2707/A/1/6/6A and B.
39. Idem.

best judgment, and for them not to offer it to the king's English ministers would be criminal. In the end, however, if a money bill had to be certified and transmitted, the present lords justices begged to be relieved from the necessity of themselves as chief governors signing the appropriate transmittal documents. They had no intention to obstruct, but firmly believed they had no authority to transmit such a bill. Stone, Boyle, and Ponsonby offered to retire from their present stations rather than perform an action they now considered to be contrary to the constitution and to the well-being of their country.[40]

About the same time that the lords justices wrote to Bedford, Ponsonby sent an abbreviated version of the letter to the lord lieutenant to his brother, Lord Bessborough. Ponsonby summarized the arguments of the lords justices' letter and mentioned also an additional one derived from his special circumstances as speaker in the last parliament and a candidate for the post in the next one. He insisted that a technical resolution of the house of commons in 1727 prevented him from signing any transmittal of a money bill. That resolution required that no money bill should be read in the house of commons until after the committee of accounts had reported to the house. In Ponsonby's judgment there was no discretion in this matter. Though professing the strongest regard for the present English government, the speaker urged his brother to procure for him an immediate discharge as lord justice.[41]

Bessborough was outraged by this letter and immediately showed it to Rigby. Bessborough agreed absolutely with all that had been done in England on this issue and promised to advise his brother accordingly. His lordship could not believe that the lords justices would persist in their refusal to transmit a money bill and indicated an intention to use what ever influence he had with the speaker to settle this matter.[42] Rigby was grateful for Bessborough's promise of assistance but doubted whether it would have any effect. Knowing the lords justices as he did, the chief secretary feared that they would remain steadfast and no money bill would be forthcoming. He communicated his thinking to Bedford, who was still struggling

40. *Idem.*
41. Rigby to Bedford, December 20, 1760. Bedford Mss., T.2915/10/69.
42. *Idem.*

to develop arguments to respond to the lords justices' letters of November 23 and December 27. Rigby's fears about the intransigence of the lords justices appears to have persuaded the duke to keep his arguments simple and short.

At first Bedford contemplated answering in detail the arguments raised in the lords justices' letters of November 23 and December 27, but after trying his hand at several drafts on January 8,[43] the duke agreed with the lords of the English privy council that no useful purpose would be served by doing so. Instead, Bedford signed and the English privy council approved a response prepared by Rigby, which was sent off to Ireland on January 17, 1761. While this version mentioned some of the arguments rehearsed in the lords justices' letter of December 27, the duke simply reported the fact that the lords justices' letters had been considered by the cabinet and that a determination had been made. All of the cabinet members present agreed that the lords justices "should not have deviated from the ancient usage of certifying a money bill as one of the causes and considerations for calling a new Parliament."[44] Furthermore, Bedford continued, the lords of the cabinet believed that the letter sent from the lords of the English privy council to the lords justices on December 3, 1761, should have convinced your excellencies and the privy council of Ireland "that you erred in your judgement in quitting for the sake of expedience the legal and accustomed form of proceeding in . . . summoning a new Parliament" and should have complied with the directions of the king in council.[45] The duke concluded by urging the lords justices to certify and transmit the required money bill. Bedford's letter of January 17 reached the lords justices in about five days' time and immediately precipitated on January 23, 1761, one of the most extraordinary and consequential meetings of the Irish privy council since the crisis over Wood's halfpence.

After opening ceremonies were concluded, Lord Kildare introduced his bill for continuing the additional duties for three months

43. Draft of Letter from Bedford to the Lords Justices, January 8, 1761. Bedford Mss., T.2915/11/6.
44. Bedford to the Lords Justices, January 17, 1761. Shannon Mss., D.2207/A/1/6/7A and B.
45. *Idem.*

from the 24th of December next. The bill was read for the first time, followed by a motion for a second reading paragraph by paragraph. Lord Carrick, Shannon's son-in-law, opposed the motion without developing serious reasons for doing so.[46] Malone spoke next and much longer against the motion but not with his usual eloquence. The reason for this minimal effort became clear enough when the question was put. Malone knew that he had a majority with him. The motion for a second reading of Kildare's bill was lost 15 to 9.[47] Next, Carrick rose and introduced a bill to continue the additional duties voted in the last session of parliament for payment of the money borrowed for financing defense measures. Though no division was taken on this motion to introduce and read Carrick's bill for the first time, the chief justices and lord chancellor spoke against it. Their lordships contended that although Carrick's bill was one for granting money, it was not a bill for a future supply for his majesty. Therefore, Carrick's measure was not a money bill within the meaning and intent of the letter sent from the English privy council or in the opinion of the English cabinet as communicated by the lord lieutenant's letter of January 17.[48] Proceedings were terminated and further action on Carrick's bill was delayed until the next day.

After the privy council assembled on January 24, a motion was made to read Carrick's bill a second time and desultory speeches followed. The speeches were desultory because many who supported the measure publicly were in private candid enough to admit that the bill was unnecessary and probably improper. Specifically, this bill was an unnecessary meddling with what the commons had undertaken by their vote of credit in the previous session. A few members of the council with seats in the house of commons feared that the house would probably throw it out when returned on those grounds. However, a substantial number of those present favored the bill because they believed that the English ministry wanted a pretext to end the controversy. The lords justices and their supporters agreed that the government of England wanted a money bill, so why not send them one? Whether the money bill sent complied

46. York to Rigby, January 24, 1761. Bedford Mss., T.2915/11/16.
47. *Idem.*   48. *Idem.*

with custom and usage was immaterial. What mattered was that a money bill of some sort should be dispatched. In addition, the lords justices insisted that the king's English ministers would take whatever sort of bill was sent because they feared that greater evils rejection would bring.[49] The chief justice reported that entire weight of the Irish government had been put behind this bill of Lord Carrick. Numbers prevailed, and the bill passed without a division.

Bowes and Yorke were distressed by the behavior of the lords justices and the council on this matter but admitted to Bedford that if this bill had not been certified, no bill would have cleared the Irish privy council. Though the lord chancellor and chief justice maintained their consistency by refusing to sign the transmittal documents, they were both clear enough in their communications with Bedford that this bill was as far as the Irish privy council would go.[50] John Ryder, Archbishop of Tuam, gave similar advice to the English ministry. If the usual sort of bill was expected, wrote the archbishop, then alterations in the government and privy council of Ireland would have to be effected. However, if the bill sent over is accepted, Ryder concluded, the Duke of Bedford "may as well return, and will do the King's business as effectually as any other new Lord Lieutenant."[51] Quite correctly, there were genuine concerns in both England and Ireland that if the bill was approved as sent neither Bedford nor Rigby would return.[52] The decision, therefore, whether the immediate controversy ought to be ended by obtaining approval and certification of the bill in the English privy council or whether ancient usage ought to be defended by rejection in that body was one only the English ministry could make.

The English ministers wasted little time in taking up the matter. Rigby learned as early as February 1, 1761, that Lord Granville, Lord President of the English Privy Council and former lord lieutenant of Ireland, had raised a hue and cry about the money bill, but after reflection he concluded that in reality the dispute was about moonshine and that the lords justices had sent the English

49. *Idem.*

50. Bowes to Bedford, January 25, 1761. Bedford Mss., T.2915/11/17.

51. Archbishop of Tuam to Wilmot, January 31, 1761. Wilmot Mss., T.3019/6762/630.

52. Waite to Wilmot, January 30, 1761. Wilmot Mss., T.3019/6762/629.

ministers nothing but moonshine. Rigby commented sarcastically
upon the quality of the lord president's reasoning but reported that
English privy councilors had submitted and had certified the bill.[53]
A point that must have been most persuasive in the discussion
among the English ministers was the fact that the Irish lords justices
were honor-bound to support this bill in the next session, and
therefore a money bill issue would not be one that the lord lieutenant or English ministry would have to face in the new Irish parliament.

Whatever the reasoning, Carrick's bill was certified by the English
privy council, and in the process an extraordinary event had occurred in the history of Irish politics. The lords justices and a
majority of the Irish privy council had successfully defied the lord
lieutenant, the English cabinet, and the English privy council on
the issue of certifying a money bill in the traditional form. In
Ireland an unprecedented degree of political and constitutional
independence from an English government had been asserted by
a Dublin administration. What was even more unusual about this
defiance and assertion of independent action was that with one
significant exception these Irish lords and gentlemen, all presently
holding places of power and profit under the crown and led by
an English-born Archbishop of Armagh, got away with it without
suffering dismissal or financial loss. This circumstance is a measure
of how much Irish politics had changed since 1754.

The one person who did not escape reprisal was Anthony Malone.
Bedford recommended immediate dismissal of Malone from his
sinecure as Irish chancellor of the exchequer to the king and his
majesty approved the recommendation forthwith. What was curi-
ous about this action was the fact that it was implemented without
consultation with Pitt. Pitt only learned of Malone's dismissal after it
had been effected. Moreover, he received that belated information
from Bedford, not from the new king or from the people close to
his majesty. Pitt doubted the expediency of dismissing Malone
and believed that such a step should have been more maturely
weighed.[54] Pitt's opinions notwithstanding, Malone was dismissed;

53. Rigby to Bedford, Received February 2, 1761. Bedford Mss., T.2915/11/20.
54. Russell Correspondence, III, 6.

appropriately his office was given to William Yorke, who then gave up his place on the bench to a wealthy, English, king's counsel of only one year's standing, Richard Aston.

Yorke's appointment was not popular. Not a single member of the privy council or of any of the grand juries wished him well. Yorke fully expected to be burnt in effigy, as had been Eaton Stannard when that gentleman replaced Malone as prime serjeant in 1754.[55] Yorke appears to have taken Rigby's advice and moved to England within a year of his appointment. One other person who played a major role in the money bill proceedings in the Irish privy council was also grandly rewarded. Bedford recommended that the Earl of Kildare be raised to the dignity of marquess. The king agreed and added a promise that Kildare would be created a duke whenever his majesty should think proper "to make one of that degree either in England or Ireland, exclusive of his own family."[56] Again, this circumstance is also a measure of how much Irish politics had changed since 1754. In the course of the last seven years, Kildare and Stone continued to despise one another, but they had changed sides. The great patriot of the past had come to court. The arch-courtier and defender of the English interest in 1754 had become the leading Irish patriot politician in 1761.

With the matter of the money bill settled and settled in a manner the Duke of Bedford could not accept, his grace had no alternative but to tender the resignation with which he had been threatening the ministry since mid-January. Once the English ministry had decided to approve the money bill sent by the lords justices and privy council they were obliged to search for a new lord lieutenant. Lord Bute, confidant of the new king, approached Pitt's brother-in-law, Lord Temple, in early February; but Pitt would not give his blessing.[57] The minister wanted Temple to remain in the English house of lords, where his supporters were already too few. Bute turned next to George Montagu Dunk, Earl of Halifax, President of the Board of Trade. Lord Halifax was an ambitious politician

55. Rigby to Wilmot, March 25, 1761. Bedford Mss., T.2915/11/48.
56. Russell Correspondence, III, 5.
57. Robert Blackey, "A Politician in Ireland: The Lord Lieutenancy of the Early of Halifax, 1761–63," *Eire-Ireland*, vol. XIV, n 4 (Winter), 1979, 68.

whose career seemed stalled at the board of trade. The earl had publicly disagreed with Pitt on foreign policy and therefore relations with the head of the ministry of which he was a part were cool. Despite this and the fact that Halifax's financial affairs and personal life were extremely disordered, a successor for Bedford had to be found. On March 20, 1761, the king in council declared Halifax to be the new lord lieutenant of Ireland. For chief secretary, Halifax chose William Gerard Hamilton, a man of unusual oratorical talent who was well connected in the literary world and with whom the earl had served on the board of trade. Bedford was offered the post of Master of the Horse, where, in Lord Shannon's words, he could "tyrannize over poor grooms and horses."[58]

News of the impending change reached Ireland in late March at the moment when Bedford was performing his last significant act as lord lieutenant. The duke issued the writs authorizing an election for a new parliament. Irishmen high and low forsook speculation about the character of their new chief governors and turned their attention to the very serious business of the first general election in Ireland in thirty-four years. Since there was neither a lord lieutenant nor a chief secretary present in Ireland in March 1761, the task of managing the election fell to the lords justices. For Stone, Ponsonby, and Shannon, election arranging became a near-total preoccupation. Under Stone's leadership, the lords justices had reached a position of independent power and authority in Ireland that no other previous group of Irish politicians in the present century had ever achieved. The basis of that power was effective management of the Irish house of commons. For the lords justices the election was an opportunity to consolidate and perhaps expand their present dominant political position by electing their own men, discouraging independents from seeking seats, and defeating candidates with ties to friends of the former lord lieutenant and chief secretary. All such strategies were employed and in the end patience and attention to detail seemed to be rewarded. A great many of the gentlemen returned in 1761 appeared ready to begin their careers in the Irish house of commons by taking orders from Stone,

58. Shannon to Dennis, March 21, 1761. Shannon Mss., D.2707/A/1/5/42.

Ponsonby, or Boyle. Such at least was the message the lord justices privately put out and wanted the new lord lieutenant and present English ministers to believe.

As the election progressed, Rigby learned, much to his chagrin, that an engagement about the return of members for Old Leighlin, made to him when he was chief secretary, was no longer binding because another now held that office. Rigby had arranged with Richard Robinson, Bishop of Ferns, for the election of Provost Francis Andrews and another friend. He was outraged to discover that the bishop had made a second and later commitment to Ponsonby.[59] However interesting the views of Bedford and Rigby about Bishop Robinson's honor, the fate of Old Leighlin was totally overshadowed by a much more spectacular election in Dublin city. A celebrated Irish political exile had come home. Charles Lucas had returned to contest the seat he believed had been illegally denied him twelve years before.

With an indictment for libel and an arrest warrant outstanding since November 1749, the return of Lucas to Irish politics had to be preceded by successful rehabilitative efforts by high-placed friends in England. The death of the king in late October provided an opportunity, and little time was wasted. Lucas' rehabilitation was clearly underway by mid-November. First, some approaches were made to Rigby and Bedford. Lucas was introduced to Rigby in the gallery of the English house of commons by Francis Andrews in late November, whereupon pleasantries were exchanged. Lucas' most recent pamphlet on the forthcoming election and a memorial on the state of his outlawry was sent to Bedford.[60] When neither of these approaches yielded any result, Lucas drafted a petition to the king and made arrangements to present it himself at a royal levee shortly before Christmas. Lord Hertford escorted Lucas into the royal presence, where the young king not only accepted the petition but also took Lucas by the hand and raised him off his knee. Lucas' hopes soared. He advised Lord Charlemont that all that stood between himself and a pardon was the necessity of finding

59. Rigby to Wilmot, April 11, 1761. Wilmot Mss., T.3019/6762/642.
60. HMC Charlemont, I, 266, 268.

someone to remind the king to issue it. To that end, Lucas asked Charlemont, Powerscourt, and other aristocratic Irish friends to write to acquaintances on the English privy council or in the royal bedchamber recommending Lucas' situation to their attention.[61]

Meanwhile matters were progressing in Dublin as well. Pery appeared in the Court of King's Bench on behalf of Lucas in early February and moved that his client might have copies of the information and processes lodged against him. Since the attorney general offered no opposition, Pery's motion was granted.[62] A few days later, Sir Edward King and Montgomery, a Dublin Merchant, appeared in court and each posted a recognizance of £1,000 that Charles Lucas would appear in court on the first day of the next term and stand trial for libel.[63] That trial never occurred. On February 27, 1761, the lords justices wrote to Bedford urging that Lucas be pardoned. The lords justices argued that the affair was of such long standing that all evidence against Lucas must be lost. Moreover, if Lucas were ever brought to trial, he most assuredly would be acquitted for want of evidence and that an acquittal would make as much noise[64] in Dublin as the trial of seven bishops had made in London in James II's time. The arguments of the lords justices prevailed and Lucas received his pardon in March.

Lucas returned to Dublin forthwith and immediately turned all of his energy to winning a seat in the forthcoming general election. He set his sights upon one of the seats for Dublin city. Though very popular in the city, Lucas' election was by no means assured. His prospects remained uncertain until one other popular candidate withdrew shortly before the polling date. In the end, after a poll of thirteen days, he was returned, along with James Grattan, as duly elected for the city of Dublin. Reflecting on the results, Lord Bowes believed that with the proper management Lucas probably could have been defeated.[65] However, in this instance such management did not occur, and in Bowes' view a very popular and

61. *Ibid.*, 269.
62. Waite to Wilmot, February 10, 1761. Wilmot Mss., T.3019/6762/632.
63. Waite to Wilmot, February 12, 1761. Wilmot Mss., T.3019/6762/634.
64. Waite to Wilmot, March 1, 1761. Wilmot Mss., T.3019/6762/637.
65. Bowes to Wilmot, May 19, 1761. Wilmot Mss., T.3019/6762/640.

practiced demagogue, much enamoured of agitating constitutional issues and causes, would be present to enliven the opening session of parliament for the new chief governors.

If proper electoral management did not prevail in Dublin city, it did elsewhere. Stone, Ponsonby, and Shannon spoke or wrote to hundreds of people with electoral interests, and significant if not excessive amounts of money were spent, as much as several hundred pounds to a variety of interest groups in some contested constituencies.[66] An example occurred at Youghal where £760 was spent in a single morning entertaining freemen, and sums in the following amounts were distributed: ten guineas for the poor, five guineas to the dissenters for their meetinghouse, one guinea to the mayor's serjeants, and another eighty-four guineas to the mayor to stop mouths that might need to be stopped.[67]

One new element in the election was the extent to which a particular constitutional issue was seriously agitated in several constituencies. The issue was more frequent parliamentary elections. The mode of agitation was to secure from candidates prior to the election a commitment to support a bill for septennial parliaments in Ireland. Both the bill itself and the manner of procuring support for it were matters of great concern to the new chief governors. Halifax viewed commitments thus obtained—previous promises—as a thoroughly unconstitutional engagement. He was distressed further by the fact that promises of support for this bill had been obtained from several of the king's servants and from other known supporters of the lord lieutenant. The point of this strategy appears to have been to deprive the Irish government of its best speakers when this bill came before the house of commons and thereby ensure passage. This strategy proved to be so effective that Halifax recommended a policy of absolute neutrality on the bill in the house of commons and rejection of it in the English privy council.[68]

It was clear enough when the polling ended that the lords justices had done their work well. Though Shannon would be well represented in the new house of commons, the predominant interest in that body would be that of the speaker and the predominant influ-

66. HMC Charlemont, I, 266.
67. Pratt to Lord Shannon, December 2, 1760. Shannon Mss., D.2707/A/1/5/32.
68. Halifax to Egremont, December 4, 1761. SP63/419/116.

ence over the speaker would be that of Archbishop Stone. Given the behavior of the lords justices and the privy council during the late controversy over certifying a money bill, the prospect of a new house of commons heavily populated with close friends of Stone, Ponsonby, and Shannon was not reassuring. As the nature of probable political alignments in the new parliament began to clarify, so also did the need of the new chief governors for alternatives to dependence on the parliamentary numbers commanded by the lords justices. Such an alternative could be independents and unaffiliated new members. While the numbers of such gentlemen in the house of commons would remain uncertain until parliament actually opened, one obvious strategy for attracting as many of such people as possible to the interest of the lord lieutenant was through parliamentary oratory. The best way for the new chief governors to persuade uncommitted members to support the Irish government was to obtain the services of the most gifted and successful parliamentary speakers before the session began. Lord Halifax and his chief secretary proposed to counter the lord justices' numbers with argument and eloquence. To that end, Hamilton paid special attention to Edmund Pery and John Hely Hutchinson. Pery would have nothing to do with Hamilton, but Hely Hutchinson was willing to listen.

Hely Hutchinson had been the most irrepressible parliamentary orator of the last session. He had spoken at length and often, on a range of popular questions. Rigby had sensed early in the session that Hely Hutchinson's present infatuation with popular questions was more apparent than real. The chief secretary suspected that the young man's ambition was much stronger than his attachment to patriotism. Rigby believed that Hely Hutchinson could be bought but seemed uncertain about the man's reliability after a purchase price had been paid. The probability that Hely Hutchinson could ever be permanently attached to government for a single reward was not high. Most likely, rewards would have to be frequent and continuing if the Irish government was to have his services on a permanent basis.

Stone also had recognized Hely Hutchinson's ability and had hopes that perhaps the young man might be attached to his own political interest. The primate pressed his brother, Andrew Stone, to arrange an interview for Hely Hutchinson with Halifax while the lord lieutenant was still in England.[69] Whether, if bought, Hely Hutchinson would serve the lord lieutenant, the primate, or himself no one could be sure, but serious efforts were made to obtain him. When Hely Hutchinson visited England during the summer of 1761[70] discussions about his future were undertaken by Hamilton and promises were made about a pension of £500 a year and about the office of prime serjeant as soon as the present incumbent, Thomas Tennison, went on the bench. In mid-October an agreement was reached, and two months later Hely Hutchinson was formally appointed prime serjeant.[71] A fine speaker was obtained and a precedent had been set. Hely Hutchinson was the first in a series of gifted young orators who would debut in the Irish house of commons as severe critics of government policy and then, in time, accept employment under the very government whose policies they had been criticizing. Hely Hutchinson was the first, but in the course of the next forty years several others would follow his example.

The recruitment of Hely Hutchinson for his speaking and parliamentary prowess, the introduction of constitutional issues into electoral contests, and the electoral success of the lords justices were three clear signs that Irish politics had changed. It was clear to many in Ireland and to some in England that a turning point in Irish politics and in Anglo-Irish relations had been reached. The country could no longer be governed in the manner of the last thirty years. The present lords justices had achieved a degree of political autonomy and administrative power hitherto unknown. There was a generation of new men coming into the house of commons, young and impatient with the past, who were anxious to make their marks in public life. There was also a growing awareness by all politicians that social discontent in Ireland was deepening and that the ability of the Irish government to maintain law and order in both urban and rural areas was limited. It was a time of opportu-

---

69. *Historical Manuscripts Commission, Twelfth Report, Appendix, Part IX, The Manuscripts of the Duke of Beaufort, C. G., The Earl of Donoughmore, and Others*, London, 1891, 231–232.

70. Rigby to Wilmot, September 20, 1761. Wilmot Mss., T.3019/6762/671.

71. Waite to Wilmot, October 14, 1761. Wilmot Mss., T.3019/6762/676.

nity and danger, when knowledgeable men took stock of themselves and thought about the future.

Most observers agreed that Irish landowners had prospered greatly during the last half century. Lord Bowes insisted that the prices of land and the value of personal property in Ireland had increased so much that the proportion of real property held by members of the Irish parliament probably exceeded that possessed by their opposite numbers in the English parliament.[72] Moreover, as an investment, generally Irish estates produced more ready money than English ones. In England, taxes, upkeep, and repairs took about twenty percent out of every pound of rent collected. Irish landlords paid virtually no taxes and usually rented raw land only with no liability for upkeep or repairs.[73]

Yet prosperity for Irish landlords had not brought social peace. Troops had to be sent into Kildare in the early summer of 1753 to protect improved property, recently enclosed common lands, and parks. Disturbances were widespread in Antrim and Down in the summer and fall of 1755, when leases expired on properties owned by the Marquis of Donegal and where heavy fines were demanded for renewal. Food shortages and near-famine conditions in parts of the north in the fall and winter of 1757 had been accompanied by attempts to clear farms and increase rents. Those attempts encountered strong resistance ranging from assaults on property to threats against persons. Dublin city exploded in riot in December 1759, and in the spring of 1760 a series of outrages occurred on Lord Milton's property near Burriss in Tipperary that exemplified at once the nature and some of the causes of the violence that had been increasing throughout the country.

Two leases held by George Cooke, one of Lord Milton's tenants, expired on March 25, 1760. Those two leases had brought his lordship £250 a year. Milton advertised the two leases to be let as three separate farms and received proposals from three prospective tenants for upwards of £700 a year. Once agreements with the prospective tenants had been reached, Cooke was ordered to vacate Burriss farm, on which he and his family lived. Immediately there-

72. HMC Various Collections, VI, 77.
73. Southwell to Coghill, July 28, 1756. Mss. 876, National Library, Dublin.

after, mobs attacked Milton's property and also the houses and persons of the prospective tenants. Milton requested that troops be dispatched to Burriss to protect his tenants and apprehend the authors of this violence, who were, in his lordship's judgment, none other than George Cooke and his sons.[74] In this instance, Milton had done only what many other landlords were doing, using lease expirations to increase income. He complained to Bedford that presuming "to let my land to whom I please"[75] had been the sole cause of the violence visited upon himself and his tenants. Neither Lord Milton nor other Munster landlords were willing to abandon that presumption. It was a fact that in the environs of Burriss and in other parts of that province there was to be little peace and much destruction of property during the next three years.

If Lord Bowes can be believed, Irish landlords had done very well during his time in Ireland, and they were determined to do better in the years ahead. One clear consequence of that determination was agrarian violence. In Bowes' view, other such consequences were legal, constitutional, and political controversy with the government and parliament of England. "Power, or attempts to acquire it," added the lord chancellor, "have accompanied opulence."[76] Opulence for some and ever rising expectations for many among the propertied classes had created a political situation in Ireland where change could be resisted and thereby delayed, but it could not be stopped. To be sure, during all of the political uproar of the last decade, Irish politicians had been hard put to specify genuine grievances that government policies had visited upon the country. Nonetheless, as the prosperity of the political classes improved, a large segment of them had become disenchanted with existing constitutional and political arrangements.[77] Such persons aspired to have a constitution in Ireland with the same privileges and protections enjoyed by men of similar wealth and rank in England. The British house of commons was seen as a proper model for Ireland; and insofar as the Dublin parliament differed in authority and power from the parliament in Westminster, increasing numbers of

74. Milton to Bedford, April 3, 1760. Bedford Mss., T.2915/9/32.
75. *Idem.*
76. HMC Various Collections, VI, 77.
77. *Idem.*

Irish lords and gentlemen believed themselves demeaned and injured. By 1760, a state of mind had developed among the Irish political classes that awaited only the proper leadership to exploit it.

There was no doubt that the present lords justices had achieved an extraordinary degree of autonomy from the lord lieutenant and from the English ministry.[78] Two circumstances had made possible that autonomy. The first was the ability of Stone, Ponsonby, and Shannon to influence votes in the Irish house of commons, and a clear sense by these men that all of the chief governors sent out from England during the last fifteen years had been uncertain about their own relations with the English ministry of the day. Every lord lieutenant from Harrington to Bedford had moments of doubt about the amount of support on a given point that he would receive from friends or rivals in the English ministry. Those who were uncertain about their positions at home, especially when the extent of that uncertainty was either widely known or wildly rumored in Dublin, were inevitably compromised in their dealings with Irish politicians.

What had happened was clear enough to observers. In Bowes' mind, Stone, Ponsonby, and Shannon had become parliamentary undertakers, that is, men who would undertake or see that the king's business in the Irish parliament was accomplished with minimum difficulty. As undertakers, the lords justices performed these services for a price. The price was patronage for their friends. In Bedford's time, Stone, Ponsonby, and Shannon had achieved sufficient influence in the Irish house of commons to bargain effectively with the duke's successors about men and also about measures. In Bowes' view, the influence of the lord justices in the Irish parliament had become so strong that no lord lieutenant could govern without them. They were able to tell a chief governor that "he must come into their measures or be rendered too uneasy for men of rank to remain under."[79] The lord lieutenant, wrote Bowes, "may parade but must submit . . . . [C]hange hands as oft as you please, you can only be furnished from this shop."[80]

From the point of view of the English ministry, the problems of

78. *Ibid.*, 78.
79. *Idem.*
80. *Ibid.*, 77.

governing Ireland were difficult but not desperate. One reason why the problem of governing Ireland was not viewed as desperate in Westminster was the situation of the present lords justices. Stone was fifty-six years of age and the most brilliant and accomplished of the three. However, he was rumored to be in poor health, and in any case the nomination of next Archbishop of Armagh was in the absolute control of the Crown. Shannon was already seventy-nine and certainly very soon destined to pass from the political scene. Ponsonby was only forty-eight but was the least competent of the three; and without Stone to help make up his mind he would be a much less formidable person. Another reason for avoiding hasty decisions was the growing entrepreneurial nature of Irish politics. After the general election, even Stone had all he could do to cope with demands and requests. Rigby described the primate's situation with tongue in cheek. Pity the poor primate, he wrote, the man was "environed not with two but with two and twenty factions."[81]

Pery, Malone, Hely Hutchinson, and Lucas were all tugging at his grace of Armagh with "contrary and discordant ropes." The first, continued Rigby, tugged for his country, the second for restoration, the third for instant possession of the attorney general's place, and the fourth for the easy task of stopping the gaping mouth of the Dublin mob. The extraordinary olio of Irish politics contained far too many piquant ingredients for any one man to digest.[82] In the long run, Rigby believed that the Irish political scene was too personal and unpredictable for the lords justices or for any similar combination of Irish politicians to dominate for very long.

Nonetheless, in the short run, it was clear that the English ministry had a problem with the present lords justices that would have to be resolved. There was talk enough in Westminster about what to do but much uncertainty about finding the moment and the man to do it. Only a permanent resident lord lieutenant seemed likely to effect a return of the country to what English ministers called a proper constitutional footing. If the lord lieutenant resided perma-

81. Rigby to Wilmot, June 28, 1761. Wilmot Mss., T.3019/6762/657.
82. *Idem.*

nently in Ireland throughout his entire tenure, there would be no
necessity for appointing any lords justices at all. As one of Shannon's sons writing from London in 1764 put the matter, "I have
heard it mentioned that the form of Irish government will be
changed, and you all unexcellencied."[83] Actually, the possibility of
a resident lord lieutenant was rumored shortly after the news of
Bedford's resignation reached Dublin. Some Irish politicians expected that "sometime or other residence will be found necessary."[84]
However, the moment was not to occur in 1761 and the man was
not to be Lord Halifax.

Thomas Waite insisted to Wilmot that very few if any English
noblemen were prepared to accept the post of lord lieutenant if
they had to reside in Ireland. Depend on it, he continued, few
would do it. A lord lieutenant had only one course to follow if he
intended to have his business done quietly and creditably. He would
have to do "what Lord Harrington did," Waite concluded, "I mean
employing and giving up to those here who are able to do it."[85]
That was precisely what Lord Halifax and his immediate successors
would have to do. Arrangements about expeditious handling of
the king's business were settled before the next session began,[86] and
both viceregal and royal approval for patronage requests from the
primate, Lord Shannon, and the speaker were obtained shortly
after it ended.[87]

In 1761, this bargaining between lord lieutenant and lords justices
was securely established as the basis of the political system by which
Ireland was to be governed. It had taken more than thirty-five
years to develop but would remain operative for not more than a
decade. This system could not long survive the demise of George
Stone, the man who had done so much to fashion and establish
it. However, efforts to reform the undertaker system would be
traumatic. Pursuing constitutional, administrative, economic, or
social reform in Ireland during the 1760s was much like Pandora

83. Lord Boyle to Shannon, October 6, 1764. Shannon Mss., D.2707/A/1/5/5.
84. Cavendish to Wilmot, March 31, 1761. Wilmot Mss., T.3019/6762/641.
85. Waite to Wilmot, November 28, 1760. Wilmot Mss., T.3019/6762/622.
86. Halifax to Egremont, November 3, 1761. SP63/419/62–63.
87. Pension Agreed to by His Majesty, April 12, 1763. Wilmot Mss., T.3019/6762/
717.

opening her mythical box. Once the box had been opened, was there anyone who could ever close it again? The next generation of Irish politicians would be at once blessed and cursed by the presence of a great many Pandoras with a variety of different boxes. Change was coming to Ireland in the last third of the eighteenth century and closely following change was first triumph and then pain.

APPENDIX

Some Historians of Early and Mid-Eighteenth Century Irish Parliamentary Politics

The history of Irish parliamentary politics during the reign of George II has not received the kind of systematic treatment that its importance warrants. For the most part, early writers and scholars addressing the subject of Irish parliamentary politics during the first sixty years of the eighteenth century have tended to view the subject through a screen of whatever was the current state of Anglo-Irish relations at the time of their writing. Some of the later writers have tended only to study dramatic episodes or particular themes rather than the period as a whole.

Of the great nineteenth century Protestant historians of eighteenth century Ireland, Froude gave the period the most attention, but he regarded it as a most shameful time when the fruits of English misgovernment in Ireland were steadily growing. Froude stated explicitly that during the half-century between the departure of the Duke of Grafton in 1725 and the outbreak of war in the American colonies in 1775, "Ireland was without a history."[1] The intricacies of eighteenth century Irish parliamentary politics had no special fascination for Froude, and he described the periodic agitations as being without defined purpose and as "expressions merely of pain from chronic sores, which day by day grew more inflamed."[2]

Lecky virtually ignored Irish parliamentary politics during George II's time. He devoted less than 10 pages out of 470 in the first volume of his Irish history to events occurring between 1730 and 1760 and saw the decade of the 1750s as a long contest for

1. James Anthony Froude, *The English in Ireland in the Eighteenth Century* (Longmans, Green, London, 1882), Vol. I, 652.
2. *Idem.*

preeminence between the great Irish Protestant families and the English ministers.[3] According to Lecky, Irish political leaders of that time were driven by chequered motives. They were neither mere selfish place-hunters nor disinterested patriots. The great men of the country were determined to make parliamentary control a reality in Ireland, and to put an end to what he called "a system under which Irish interests were habitually sacrificed, and Irish patronage was regarded as a reward for the most questionable services to English ministers."[4] Lecky simply did not go very far into the Irish parliamentary politics of those years. He much preferred to study the events and personalities of the last half of the century, which for him were at once more worthy and interesting.

One scholar writing, at the turn of the century, who studied in some detail one of the major events of Irish parliamentary politics during George II's time was the lawyer and sometime Unionist politician, C. Litton Falkiner. A writer of essays and articles rather than books, Falkiner's first contribution to the study of mid-century Irish parliamentary politics was the publication of parts of the Archbishop Stone–Newcastle correspondence in two articles appearing in the *English Historical Review* in 1905. This correspondence and the brief introductory material that accompanied it was followed by a long essay on Archbishop Stone, published first in the *Edinburgh Review* and later in a posthumous volume of essays in 1909. In these articles and this essay, Falkiner provided source material and described the development and course of the conflict between the Irish administration and the Boyle–Kildare party between 1751 and 1755. He also provided an interpretation of those events as well as an interpretation of how Ireland had been governed and how the Irish parliament was managed during the first half of the century.

Following Froude and Lecky, Falkiner described those years as "the heyday of that extraordinary system of government by Undertakers which prevailed through the earlier parts of the century, and was only destroyed by the Octennial Act of 1767."[5] According to Falkiner, undertakers were powerful members of parliament who undertook to conduct government business through the house of commons in return for a voice in policymaking and a share in the

3. William Edward Hartpole Lecky, *A History of Ireland in the Eighteenth Century* (Longmans, Green, London, 1892), Vol. I, 465).

4. *Ibid.*, 465–466.

5. C. Litton Falkiner, *Essays Relating to Ireland: Biographical Historical and Topographical* (Longmans, Green, London, 1909), 84.

disposal of patronage. It was a system, Falkiner argued, whereby "so many successive Viceroys practically abrogated their functions in favour of certain of the more wealthy and ambitious members of the Irish aristocracy."[6] Falkiner derived his notions about such an undertaker system in Ireland from some self-serving letters written by Stone to Newcastle during the early stages of the conflict between the Dorset administration and the Boyle–Kildare party in March and May 1752, and more directly from a letter written by Chesterfield to the Bishop of Waterford on May 23, 1758.[7] Chesterfield's letter was written shortly after news reached London that an arrangement about carrying out government business and sharing patronage had been formally concluded by the Duke of Bedford as lord lieutenant with Stone, Ponsonby, and Shannon (Boyle) as undertakers. Falkiner assumed that Chesterfield was describing the sort of formal arrangements that had existed between chief governors and parliamentary leaders for many years instead of only for two months.

Falkiner tended to see the struggle between the Dorset administration and the Boyle–Kildare party as an attempt by the lord lieutenant to recapture control of the government of Ireland lost to prominent politicians during the previous twenty-five years. He asserted that a decision to reform the undertaker system antedated the Harrington administration but was not implemented until Dorset came to Ireland in 1751. Falkiner attributed the awareness of a need for reform to Chesterfield but said very little about the events and very special circumstances of the Harrington administration.[8] What Falkiner wrote about the operation of an undertaker system between 1700 and 1750, as well as the indolence of Ireland's chief governors in allowing such a system to develop, was entirely *obiter dicta*. However, this *obiter dicta* had more influence upon the work of later historians than his well-written account of Stone's central role in the crises of the 1750s or his insightful observations about Stone's restoration as lord justice by the Duke of Bedford in 1758.

Generally, the interpretation of mid-century Irish parliamentary politics remained where Falkiner's essay had left it until J. L. McCracken published his very influential article, "The Conflict Between the Irish Administration and Parliament, 1753–1756," in *Irish Historical Studies* in 1943. McCracken accepted Falkiner's pro-

6. *Idem.*   7. *Ibid.*, 84–85.
8. *Ibid.*, 94–95.

jection of a formal undertaker system back in time but not back to the early years of the century. Before 1724, McCracken assumed that the tasks of parliamentary management had been performed by the lord lieutenant who employed persuasion and patronage to organize a court party. That style of management was supposed to have collapsed during the crisis over Wood's Halfpence, and in a moment of desperation the English ministry decided to transfer responsibility for parliamentary management from the lord lieutenant to those who could do it better, namely, purchased influentials in the Irish parliament or undertakers.

In other words, the undertaker system was a reform conceived and implemented by the English ministry as an alternative to failed viceregal parliamentary management and was continued for almost a half-century. It remained in place for so long because it provided a succession of English ministries with short, tranquil, and well-managed sessions of the Irish parliament. McCracken attributed the outbreak of the dispute between the Dorset administration and the Boyle–Kildare party to the evolution of that system.[9] He also accepted Falkiner's notion that viceregal indolence allowed such a system to develop and thrive. Also following Falkiner, McCracken did not question why eminent noblemen and cabinet officers in England such as Carteret, Dorset, two Dukes of Devonshire, Chesterfield, and Harrington would allow themselves, while serving in Ireland, to be led, directed, and otherwise imposed upon by gentlemen party leaders in the Irish parliament.

While accepting Falkiner's assumptions about the evolution of the undertaker system between 1724 and 1750, McCracken departed from Falkiner's interpretation of the events of the 1750s and saw them as a struggle between two rival parties in the Irish parliament for control of the government. McCracken found no evidence save some statements by Stone of an attempt by Dorset and the English ministers to recapture lost authority. By adding a close reading of contemporary pamphlet literature to information gleaned from the Stone–Newcastle correspondence, McCracken believed that the struggle between the Ponsonby and Boyle parties in the 1750s had very deep roots and was a continuation or revival of the old Conolly-Midleton conflicts occurring during George I's time.[10]

9. J. L. McCracken "The Conflict Between the Irish Administration and Parliament, 1753–1756," in *Irish Historical Studies*, III, 1942–1943, 159.
10. *Ibid.*, 160.

McCracken interpreted the crises of the 1750s as a struggle for paramount political influence in the parliament and government of Ireland. The Boyle party and their allies had that paramount influence, and the Ponsonbys and their friends wanted to wrest it from them. The English government of the day might have preferred one group over another, but they were content to live with the undertaker system as it was because the times were too parlous to risk the kind of effort required to change it. McCracken's interpretation of Irish political and parliamentary history in the second quarter of the century became canonical and long-lasting. As a matter of fact, parts of this McCracken orthodoxy have found its way into the long-delayed volume on eighteenth century Ireland in the celebrated New History of Ireland series published in 1986.[11]

In the New History, McCracken changed his views about the viceroys organizing their own court parties in the Irish parliament between 1714 and 1724. He adopted the conclusions of recent scholarship about Bolton and Grafton employing William Conolly, speaker of the Irish house of commons, as the principal undertaker for the Irish government.[12] However, for the period 1731–1760, most of the interpretative orthodoxy of McCracken's earlier work was restated. In the seven pages of the New History devoted to the history of Irish parliamentary politics during those years, McCracken suggested that Boyle and his friends as undertakers were able to establish an ascendancy over most of the serving viceroys of that period. Consequently, when Dorset returned to Ireland as chief governor for the second time in 1751, the combined parties of Stone and the Ponsonby family were ready to challenge that ascendancy and try to win paramount political influence in the parliament and government of Ireland for themselves.[13] In the very brief sections on Irish parliamentary politics in the New History that were written before 1973, revised in 1981–1982,[14] and not published until 1986, McCracken provided some new information but did not substantially alter the interpretation first presented in 1943.

J. C. Beckett's much respected The Making of Modern Ireland (1966) mentioned the practice of entrusting the management of the house of commons to a group of politicians who were rewarded

11. T. W. Moody, et al., eds., Eighteenth Century Ireland, 1691–1800, Vol. 4, New History of Ireland (Oxford University Press, 1986).

12. Ibid., 60; see note 3. 13. Ibid., 116–122.

14. Ibid., Preface.

with lucrative offices and a share of patronage being continued by a succession of viceroys but provided few details about the political or parliamentary history of the period. At the same time, Beckett denied the existence of any conscious policy in 1751 by English or Irish ministers to recapture lost control of the Irish house of commons.[15]

F. G. James's *Ireland in the British Empire, 1688–1770* (1973) tended also to follow McCracken, supplemented by James's own reading of the state papers and pamphlet literature. In other words, James followed McCracken's overall interpretation and provided additional details about the events and issues occupying Irish politicians between 1724 and 1750. After 1750, however, Irish parliamentary politics were only lightly considered. James devoted only a few lines to the struggle between the Dorset administration and the Boyle–Kildare party and not very much at all to the later history of Archbishop Stone.[16]

One of the most interesting efforts to present an account of Irish parliamentary politics between 1724 and 1767 is Edith Mary Johnston's *Ireland in the Eighteenth Century* (1974). She made use of materials only recently available in a much larger scholarly study and drew upon that work for this briefer but more generalized book. Consequently, because of space limitations, she presented mainly descriptive historical highlights selected out of the period. Nevertheless, in her thinking about the period, Johnston clearly has gone beyond the *obiter dicta* of Falkiner and the assumptions of McCracken about the undertaker system. She also recognized that the quarrel between the Dorset administration and the Boyle–Kildare party operated at several levels and was far more complicated than Falkiner or McCracken had thought. In particular, she emphasized the roles of Carter and Malone in persuading Boyle to challenge the Dorset administration and make banishment of Stone from Irish politics a party objective.[17] One can only wish that she had had space enough to develop her arguments and address interpretative issues more directly.

More recent work by David Hayton and Declan O'Donovan, and

15. J. C. Beckett, *The Making of Modern Ireland* (Alfred A. Knopf, New York, 1966), 190.
16. F. G. James, *Ireland in the British Empire, 1688–1770* (Harvard University Press, Cambridge, Massachusetts, 1973), 189.
17. Edith Mary Johnston, *Ireland in the Eighteenth Century* (Gill and Macmillan, Dublin, 1974), 115.

J. C. D. Clark has examined some of the interpretative points of mid-eighteenth century Irish parliamentary politics not addressed by Johnston. In two articles published in 1978 and 1984 respectively, Hayton reexamined the problems encountered and the methods of managing the Irish parliament employed by Ireland's chief governors between 1691 and the fall of Walpole in 1742. In so doing, Hayton directly challenged a large part of the reigning McCracken orthodoxy about the evolution of the undertaker system. Hayton has argued very persuasively that from Lord Capel's time in 1694 and continuing throughout our period the lords lieutenants employed parliamentary managers, many of whom also functioned as undertakers.[18] According to Hayton, the distinction between managers and undertakers was clear enough in early eighteenth century Ireland. Undertakers were politicians who undertook completion of the king's business for specific concessions. Evidence of some sort of contract or treaty between the lord lieutenant and one or more parliamentary leaders was required to substantiate an undertaker arrangement.[19] Hayton admitted that evidence of such contracts or treaties is difficult to find in the early eighteenth century because managers thus engaged were reluctant to let the world know about their arrangements. Nonetheless, Hayton cited two examples between 1694 and 1714, when two such treaties were worked out between lords lieutenants and several parliamentary leaders, and one example where negotiations were begun but no mutually satisfactory conclusion was reached.[20] In Hayton's view, undertakers of a sort operated in the Irish parliaments of William and Anne.

After 1714, political conditions in Ireland changed significantly. Power and influence in the Irish parliament at first fragmented and then became concentrated in the hands of three or four principals. Conolly emerged first as the most dependable parliamentary manager, but by 1725, according to Hayton, the speaker had become indispensable and was the leading, and virtually unrivaled, undertaker. Moreover, Hayton insisted, by the time George I died, the undertaker system in Ireland, evolving since the 1690s had totally changed its character. It had evolved from an oligarchy of three or four leading politicians to a monarchy with Conolly as king.[21]

18. David Hayton, "The Beginnings of the 'Undertaker System,'" in *Penal Era and Golden Age*, ed. Thomas Bartlett and D. W. Hayton (Ulster Historical Foundation, Belfast, 1979), 41.

19. *Ibid.*, 37.   20. *Ibid.*, 39–41.

21. *Ibid.*, 54.

In Hayton's view, this Conolly pattern of a single all-powerful undertaker serving as speaker and lord justice should have been the model for the future. He faulted Walpole for not appreciating how easily the Irish house of commons could have been managed if a chosen undertaker, or undertakers, had been offered clear and unequivocal support.[22] Pursuit of such a policy was impossible because Conolly died in 1729, and his successors, Gore and Boyle, turned out to be men with very different intellectual and political resources. Hayton sketched out a brief outline of English ministerial and viceregal relations with Henry Boyle, speaker, lord justice, and principal candidate for parliamentary manager and undertaker between 1733 and 1742. He found those relations characterized by uncertainty and inconsistency, Walpole and his colleagues sometimes reluctantly accepting the Conolly model of undertaker and other times working against it. Whatever management problems Walpole, Dorset, and Devonshire experienced with the Irish parliament, Hayton concluded, were largely of their own making.[23]

Declan O'Donovan, exploiting the hitherto largely unused Wilmot Correspondence, reexamined in detail the conflict between the Dorset administration and the Boyle–Kildare party during the parliamentary session of 1753. In explaining the origin of this conflict, O'Donovan also challenged the McCracken orthodoxy that the conflict was really a contest for paramount political power between the Boyle party and allies and the Ponsonbys and their friends. By assigning initiative in starting this conflict to Stone and Sackville, O'Donovan made an interpretative tilt toward Falkiner and away from McCracken. According to O'Donovan, the objectives of Stone and Sackville were to smash the considerable interest of the speaker's party and thereby establish a direct Castle control over the house of commons.[24]

In O'Donovan's judgment, the period 1720–1770, the age of the undertakers, has been misnamed. He saw those years as a time of steady retreat from places of power and influence in the government of Ireland by the great men of the Protestant Ascendancy. Englishmen had been installed as a majority in the commission of

22. David Hayton, "Walpole and Ireland," in *Britain in the Age of Walpole,* ed. Jeremy Black (St. Martin's Press, New York), 119.
23. *Idem.*
24. Declan O'Donovan, "The Money Bill Dispute of 1753," in *Penal Era and Golden Age,* ed. Thomas Bartlett and D. W. Hayton (Ulster Historical Foundation, 1979), 57.

lords justices and advanced to many places in the privy council, on the episcopal bench, in the courts, in the army, and on the revenue board. According to O'Donovan, the one institution not thus infiltrated was the Irish house of commons. On the basis of such developments, O'Donovan wondered why Irish politicians were accused of trying to subject the lord lieutenant to their power. He was willing to argue that it was the attempt of Stone and Sackville to achieve a direct control over the Irish house of commons that forced the Boyle party into opposition.

O'Donovan also related the political uproar of 1753 to deteriorating economic conditions during that year.[25] Food prices were up; cloth and yarn prices were down. Credit was scarce and expensive; bankruptcies had increased. All of these conditions helped to sustain popular impressions that the Englishmen holding Irish offices and places were up to no good and that somehow Ireland was being exploited for the benefit of English monied interests. O'Donovan concluded that this dispute was much more than a struggle between Irish parties for paramount political power. He saw it as providing a focus and acting as an accelerator of gathering patriotic sentiments, which were to culminate in the establishment of legislative independence in 1782.[26]

J. C. D. Clark's essay into eighteenth century Irish parliamentary politics was a by-product of his massive study of English party politics during the 1750s. Appearing in 1978, Clark's "Whig Tactics and Parliamentary Precedent: The English Management of Irish Politics, 1754–1756" examined the tactical complexities underlying Hartington's settlement of Irish affairs after the Boyle–Kildare party had succeeded in driving Dorset out of Ireland and out of office in 1754. Of the scholarship on mid-eighteenth century Irish parliamentary politics, Clark looked at everything available at the time of his writing. He criticized James for overlooking major source collections and for insufficient knowledge of the course of English party politics. Clark described some of James's conclusions and analogies as "deeply misleading."[27] Generally, Clark followed Hayton for historical background on the Irish political scene. Clark eschewed any effort to apportion blame among the antagonists in Dublin for the crisis of 1753–54. Instead, he sought to account for

25. *Ibid.*, 74–79.   26. *Ibid.*, 56.
27. J. C. D. Clark, "Whig Tactics and Parliamentary Precedent: The English Management of Irish Politics, 1754–1756," in *The Historical Journal*, 21, 2, 1978, 275, n. 2.

the English ministry's handling of the Irish crisis and to explain how it impacted upon events at Westminster.[28]

For Clark what is important about this Irish affair is a realization that similar models of government produced similar problems. He believed that in several respects England and Ireland can be treated as a single political arena during the 1750s. What emerged in Clark's study is a view of the pattern of Irish parliamentary politics as a mirror of, a response to, and a precedent for English political crises during the parliamentary sessions of 1754–55 and 1755–56. Clark insisted that to understand the crisis in Dublin in 1753, the detailed course of events in both Dublin and London must be explained together and in parallel.[29] Moreover, many of the long-term developments in English politics can be found echoed in Dublin in ways that suggest that Irish examples often served as unacknowledged precedents for English innovations.[30]

According to Clark, historians have much to learn from the lessons drawn by English ministers about the ways in which Irish opposition factions might be controlled, resisted, or accommodated.[31] Whether the government ought to punish opposition leaders by dismissal and deprivation of pensions, as did Dorset in 1754, or seek political peace through accommodation and restoration, as did Hartington in 1755, were questions that Newcastle would have to ask and answer in London during 1755 and 1756. Clark believed that the experiences of Dorset and Hartington in Ireland profoundly influenced Newcastle's thinking about whether and when to punish or to try to accommodate opposition leaders at Westminster.

Irish Parliamentary Politics in the Eighteenth Century, 1730–1760, profits from and builds upon the work of previous scholars. Exploiting the State Papers, the Wilmot Correspondence, and other manuscript sources, this book contains information that has not been available to other scholars. In design, the book differs from earlier works insofar as it treats the period 1730–1760 systematically and as a whole. Every session of the Irish parliament during the time period of the study is examined. What emerges from such systematic treatment is a different view of the so-called age of the undertakers.

First of all, this book argues that apart from pressing for the appointment of Englishmen to key positions in Irish church and

28. *Ibid.*, 278.   29. *Idem.*
30. *Ibid.*, 276.   31. *Idem.*

state offices during the early and middle 1730s, the English government had no consistent strategy for managing the Irish parliament or governing the country during this period. The chief governors of Ireland were largely left to their own devices regarding how they were to complete the king's business. Most of the lords lieutenants preferred not to favor one party and govern through them. With the exception of Chesterfield, who was not in Ireland long enough to make any impact on parliamentary management strategies, Ireland's chief governors tended initially to cultivate or otherwise favor those members and influentials in the Irish parliament who had harassed their predecessors.

Relations between Boyle as speaker and Dorset and Devonshire as lords lieutenants alternated between hostility and toleration. To be sure, Boyle's patronage needs were satisfied from time to time by both of these noblemen, but neither of them regarded Boyle and his party as reliable, purchased managers. Many of the details of parliamentary management were handled by those of the king's law officers with seats in parliament. Such had been the practice in the past and so it was in our period. For his part, Boyle rarely gave unsolicited policy advice to Dorset or Devonshire. When a particular measure, such as relief for Protestant Dissenters from the Test Act, was intensely unpopular in the house of commons, he communicated that fact to Dorset along with perhaps a dozen other gentlemen. The speaker and the lord lieutenant cooperated, but neither of them were parties to treaties or contracts about what had to be done in the house of commons or what the price would be for carrying a piece of controversial legislation.

Circumstances changed somewhat after the outbreak of war in Europe in 1740 and particularly after the fall of Walpole from office in early 1742. The combination of war in Europe and ministerial instability in England complicated the later years of Devonshire's long viceroyalty. Though Devonshire had facilitated the rise of his new in-laws, the Ponsonby family, as an alternative to Boyle and his friends, he put himself into the hands of Boyle during his third session of parliament, 1741–42. Following the brief Chesterfield interlude, during Harrington's administration, 1747–50, Boyle and his friends were able to play the role of undertaker as Falkiner and McCracken imagined that it had been played. The Boyle party monopolized patronage and dominated the Irish house of commons and the lord lieutenant. They succeeded grandly in driving Charles Lucas out of politics and out of the country, and in dictating policy to the lord lieutenant. They were able to do so because Harrington was politically helpless in England and utterly dependent upon the Boyle party in Ireland. The circumstances of the Harrington administration were very special because the king personally despised his lord lieutenant of Ireland, and the whole world knew it.

The origin of the great crisis of 1753 was rooted in Harrington's years and in the efforts of Stone and Sackville to recover the influence and authority lost to the Boyle party since 1747. Appalled by what he perceived to be the unreasonable demands and unbridled arrogance of Malone and Carter during the hegemony of the Boyle party over Harrington, Stone managed to offend those two gentlemen severely. Bad personal relations with Malone and Carter, as well as with the Earl of Kildare, accounted in large part for the intensity of their response to political moves by the Dorset administration. The settlement of this crisis by Hartington put Stone out of office but not out of politics and left Kildare as a candidate for the role of principal undertaker. Another Conolly, Kildare could not be. Because parties in the Irish house of commons were so evenly divided and because Hartington's successor, the Duke of Bedford, had such a difficult first session, the duke responded to Stone's initiative about establishing in 1758 what became the classic undertaker situation. Stone, Ponsonby, and Shannon (Boyle) were installed as lords justices with formal viceregal promises that patronage would be shared equally among their respective friends. Though patronage was to be shared equally, Stone was clearly the dominant personality among the three, and he remained the most powerful figure in Irish politics until his death in 1764.

The high point of Stone's political ascendancy occurred in early 1761. At that time Stone, supported by the other two lords justices, captured control of the Irish privy council, forced the lord lieutenant out of office, and compelled the English government to abandon its traditional insistence upon certifying a money bill as a reason for calling a parliament. In this instance, the lords justices and their majority in the Irish privy council had asserted an unprecedented degree of political and constitutional independence from an English government. George Stone, the English-born Archbishop of Armagh and the great assertor of viceregal authority in the crisis of 1753, had by 1760 become a leading Irish patriot and a champion of the sole right of the Irish house of commons to originate money bills. No wonder English ministers had difficulties devising strategies for managing the Irish parliament and governing the country. They could never be certain who in Ireland could be trusted with political power or for how long, what would satisfy, or what would work. The age of the undertakers was far more complicated and challenging for English ministers to understand and cope with than Falkiner and McCracken, and those writers who depended on their research and interpretations, would have us believe.

BIBLIOGRAPHY

MANUSCRIPT MATERIAL

British Library, London

Hardwicke Mss.: Mss. of the Second Earl of Hardwicke, Lord Chancellor of England, especially letters from Lord Newport 1719–1756 (Add. Mss. 35,585–35,586).
Herring, Mss.: Mss. of Thomas Herring, Archbishop of Canterbury, 1747–1757, letters from Irish correspondents (Add. Mss. 35,592).
Newcastle Mss.: Mss. of the Duke of Newcastle, letters from Irish correspondents (Add. Mss. 32,737; 32,863).
Southwell Mss.: Mss. of Edward Southwell as Secretary of State for Ireland, letters from Sir Richard Cox, Archbishop William King, and Dr. Marmaduke Coghill, 1714 to 1735 (Add. Mss. 9712; 9713; 9715; 21,121; 21,122; 21,123; 38,016; 38,156; 38,157).
Willes, Mss.: Mss. of Edward Willes, Chief Baron of the Irish Court of the Exchequer 1757–1766 (Add. Mss. 29,252).

National Library of Ireland, Dublin

Southwell Mss.: Mss. of Edward Southwell as Secretary of State for Ireland, 1714–1735 (Mss. 875; 876; 2,055; 2,056).

Public Records Office, London

Secretary of State Mss. (SP63 360–419); Available on microfilm in the University of Notre Dame Library.

Public Records Office of Northern Ireland, Belfast

Bedford Mss.: Mss. of the 4th Duke of Bedford as Lord Lieutenant 1756–1761 (T.2915).
Chatsworth Mss.: Mss. of the 3rd and 4th Dukes of Devonshire as Lords Lieutenants, 1737–1744 and 1754–1756 (T.3158).
Emly Mss.: Mss. of Edmund Sexton Pery, 1756–1758 (T.3087). Copies available in the University of Notre Dame Library.
Macartney Mss.: Mss. of Sir George Macartney, Earl Macartney, occasional letters 1755 (D.572).
Shannon Mss.: Mss. of Henry Boyle, 1st Earl of Shannon, 1730–1763 (D.2707); copies available in the University of Notre Dame Library.
Tickell Mss.: Mss. of Thomas Tickell, Undersecretary to the chief secretary, 1724–1740.
Wilmot Mss.: Mss. of Sir Robert Wilmot, Secretary for the Lord Lieutenant

resident in England, 1740–1772 (T.3019). Copies available in the University of Notre Dame Library.

Trinity College Library, Dublin

Clements Mss.: Mss. of Nathaniel Clements, TC 1741–43.

PRINTED MATERIAL

Bedford: *Correspondence of John, Fourth Duke of Bedford,* ed. Lord John Russell (Brown, Green, and Longmans, 3 vols., London, 1842–1846).

Boulter: *Letters Written by His Excellency Hugh* Boulter, D. D., *Lord Primate of All Ireland, etc. . . .* (2 vols., Dublin, 1770).

Chesterfield: *Private Correspondence of Chesterfield and Newcastle, 1744–46,* ed. Sir Richard-Lodge (Royal Historical Society, London, 1930).

Chesterfield: *The Letters of Philip Dormer Stanhope, 4th Earl of Chesterfield,* ed. Bonamy Dobree (King's Printer's Edition, Viking Press, 3 vols., New York, 1932).

Delaney: Mrs. Delaney, *A Memoir 1700–1788,* (ed. George Paston, London, 1900).

Hervey: Lord John Hervey, *Some Materials Toward Memoirs of the Person of George II,* ed. Rommey Sedgwich (Eyre and Spottiswoode, Ltd., 3 vols., London, 1931).

O'Brien: *The Inchiquinn Manuscripts,* ed. John Ainsworth (Irish Manuscripts Commission, Dublin, 1961).

Leinster: *Letters to Henry Fox, Lord Holland with a few addressed to his brother Stephen, Earl of Ilchester* (privately printed for presentation to the members of the Roxburghe Club, London, 1915).

Leinster: *Correspondence of Emily Duchess of Leinster (1731–1814),* ed. Brian Fitzgerald (Irish Manuscripts Commission, 3 vols., Dublin, 1949–1957).

Stone: "Correspondence of Stone and Newcastle," in *English Historical Review,* Vol. 20, 1905, 509–542; 735–763.

Walpole: Horace Walpole Memoirs of George II (Henry Colburn, London, Vol. 1, 1846).

Publications of the Historical Manuscripts Commission

Charlemont Mss. (Mss. of the 1st Earl of Charlemont), *12th Report, Appendix Part X. Vol. I.*

Donoughmore Mss. (Mss. of John Hely-Hutchinson), *12th Report, Appendix, Part IX.*

Egmont Mss. (Diary of Viscount Percival, afterwards 1st Earl of Egmont, 3 vols.).

Emly Mss. (Mss. of Edmund Sexton Pery), *8th Report, Appendix, Part I,* and *14 Report, Appendix IX* (2 sections).

House of Lords (Mss. (The Manuscripts of the House of Lords, 1697–1699, Vol. 3), New Series.

Stopford-Sackville Mss. (Mss. of Lord George Germaine, 1st Viscount Sackville), Vol. 1.

Various Collections of Mss. (Mss. of John Lord Bowes), Vol. 6. Weston Mss. (Mss. of Edward Weston), *10 Report, Part I.*

Newspapers and Periodicals

Belfast News Letter, 1755.
Censor, September and October, 1749.
The Gentleman's Magazine, 1741, 1753, and 1760.

Calendars, Records, and Journals

Calendar of the Ancient Records of Dublin, ed. John T. Gilbert (Joseph Dollard, 18 vols., Dublin, 1891–1922).
Calendar of the State Papers, Domestic Series, 1689 to 1703 (HMSO, 7 vols., London, 1895–1937).
Eighteen Century Irish Official Papers in Great Britain, Private Collections (HMSO, Belfast, Vol. 1, 1973).
Journals of the House of Commons of the Kingdom of Ireland. 3rd ed. (20 vols., Dublin, 1796–1800).
Journals of the House of Lords of the Kingdom of Ireland, 1634–1800 (8 vols., Dublin, 1799–1800).

Contemporary Pamphlets and Other Publications

Briton, A. *History of the Dublin Election with a Sketch of the present State of Parties in the Kingdom of Ireland* (Dublin, 1753).
Lucas, Charles. *Pharmacostix: or the use and abuse of Apothecaries explained* (Dublin, 1741).
Lucas, Charles. *Remonstrance against certain Infringements on the Rights and Liberties of the Commons and Citizens of Dublin* (Dublin, 1743).
Lucas, Charles. *The Complaints of Dublin* (Dublin, 1747).
Lucas, Charles. *Addresses to the Free Citizens and Free-Holders of the City of Dublin* (Dublin, 1748–1749).
Lucas, Charles. *The Great Charter of the City of Dublin* (Dublin, 1749).
Lucas, Charles. *An Address to His Excellency William Earl of Harrington . . . of Ireland . . . with a preface to the free and loyal subjects of Ireland in general* (Dublin, 1749).

Books and Articles

Akenson, Donald Harman: The *Church of Ireland: Ecclesiastical Reform and Revolution, 1800–1855* (Yale University Press, 1971).
Ashton, T. S.: *Economic Fluctuations in England, 1700–1800* (Oxford University Press, 1959).
Ayling, Stanley: *The Elder Pitt, Earl of Chatham* (David McKay Company, New York, 1976).
Ball, F. Elrington: The *Judges in Ireland, 1221–1921* (Dutton and Company, New York, 2 vols., 1927).
Beckett, James C.: *Protestant Dissent in Ireland, 1687–1780* (Faber and Faber, London, 1946).
Beresford, Marcus: "Francis Thurot and the French Attack at Carrickfeargus, 1759–60," *The Irish Sword*, 10, 1970–72, 255–274.

Blackey, Robert: "A Politician in Ireland: The Lord Lieutenancy of the Earl of Halifax, 1761–63," *Eire-Ireland* 14, (Winter), 1979, 62–82.

Burke, Rev. William: *The Irish Priests in the Penal Times (1660–1760)*, printed by N. Harvey for the author (Waterford, 1914).

Carswell, John: *The South Sea Bubble* (Stanford University Press, 1969).

Clarke, J. C. D.: "Whig Tactics and parliamentary Precedent: The English Management of Irish Politics, 1754–1756," *The Historical Journal*, 21, 2 (1978), 275–301.

Coxe, William: *Memoir of the Life and Administration of Sir Robert Walpole, Earl of Orford* (3 vols., London, 1798).

Coxe, William: *Memoirs of the Administration of . . . Henry Pelham . . .* (Longmans, Rees, Orme, Brown, and Green, London, 2 vols., 1829).

Cullen, L. M.: *An Economic History of Ireland since 1660* (B. T. Batsford, Ltd., London, 1972).

Donnelly, Jr., James S.: "The Whiteboy Movement, 1761–65," *Irish Historical Studies*, March 1978, 20–54.

Drake, Michael: "The Irish Demographic Crisis of 1740–41," *Historical Studies*, 6, London, 1968, 101–124.

Englefield, D. J. T.: "The Irish House of Parliament in the Eighteenth Century," *Parliamentary Affairs*, IX (1956), 57–64.

Edwards, R. Dudley, and Moody, T. W.: "The History of Poynings' Law: Part I, 1494–1615," *Irish Historical Studies*, September, 1941, 415–424.

Fitzgerald, Brian: *Emily, Duchess of Leinster, 1731–1814* (Staples Press, London, 1950).

Gilbert, John T.: *A History of The City of Dublin* (Irish University Press, Shannon, Ireland, 3 vols., 1972).

Hall, F. G.: *History of the Bank of Ireland* (Hodges, Figgis and Company, Dublin, 1949).

Hayton, David: "The Beginnings of the Undertaker System," *Penal Era and Golden Age Essays in Irish History 1690–1800,* ed. Thomas Bartlett and D. W. Hayton, Ulster Historical Foundation, 1979, 55–87.

Hayton, David: "Walpole and Ireland," *Britain in the Age of Walpole*, ed. Jeremy Black (St. Martin's Press, New York, 1984).

Kiernan, T. J.: *History of the Financial Administration of Ireland to 1817* (London, 1930).

James, Francis Godwin: *Ireland in the Empire, 1688–1770* (Harvard University Press, Cambridge, 1973).

Johnston, Edith M.: *Great Britain and Ireland, 1760–1800, A Study in Political Administration* (St. Andrews University Publication 55, Oliver and Boyd, London, 1963).

Johnson, Edith M. *Ireland in the Eighteenth Century* (Dublin, 1974).

Landa, Louis A.: *Swift and the Church of Ireland* (Oxford, 1954).

Large, David: "The Wealth of the Greater Irish Landowners, 1750–1815," *Irish Historical Studies*, March 1966, 21–47.

Lecky, W. E. H.: *History of Ireland in the Eighteenth Century* (Longmans, Green, and Company, London, 5 vols., 1892).

Maguire, James I.: "The Irish Parliament of 1692," *Penal Era and Golden Age Essays in Irish History* (Ulster Historical Foundation, Belfast, 1979, 1–31).

McCracken, J. L.: "The Conflict between the Irish Administration and Parliament, 1753–6," *Irish Historical Studies*, 1942–43, 159–179.

McDowell, R. B.: *Irish Public Opinion 1750–1800* (London, 1944).

Malcomson, A. P. W.: "John Foster and the Speakership of the Irish House of Commons," *Proceedings of the Royal Irish Academy*, Vol. 72, sec. c, no. 11 (Dublin, 1972), 271–303.

Malcomson, A. P. W.: "The Newtown Act of 1748: Revision and Reconstruction," *Irish Historical Studies*, March 1973, 313–144.

Moody, T. W., and Vaughan, W. E.: *A New History of Ireland, Volume 4, Eighteenth-Century Ireland, 1691–1800* (New York: Clarendon Press of Oxford University, 1986).

Munter, Robert: *The History of Irish Newspapers, 1688–1760* (Harvard University Press, Cambridge, 1967).

O'Donavan, Declan: "The Money Bill Dispute," *Penal Era and Golden Age Essays in Irish History, 1690–1800*, ed. Thomas Bartlett and D. W. Hayton (Ulster Historical Foundation, Belfast, 1979, 55–87).

Plumb, John Harold: *Sir Robert Walpole; The King's Minister* (Houghton Mifflin Co., Boston, 1963).

"The Church of Ireland," *Church Quarterly Review*, January, 1985.

Trainor, B., and Crawford, W. H.: *Aspects of Irish Social History, 1750–1800* (HMSO, Belfast, 1969).

Wall, Maureen: *The Penal Laws, 1691–1760* (Dundalk, 1961).

Whyte, J. H.: "Landlord Influence at Elections in Ireland," *English Historical Review*, 75 (1960).

Williams, Basil: *Carteret and Newcastle: A Contrast in Contemporaries* (Cambridge University Press, 1943).

Reference Books

Hughes, J. L. T.: "The Chief Secretaries in Ireland, 1561–1921," *Irish Historical Studies*, 8 (1952–1953).

Powicke, F. M.: *Handbook of British Chronology*, 2nd ed. (London, 1961).

Sainty, J. C.: "The Secretariat of the Chief Governors of Ireland, 1690–1800," *Proceedings of the Royal Irish Academy*, Vol. 77, Sec C, No. 1 (1977).

Sedgwick, Romney: *The History of Parliament: The House of Commons 1715–1754*, 2 vols. (published for The History of Parliament Trust by Oxford University Press, New York, 1970).

INDEX

Absentee tax, 160–61

Acheson, Sir Archibald, moves a secret committee to investigate the state of the revenue, 238

Armagh election, 144–45, 159, 160

Armagh election petition, trial of strength between government and Boyle party, 168

Athy, Borough of, 142

Barracks construction project, 91, 126

Beckett, J. C., views of the crisis of 1751–1754, 329–30

Bedford John Russell, Duke of, 94, 111, 112, 220, 225, 228, 231, 239, 254, 262, 263, 264, 265, 288, 292, 307; appointed Lord lieutenant of Ireland, January 28, 1757, 221; spends his own money to relieve food shortages in the north of Ireland, 224; supports revival of Clanbrassil's Catholic proposal, 226–27; consults with Devonshire and Hillsborough about Irish politics, 227; does not trust Stone, 227; hears rumors about an attack on the pension list, 229; on the proposed pension for the king's daughter, 230, 252; speech from the throne October 11, 1757, 230; disapproval of resolutions attacking pensions to non-residents, 231; party animosities divide officeholders, 232; capitulates on transmitting resolutions attacking the pension list, 234; wants authority to put down factionalism, 234–35, 241; no hope a policy of reconciliation will succeed, 237; country gone mad over politics, 240; promises to do his best without further complaints, 242; accepts Stone's proposed new system of undertakers, 244;

presses English ministers to approve inland carriage of corn bill, 248; supports Clanbrassil's Catholic relief measure in the Irish privy council, 249; on the role of patronage in Irish parliamentary politics, 251; attends cabinet meeting on military preparations, 257; authorizes recruitment of Protestants in the north of Ireland, 258; speech from the throne October 16, 1759, 262; strategy for the defense of Ireland, 265–66; causes of the Dublin riot examined, 272–73; no optimism about apprehending and punishing rioters, 274; principal rioters were New Light Presbyterians, 274; denies the financial dealings of Malone and Clements were causes of the riot; 275; proposes a scheme to recruit Catholics for the Royal Marines, 278–79; difficulties in attempting to prosecute the lord mayor and magistrates, 280; compassion for Malone and Clements, 282; praises Jennings' performance at Carrickfeargus, 286; outraged at Haven's misrepresentations to Pitt about preparedness in the north, 286; held meeting to decide how to deal with the Dublin merchant's petition, 290; assessment, 293; orders dissolution of parliament after the death of the king, 300; urges lords justices to comply in transmitting a money bill, 312; resigned, 312

Belleisle, Marshal, strategy, 215

Berkeley, George, appointed Bishop of Cloyne, 23; Boulter's opinion of, 23

Bessborough, Brabazon Ponsonby, first Earl of, 36, 37, 42, 69, 70, 87, 92, 93, 94, 121, 128, 190, 196, 210; supported

124; on Malone's place in parliamentary politics, 124–25; believes Boyle party planned to drive him from office, 131; argues issues at trial in Ireland are constitutional, 135; attacked in house of commons, 138; argues that the future role of Englishmen in the government of Ireland is the real issue, 139–40; wants authority to dismiss officeholders for voting against the government, 140; dines with members of the house of commons and argues government's case, 142; states that Clements works against the government, 144; contends power of the Boyle party has been weakened, 145; prepares refutation of Kildare's memorial, 148; thinks about an accommodation, 149; response to Gardiner's peace initiative, 151–52; sees attack on the prerogative as an effort to keep the Kildare faction from deserting the Boyle party, 162; insists old independency doctrines have been resurrected by Malone, 166; argues that Boyle has been manipulated by Malone, 167; states that Brownlow must be supported in the Armagh election petition to keep the government party together, 167–68; blames defeat on the amended money bill to bad luck and treachery, 172–73; offers his resignation to Newcastle, 179; suggests John Ponsonby as government leader in the house of commons, 176–77; urges dismissal of Clements, 179, 181; suspects that Clements will not be dismissed, 185; spirit of patriotism never higher, 186; on fighting with halters around their necks, 188; offers compromise plans on the Clements matter, 190–91, 196; recommends Hartington as Dorset's successor, 194; withdraws name from future consideration for appointment as lord justice, 206; on enduring disgrace, 217; negotiations to bring Pitt and Newcastle together, 224, 225; returns to Ireland, 228; as principal leader of the opposition,

235; proposes to stop factionalism by sharing power and patronage, 243; as master of the Irish house of commons, 246–47; management skills, 252; condition of the country, 253; orders disposition of troops, 258; on dangers from the Catholics if the French invade, 258–59; patronage requests under the new undertaker system, 296; seeks advice about the type of bill required as a cause for calling a parliament, 301; revived sole right controversy, 301, 303; delays considering Kildare's motion on a supply bill, 305; offers justification of patriot position on transmitting money bill, 306; prepared to resign rather than transmit a money bill, 307; successful on the money bill issue, 311; manages the general election, 313; difficulties in managing entrepreneurial politics, 317

Stratford, Mr., 230, 234
Strode, General, 284
Stuart, Charles Edward, Young Pretender, 75
Swift, Jonathan, 37

Tax on dogs, 240
Tax on pensions paid to absentees, 240
Test Act, Ireland, efforts to repeal, 1731–1732, 10–12; 1733–1734, 17–20
Thurot, Francois, 263, 264, 268; captures and plunders Carrickfeargus, 282–83; killed, 285
Tickell, Thomas, secretary to the lord justices, 9
Tillage promotion schemes, 151, 224; bounty for inland carriage of corn to Dublin, 240, 247–48
Tisdale, Charles, 142
Tisdale, Philip, 232, 233; considered for prime serjeant, 63; appointed solicitor general, 124; withdraws request for sinecure of master of the rolls, 267–68
Tithe of agistment controversy, 30–32; intimidation of clergy, 35–36